nai010 publishers intend the Reflect series to focus attention on socially relevant themes for architecture, urban planning, fine art and design.

Reflect #13

Previously published in
the Reflect series:

reflect # 01
New Commitment
In Architecture, Art and design
Various authors

reflect #02
Stadswijk
Stedenbouw in het dagelijks leven
Arnold Reijndorp

reflect #03
The Capsular Civilization
On the City in the Age of Fear
Lieven De Cauter

reflect #04
Documentary now!
Contemporary strategies in photography, film and the visual arts
Various authors

reflect #05
Creativity and the city
How the creative economy changes the city
Various authors

reflect #06
Urban Polictics Now
Re-Imagining Democracy in the Neoliberal City
Various authors

reflect #07
Questioning History
Imagining the Past in Contemporary Art
Various authors

reflect #08
Art and Activism in the Age of Globalization
Various authors

reflect #09
Entropic Empire
On the City of Man in the Age of Disaster
Lieven De Cauter

reflect #10
The City as Interface
How Digital Media are Changing the City
Martijn de Waal

reflect #11
The Dwarf in the Chess Machine
Benjamin's Hidden Doctrine
Lieven De Cauter

reflect #12
Ending the Anthropocene
Essays on Activism in the Age of Collapse
Lieven De Cauter

Discursive Architecture

Tactics for Critical Intervention in the Work of BAVO

Gideon Boie

nai010 publishers

'There is nothing more practical than a good theory.'

(Kurt Lewin)

Contents

	Introduction	7
1.	The Problem Called BAVO	14
2.	Stop Criticizing and Judging	30
3.	Work Through Inherent Criticism	48
4.	Take Away Critical Distance	60
5.	Hystericize the Subject	76
6.	Provoke Full Spectrum	90
7.	Shoot at Your Own People	108
8.	Choose Hyperidealism	122
9.	Keep the Paradox Alive	142
10.	Design Your Symptom	164
11.	Stay True to Ignorance	190
12.	Make Things Public	210
	Conclusion	231
	List of Abbreviations	250
	Bibliography	252
	List of Images	268
	Acknowledgements	269
	Credits	272

Introduction

This book explores how to reactivate criticism in the field of architecture on the basis of a more or less academic retrospective of the work of BAVO, the collective co-founded by the author and Matthias Pauwels. BAVO established criticism as a practice on the threshold of architecture and philosophy, starting in Rotterdam and later based in Brussels. The main research question is whether a strategy of overidentification can function as a crowbar by which to break open the ideological function of what we call inherent criticism. There is an awful lot of criticism in daily practice but, following the Freudo-Marxist philosophy of Slavoj Žižek, this inherent criticism is actually not meant to be taken seriously: critical thinking merely establishes an ideological distance that safeguards the actors from the situation that they are fully immersed in. The strategy of overidentification is also taken from Žižek; it refrains from direct criticism and aims to undermine a situation by taking lost ideals and their obscene supplements a little bit too seriously.

The question that follows on this first question is whether and how the strategy of overidentification translates to the field of architecture, making it possible to forge tactics that instigate processes of awareness and change. The strategy of overidentification has mainly been theorized by Slavoj Žižek in relation to art practices, in the first place in relation to Neue Slowenische Kunst (NSK), later in relation to the gesture of orthodoxy within religious studies (in the case of G.K. Chesterton) and the saving grace of autism in the climate crisis (in the case of Greta Thunberg). After first studying the art of overidentification as a strategy for cultural activism, BAVO has been applying the strategy in the work of criticism, using it as a methodological tool to intervene in different debates. The hypothesis is that the inherent criticism lingering in debates functions as an ideal anchor point for overidentification and thus opens a window to redefine design challenges, construct alternative design intelligence and trace new lines of flight.

Over the years, the different contexts of intervention have made it possible to turn the screw of overidentification as a critical method. In the first project on regional development, we applied a rather classical overidentification in the style of the Yes Men. In later projects on city marketing and art in the public space, we implemented more complex and total forms of overidentification by including both peers and ourselves in the performance. The work on spatial management was a first experiment in hyperidealism. Still later, other critical strategies were put in the mix, such as the politics of commoning and the pedagogy of ignorance, to engage with the design challenges of detention and mental healthcare.

The critical interventions by BAVO play on different registers to provoke processes of awareness and change, including visual and performative elements. Besides articles and lectures – the critic's usual weapons – formats were adopted from the cultural sphere (exhibitions, pamphlets, posters, billboards, propaganda, press releases, etc.) and from design practice (workshops, master plans, dummy sketches, project definitions, etc.). The cultural sphere is used as a platform for the critical interventions, first acting with one foot in the protected white cube of art, later fully exploiting the parallel sphere of architecture culture as a field for playful action. In the search for impact, the interventions set up engagements with the usual suspects in architecture culture and with professional partners. Engagement with the public debate is used as an essential element in the labour of criticism, not only as a means to reach out to unusual partners, but also using the perspective of architecture to shed a different light on urgent social issues.

This book is a narrative account of each critical intervention, reflecting on defining moments, successes as much as failures. The goal of the retrospective is to show how different tactics for critical intervention were forged within the scope of overidentification but that depend on the specific context, network of actors, overall choreography and, perhaps most importantly, lessons learned from previous actions. The overview skips the full documentation of the different interventions to keep the focus on the tactical considerations in the labour of criticism, not without noticing that most case studies are published in different formats and on different platforms: just google them! The field survey and research articles have been published elsewhere, using academic, professional and popular platforms. Results have also been included in exhibitions and museum collections. Part of the modus vivendi developed by BAVO is to publish findings immediately, even in preliminary form, on whatever platform that makes sense, in order to have the maximum impact and, more importantly, to include feedback loops in the labour of criticism.

*

The book starts with four chapters that discuss the main research question through an outline of the genealogy, conceptual biography and overall strategic development in BAVO's work. Chapter 1, 'The Problem Called BAVO', describes the development of a critical practice along the lines of Crimson Architectural Historians, in our case operating at the intersection of architecture and philosophy. In Chapter 2, 'Stop Criticizing and Judging', we describe how the work developed as a psychoanalysis of the architectural field, inspired by the Freudo-Marxist work of Slavoj Žižek, who theorized the strategy of overidentification mainly in relation to art practices. Chapter 3, 'Work Through Inherent Criticism', describes the repositioning of the criticism practice using the conceptual framework of Lacanian psychoanalysis. A defining turn in BAVO's work occurred when we began to employ psychoanalytic techniques, particularly overidentification, within our own critical practice. Using early works by BAVO, Chapter 4, 'Take Away Critical Distance', describes BAVO's questioning of the embedded role of artists in urban development and the ensuing resistance we faced after criticizing it. The embedded nature of artists appears to be a fundamental feature of architectural culture.

The main body of the book (Chapters 5 to 11) provide a retrospective on seven critical interventions in the field of architecture set up by the author as part of the BAVO collective. Chapter 5, 'Hystericize the Subject', discusses how to heighten the impact of criticism by shifting the debate from a cock fight between public and critic to an articulation of internal divides. In Chapter 6, 'Provoke Full Spectrum', we hope to ensure that criticism includes all actors involved in a certain situation and prevent enlightened architects from retreating into apolitical conceptions of architecture. Chapter 7, 'Shoot at Your Own People', is about preventing architects (and artists) from projecting responsibilities onto the other scene of politics and showing how they are always involved in the manipulation of politics. In Chapter 8, 'Choose Hyperidealism', we argue that criticism should stop revealing all sorts of dirty little secrets and instead use hysteria as a positive force to rearticulate the vested interests in architecture. Chapter 9, 'Keep the Paradox Alive', develops the tactic used to stop actors from compromising noble intentions and helps them understand the inherent complexity and contradiction of certain situations. The tactic is further developed in Chapter 10, 'Design Your Symptom', where the commoning of the inherent paradoxes to a situation is a means to construct new design intelligence and trace lines of flight for future development. Lastly, Chapter 11, 'Stay True to Ignorance', redefines the role of architect-critic to prevent it from falling into the trap of expertocracy and ensure that actors take their own responsibilities towards the paradoxes of the situation.

The seven chapters make up the main part of the handbook of tactics for critical intervention in the field of architecture, based on the work of BAVO. Although building upon each other and following a more or less chronological order, the chapters can be read separately as presentations of systematically different tactics for critical intervention. The handbook uses the findings in the different chapters to broaden the scope of architecture criticism and to situate its potential role in the process of architectural production and, even more importantly, in the public debate dealing with the sustainable, social and just organization of society. Therefore the book ends with the special Chapter 12, 'Make Things Public', that discusses the author's involvement in recent moments of urban activism in Brussels. The engagement with urban activism forms a parallel in which academic and professional knowledge is deployed within heated issues, such as traffic safety and air quality. At the same time, urban activism constitutes a lesson in urgency that encourages a more explicit use of architectural criticism as entry into public debate and a catalyst for processes of awareness and change. Lastly, the Conclusion brings the debate back to the architecture culture in Flanders. The starting point was the impact of criticism in the context of an architecture culture that proclaims depoliticization as its fundamental principle. The strategy of overidentification was not just an abstract experiment but an explicit part of situated interventions to re-politicize the role of architecture in discussion with its main actors and its willing executioners.

*

In fact, the exploration of how to re-activate criticism in the field of architecture became the main focus of my research. In writing the methodological chapter for my PhD research on the architecture of psychiatry and detention, I could not but relate to earlier work of BAVO. In the early 2000s Matthias Pauwels and I studied the strategy of overidentification in relation to art and used it to advocate a radical 'activist' art practice. Later, we started to experiment with the strategy of overidentification in our own work as critics in relation to architecture. I must admit that the writing of the genealogy, conceptual inspirations and tactical moves in different projects stimulated me to readjust the focus of the research towards the question of how to re-politicize architecture. The question is especially crucial in the trendsetting architecture culture in Flanders and the Netherlands that has de-politicization as its fundamental concept, and rightly so.

Architecture culture usually takes the form of discursive programmes that delve into the sublime qualities of objects, identify best practices and enlighten emerging oeuvres. The historical perspective therefore reigns supreme in architecture culture, even in dealing with contemporary architecture. Learning from the past is certainly necessary, but the questions that keep me busy are: Are we, architects, doomed to react belatedly to the urgencies of our time? Can we merge architecture criticism with the public debate? Can we use architecture culture as a platform to trace new lines of flight? Does architecture culture provide criticism with an agency of its own? Is the critic allowed to cross the thin line between architecture culture and design practice? These are very basic questions when it comes to the use of criticism as a catalyst for processes of awareness and change.

The result is an 'autobiographical action research', as Lieven

De Cauter has called it. The first sketch of the methodological chapter was discussed in an elective master's course on architecture and activism during our year-and-a-half stay on the 24st floor of the Brussels World Trade Center (WTC), around 2019. In the following years, I slowly but consistently unpacked the outline for the one chapter into a full book that looks back at BAVO's twenty years of critical practice. In building up the chapters for the different critical interventions, I felt obliged to be equally consistent with my starting point in psychoanalysis – cut the crap and start with the by-thoughts. Admittedly, the drastic choice drains away a lot of detail on the specific questions of psychiatry and detention. The good news, however, is that a lot of the research pieces have been published on different platforms, so there is little reason to republish the articles here.

The clear choice to skip the research pieces and field surveys makes it possible to foreground how experiments with the strategy of overidentification gave way to a practice of what I call 'discursive architecture'. The topic of discussion is architecture as discourse, based on Lacanian philosophy that acknowledges that a social formation like architecture interacts with speech and language, not to forget discipline. The poststructuralist discourse theory of Michel Foucault is in the background. It is not by accident that the title and profession of architect in Belgium is still juridically protected by the 'Orde van architecten/Ordre des architectes' (Order of Architects). In this line we can talk about an 'order of architecture' safeguarded through cultural institutions such as the architecture institutes, government architects, together with starchitects, theorists and historians, property developers, politicians and magazines. Critically intervening in the field of architecture means challenging the order of architecture, i.e. questioning first of all accepted bodies of knowledge about what is true or not, but also the social power relations that define who has the right to speak or not.

Publishing on architecture criticism is exceptional as critics are supposed to talk about work by others from the sidelines, in the form of either praise or commentary. Criticism is largely an unprofessional affair, more often than not a friendly service, at best a civil service for the good cause of architecture culture; in any case, it is poorly paid and there is no market for criticism. Still, BAVO has managed to practise criticism as a quasi-professional affair and produce work thanks to rare subsidies, commissions, and teaching and research activities. In this context, BAVO is used as an empty signifier to steer interventions, claim a space for speech, make the work anonymous, project a collective, and protect collaborators engaged in action. I used my personal name and academic affiliation only when deemed necessary or strategically useful. And yet BAVO remains a thing of nothing. It makes me even happier to present the practice of BAVO in this book. I see it as an honour to the masters that have introduced me into the fine art of criticism, the many collaborators throughout the years *and* the persons who, wittingly or not, have been adding to the dream labour. My gratitude extends to those persons and offices that I fiercely oppose in my writings. The practice of criticism never shies away from what Slavoj Žižek called the 'cruelty of true friendship' – the same counts for my deep love of architecture.

The Problem Called BAVO

Chapter 1

This book is a theoretical, more or less academic reflection on the critical architectural practice of the office called BAVO, the collective of architect-philosophers co-founded by the author and Matthias Pauwels in the early 2000s, operating as a practice in architecture criticism and research. Closely following the Freudo-Marxist version of Slavoj Žižek, the psychoanalytical framework is used to set up critical interventions that address the complexities and contradictions at stake in societal organization and utilize it as a window for change. After first putting forward the strategy of overidentification as a proposal for the radicalization of cultural practice in several essays and books, BAVO started to apply the strategy within its own critical practice.[1] The strategy of overidentification came into play as a criticism of the dominant logic of embedded art in the Netherlands in the first place. However, we had to prevent the call for the radicalization of cultural production from ending up as an equally empty embedded gesture. Also, the architecture culture in Flanders (Belgium) challenged us to further experiment with the strategy of overidentification, especially given its instrumental and apolitical tradition in criticism. Obviously, the strategy of overidentification shifted the role of criticism, moving away from the calm waters of reflective distance and searching for critical proximity in the muddy terrain of ideology. Further experimentation with the strategy of overidentification was part of a continuous effort to prevent critical labour from ending up in exactly the same logic of embedded art. In practising criticism, our main questions are: Where to land in the muddy terrain of ideology? How to escape the thin air of history and theory? How to make sure the message reaches its destination? How to bring the audience to the threshold where the real work begins?

The Early Years

Before we discuss the origin and conceptual inspiration of BAVO in the next chapter, let's sketch the genealogy. The work of BAVO can be divided into roughly three periods. In the initial period from around 2001, Matthias Pauwels and I started to operate under the name of BAVO while writing texts together, first as an extension of our student work, later as an autonomous production. In 2002 an article on security syndromes in safety architecture for *Archis* (now called *Volume*) was published under the name BAVO, described in the short bio as a 'research team'.[2] Soon we started to publish under the name 'BAVO Research': for instance, *De on-*

verdeelde stad en haar gewillige beulen: 7 essays over Transvaal, stadsontwikkeling en aanverwante kwesties (The undivided city and its willing executioners: Seven essays on Transvaal, urban development and related issues) published by Stroom in The Hague (2003) as the outcome of a study on the Transvaal district.³ Adding the notion of research to the name was somehow influenced by Stroom (at the time headed by Lily Van Ginneken) to justify our participation as a critical watchdog in the exhibition *De Stad, de Kloof en de Regels* (The city, the gap and the rules) on the contested redevelopment of Transvaal, part of the Grote Stedenbeleid (Big cities policy). Perhaps for the same reason, the text 'Rediscover Your Wholeness! Vijf manieren om de spanning tussen economie en identiteit op te lossen' (Rediscover your wholeness! Five ways to solve the tension between economy and identity) was published under the name of BAVO Research; it was the outcome of a study on regional development in the Tuin- en Bollenstreek, led by artist Hans Venhuizen and involving many artists in the cultural planning of the region.⁴

The study for Stroom was defining insofar as we were somehow forced to expand the notion of architecture and engage with art and urban planning. This brought us to the BAVO tagline, 'Research into the political dimension of art, architecture and planning'. In the case of Transvaal, one would have to be half blind to talk about architectural production and leave the framework out of the discussion: the urban redevelopment scheme part of the Grote Stedenbeleid. Urban development is not only the framework for architecture production; architecture is in fact the key piece that puts the urban redevelopment plan in motion by giving it substance. At the same time, art couldn't be left out of the discussion as the urban redevelopment of Transvaal was an opportunity for many artists to produce critical art. The programme was managed by Stroom in their chapter on art in the public space (managed by Jan Wijle). In the context of urban development in the Netherlands, it is a classic procedure for government agencies to sponsor an army of embedded artists and allow them to critically engage with the process, ourselves included.

The research stay at the Jan van Eyck Academie in Maastricht (January 2004-December 2005) was a springboard for BAVO, not only in terms of public relations and output, but in the first place in the definition of our research topics and methods. Matthias Pauwels and I applied for a residency on the basis of the research plan 'Scumspace: Mapping the Illegal Users of the Dutch MUD' in the framework of the Authoring the City programme organized by the Charles Nypels Foundation. But we were both granted a position as researchers in the Theory Department to work on our research plan independently. The post-academic research context of the Jan van Eyck Academie, at the time headed by Koen Brams, was extremely open. In fact there was no fixed programme; this ignited a vibrant atmosphere in which researchers were themselves organizing exhibits, reading groups, film screenings, colloquiums and more. Researchers were encouraged to cross the disciplinary boundaries of the three departments at the Jan van Eyck Academie: arts, design and theory. The course of the research took a decisive turn in organizing two symposiums. The first, 'Psychoanalysis, Urban Theory and the City of Late-Capitalism', was a three-day colloquium organized by BAVO and Lorenzo Chiesa at the Jan van Eyck Academie (18-20 November 2005) with Edward W. Soja, Juliet Flower MacCannell, Friedrich von Borries, Yannis Stavrakakis and others. In parallel, 'Cultural Activism Today: Strategies of Over-Identification' was organized at the Stedelijk Museum CS (19 January 2006) with Boris Groys, Joep Van Lieshout, Alexei Monroe, Dieter Lesage and others.[5] The theoretical contributions were published in 2007 in two volumes edited by BAVO: *Urban Politics Now: Re-Imagining Democracy in the Neoliberal City* (Rotterdam: nai, 2007) and *Cultural Activism Today: The Art of Over-Identification* (Rotterdam: Episode, 2007).[6]

The second period (2007-12) in the work of BAVO coincided with the application of the strategy of overidentification in our own work, instead of merely constructing ideology-critical arguments in reference to other art practices and promoting it as an alternative activist strategy. The notion of overidentification was proposed as counter-strategy in which artists identify with the current trends in such an excessive way that it becomes rather difficult to digest, I will discuss the strategy later. The performances of overidentification were a joint venture of Matthias Pauwels and myself. We started to use the format of lectures – the critic's primary tool – as a means of overidentification, at first in the pretty straightforward modus of the Yes Men, for example in *10 Must-Dos for the Spatial Development of a Top Region* (2007), discussed in Chapter 5, and the lecture-performance on the Creative Up-Scaling of The Hague and Environs at DCR The Hague. Another try-out was the Euregional Forum (2006-10), a discursive programme at the Jan van Eyck Academie set up to critically deal with the cross-border development of the Limburg-Liège-Aachen region. Director Koen Brams encouraged us to engage with (local) art institutions, academia, civil society and political actors. The programme was used to experiment with the strategy of overidentification in different ways, including the setting of debate and the communication formats. Later, more complex but sharply directed performances of overidentification were set up using exhibitions as the basis to make public statements through press releases, publications, pamphlets, lectures and debates, such as De Janssens Werken (Flanders Architecture Institute, VAi and De Singel), Bureau Kunstenaarsparticipatie (TENT. Rotterdam), discussed in Chapters 6 and 7, respectively, and Dutch Design Lobby (Van Abbemuseum), discussed briefly in Chapters 2 and 7.

All the interventions were co-authored by Matthias Pauwels and myself, operating as BAVO, in the same way as we published books and articles from the beginning under the common name. Part of the overidentification was the use of project names as alter ego, only mentioning BAVO in the margin of the production notes, sometimes including the logo among the other partners. We were considering the project names – Euregional Forum, De Janssens Werken, Bureau Kunstenaarsparticipatie (Office for artist participation), Dutch Design Lobby, etc. – as avatars. Still, having the name BAVO in the background raised suspicion as some couldn't understand why we had suddenly shifted from an ideology-critical oeuvre to promoting the reconquest of the city through architecture (in the case of De Janssens Werken) and neoliberal policies in the arts (in the case of Bureau Kunstenaarsparticipatie). Against the easy countercriticism of being a hoax, we argued that we were convinced after a long study, as happened with Saint Paul after his years-long persecution of early Christians, even making the conversion an explicit part of the performance. The many avatars functioned in much the same way as Soren Kierkegaard's many pseudonyms. The figures may contradict each other, but what counts are the internal coherence and the differential view.

The strategy of overidentification also became the standard method of my individual writings on architecture at that time, for example in case studies and essays for the *Flanders Architectural Yearbook* published by the VAi, on whose editorial board I sat. For example, the essay 'Taskforce for Architecture and Administrative Modernisation: Here the Citizen is at Home', published in the 2008 edition of the yearbook, discussed four new administrative buildings designed by leading firms such as Van Broeck Meuwissen Architecten, Jo Crepain, META architecten and noAarchitecten.[7] The essay – still authored under the common name BAVO – discussed the different ways the designs not only answered, but rather laid the foundations of, the political programme of modernization and the specific ideologies of democracy at work in each case. Overidentification also underlies the short essay 'A Lesson in Added Architectural Value', published under my name in the 2010 edition of the yearbook and discussing the Wet89 headquarters of the Flemish Christian democratic party CD&V designed by 51N4E.[8] Based on interviews, the article reconstructs the narrative of the Wet89 project in terms of a win-win where architectural design generates political added value by sticking to questions of identity and urbanity, thus going beyond ideological kinship between architect and client. Another essay for the 2010 edition of the yearbook is 'Plea for Care Architecture', which marked the start of my engagement with the architecture for care and mental healthcare in particular. The use of overidentification as a normal part of critical architecture discourse culminated in the project I developed on the Provincial Government Architect in Limburg for *Architectuurwijzer*, discussed in Chapter 8, in terms of both form (setting up an advocacy campaign) and content (immediately drafting the future programme).

Criticism, Research, Practice

From around 2012, the work of BAVO reached another magnitude in the explicit use of the strategy of overidentification as a research method for vision development on the architecture of detention and psychiatry. In this third period (2012-today,) the work of criticism is enveloped in larger, self-initiated research projects, partly in the context of my research at the KU Leuven Faculty of Architecture and at different stages supported by the Arts Decree of the Flemish Government. 'Prison Gear: Knowledge platform for humane detention architecture' is a long-running research project focusing on the inherent paradox in the Prison Act 2005, discussed in Chapter 9. Prison Gear was used, again, as an avatar featuring BAVO as initiator and also as an indication of the cultural background of the initiative. The academic profile of KU Leuven was certainly useful for building up credibility and finding legitimacy for sharp criticism. Over the years, close collaborations were set up with prison directors, the non-profit association De Huizen, architecture-culture non-profit associations Architectuurwijzer and AR-TUR, and finally also the FPS Justice.

The collaboration of other researchers in the Prison Gear project, mostly (former) students at the KU Leuven Faculty of Architecture, allowed us to present BAVO as a research collective again or 'research office' if a more institutional presentation was thought necessary. First, Wim Vandendriessche was engaged in the set-up of the project for BAVO and the preparation of the subsidy dossier. The studio work of master's students Maarten Moonens and Fie Vandamme was exhibited at the triennial 'Conflict & Design' in C-mine (Genk), showing and publishing the work under their own name as part of Prison Gear's contribution. The preparation of Prison Gear's contribution to the triennial was due to Rūta Valiūnaitė-Aleks. After graduating, Fie Vandamme became the driving force for BAVO in the work on Haren Prison Village and the design workshop series in the prisons of Dendermonde and Hasselt, also operating as co-author of articles and participating in debates. Paoletta Holst was engaged in the set-up of the Prison Gear website and the production of online content, the workshops at Dendermonde Prison and the preparation of the second subsidy dossier (leading to the collaboration with AR-TUR and the FPS Justice). Finally, Heleen Verheyden was involved in the programme at Merksplas Prison, following on her master's thesis dealing with detained mothers at Berkendaal Women's Prison.

The research in psychiatry started with publishing case studies on care architecture in Flanders for the quarterly magazine of the non-profit association *Psyche* (then called Flemish Association for Mental Health, VVGG). The research in psychiatry was running in parallel to the work in prison, but both topics were kept separate for obvious reasons. From 2011, it was a voluntary continuation of the 'Plea for Care Architecture' published in the *Flanders Architectural Yearbook*. The research project took off in the work on the KARUS psychiatric centre in Melle (then called Caritas psychiatric centre), starting in the summer of 2014. The research project received massive attention with the opening in 2016 of the Kanunnik Petrus Jozef Triest Plein, also known as the 'Caritas' project, designed by architecten de vylder vinck taillieu. Again, BAVO's activities wouldn't have been possible without the close collaboration of many former students. Fie Vandamme was the driving force for the work at KARUS from 2014 until around 2017. Vjera Sleutel got involved, first voluntarily as part of her master's thesis, later as part of the preparation for the entry to the 2018 Venice Architecture Biennale, together with architecten de vylder vinck taillieu and Filip Dujardin. The work on psychiatry is discussed in Chapter 10.

Research on the seclusion room within crisis psychiatry was initially set up with Fie Vandamme during the work at KARUS and later developed as a research in itself involving different psychiatric institutions. The work in the Sint-Jan acute admissions department of Sint-Annendael Diest psychiatric hospital was set up as a joint project with Heleen Verheyden, starting in the summer of 2017 (discussed in Chapter 11). The research was continued the following years at psychiatric centre Gent-Sleidinge, psychiatric hospital Bethaniënhuis in Zoersel, university psychiatric centre KU Leuven and KARUS in Melle with Vjera Sleutel. Verheyden and Sleutel co-authored many articles on the topic. Rosa Fens and Helen Van der Vloet were involved in working through the material on the seclusion room as part of the contribution to the *Prikkels* exhibition at Museum Dr. Guislain (Ghent), October 2018 to May 2019. Finally, Marine Boey was involved in the artwork *Don't Eat the Microphone* by Veridiana Zurita and others at the psychiatric centre Dr. Guislain (Ghent) and working on artwork for different publications.

Parallel Engagements

The third phase in the work of BAVO runs parallel to teaching assignments with Lieven De Cauter at the KU Leuven Faculty of Architecture, in particular the Criticism and Ethics master's course that we taught together from the academic year 2013-14. It goes without saying that the joint course with Lieven De Cauter left a huge mark on the work of BAVO. There was never a real collaboration outside the university context; worse still, we only managed in 2021 to co-author a text as part of our contribution to the *Institution Building* exhibition at CIVA. And yet the work at Prison Gear and KARUS was in fact directly influenced by the teaching on the commons. In the first years of teaching Criticism and Ethics, we were voluntarily engaging in each other's classes – playing best student to each other – and teaching on the topic of the commons through readings of texts by Massimo De Angelis, David Harvey, David Linebaugh, Karl Marx, Thomas More, Doina Petrescu and more. Teaching the elective master's course Architecture and Activism with Lieven De Cauter (from the academic year 2015-16) also impacted the work of BAVO. The reading of texts with students, followed by lively discussions, including the festive sofa-talks and the publication of many reports, all part of the desire to embrace the public character of education, made the different elements of my work further merge into one and the same discursive practice. The joint teaching with Lieven De Cauter inspired me to directly engage from the architecture field with the public debate, using design practice as a prism to better understand the psychological, social and environmental ecology of today and to critically intervene in it. This engagement is not documented in the book, since it would lead us too far from the question of how overidentification enables the critic to operate differently.

Another parallel to the third phase of BAVO can be traced back to the flowing over of professional activities into personal engagement with urban issues in my home town, Brussels. After a traumatic event involving a traffic accident with my young children, I started to explicitly mobilize all the theoretical baggage acquired to advocate road safety in Brussels. A few years later I joined forces with citizen movement 1030/0, using the zip code of the municipality of Schaarbeek with the 0 of Vision Zero, a European policy to reduce traffic death. The mix of moral indignation and professional anger over the weak political response proved to be a strong drive to common the streets of Brussels, organize joyful rebellious actions and advocate infrastructure improvements. The movement spread across Brussels and resulted in the umbrella organization Heroes for Zero. This activism in the field was equally about spreading the message in the main news platforms, such as the newspaper *De Standaard* and the news website *VRT NWS*, something I have devoted myself to fully, playing the critical commentator and even instigator of many actions. My inclusion of the activist work by Heroes for Zero and Filter Café Filtré in this book (see Chapter 12) is not to claim authorship in any way, but rather to show how the desire for urban change was strengthened by the power of the activist commons. It is also to acknowledge how activist work gave me so much in return, not only allowing me to practise architecture criticism as a public affair, but also better understanding the theoretical issues I was always professionally busy with, such as urban politics, democracy in the city, architecture of the commons and more.

Discursive Architecture

Let us now briefly introduce the origin and inspiration of BAVO to both rethink criticism on the basis of the strategy of overidentification and develop it as a practice that takes part in the architectural production process. The starting point is the acknowledgement that most criticism is not intended to be taken seriously. Criticism is usually ushered in to deal with messy politics and blurry ethics, making it possible to navigate the complex choreography that defines the unstable field of architecture and to define an agency of its own. Criticism makes it possible to maintain a healthy distance towards the practices one is engaged in and to cling to certain ideals without assuming responsibility for the practical implementation. Hire a critic and you can get away with murder. The paradoxical function of maintaining the status quo in the sign of its opposite leads to what we call inherent criticism, taking our inspiration from the conceptualization of the inherent transgression introduced by Slavoj Žižek.[9] This interdependence of criticism and the status quo runs in two directions. Criticism is not meant to politicize or undermine anything at all; on the contrary, it is an inherent function of the status quo that makes it possible to get away with it by pretending the opposite. At the same time, criticism has become an automated function in the daily operation of the system as the symbolical institute fully counts on voluntary identification. The system feeds on autonomous agents and critical minds, not faceless bureaucrats.

The twisted ideological function of criticism is not just an abstract reflection, but is supported by the state of affairs when it comes to criticism in the field of architecture in Flanders. An exemplary figure is the work of architecture critic Christophe Van Gerrewey. Take his essay 'Order, Disorder: Ten Choices and Contradictions in the Work of OFFICE'.[10] All sort of contradictions are mobilized to situate the work of Office Kersten Geers David Van Severen (Office KGDVS) in relation to many references that are part of the canon of architectural history and theory. The contradictions do not politicize the architectural work, hell no; rather, they depoliticize the work by claiming that 'only swaying between the two [opposites] does justice to the rich difficulty of contemporary life'. Moreover, the list conveniently omits one quite basic contradiction that is overly present in the portfolio of Office KGDVS, the identification of every project by a number: Office 51, Office 52, Office 53, etc. Clearly the numbering follows the logic of the oeuvre and suggests a sort of artistic autonomy, but fails to recognize the framework of architectural production, such as the service-oriented relationship with the client, the specifications of the project brief, and so on. Business interests are also repressed, such as the many joint ventures of Office KGDVS with Jaspers Eyers Architects in recent work: in Brussels, the new headquarters for the VRT public broadcasting company, the redevelopment of the headquarters of KBC Bank and the Commerce 46 office block, and in Antwerp, the AP University College Campus Hallenplein.[11]

The joint venture of Office KGDVS and Jaspers Eyers Architects is problematic considering their dubious role in devastating urban project developments in recent decades in Brussels and elsewhere. This specific history, commonly known as the period of 'Brusselization', is not just something external to architecture culture in Flanders; on the contrary, it is at its very heart, not to say it is its *raison d'être*. In the late 1990s an 'architecture civil society' was engineered in Flanders to put up a dam against devastating urban developments caused by project developers with their corporate architect and political friends. The office of the Flemish Government Architect was set up to advise the government when it came to the selection of architects. In parallel the VAi was established to promote best practices and highlight emergent oeuvres. Suddenly, the young gods of Flemish architecture, the proud heirs of the long struggle for architecture civil society in the past century, now emerged as allies of the establishment their great patrons had rebelled against. Part of the problem is an architecture criticism that presents itself as willing executioner that invites to swing between contradictions, that sings the praise of brave innocuous choices and helps to cope with situations that demand a firm ethical stance.

Remember how Michael Sorkin called upon his colleagues to 'draw the line' and put an end to their participation in the design of the death chambers in prisons.[12] I cannot recall any architectural critic in Flanders doing the same in respect to the construction of new prisons for Beveren and Dendermonde designed by Stéphane Beel Architects – one of the early acclaimed architects in Flemish architecture culture. In this case, Stéphane Beel Architects collaborated with, again, Jaspers Eyers Architects – no wonder the prison design merely refashioned the century-old Ducpétiaux model. The joint venture can be seen as an early precedent of the success formula through which the status quo survived its near-death and smartly countered the Flemish architecture culture to their benefit. The same holds for the use of OMA and Neutelings-Riedijk – pioneers from the Netherlands, a guiding country for architecture culture – as a signboard for Jaspers Eyers Architects for the design of respectively the headquarters of the Belgian public railway company NMBS/SNCB at Brussels-South Station and the Proximus towers at Brussels-North Station.[13] The highly productive collaboration of Office KGDVS with Jaspers Eyers Architects is just another case in point.

The affirmation of the status quo through the new is key to understanding why the artist was considered the typical split subject that sustains the 'end of history', once proclaimed and later criticized by Francis Fukuyama, but nonetheless holding consensus: although art no longer has any social usefulness, it enables us to hold on to the idea that something different is still possible.[14] The post-historical framework defines what we will call inherent criticism: it is a figure that criticizes everything in order to keep the situation in check, a figure that indulges in severe self-criticism in order to avoid fundamental questions.[15] Going against the blackmail, the strategy of overidentification gave way to another conception of architecture criticism, no longer acting as willing executioner, no longer arguing from an opposite standpoint, no longer nesting in the safe hearth of frustration, but feeding on the inherent criticism present in a certain situation, affirming the complexities and contradictions and taking it more seriously than anyone is prepared to do. The inherent criticism may well function as a support for the system at the same time as it provides the possibility of subversion and offers new lines of flight, something which may well pass through moments of closure.

The strategy of overidentification is about the radicalization of criticism by acknowledging that even the most heated ideological debate will be decided in practice, not theory. You can also see it as the inverse Kurt Lewin aphorism that 'there is nothing more practical than a good theory'. Over twenty years, BAVO has been engaging with different debates in the expanded field of architecture, ranging from regional development, city marketing and policy on architecture quality to the architecture of prisons and mental healthcare, ending with the design of the seclusion room. The practical element was not just about finding the right illustration of theory, but lay rather in the opposite, Žižekian meaning: the practical situation makes it possible to shed a different light on the theory.[16] The continuous search for impact in the practical situations made the application of the general strategy of overidentification shift in response to the context of intervention. First, the strategy of overidentification got narrowed down by understanding it in terms of full spectrum provocation and hyperidealism (still working in line with the psychoanalytical tradition). Next, other critical strategies were put in the mix, such as the emancipatory pedagogies of ignorance (taking our inspiration from the work of Jacques

Rancière) and the relational architecture of the commons (inspired
by the work of Doina Petrescu). Taking into account the specific
field of intervention – actors, initiative, platform, public attention,
duration, reception and other dynamics – led us to experiment
with different tactical moves. Over the years, the different critical
interventions enabled us to turn the screw of overidentification at
every step, shifting from identity correction to provocative affirmation and ignorant mediation.

The resulting practice may have turned into physical results
at some points, especially in the Caritas project, but the outcome
is still first situated at the discursive level. Clearly the topic of discursivity is not about the linguistics of a formal discipline like architecture nor about the relation of literature and architecture.[17]
Discursive architecture is used in reference to Lacanian psychoanalysis and rather hints at the awareness that, besides form,
proportion and matter, architecture is always about knowledge.
Discourse is the apparatus that makes it possible to articulate the
world we live in and imagine our future.[18] However, discourse has
a double meaning in Lacanese and also hints at the social link established through architecture, not only between the users of the
built environment, but first starting with the agent of the architectural production process. Jacques Lacan defined four different
social links (Master, University, Hysteric, Analyst) that dynamically relate to each other, later outlining the fifth, Capitalist, as a
variation on the first, Master discourse.[19] Each discourse may have
its specific critical effect. The hysteric is most known for its endless questioning. The university is about commenting practice and
historicizing specific oeuvres. The master fits practise in abstract
metanarratives, refits if necessary. Still, we will situate the critical
function in the analytic position; it is about showing how, to paraphrase Slavoj Žižek, old knowledge can function differently, and
awaken earlier unthought-of visions from there.[20]

Discursive architecture also hints at the ambition to intervene in the field of architecture by challenging its order of speech,
following the poststructuralist philosophy of Michel Foucault.[21] In
Belgium, the 'Orde van architecten/Ordre des architectes' (Order
of Architects) quite literally limits speech in the field of architecture, and so do other players, such as the Flemish Government Architect, VAi, architectural magazines, cultural institutions, project developers, politicians and faculties. Other limits to the field of
architecture involve daily design practices and the specific procedures that allow them to be recognized, appreciated and distributed within communities or schools. The role of critics is crucial in
the order of architecture; they function as gatekeepers and have
the power to limit or delimit the field. Again, Christophe Van Gerrewey is exemplary. Discussing the Design Museum competition
in Ghent, the critic regretted the choice of the dullest design by

Carmody Groarke, ATAMA and RE-ST – the quality was similar to that of many Zara stores, he argued – over his favourite, Office KGDVS, which he called the most important architectural office of the Flemish golden generation. In the same breath, Van Gerrewey accused the Flemish Government Architect of bad intentions and suggested that the Design Museum competition proved the total bankruptcy of architecture culture in Flanders.[22] Was it criticism or flagrant idolatry? In any case, Van Gerrewey blindly negated the basic principles of the Open Call procedure by the Flemish Government Architect in an attempt to brutally restore order in the canon of Flemish architecture.[23]

By contrast, BAVO's critical interventions in the field of architecture aimed to challenge the order of speech by questioning first of all accepted bodies of knowledge about what is true or not, and also the social power relations that define who has the right to take the stage or not. Therefore, the spectral office of BAVO was a rhetorical strategy to claim a space for criticism in the absence of legitimacy and with the clear goal of undermining vested subject positions in the order of speech. The office was a mirage of the author, much the same way as the relationship of Rem Koolhaas with the Office for Metropolitan Architecture (OMA) or, even more fittingly, the group of historians acting as a quasi-office under the name Crimson Architecture Historians. The empty signifier of BAVO made it possible to project a collective that grants anonymity and gives collaborators space for play while also protecting them. In certain situations, I used my academic affiliation with KU Leuven to bolster BAVO's credibility; this was especially useful in relation to government institutions and, on the opposite side of the spectrum, as support for urban activism. Besides rhetoric, BAVO's spectral role was also a necessity as there is little money available in the field of architecture for criticism, let alone that it makes sense to be paid for activism. Therefore, the discursive practice of BAVO necessarily remained an 'activism without a business plan', in spite of occasional subsidies and commissions for specific projects. Still, BAVO embraced its position of being 'nothing' as it enabled BAVO to work through the internal contradictions of a situation while leaving the initiative to the main actors.

Notes
1. BAVO, 'Always Choose the Worst Option: Artistic Resistance and the Strategy of Over-Identification', in *Cultural Activism Today: The Art of Over-Identification*, ed. BAVO (Rotterdam: Episode, 2007), 18-39. See also the other essays by BAVO from that period.
2. BAVO, 'When it Comes to Security, There Is No Normality: een klinische benadering van de hedendaagse beveiligings- en bewakingscultuur', *Archis* 3 (Mar. 2002), 36-42.

3. BAVO Research, *De onverdeelde stad en haar gewillige beulen* (The Hague: Stroom, 2003).
4. Gideon Boie and Matthias Pauwels (BAVO Research), 'Rediscover Your Wholeness! Vijf manieren om de spanning tussen economie en identiteit op te lossen', in *Geest en Grond, culturele planologie in de Duin- en Bollenstreek*, ed. Hans Venhuizen (Rotterdam: Bureau Venhuizen and Erfgoedhuis Zuid-Holland, 2003), 138-46.
5. The conference at Stedelijk CS was the final outcome of the series of research seminars 'The Spectre of the Avant-Garde: Reasserting the Programme of Subversion in Contemporary Artistic-Cultural Practices' organized by BAVO at the Jan van Eyck Academie, 15-16 Mar. and 12-13 Apr. 2005. The proceedings of the research seminar programme 'The Spectre of the Avant-Garde' were published in an issue of *Andere Sinema* guest-edited by BAVO and Dieter Roelstraete under the title 'Spectres de l'Avant-Garde', *Andere Sinema AS* 176 (Sep.-Oct. 2006).
6. BAVO, ed., *Urban Politics Now: Re-Imagining Democracy in the Neoliberal City* (Rotterdam: nai, 2007). BAVO, ed., *Cultural Activism Today: The Art of Over-Identification* (Rotterdam: Episode, 2007).
7. Gideon Boie, 'Report by the Taskforce for Architecture and Administrative Modernisation: Here the Citizen is at Home', in *Flanders Architectural Yearbook 2006-2007: edition 2008*, eds. Katrien Vandermarliere et al. (Antwerp: VAi, 2008), 21-26.
8. Gideon Boie, 'A Lesson in Added Architectural Value', in *Flanders Architectural Yearbook 2008-2009* (Antwerp: VAi, 2010), 175-77. Later republished as: Gideon Boie, 'Wet89', in *Double or Nothing*, ed. 51N4E (London: AA Publications, 2011).
9. Slavoj Žižek, *The Plague of Fantasies* (London: Verso, 1997), 18-27.
10. Christophe Van Gerrewey, 'Order, Disorder: Ten Choices and Contradictions in the Work of OFFICE', in *OFFICE Kersten Geers David Van Severen: Volume 2*, ed. Kersten Geers, David Van Severen, Bas Princen, et al. (Cologne: Walther König, 2016), 7-14.
11. Gideon Boie, 'Kwaliteit als katalysator van sloop', *De Architect : Vakblad voor de Architect, 48, no. 5* (2017): 164-65. Gideon Boie, 'Vernieuwing en gevestigde orde gaan niet samen', *De Standaard*, 28 Jun. 2021, 30-31.
12. Michael Sorkin, 'Drawing the Line: Architects and Prisons', *The Nation*, 27 Aug. 2013.
13. Geert Sels, 'Eerste project van Rem Koolhaas in België', *De Standaard*, 22 Feb. 2020, 30-31. Lukas Vanacker, 'Immobel plant 400 woningen en koten in Proximus-torens', *De Tijd*, 14 Jul. 2022.
14. Francis Fukuyama, *The End of History and the Last Man* (New York: Free Press, 1992), 321; Francis Fukuyama, *America at the Crossroads: Democracy, Power and the Neoconservative Legacy* (New Haven: Yale University Press, 2006).
15. The argument is developed in: BAVO, 'Always Choose the Worst Option'. BAVO, *Too Active to Act: Cultureel activisme na het einde van de geschiedenis* (Amsterdam: Valiz, 2010), 43-50 and 63-70.
16. Slavoj Žižek, *Looking Awry: An Introduction to Jacques Lacan through Popular Culture* (Cambridge, MA: MIT Press, 1991), 3.
17. Wim Cuyvers, 'From the Dream of the Novel Turned to Stone to the Acknowledgment of Public Space', *OASE* 70 (Jun. 2006), 20-29.

18. Giorgio Agamben, *What Is an Apparatus? And Other Essays* (Stanford: Stanford University Press, 2009), 14.
19. Jacques Lacan, *The Seminar of Jacques Lacan, Book XVII: The Other Side of Psychoanalysis* (1973; New York: Norton, 2008), 29-53. See also Chapter 2 in this book.
20. Žižek, *The Parallax View*, 304. View (Cambridge MA: MIT Press, 2006), 304.
21. Michel Foucault, 'The Order of Discourse', in *Untying the Text: A Post-Structuralist Reader*, ed. Robert Young (Boston: Routledge & Kegan Paul, 1981), 48-78. Inaugural lecture at the Collège de France, given 2 Dec. 1970.
22. Christophe Van Gerrewey, 'Het saaiste ontwerp heeft gewonnen', *De Standaard*, 25 Oct. 2019.
23. Gideon Boie, 'Weg met de architectuurwedstrijden?', *De Standaard*, 31 Oct. 2019, 37.

Stop Criticizing and Judging

Chapter 2

From the early years, psychoanalytical theory has been the main guide for the practice of BAVO, especially in the political and ideology-critical version developed by Slavoj Žižek. After studying architecture and later philosophy at the same universities, an academic friendship spontaneously evolved into a common writing practice, critically engaging with the architecture debates. BAVO was founded as a collaboration with Matthias Pauwels around 2001 in Rotterdam. Clearly, the idea was to practice architecture philosophy, but for different reasons we didn't brand it as such. Architecture philosophy was rather inexistent as a disciplinary field, or at least undefined, and it lacked the sense of urgency that is a necessary part of criticism. Instead, we established the practice of BAVO using the tag line 'Research into the political dimension of art, architecture and urban planning'. The political was used as a stand-in for philosophy, referring to our background in political philosophy and introducing the basic difference between everyday politics and the political, the latter refers to the basic antagonisms driving society.[1] The reference to the political was uncommon in the field of architecture, especially in Flanders where de-politicization was – and still is, rightly so – the watchword for architecture culture.[2] Still, de-politicization and re-politicization should be considered together, having in mind the basic difference with politics introduced by the political (we will return to it below). From 2009 onward, BAVO continued as a parallel practice to my teaching and research at the KU Leuven Faculty of Architecture and as an ever changing collective operating in various configurations, temporarily involving different collaborators, often former students. In this chapter, I briefly sketch the main motivations and inspirations underlying BAVO and how specific twists in the conceptual framework came about.

The Office Is Nothing

BAVO was explicitly established as an office, the typical agency in the field of architecture, but not having the slightest intention to conform to conventional design discipline in the service of building practice and urban development. The ambition was explicitly to practise architecture criticism by rearticulating the ongoing debates through the use of our philosophical background, expanding the architectural discourse for that matter. A prime example was Crimson Architectural Historians, the Rotterdam-based collective of historians operating as an office, outside academia, but producing a body of work no less profound and rigorous, and clearly written with a surplus of joy.[3] Crimson was using architecture history as a means to engage with ongoing debates about architecture in the Netherlands, the home base Rotterdam more particularly, and showing a fine taste for visual aesthetics.[4] Another example was Maurice Nio, an architect with writings heavily influenced by Jean Baudrillard, first publishing under the name NOX (with Kas Oosterhuis) and later under his own name.[5] Soon the desire grew to undertake something similar, this time enlarging architecture discourse from the perspective of (political) philosophy and, in turn, using architecture as the main material to engage with urgent social and political issues.

The name of BAVO mimicked the typical brand names of architecture offices consisting of an acronym referring either to intellectual manifestos (OMA standing for 'Office for Metropolitan Architecture') or just the names of the founders (MVRDV standing for 'Maas, van Rijs and De Vries'). BAVO, by contrast, was used as an empty signifier, lacking direct meaning and not referring to anything specific, although we had borrowed the first name of Bavo Claes, a news anchor with a longstanding career for the Flemish broadcasting network VRT. He was known for his earnest style and stern look, not afraid of putting uncomfortable questions to people in high places while keeping a reserved distance (his attitude allegedly led him to being pushed to ever-later news shows). Unknown as a media personality in the Netherlands and certainly irrelevant in the field of architecture, the name BAVO became a sort of enigma, mainly suggesting an institutional context. The name was often understood in line with the typical acronyms defining the Dutch educational system such as Mavo ('Middelbaar algemeen voortgezet onderwijs', Lower general secondary education) and Havo ('Hoger algemeen voortgezet onderwijs', Senior general secondary education). In this series, the term Bavo was less commonly known but stood for 'Basis algemeen voortgezet onderwijs' (Basic general secondary education), the first two years of basic education. Another interpretation people suggested referred to Saint Bavo, who was active in the Christianization of the Low Lands and therefore the patron of churches in many cities, the best known being in Ghent and Haarlem. The Catholic tradition meant that Bavo was also known as a name for schools (in Ghent there is the secondary school 'Sint-Bavohumaniora') and psychiatric institutions (we often got calls from people asking about their relatives in therapy at the Bavo RNO psychiatric hospital in Rotterdam). We acknowledged all interpretations with pleasure, while resisting any invitation to elucidate the name.

The BAVO enigma was heightened by eclipsing our personal names in public communications and appearances. In the early years of our activity, we published texts under the name BAVO, presented lectures as BAVO, engaged in meetings as BAVO, took commissions as BAVO, mostly without mentioning our identity and without informing the host in advance whether we would show up solo or as a duo. The identification with the brand name was total, up to the point that I once introduced myself at the *Cinema Clash Continuum Conference* (28 Mar.-1 Apr. 2011) at the Gerrit Rietveld Academie (Utrecht) as 'Gideon Bavo'. BAVO's impersonal appearance meant that the public was unaware of its nature, intention and seriousness, who was actually behind it, how many we were, where we got the money and, perhaps the most recurrent question, what we wanted of them. Actually, the issues of money and desire were entangled, just as in psychoanalytical practice. As we were strictly making a living from writing (not being engaged in teaching, as most critics are, nor any other engagement), it was impossible to pinpoint our position. We were proudly labelling BAVO as an independent research office. Keeping up the spectre of BAVO became more difficult after Matthias Pauwels and I moved to, respectively, Pretoria in 2009 and Brussels in 2007. It was soon clear that it was mostly myself who took the honours in public, although engagements were still common until around 2010.

The use of BAVO took another turn when we started to present BAVO as a research collective after engaging mostly former students from the KU Leuven Faculty of Architecture (where I had been teaching and researching) since 2009. Collaborators include, in chronological order, Wim Vandendriessche, Rūta Valiūnaitė-Aleks, Paoletta Holst, Fie Vandamme, Lydia Karagiannaki, Heleen Verheyden, Vjera Sleutel, Marine Boey, Rosa Fens, Helen Van der Vloet, Erro Rasker and Tom Schoonjans. The open format of the collective made it possible to appear in different formations and publish under different names, again making the public believe that we were many, which was clearly never the case. The confusion also concerned the structural basis of BAVO, making people (even superiors, colleagues and friends) doubt whether it was an independent practice like any other architecture office or a research unit at the university – again, neither was the case. In terms of content, BAVO operated more and more as a parallel practice to academic research, but hardly possible to distinguish. In fact, both activities were interchangeable and employed for mutual benefit. Still, BAVO was effectively nothing; it started as an alter ego, an office as mask of the author, and remained so throughout the years, even when operating as a collective. The collaborations in the BAVO collective, mainly involving former students, happened on a project basis and for loose engagements, allowing them to use the work as a stepping stone for their careers. The office of BAVO was purely performative, never inscribed as a trading company; it neither operated during office hours nor did it separate work engagements for KU Leuven, BAVO and civil society.

The confusion was partly due to the publication of articles identifying me as affiliated with 'BAVO/KU Leuven Faculty of Architecture', in contrast to the previous common authorship with Matthias Pauwels under the name of BAVO. A constant element in BAVO's operation has been the frenetic publishing policy, understanding articles not just as a means to distribute ideas and arguments, but considering publication in itself an intervention in the public space, provoking different types of public. The publications consisted of research findings in academic magazines, field notes in professional magazines, critical arguments in popular media and other propaganda on direct publication platforms. Using my personal name as the author of publications was done to take the flak in delicate or contested issues and keep freelance collaborators out of reach. The academic affiliation added credibility not without immediately fuelling question marks, though the work was exactly the same in terms of topic, output and presentation. Even more, through the years the practice of BAVO became increasingly interchangeable with the academic work, perhaps the only difference being public perception.

Psychoanalysis of the Architecture Field

The set-up of BAVO as a practice on the threshold of architecture and philosophy was a strange thing in both the field of philosophy and that of architecture. During our architecture studies at Sint-Lucas in Ghent (now called KU Leuven Faculty of Architecture, campus Ghent), Matthias Pauwels and I were triggered into the unknown terrain of architecture philosophy by the phenomenological work of philosopher Jacques De Visscher and the writings of architect Wim Cuyvers, the latter heavily influenced by Georges Bataille. Thanks to a stipend from the Thomas More Foundation, I was able to spend a year studying philosophy at the Radboud University Nijmegen (1999-2000), where Jacques De Visscher was also holding a professorship. A year later, Matthias Pauwels followed with the same stipend. It was Philippe Van Haute who put us on the path of psychoanalysis in the philosophical anthropology course through close readings of Sigmund Freud and Jacques Lacan. We continued studying at the Erasmus University Rotterdam (from 2000), where Henk Oosterling introduced us to the world of Slavoj Žižek, starting with the *Pleidooi voor intolerantie* (Plea for intolerance), a short essay originally published in an early English version as 'Multiculturalism, Or, the Cultural Logic of Multinational Capitalism'.[6] The knowledge of Lacanese was deepened during our two-year stay at the Jan van Eyck Academie Maastricht (2004-05), where we enjoyed the exegesis of the Seminars of Jacques Lacan led by Marc De Kesel as part of the Circle for Lacanian Ideology Critique (CLiC). The work of Slavoj Žižek was most inspiring, not only because of the introduction of psychoanalytical theory into philosophy, following in the footsteps of Jacques Lacan, but especially for the use of popular culture as the main analytical material in a post-Marxist philosophical critique of capitalist society today. After all, Žižek's work is very practical and casuistic: the eclectic mixture of philosophy, psychoanalysis and pop culture is, perhaps in the first place, a means to critically intervene in ongoing social and political debates. In an early work, Žižek describes the critical strategy of 'looking awry': 'What is at stake in the endeavour to "look awry" at theoretical motifs is not just a kind of contrived attempt to "illustrate" high theory, [...] The point is rather that such an exemplification, such a mise-en-scène of theoretical motifs renders visible aspects that would otherwise remain unnoticed.'[7] The strategic note can be understood as the manifesto underlying much of Žižek's work. He frames the strategy as follows: 'to undermine a given theoretical position by "staging" it as an existential subjective attitude [...] and to reveal its otherwise hidden inconsistencies, that is, to exhibit the way its very subjective position of enunciation undermines its "enunciated", its positive contents.'[8]

In line with Žižek's Freudo-Marxist philosophy, we started with BAVO to develop what you could call a psychoanalysis of the architecture field, except that the clinical connotation is somehow inappropriate within the context of architectural criticism. Architecture might be ugly or terrible, buildings might be considered sick or sick-making, you might even construct a whole symptomatology of spaces, but the critic can offer no healing. Our central focus became the entanglement of the architectural object and the discourse that envelops it, discourse understood in the double Lacanian meaning of language and social relationship. Beyond intrinsic qualities such as form, proportion and texture, architecture is a product answering a demand by the client, following specific regulations, social expectations and business plans, often reduced to mere prehistory, but therefore all the more defining.[9] Equally important in understanding architecture, as we know, are the processes of consumption and distribution, often located in the afterlife of architecture, but no less defining for the architectural object.[10] We considered the articulation of these moments as a way to engage the 'other scene' of architecture, just as Étienne Balibar defined the autonomy of politics not without immediately discussing its heteronomy.[11] Architecture is a cultural product bearing logical, ethical and political implications that accompany the different actors in the production process and their complex social relationships. Architects, commissioners, users and others, they all have often contradictory stakes in a design project and make up their own narrative on the beauty, meaning, use and surplus of architecture. There might even be myths of origin, primary identifications, intimate fears and collective imaginations at stake in architecture, just as Balibar talked about the 'heteronomy of heteronomy' active in politics.[12]

Developing a psychoanalysis of the architecture field gave a twist to BAVO's practice, avoiding the typical oppositional approach of criticism. 'Blame the architect!' is certainly the easiest game for criticism, Wouter Vanstiphout has argued, using the architect as scapegoat for whatever social and political wrong.[13] Spatial environments condensate urban policies and market operations, they provide material, tangible form to abstract logics and, therefore, architecture often symbolizes processes of inequality, injustice, exclusion, exploitation, especially in times of unrest and riots. However, the reverse game of 'Blame the Other!' is equally easy and cheap. In the criticism of the *Flanders Architectural Review* (previously the *Flanders Architectural Yearbook*) published by the VAi, architecture is typically presented as pristine while everything that goes wrong is said to come from external forces (client, market, politics, NIMBYs, etc.). Architecture follows the publishing format. The ambition of the VAi to showcase best-practices in architectural production results in the caricature of architecture as always situated on the right side of history, conveniently forgetting the wisdom of Walter Benjamin that 'there is no document of civilization which is not at the same time a document of barbarism'.[14] Going beyond good and evil, the main task in BAVO's psychoanalysis of the architecture field was to shed light on the different subject positions in a certain situation and analyse how it colours the content of architecture. This meant articulating and visualizing the needs and desires of the actors engaged in the process of architectural production, their intentions and motivations, engagements and interests, inspirations and dreams, obstacles and limitations, frustrations and fears, while including processes of consumption and distribution, and not forgetting eventual complexities and contradictions.

A shift in BAVO's work became visible the moment psychoanalysis became the method for critical intervention, not just providing the conceptual tools and strategies. In the early years we used the psychoanalytical framework to construct ideology-critical arguments, presented in debates and published in articles and books. For instance, the critique of the embedded artist was inspired by Slavoj Žižek's notion of interpassivity, summarized in the formula 'Let's go on changing something all the time so that, globally, things will remain the same!' and used to understand the frenetic engagement of cultural actors in urban redevelopment as contradictory key to the status quo.[15] The notion of overidentification was proposed as counter-strategy in which artists no longer act as the last of idealists, but identify with the current trends in such a way that it becomes unbearable.¹⁶ The early prescriptive criticism was justified, but it always ran the danger of preaching to the converted while frustrating the main actors in such a way that any window for change would be shut closed from the outset. How many times does a critical debate or lecture not end with the critic being accused of lacking information, making false interpretations or having bad intentions? In seeking to have an impact, we soon started to assume the conceptual tools and strategies of psychoanalysis in the labour of criticism itself, no longer prescribing others what to do, but overidentifying with the interpassivity. We stopped playing the critic preaching about the interpassivity that pervades design practice and demand architects to change their action in the light of whatever doom; on the contrary, we abandoned all hope and started to embody the interpassivity of architecture practice, articulate and visualize its motivations, and stage its nullifying effects. Covering all sins of the world of architecture, the job of criticism changed in allowing the public to work through the ideological identifications and other passionate attachments underpinning their work.

The shift in strategy brought us to the establishment of a therapeutical relationship. This can be considered the most important part of criticism, i.e. setting a scene where it is accepted to work through the complexities and contradictions in a certain project. The therapeutical relationship doesn't come naturally and needs attention if digesting the outcome is the goal; even more, entertaining the relationship is perhaps the most difficult part. Criticism in the traditional form of endless questioning runs the danger of hysteria. Criticism in the form of providing data and fact-checking gets trapped in the university discourse. Criticism in the form of alternative proposals is vulnerable to new master discourses. The strategy of overidentification was helpful in this regard; it meant that the critic no longer fought over the right interpretation, no longer cast doubt on motivations, no longer even longed for alternatives, but fully identified with the movement at work. Facing such inverted criticism, the public can no longer hide behind the critic's alleged shortage of information, false interpretations or bad intentions. On the contrary, the public is confronted with an image of their own, though in a slightly exaggerated way. If there is any therapeutical result, it is the stirring of hope that lines of flight will appear in working through the phantasy that sustains a certain situation, lines which in turn start to function as a catalyst for processes of change and emancipation. Call it the critical impact, the opening of possibilities to reconsider and eventually reposition the set engagements.

Bend It Like the Yes Men

The strategy of overidentification came into play through the work of Slavoj Žižek, who was personally involved in NSK, a subversive movement of artists, designers and theorists in the late days of the Yugoslav Republic. Part of the NSK movement was the rock-band Laibach, famous for its quasi-fascist motifs as a criticism of the Yugoslav socialism-in-one-state solution; think of the song 'Geburt einer Nation' (1987), the proto-fascist version of Queen's 'One Vision' (1985). The celebration of 'Ein Fleisch, ein Blut, ein wahrer Glaube, eine Rasse und ein Traum, ein starker Wille, Jawohl!' was actualizing the Germanic trauma of the Yugoslav nation. Slavoj Žižek called Laibach's strategy the 'public staging of the obscene phantasmatic kernel of an ideological edifice', a play that was even present in the use of the old Germanic name of Ljubljana, the capital of Slovenia.[17] Interestingly, Laibach employed the same strategy in their songs after the fall of the Eastern Bloc, this time addressing the new post-historical world order. The song 'War' on the album *NATO* (1994) was a cover of the original anti-war song by The Temptations (1970), now issued in the context of the bombing of Serbia by NATO forces, but changing the famous chorus: 'War, what is it good for? Absolutely nothing uh-uh'. In Laibach's version, the pathetic outcry 'War, what is it good for?' is immediately answered by a list of all the fields that profit from war (religion, industry, communications, etc.), even explicitly naming multinational firms that are part of the war industry (GM, IBM, Newsweek, CNN, Universal, ITT, etc.). Another example is the song 'Tanz mit Laibach' on the album *WAT* (2003), in which Laibach praises the union of former arch-enemies in the invasion of Iraq: 'Mit Totalitarismus, und mit Demokratie, wir tanzen mit Fascismus, und roter Anarchie, eins, zwei, drei, vier, Kamerad, komm tanz mit mir, eins, zwei, drei, vier, beide Hände reich ich dir [...] Amerikano Freunde, und Deutscher Kamerad, wir tanzen gut zusammen, wir tanzen nach Baghdad.'[18] The strategy of overidentification reappears in Žižek's later philosophical writings, especially in conceptualizing the figure of orthodoxy (e.g., with G.K. Chesterton) as a critical gesture against the cynical logic of ideology: that is, ideology is only effective insofar as it always keeps a distance.[19] Still later, Žižek praises Greta Thunberg for exposing the weak response of world leaders and captains of industry by presenting the climate issue in black and white, refusing to think in shades of grey and taking the issue of survival predicted by the Intergovernmental Panel on Climate Change (IPCC) seriously.[20]

The artist duo Yes Men was the main example in BAVO's theoretical exploration of the use of overidentification for cultural activism today in the symposium and publication mentioned above in the short genealogy. The Yes Men are famous for hoaxes in which they put forward, with a poker face and under false identities, the most scandalous proposals. For example, a WTO business plan to solve starvation in the Third World by recycling the faeces of McDonald's customers into hamburgers for Africa. Their most famous hoax is perhaps Jacques 'Andy Bichlbaum' Servin appearing on BBC World (3 December 2004) as 'Jude Finesterra', a Dow Chemical spokesman, announcing that the multinational was finally going to assume full responsibility for the Bhopal disaster on 3 December 1984, exactly twenty years earlier. The interview lasted more than five minutes, 'Finesterra' giving details on reparation, site clearance, future transparency, extradition of the former CEO, and so on, while the BBC changed its caption to 'Breaking News'. Although the performance was rapidly denounced as fake by Dow Chemical, the impact was nonetheless devastating. Dow Chemical was forced to release a press brief in which they denied the statement made by the fake spokesman about proper action towards the Bhopal disaster. This also meant putting an end to the vague promises Dow Chemical had made earlier. The intervention by the Yes Men – they call it 'identity correction' – turned the usual gesture of criticism upside down: instead of denouncing the multinational for being unethical and only acting for the sake of its profits, they took the ideal of corporate governance and business ethics deadly seriously, leaving no room for compromise. The gesture meant that the target of the criticism – Dow Chemical – could no longer hide behind vague ideals and was forced to make absolutely clear that it did not care one bit about the local community.

Although the strategy of identity correction is a powerful tool for criticism, the impact is limited insofar as the Yes Men expose the bad guys for their wrongdoing while other subject positions are kept out of the picture. It is easy to blame capitalist firms, but what about the rather weak response to the Bhopal disaster by progressive governments and human-rights movements? What about the public having a laugh with the cunning of the artist duo, but continuing to buy products from the multinational, perhaps even checking their stock market return in the evening? And what about the enlightened artist duo, active in an art context that benefits from corporate sponsorship and is driven by short-lived critical engagements? All this drove BAVO to shift strategy and present the work of theatre-maker Christoph Schlingensief as next-level overidentification, one that doesn't allow the public easy identification with the good guys while mocking the bad ones. *Bitte Liebt Österreich* (2000) was a sort of 'Big Brother' theatre show, set up in front of the Vienna Burgtheater, in which twelve undocumented refugees could compete for the vote of the public to be accepted in the country by showing how well they knew the local language, culture and traditions.[21] The most convincing of them was promised a residence permit, through marriage, while the public could watch how the losers were removed from the show by security, put in a taxi and brought to an unknown location. The performance caused an outroar, with people from all sides protesting against the show: not only right-wing people who felt offended – clearly the show was created after Jörg Haider's far-right FPÖ party took power – but also left-wing people who bemoaned the inhumane character of the show.

Bitte Liebt Österreich went beyond the one-sided provocation of multinational capitalism or nationalist populism. It could be labelled as what Alexei Monroe called 'Full Spectrum Provocation', referring to the cultural practices of NSK, accepting of the fact that there is no proper criticism except for criticism that provokes all sides equally, at the risk of alienating friends and foes alike.[22] Interestingly, the director was present at *Bitte Liebt Österreich*: Christoph Schlingensief stood on the roof of the container village with a megaphone, commenting on the show and provoking the public with obscene remarks, just like the voice-over in *Big Brother*. The director addressed right-wing people – 'I count six, seven fascists on the square! Welcome to Nazi-land. Österreich is Nazi-land. How much love do you have for the country?' – while calling out the bleeding hearts on the left ('How brave of you to free refugees from a play while allowing your country to become a prison!').[23] The critical position in this case is not occupied by a neutral outsider or a questioning hysteric but by one who makes a big mess, embodies complexities and contradictions, stages the identity of opposites, etc. Commenting on humanitarian critique, Schlingensief said: 'It's not an Amnesty International project, it's not a "Show me your wounds" project, it's a "schweinische Unternehmung", a swinish enterprise!' The show was announced as '6 days, 12 asylum seekers, 1 container, 1 case, "eine Woche Kulturterror"'.[24] And cultural terror it was.

In *Cultural Activism Today: The Art of Over-Identification*, we listed more self-reflective performances that allow no one to escape with an easy interpretation, but that rather address the criticism to everyone and everything at the same time, rendering futile the difference between left and right, good and evil, ideology and commonsense, phantasy and reality.[25] Many examples could be found in the visual arts: Santiago Sierra (using his arts budget to tattoo impoverished migrant labourers), Jens Haaning (importing and selling household products as artworks to avoid taxes between Denmark and Sweden), Martijn Engelbregt (distributing a questionnaire asking Amsterdammers if they have seen undocumented refugees in their neighbourhood and, if so, whether they are ready to report them), etc. These works could be considered an antidote to the typical idealist reflex in the labour of criticism: the critic is a prophet of the awful truth, announcing the flooding of the Earth and calling us to do the right thing, but who forgets how progressives might well be included in the imminent catastrophe, even forgetting to include his own position in the picture. Instead, the works of art mentioned here use the strategy of overidentification as a critical gesture that is at the same time a full-spectrum provocation and self-reflective: the artist/critic willingly covers all sins of the world and stages it for everyone to see, even calling everyone to enjoy the beauty of barbarism.

Shifting Uses of Overidentification

The defining moment in the work of BAVO is when we started to apply the strategy of overidentification in the interventions themselves, instead of merely constructing ideology-critical arguments referring to other practices in the field of art and promoting this as an alternative activist strategy. We used the format of invited lectures – a primary tool for the critic – as an opportunity to set up critical interventions that followed strictly the strategy of overidentification. The first experiment happened in the pretty straightforward mode of the Yes Men, for example in the study on the spatial development of the Zuidvleugel (2007), commissioned by Atelier Zuidvleugel and the Province of South Holland.[26] Although asked to critically deconstruct the fundamental concepts of the regional development in the Rotterdam-The Hague-Dordrecht urban cluster, we listed '10 Must-Dos' for spatial development that merge neoliberal dogma with its supposed social and green counterparts. Applying the strategy of overidentification made it possible to avoid to usual game of criticism in which first someone is invited to critically research a certain situation and next he is confronted with what is called resistance in psychoanalytic terms, i.e. counter-criticism meant to debunk the arguments by the critic, cast doubt over his or her honesty and even delegitimize his or her position. Instead, the strategy of overidentification was necessary to divert the typical shooting of the messenger and fuel the debate where it belongs, among the public itself.

We were forced to change tactics once we started to deal with the obsessions of the art sector and addressed artists themselves, i.e. subjects known for their critical engagement with society and hypersensitive when it comes to their autonomy. A game changer was the lecture performance 'Een wereldstad benut haar creatief kapitaal: zeven aanbevelingen van de Rijksadviseurs voor de creatieve schaalsprong van Rotterdam en omstreken' (A global city exploits its creative capital: Seven recommendations from the chief government advisers for the creative upscaling of Rotterdam and environs) in the exhibition *Rondom* (31 January 2008) curated by Jack Segbars at the DCR arts centre in The Hague.[27] The speech drew on the conclusions of the Zuidvleugel project to situate the embedded role of artists in the development of Rotterdam as a creative city, praising its trickle-down effects in the urban development of neighbouring cities, such as The Hague and Dordecht, reducing these cities to the status of 'environs'. However, the overidentification in the style of the Yes Men met with resistance from the public of mainly artists who are somewhat trained in critical engagement with the world and have less faith in whatever happens. The artists proved to be an unanalysable subject, immediately seeing through the overidentification, just fair enough to give the benefit of the doubt to an interesting thought experiment, but not willing to take it quite seriously and to position themselves.

We encountered the same hypersensitivity when dealing with architects who disavow the obvious entanglement of politics with architecture and space and who tend to confuse criticism with praise of the sublime object. One of the first experiences with overidentification in the field of architecture was the 'Office of the Royal Explorers, entrusted with the task of unravelling the deadlock around the Belgian and European Capital', an exhibition proposal in the '1907' invited competition for the 2008 Venice Architecture Biennale, organized by the Flemish Government Architect and VAi.[28] The entry by BAVO was a proposal to call upon the international architecture scene gathering in Venice to help solve the dysfunctions of the Belgian federal state, using Brussels as a case to frame the issue in spatial terms (it was around this time that the formation of the federal government took almost a year). Allegedly, the international jury (which included Petra Blaise and Anne Lacaton) praised BAVO's submission, while national jury members saw the political narrative as a distraction from architecture, and curator Moritz Küng believed the government would be formed before the biennial started (that didn't happen). The resistance made BAVO further experiment with the format of exhibitions as a means for overidentification, making all sorts of public statements, not only through lectures and debates – the typical weaponry in the hands of critics – but also press releases, pamphlets, posters, billboards and other propaganda material.

The use of visual material to convey ideology-critical messages was something we inherited from the period at the Jan van Eyck Academie, especially in the Euregional Forum discursive programme (2006-10). The programme was set up as a means to reach out to provincial and local governments and interrogate them on the issue of cross-border cooperation in the Meuse-Rhine Euregio, bringing together part of the Belgian and Dutch provinces of Limburg, the province of Liège, and the Aachen urban region. The programme was established in collaboration with art institutions in the region, such as NAi Maastricht, Stadsgalerij in Heerlen, FLACC in Genk, Neuer Aachener Kunstverein and Espace 251 Nord in Liège. The programme was an early test for the strategy of overidentification, premature for the most part, but an important step for experimenting with other ways of doing criticism. Over the years, the debate programme included lectures by Wim Cuyvers, Miran Mohar (IRWIN/NSK), Lieven De Cauter, Étienne Balibar, Chantal Mouffe, Paul Scheffer, Riccardo Petrella and many others. The programme also experimented with different visual formats, such as posters, newspapers, films and more. The material was made by fellow researchers from the arts and design department, such as Metahaven (Daniel Van der Velden, Vinca Kruk and Adriaan Mellegers), Hendrik-Jan Grievink and others. The whole set-up of the Euregional Forum was based on the idea that criticism is not just about constructing a sound and just argument, but in the first place about critically intervening in a debate, trying to tickle the actors involved, and also setting a theoretical statement in motion within the local and particular sensibilities. The strategy of overidentification was applied in a hyperidealist version, fully embracing the dream of cross-border cooperation between different European nation states while at same time celebrating the petty conflicts and opportunities operative in the border regions, even calling to enjoy what we called 'geographical schizophrenia'.[29]

The first intervention to make full use of the strategy of overidentification was 'De Janssens Werken' (The Janssens Works) in 2008, an exhibition organized by the VAi and the arts campus De Singel.[30] The invitation to exhibit work by BAVO in the *35m³ Young Architecture* exhibition series was used as an opportunity to showcase the perfect union of architecture and politics in Antwerp. The exhibition deliberately transgressed the taboo on politics in Flemish architecture culture by praising the good works of well-known Flemish architects in the political project of Mayor Patrick Janssens. The exhibition material was about posters, brochures, press releases and other propaganda designed according to the visual guidelines for the official communications of the City of Antwerp, something said to have been influenced by the mayor being a former 'mad man'. The whole purpose of the exhibition shifted from a means for self-promotion to the identity correction of architecture culture in Antwerp. The *35m3* series was promoting the emergent oeuvres of Jan De Vylder, Office Kersten Geers David Van Severen (Office KGDVS), Jo Taillieu, URA, noAarchitecten and other names that would later define the architecture scene in Flanders, and still do today. The exhibition by BAVO was different as it didn't promote itself, but staged the best practices of architecture in Antwerp, including the political framework set by Mayor Janssens, and encouraging our colleagues to come out of the box when it comes to politics.

The tactic was brought to the next level in 'Bureau Kunstenaarsparticipatie' (Office for artist participation) (2010, but already started in 2009), part of the exhibition *The People United*

Will Never be Defeated at TENT. Rotterdam, again showcasing the value of art in the new regime of the populist right-wing (neo)liberalism in the Netherlands.[31] The exhibition entry took the form of a presentation of specific arrangements to reform the arts sector following the new political trends, recognizing how artists have always already been more right-wing liberals then they might care to admit. The museum space was organized as a booth, with posters and a table with chairs for the distribution of propaganda material. Going beyond the four walls of the museum, the exhibition was also held in the town hall and later extended into discussing the budget cuts by the new liberal state secretary for culture, Halbe Zijlstra (instead of criticizing his policies, exposing him as being not liberal enough).

The same topic was brought forward in the 'Dutch Design Lobby' (2010), our contribution to the *Tricksters Tricked* exhibition at the Van Abbemuseum and set up as a promotion campaign for artists to fully embrace the business opportunities present in the Dutch Design Week industry.[32] The object on show was a campaign brochure that reused the images distributed by the Dutch Design Week (DDW) for promotional purposes, providing it with an alternative text highlighting the business potential of art and design. More important was the gesture of leaving behind the museum space and taking the stage in the ABN-AMRO booth at the main venue of the DDW. After the Dutch Design Foundation complained about the misuse of the logo, the directors of Van Abbemuseum quickly retired the brochure from the exhibition and website in a desperate attempt to maintain good relations with the Dutch Design Foundation (which functions as a business with the Dutch Design Week as one of its protected labels) and ABN-AMRO (the bank which is the main sponsor for both the museum and the design fair). Still, the withdrawal, by the Van Abbemuseum management, of the Dutch Design Lobby brochure from the exhibition contrasted sharply with the museum's official ambition to connect with society (in the typical attempt to break out of the white cube). Ironically enough, the Van Abbemuseum did not realize that we were hosted by ABN-AMRO at the main venue of DDW at Strijp-S, thus effectively breaking out of the white cube and realizing the museum's fantasy. Even more, ABN-AMRO showed much interest in the Dutch Design Lobby and was ready to invest money in the follow-up pilot programme.

In the projects that followed, we continuously shifted the strategy of overidentification depending on the specific topic, situation and actors. The advocacy project on the Limburg Government Architect, set up for the architecture-cultural organization Architectuurwijzer, can be seen as stepping stone to the new phase, employing what we theorized earlier as the hyper-idealist version of the strategy of overidentification in the context of building architecture culture in the Belgian province of Limburg.[33] The project was also a step-out of the world of exhibitions, call it a walk-out, fully embracing architecture culture as a parallel platform for advocacy around urgent issues. Although successful in launching the debate, the use of overidentification by BAVO was still overdetermined by the cultural context that feeds upon all sort of critical performances and statements, only on the condition that it doesn't interfere (at least not too much) with everyday reality. The dynamic is especially worrisome in the context of architecture culture: you can discuss the most burning issues in critical lectures and debates, but only insofar as it doesn't interfere too much with design practice, considered the holy ground of 'The Architect'. This meant that we started to look for ways of transgressing the limits of architecture culture and mobilizing the strategy of overidentification as a means to construct alternative design intelligence, in particular on the architecture of detention and psychiatry. The following projects – 'Prison Gear: Knowledge Platform for Humane Prison Architecture' (started 2012) and 'The Caritas Project: Vision Development on the Psychiatric Clinic of the Future' (started 2014, but dating back to 2010) – were self-initiated and developed in close collaboration with professional actors in the respective fields.[34]

The research on the architecture of detention and psychiatry still leaned on the strategy of overidentification, but the institutional and sensitive context made us realize the performances of the Yes Men weren't even close enough to reality. We expanded the strategy of overidentification by introducing the lessons of the 'ignorant master', a pedagogical method theorized by Jacques Rancière.[35] In terms of criticism, this meant that we accepted the need *not* to know anything of a certain topic to set up a critical debate about it; even more, the critic doesn't even have to talk the same language and share the same expertise. The strategy of ignorance introduced the idea of emancipation when talking about design intelligence and thus the question how to democratize design practice. This led us to put theories on the commons in the mix, after I started teaching on this topic with Lieven De Cauter as part of the master's course Criticism and Ethics at the KU Leuven Faculty of Architecture. Especially the hybrid work of architect-philosopher Doina Petrescu, who co-founded the Atelier d'Architecture Autogerée (AAA) with Constantin Petcou, was an inspiration to think architecture in relational terms and start the vision development as a process of knowledge commoning. Setting up talks with psychiatrists, managers, nursing staff *and* patients proved to be an effective means to articulate and visualize the main paradoxes underpinning the architecture of the psychiatric clinic. The same counts for prisons, monopolized by the power of the state, therefore an institute typically immune to any criticism, where we started to engage directors, staff *and* prisoners in different ways when thinking about humane prison architecture. The idea of humanizing the prison infrastructure might sound like an oxymoron – how can the deprivation of freedom ever be made humane? – but still it was an overidentification in hyperidealist form of the official policy line that actually underpins the modernization of prisons in Belgium.

Notes

1. Judith Butler, Ernesto Laclau and Slavoj Žižek, *Contingency, Hegemony, Universality: Contemporary Dialogues on the Left* (London/New York: Verso, 2000).
2. Gideon Boie, 'Flemish Architecture Culture for Beginners', in *The Persistence of Questioning: Critical Reflections on the Future, on Architecture and More – What Is The State of Architecture Culture?*, eds. Marina van den Bergen, Paul van den Bergh en Leonieke van Dipten (Rotterdam: Archined, 2022).
3. Crimson Architectural Historians, *Mart Stam's Trousers: Stories from behind the Scenes of Dutch Moral Modernism* (Rotterdam: 010, 1999) and *Too Blessed to Be Depressed: 1994-2001* (Rotterdam: 010, 2002).
4. Felix Rottenberg and Crimson, *WIMBY! Hoogvliet toekomst, verleden en heden van een New Town* (Rotterdam: nai, 2007).
5. Maurice Nio, *You Have The Right To Remain Silent* (Amsterdam: 1001, 1998). NOX published four books: *Actiones in Distans* (Amsterdam: 1001, 1991), *Biotech* (Amsterdam: 1001, 1992), *Chloroform* (Amsterdam: 1001, 1993) and *Djihad* (Amsterdam: 1001, 1995).
6. Slavoj Žižek, *Pleidooi voor Intolerantie* (Amsterdam: Uitgeverij Boom, 1998). Originally published as 'Multiculturalism, Or, the Cultural Logic of Multinational Capitalism', *New Left Review* 225 (Sep.-Oct. 1997), 28-51. The essay was later reworked in the chapter 'Political Subjectivization and Its Vicissitudes', in Slavoj Žižek, *The Ticklish Subject: The Absent Centre of Political Ontology* (London: Verso, 1997), 171-245.
7. Žižek, *Looking Awry*, 3.
8. Žižek, *Looking Awry*, 3.
9. Alain Findeli and Rabah Bousbaci, 'L'éclipse de l'object dans les théories du projet en design', *The Design Journal* 8, no. 1 (2005), 35-49.
10. Findeli and Bousbaci, 'L'éclipse de l'object'.
11. Étienne Balibar, 'Three Concepts of Politics: Emancipation, Transformation, Civility' in *Politics and the Other Scene* (London: Verso, 2002), 1-39.
12. Balibar, 'Three Concepts of Politics', 21-39.
13. Wouter Vanstiphout, 'Blame the Architect!', lecture organized by Stad en Architectuur (Leuven, STUK, 3 Mar. 2011). The title was used as general title for the autumn lecture series by Wouter Vanstiphout as Chair of Design as Politics at TU Delft in 2011.
14. Walter Benjamin, 'On the Concept of History', originally written 1940, online English trans., https://www.sfu.ca/~andrewf/CONCEPT2.html.
15. Slavoj Žižek, *Repeating Lenin* (Zagreb: Bastard, 2001), 12.

16. BAVO, 'Always Choose the Worst Option', 18-39.
17. Slavoj Žižek, 'Why Are Laibach and NSK not Fascists?', *M'ARS Moderna Galerija Ljubljana Magazine* 3-4 (1993). See also Boris Groys, 'The Irwin Group: More Total than Totalitarianism', in *Primary Documents: A Sourcebook for Eastern and Central European Art Since the 1950s*, eds. Laura Hoptman and Tomaš Pospisyl (New York: Museum of Modern Art, 2002). Originally written in 1990.
18. 'With totalitarianism, and with democracy, we are dancing with fascism, and red anarchy, one, two, three, four, comrade, come dance with me, one, two, three, four, with both hands I reach out to you [...] Americano friend, and German comrade, we're dancing nicely together, we're dancing to Baghdad.' Trans. by the author.
19. Slavoj Žižek, *The Puppet and the Dwarf: The Perverse Core of Christianity* (Cambridge, MA: MIT Press, 2003).
20. Slavoj Žižek, 'Only Autistic Children Can Save Us'.
21. BAVO, 'Always Choose the Worst Option', 18-39.
22. Alexei Monroe, 'Full Spectrum Provocation: The Retrogarde Strategies of Neue Slowenische Kunst', *Andere Sinema* 176 (Sep.-Oct. 2006), 84-101.
23. *Foreignors Out! Schlingensiefs Container*, film directed by Paul Poet, Monitorpop, 2002.
24. *Foreignors Out! Schlingensiefs Container*.
25. BAVO, 'Always Choose the Worst Option', 18-39.
26. The study on the Zuidvleugel is discussed in Chapter 6 of this book.
27. Jack Segbars, *Rondom (All Around the Periphery)* (Eindhoven: Onomatopee, 2013), 26-35.
28. Stefan Devoldere, ed., 'A+ 1907 After the Party', special issue of *A+ Belgisch tijdschrift voor architectuur*, on the occasion of the 2008 Venice Biennale.
29. BAVO, 'Come With Us and Enjoy Geographical Schizophrenia', published in the Euregional Forum newspaper (Maastricht: Jan van Eyck Academie, 2008). BAVO, 'Eigen Euregio Eerst' (Our own Euregion first), 2009, poster series designed by Hendrik-Jan Grievink.
30. 'De Janssens Werken' is discussed in Chapter 6 of this book.
31. 'Bureau Kunstenaarsparticipatie' is discussed in Chapter 7 of this book.
32. BAVO, *Dutch Design Lobby* (2010), contribution to the exhibition *Tricksters Tricked: (Un)Covering Identity* at the Van Abbemuseum, Eindhoven, 16 Oct. 2010-06 Feb. 2011, curated by Freek Lomme and Hadas Zemer Ben-Ari. Marina van der Bergen, 'De Dutch Design Lobby', *Archined*, 28 Oct. 2010.
33. The Limburg Government Architect advocacy project is discussed in Chapter 8 of this book.
34. 'Prison Gear' and the Caritas project are discussed in Chapters 9 and 10 of this book, respectively.
35. Jacques Rancière, *The Ignorant Schoolmaster: Five Lessons in Intellectual Emancipation* (1987; Stanford: Stanford University Press, 1991).

Work Through Inherent Criticism

Chapter 3

Today, cynical logic reigns supreme: we know the falsehood of ideology and we have acquired in-depth insights into the particular interests hidden behind universal values. And yet we continue to operate thanks to ideology. This has led Slavoj Žižek to argue that '[p]erhaps the greatest danger for totalitarianism is people that take its ideology seriously or literally'.[1] Even the strictest political regime anticipates the ideological misrecognition of reality; critical knowledge organizes the belief of not being fully part of ideology. The act of taking ideology deadly seriously makes cynical logic impossible as it dissolves the basic distance that supports our functioning in society and forces us to assume responsibility. If ideology is not to be taken literally, the same holds for critical labour. Criticism is not meant to be taken seriously, especially in the field of architecture. Criticism is part of the discursive programme that delves into the sublime qualities of certain objects, identifies best practices and enlightens emerging oeuvres, but only as long as it doesn't expose practice too much. Criticism also has an educational function, part of capacity-building, especially in dealing with local government administrations and agencies, preparing the field for architecture, but never assuming full responsibility. A special kind of criticism is the self-reflection of architects, discussing at length the many difficulties they experience in their daily practice, thus installing a healthy distance towards the context of their work. Against these conservative uses, we believe architecture criticism can only regain relevance in the form of analytical interventions that subvert the fundamental concepts of architectural production by taking these deadly seriously. In the following retrospective, we will show how architecture criticism is reactivated by applying the strategy called overidentification, dealing with different issues like neoliberal governance, city marketing, artist participation, spatial management, deprivation of freedom and mental healthcare.[2] The projects provide the stepping stones in the definition of as many tactics for critical intervention through all-too-literal identification with the utopias, traumas and phantasies active in architectural production today. First, we introduce how the strategy of overidentification is inspired by the hybrid politico-philosophical work of Slavoj Žižek, more specifically his use of Lacanian psychoanalytical theory, with notions such as inherent transgression and resistance.

Ideas or Actions? No Thanks!

In thinking of the uses and disadvantages of criticism for urban change, the difference between ideas and actions hangs like the sword of Damocles above the critic's head. Remember the enchanting words of Ernest Mandel, the author of *Late Capitalism* who stood at the barricades in the revolutionary year 1968: 'Ideas that float in the air, are printed on paper or carried only by the spoken word, that's something the bourgeoisie doesn't fear so strongly. What these gentlemen fear is organization, organized action, the organized attempt to realize those ideas.'[3] Following this logic, the revolution won't result from dreams about emancipation nor from grand narratives of utopian islands, but will only come about through organized action to turn these dreams into reality. No doubt Mandel's slogan contains some wisdom, but still it has put a spell on the practice of criticism, setting aside visionary brainpower as long as it's not followed with an immediate *passage à l'acte*. The opposition of idea and action starts to function as blackmail that delegitimizes and even disqualifies the critical agent who poses a sharp analysis or sketches an alternative vision without putting their hands to the plough.[4] Interestingly, the blackmail of calling for action has become a way to delegitimize criticism from the perspective of power, misusing the leftist distrust of ideas and turning it in a conservative argument. In 2019, a typical populist answer to secondary-school climate strikers was provided by Bart De Wever, the mayor of Antwerp and president of the Flemish populist party N-VA; I summarize: 'Go back to school, trust in innovation, humanity has faced big problems before and has always found pioneering solutions through innovation. Go back to school and study mathematics and physics and help us to achieve scientific breakthroughs.'[5]

The best answer to the primacy of actions over ideas in the practice of criticism was given by ... Ernest Mandel. Discussing the topic of agitation in a video interview, Mandel corrects the exaggerated hopes in the critical capacity of actions organized by small leftist movements in the face of the general passivity among the masses as a result of the monopoly of agitation in the ruling class. 'You can't make a revolution in a modern industrial society with a few hundred or a few thousand men', said Mandel, continuing: 'What the bourgeois class is frightened of is not the limited or unlimited efficiency of RAL and AMADA; what they're frightened of are the internal contradictions of their system which periodically brings hundreds of thousands of people – and tomorrow it will be millions – into the streets and which then enables those revolutionaries to educate those people, to educate them and to push their political action in a certain direction.'[6] In this reformulation, Mandel suggests that the true critical moment isn't so much the plotting of actions by small revolutionary leftist groups that cause trouble to the system – at the time, RAL and AMADA were two very small socialist movements active in Belgium. The central moment is the first appearance of the internal paradoxes of a system, which is the main cause for discontent, confusion and unrest among people and the thing that prompts them to take the streets. In this perspective, the task for revolutionary groups is not to get people into the streets, but to politicize the initial trouble by 'educating and pushing' the people already out on the street. The idea that revolutionary power has to steer people already out on the street is reminiscent of the idea of gravediggers produced by the system itself, present in *The Communist Manifesto* (1948) by Karl Marx and Friedrich Engels, and the termite theory of urban transformation, discussed by David Harvey.[7] Recall also recent moments in urban activism in Brussels, such as the 'Picnic the Streets' movement: it sketches an even more nuanced perspective in the fact that the movement called upon people to take to the streets for festive picnics, thereby externalizing discontent over urban politics that had remained implicit until then.[8]

In parallel, the first task for critical agency can be understood in its psychoanalytical function: bringing out internal contradictions already present in the system, as the cipher that opens a gateway for change to happen, but not passing the threshold where the journey begins.[9] My premise is that Slavoj Žižek provides a conceptual framework, largely derived from psychanalysis, that enables criticism to go beyond the opposition of idea and action, theory and practice, and to unfold the intermediary moment of laying bare the internal contradictions of a certain situation. The key is the different critical impact between the hysteric discourse and the analytical discourse in the theory of the four discourses, defined by Jacques Lacan.[10] The hysteric discourse starts from the agency of questioning by the split subject always addressing the figure of power (symbolized by the master signifier) while being supported by the remainder of the discourse (symbolized by the famous 'Objet petit a') in the repressed position. The analytic discourse tilts the term: it starts with the impossible position of the 'Objet a' in the position of the agent and addresses the split subject. Žižek uses the theoretical background to distinguish two critical positions. Firstly, the hysteric discourse depends on the classic critical gesture of exposing the lack in the master figure, the revelation of the lack as the moment of truth, without necessarily pushing towards a new master signifier. Secondly, in contrast with the first, the analytical discourse takes the inherent contradictions of a situation as a window for change by bringing the discontent to the point that it gives way to the renegotiation of basic choices and the reimagining of lines of flight. Of crucial importance are the different points of departure in both discourses: while the hysteric discourse mostly takes the form of an unsolicited critique and any link can fuel suspicions of collaboration, the analyst discourse may well intervene as part of a paid service and mutual agreement, using the money issue to set up a therapeutical relationship.[11]

The psychoanalytical framework thus enables us to leave behind romantic leftist feelings about critical agency: against the nostalgic idea of a true revolutionary agent, the figure of the invited critic is not an oxymoron; rather, the invitation might be crucial for critical impact. In thinking about how the analytical intervention can lead to change and how it translates to architectural criticism, many questions arise. The question is how to lay bare the internal paradoxes and use them as a catalyst for change: is it a spontaneous outcome of historical development to be deciphered by the analyst or can history be given a push through critical intervention? The question also concerns the effect of criticism: is it enough to open the wound for change to come about or is it necessary to project alternative futures and provoke practices of change? Another question concerns the threshold of critical intervention: how to bring stakeholders to the point of ignition while leaving the initiative in their hands? In seeking an answer to these questions, I'll focus on three psychanalytical notions that are prominent in the work of Slavoj Žižek: inherent critique, resistance, and overidentification.

Ideological Distance

In the first place, there is the idea that every situation is fundamentally split between the ideal and the obscene supplement since ideology necessarily feeds upon the need for inherent transgression. Žižek discussed the notion of inherent transgression in an analysis of complex subjective engagements in the Vietnam War, using popular war films like *MASH*, *An Officer and a Gentlemen*, and *Full Metal Jacket*.[12] Žižek wrote: 'Identification with the military machine is supported either by ironic distrust, indulgence of practical jokes and sexual escapades or by the awareness that behind the cruel drill-sergeant there is a "warm human person"...'[13] The war films evoke a split subjectivity that allows the protagonist to participate in the war while keeping a healthy distance, for instance stressing how an officer is at the same time a humble gentleman in the film *An Officer and a Gentleman* (directed by Taylor Hackford, 1982). In Stanley Kubrick's *Full Metal Jacket* (1987), this sort of very split subjectivity in the military complex is problematized: we see, for instance, how private J.T. 'Joker' Davies is himself quite critical of war (there is a peace sign on his helmet); he somehow got involved in the army by accident, he rationalizes his engagement as a sort of embedded journalism, and yet he never simply quits when things get worse. On the contrary, private Joker is the one who finally shoots the Vietcong sniper in the heat of the moment, pulling the trigger while knowing the sniper is just a young girl. The belief that he is not fully part of the military complex is the ideological glue that allows the subject to continue engaging in the drill and accept the atrocities of war. There are many ways to retain self-critical distance, for example by making fun of a terrible situation or deliberately transgressing the norms. The distance might seem a sign of criticality but in the end it fulfils an inherent function of ideology, even more so: the distance towards a certain complex is the ideology that secures the smooth functioning of the subject. Žižek writes: 'The subject does always maintain a minimal 'inner distance' towards the apparatuses and rituals in which ideology acquires material existence – his attitude towards this externality is always an "I am not that" (my true self does not hinge on this stupid mechanism [...]).'[14]

Underlying this is a torsion in the functioning of ideology which means that dis-identification can easily end up doing exactly the opposite, as we saw in the example of private Joker, whose self-critical subjectivity perfectly fits the war machine. Žižek explains the torsion of ideology by referencing the dialectic active in the contemporary master-slave relationship: 'the bondsman (servant) is all the more the servant, the more he (mis)perceives his position as that of an autonomous agent'.[15] In the (mis)perception, the subject is not a passive victim of the system, but an active agent for necessary reason: 'The bureaucratic/symbolic Institution not only reduces the subject to its mouthpiece, but also wants the subject to disavow the fact that he is merely a mouthpiece and to (pretend to) act as an autonomous agent – a person with a human touch and personality, not just a faceless bureaucrat.'[16] Criticizing the war subject might thus be difficult as he often acts as the most critical of all, engaged in a permanent institutional critique, and thus never fully assuming the responsibilities while at same time never fully taking sufficient distance. The logic at play means that identification with a certain cause doesn't necessarily translate one-on-one with the subject's ethical position. In the context of war, this could be the case with people engaged in anti-war movements but who still depend on a military complex that keeps the West free from war and/or outsources conflicts beyond its borders. Think also about the anti-war hero who, wittingly or not, might have subscribed to pension funds that are making profits from weapon manufacturers or at least general companies that somehow profit from war. The point in each scenario is again that the actor's identification with 'the good cause' is allowed insofar as the activities don't touch upon structural engagements (which may be excused as an inevitable outcome of forces beyond their control).

The discussion on war subjectivity touches upon art in the

tradition of institutional critique, a genre in the field of art in which artists use their art production to criticize the art institutions they largely operate in. The term is most commonly used in reference to Hans Haacke, but the conceptual framework of relational aesthetics by Nicolas Bourriaud can also be considered an institutional critique insofar as it criticizes the art museum by using its space for totally different uses.[17] One of Bourriaud's key examples is the work of Rirkrit Tiravanija, who organizes dinners and other social gatherings in the space of a museum, thereby dealing with people and situations instead of oil and canvas. The genre of institutional critique is an internal criticism as it enables artists to keep their distance from the institute while never fully retreating from it; on the contrary, the critical attitude is often a factor of success. What's important in all this is how Žižek reconceptualizes the function of ideology: 'The fundamental level of ideology [...] is not that of illusion masking the real state of things, but that of an (unconscious) fantasy structuring that social reality itself.'[18] There is nothing illusionary in the ideological belief that behind the officer is a gentleman and peace-loving human being and that behind the artist is a critical individual. This might well be the case. The point is that the image functions as a support of reality. In the jargon of psychoanalysis, it is the phantasy that structures social reality – whether the character is false or true is irrelevant at this point.

Resistance, Two Interpretations

This brings us to the second notion borrowed from psychoanalysis: resistance, which stems from the idea that the subject will always fail to recognize the passionate attachment with certain processes he may denounce publicly; even more, the subject will actively resist anything that hints at the paradox. Žižek reminds us that there are two possible uses of the term 'resistance'.[19] On the one hand, there is the typical sociopolitical interpretation in which resistance refers to an antagonistic relation with the powers that be, which one criticizes in the hope of undermining and even toppling them. In the case of World War II, resistance became the name for all movements opposing Nazi occupation. There are also social movements calling for resistance against capitalism, ecologists resisting the exploitation of Mother Earth, vegetarians resisting meat consumption, urban movements resisting gentrification, devout Christians resisting the temptations of Evil, etc. In all these cases, the resistance divides the battlefield between clearly recognizable parties, defines the right ethical position and justifies the actions. On the other hand, there is the clinical interpretation of the term 'resistance' referring to the patient's hesitation with regard to the analytic intervention, i.e. 'the patient's resistance to acknowledge the unconscious truth of his symptoms, the meaning of his dreams, etc.'.[20]

Clinical resistance is particularly complex as it is situated in the relationship between analyst and analysand, a therapeutic setting that wouldn't exist without the former being invited by the latter; and yet, still the latter does everything possible to resist the interventions by debunking the argument and/or casting doubt over the figure of the analyst. One of the strongest forms of clinical resistance is perhaps the situation in which the analysand presents himself as his own biggest critic – questioning his actions, offering an interpretation of his symptoms, searching for alternatives, inviting others to think along, and correcting the analyst for that matter. The incessant questioning is a resistance formation; at the same time, it establishes an a priori guilt in the therapeutical relationship. Žižek writes: '[T]his is what the analyst qua "subject supposed to know" is about: when the analysand enters into a transferential relationship with the analyst, he has the same absolute certainty that the analyst knows his secret (which only means that the patient is a priori "guilty", that there is a secret meaning to be drawn from his acts).'[21]

The dynamic of clinical resistance opens another meaning of power and critique. Traditionally criticism is defined by the hysteric discourse: the split subject incessantly 'hystericizes' the discourse by addressing the position of the master, who is blamed for personal profit, hidden interests, and/or secret desires.[22] Jacques Lacan's famous statement on hysteria is a sarcastic reproach to revolting students in the aula: 'What you aspire to as revolutionaries is a master. You'll get one.'[23] Žižek has argued how Lacan's underlying premise was utterly conservative.[24] Still, the hysteric discourse will never leave the position of critique facing power; it will speak truth to power by revealing the master as split subject, but never take over the power position. Moreover, the classic gesture of the hysteric no longer works in the context of ideological distance where the master takes the stage as split subject, call it a reflexive master, a master who is the first to question the official ideology, to call for an open negotiation of personal interests, and even to openly transgress the set rules, but doesn't consider it reason to resign from power, on the contrary. Žižek: 'The power edifice itself is split from within. [...] Power is always-already its own transgression, if it is to function, it has to rely on a kind of obscene supplement.'[25] Think of the ridiculous sergeant Hartman in *Full Metal Jacket*, who rules the game by openly mocking the military, who enforces discipline with obscene jokes (recruits are told they should care for their guns the way they care for their girlfriends) and leads not by example but through blasphemy (he wants the toilets in the barracks so clean that even Mother Mary will want to brush her teeth in them). Sergeant Hartman no longer hides the split subjectivity that supports his master position; on the contrary, he embodies it, showing how power only functions by openly embracing its obscene double.

In the famous Milan discourse (1972), Jacques Lacan developed the theory of the four discourses by adding a fifth variation, calling it the discourse of the Capitalist, based on 'une toute petite inversion simplement entre le S1 et le split subject'.[26] The adjective of capitalism might be misleading to understand the general implication of the master becoming hysterical, for instance in the blackmail of constructive critique and the new style of self-critical power.[27] Gone is the classic formula Master discourse with the master signifier in the position of agency while the split subjectivity is at the level of repressed truth. The contemporary master rules by showing his weak side and makes himself *incontournable* by inviting critics to bridge the gap. The result is that the new enlightened Master will always appear alongside the equally new entrepreneurial understanding of critical agency: criticism is offered in a package deal with creative problem-solving solutions. This brings us to the University discourse, part of the Lacanian scheme of four discourses, now presented as the double of the new Master discourse: knowledge takes the position of agency, it immediately solves all obstacles, thereby always postponing final answers. Lacan mockingly called it the *tout-savoir* (all-knowing) as the University discourse is always supported by the figure of 'almighty' power in the repressed position.[28]

Getting Closer to Closure

The third notion is the idea of overidentification, which brings the first two notions together. Slavoj Žižek introduced the concept of overidentification in the discussion of the performances by the rock band Laibach, part of NSK: 'it "frustrates" the system (the ruling ideology) precisely insofar as it is not its ironic imitation, but over-identification with it – by bringing to light the obscene superego underside of the system, over-identification suspends its efficiency'.[29] Bringing to light the obscene superego of the military is exactly what happens in *Full Metal Jacket*. While private Joker stands for the moment of ideological distance with the military complex, it is private Leonard 'Gomer Pyle' Lawrence that confronts us with the devastating moment of overidentification. Private Pyle is a recruit who appears unfit for war, both physically and mentally, which is why he is mocked by drill sergeant Hartman. Worse, the desperate attempts by private Pyle to meet requirements are perversely exploited by sergeant Hartman in the disciplinary exercises, as Hartman singles out the antihero as a bad example and makes the other recruits complicit in his failure. The story leads to a psychotic passage that ends in the terrible act of suicide by private Pyle, for who self-obliteration appears as the only possibility to escape the suffocating military discipline and the obscenities that support it. The act of 'overdoing it' is symbolized in the psychotic break by private Pyle, who, in the midst of despair, takes the obscene messages by sergeant Hartman deadly seriously and effectively starts to care for his gun as he would for his girlfriend. In the terrible night-time bathroom scene, private Pyle is unable anymore to distinguish military discipline from the drill sergeant's obscene orders, while private Joker watches in total despair. In the unfolding deadly moment, private Pyle suspends the cynical reason that supports the military drill by first shooting the drill sergeant and then spattering the immaculate bathroom with his own blood.

No wonder private Pyle's terrible act of suicide is the pivotal point in the film, ending the drill in the military camp and moving to the real thing, the battlefield in Vietnam, which leads to the moment of truth for private Joker. In the heat of battle when clearing a Vietcong village, private Joker forgets about the peace signs on his helmet, forgets about the ambition to act as an embedded journalist and cold-heartedly shoots a Vietcong sniper, knowing full well she's just a young girl. Private Joker proves to be the ideal war subject thanks to his critical attitude, not despite it – the belief that he isn't fully part of the army enables him to function perfectly. This brings us back to Žižek's argument: 'An ideological identification exerts a true hold on us precisely when we maintain an awareness that we are not fully identical to it.' Continuing with the formula for criticism: 'For that reason, an ideological edifice can be undermined by a too-literal identification.'[30] What interests us here is how the torsion of inherent criticism – disidentification functioning as lubricant for acceptance – also runs in the opposite direction: identification can lead to disidentification, especially when it happens a little bit too seriously. Inherent criticism opens up a window for a critical intervention that takes advantage of the contradictory mechanism inherent to the situation itself. From there, the strategy of overidentification can work in two directions: either overdoing the obscene transgression – call it the default mode of overidentification – or overdoing the lost ideal – which we have labelled hyperidealism.[31] The first version is what we get to see in *Full Metal Jacket*: private Joker's cynical distance towards the military machine is presented as the perfect war subjectivity. The second version would be the opposite: taking the peace sign on the helmet deadly seriously and not accepting any justification for the bloody ramifications both in the booth camp and on the battle field.

The strategy of overidentification reorients the practice of criticism from the hysteric discourse to that of the analyst. Usually, criticism is understood as the constant questioning of ruling power and knowledge. This is certainly effective in producing knowledge but equally ends up criticizing the new master.[32] By contrast, overidentification is a critical strategy defined by the discourse of the analyst: it takes position in the very impossibility of a certain situation and addresses the split 'self-questioning' subject. Žižek writes: 'Consequently, when we pass from perversion to the analytic social link, the agent (analyst) reduces himself to the void, which provokes the subject into confronting the truth of his desire. Knowledge in the position of "truth" below the bar under the "agent", of course, refers to the supposed knowledge of the analyst, and, simultaneously, signals that the knowledge gained here will not be the neutral objective knowledge of scientific adequacy, but the knowledge that concerns the subject (analysand) in the truth of his subjective position.'[33] Knowledge has a specific place in the analyst discourse: the analyst is positioned by the analysand as the 'subject supposed to know', meaning the analyst doesn't possess the truth but rather 'embodies the absolute certainty of the analysand's "guilt", of his unconscious desire'.[34] The analyst intervention demands nothing but the affirmation of the complexity and contradiction present in the given situation, inviting the split subject to work through it, thus opening up a potential gateway where change can come about.

Notes

1. Slavoj Žižek, *The Sublime Object of Ideology* (London: Verso, 1989), 24.
2. Žižek, *The Ticklish Subject*, 248.
3. Frans Buyens, 'Een mens genaamd Ernest Mandel (1972)', in Chris Den Hond, dir., *Ernest Mandel, een leven voor de revolutie* (Avanti Productions, 2005), video documentary.
4. BAVO, 'Always Choose the Worst Option', 18-39.
5. Ihsane Chioua Lekhli and Floor Bruggeman, 'Wat is het antwoord van Bart De Wever (N-VA) aan de 35.000 klimaatspijbelaars? Niet geloven in doemverhalen', *VRT NWS*, 1 Jan. 2019.
6. Den Hond, dir., *Ernest Mandel*.
7. Karl Marx and Friedrich Engels, *The Communist Manifesto: A Modern Edition* (1848; London: Verso, 2012), 50. David Harvey, *Rebel Cities: From the Right to the City to the Urban Revolution* (London: Verso, 2012), 124.
8. Gideon Boie, 'Pic Nic Architectuur', *A+ Architecture in Belgium* 264 (Feb. 2017), 22-24.
9. Jacques Lacan, 'The Mirror Stage as Formative of the Function of the I', in *Écrits: A Selection* (1966; London: Routledge, 2005), 1-6.
10. Lacan, *The Seminar of Jacques Lacan, Book XVII*, 29-53. Slavoj Žižek, 'The Object a in Social Links', in *Jacques Lacan and the Other*

Side of Psychoanalysis: Reflections on Seminar XVII, eds. Justin Clemens and Russel Grigg (Durham: Duke University Press, 2006), 107-28. Slavoj Žižek, *Tarrying With the Negative: Kant, Hegel and the Critique of Ideology* (Durham: Duke University Press, 1993), 165-99.

11. Dany Nobus, 'What Are Words Worth? Lacan and the Circulation of Money in the Psychoanalytic Economy', *Modern Psychoanalysis* 38, no. 2 (2013), 157-88.
12. Žižek, *The Plague of Fantasies*, 18-27.
13. Žižek, *The Plague of Fantasies,* 18-27.
14. Slavoj Žižek, *Indivisible Remainder: On Schelling and Related Matters* (London: Verso, 1996), 166.
15. Žižek, *The Ticklish Subject*, 258.
16. Žižek, *The Ticklish Subject*, 258.
17. Nicolas Bourriaud, *Relational Aesthetics* (1998; Dijon: Les Presses du réel, 2002).
18. Žižek, *The Sublime Object of Ideology*, 16 and 23-30.
19. Žižek, *The Ticklish Subject,* 262.
20. Žižek, *The Ticklish Subject,* 262.
21. Žižek, *The Plague of Fantasies,* 107.
22. Lacan, *The Seminar of Jacques Lacan, Book XVII*, 29-39. Bruce Fink, 'The Master Signifier and the Four Discourses', in *Key Concepts of Lacanian Philosophy*, ed. Dany Nobus (New York: Other Press, 1998), 29-47.
23. Lacan, *The Seminar of Jacques Lacan, Book XVII*, 207.
24. Slavoj Žižek, *On Belief* (London: Routledge, 2001), 30.
25. Žižek, *The Plague of Fantasies*, 18-27.
26. Transcript of the lecture by Jacques Lacan at Milan University on 12 May 1972 is published in: Jacques Lacan, 'Du Discours Psychanalytique', in *Lacan in Italia, 1953-1978, Lacan en Italie* (Milan: La Salmandra, 1978), 32-55.
27. BAVO, *Too Active to Act*, 43-50 and 63-70.
28. Lacan, *The Seminar of Jacques Lacan, Book XVII*, 34.
29. Žižek, 'Why Are Laibach and NSK not Fascists?'.
30. Žižek, *The Plague of Fantasies,* 18-27.
31. BAVO, 'Always Choose the Worst Option', 18-39.
32. Lacan, *The Seminar of Jacques Lacan, Book XVII*, 207.
33. Žižek, *The Parallax View*, 304.
34. Žižek, *The Plague of Fantasies,* 107.

Take Away Critical Distance

Chapter 4

The redevelopment of Transvaal, a so-called problem neighbourhood in The Hague (the Netherlands), centrally located and known for its multicultural character, was BAVO's first encounter with the ideological function of cultural production. In 2002 the Stroom Den Haag arts centre commissioned a critical survey of the makeover happening in Transvaal. The study was part of 'De Stad, de Kloof en de Regels' (The city, the gap and the regulations), a wide-ranging cultural programme mainly organized onsite in Transvaal.[1] Stroom built up a long-term engagement with the Transvaal district, using the vacant buildings as a stage for all sorts of critical art productions. Reusing the wooden floors to make an installation hanging on the façade of a house awaiting demolition, Tadashi Kawamata created an iconic installation. In fact, the work was a re-enactment of an earlier work at the last house standing at Spui (1986), when the central area in The Hague was cleared for the construction of the new Dans Theater (OMA) and City Hall (Richard Meier).[2] Other projects were the ongoing mobile art residency OpTrek and the student workshop led by Wim Cuyvers and more.[3] Strikingly, the highly critical artists were mobilized as part of a long-term cultural programme running parallel to the neighbourhood redevelopment scheme, which basically boiled down to a replacing of the existing housing stock by more or less identical blocks. Though the new housing blocks looked somewhat similar, mimicking the identity of social welfare housing from the early twentieth century, the operation drastically changed the property relations (turning the average 70/30 proportion of ownership and tenancy upside down), rationalized social services (shopping complexes with underground garages for both consumers and local inhabitants), and diversified retail (preventing streets from having five kebab snacks in a row). As the parallel art programme funds were from public and private parties involved in the redevelopment, the art programme could therefore be read as what Slavoj Žižek has framed as the ideological distance.[4] The artworks certainly did raise most interesting questions about the ongoing demolition and rebuilding of the neighbourhood, and still these questions remained internal to the development, respecting the overall framework of demolition. In this situation, the art production did function as inherent criticism, by organizing moments of deep reflection, even regretting the redevelopment of the neighbourhood. The public was allowed to keep a critical distance from the system while ensuring the smooth functioning of the process.

Embedded Artists, Inherent Critics

The outcome of our study was the very short book *De onverdeelde stad en haar gewillige beulen* (The undivided city and its willing executioners). It highlighted the underlying neoliberal logic in the urban redevelopment and defined the strange function of the socially oriented art production as its counterpart.[5] The embedded artist wasn't just an uncritical servant of corporate interests but, on the contrary, a figure who took the invitation from the arts centre as an opportunity to investigate the shadow side of urban development.[6] The cultural actor – we used the general category of 'cultural actor' to include artists, architects, planners, photographers and other creatives – appeared as perhaps the last of the idealists in the Transvaal area.[7] The position of the cultural actor in a specific context, call it the subject position, became the prime focus of our study. The idea of cultural actors as free agents finding themselves in the middle of a neoliberal onslaught – critically observing the political machinations without being part of that system, holding up an ideal while everyone has left the stage – appeared to be a post-historical pose. In his famous argument on the end of history, Francis Fukuyama describes how art also ends insofar as it was once considered socially useful. In the post-historical era, art is the empty formalistic gesture that takes the participant out of the comfort of petty bourgeois existence, if only momentarily.[8] The post-historical formal gesture of Japanese art comes close to Slavoj Žižek's critique of the Tamagotchi as an interpassive object, the permanent activity required to nurture the toy being intended to confirm the underlying passivity of the status quo.[9] The interpassive logic was summarized in the formula: 'Let's go on changing something all the time so that, globally, things will remain the same!'[10] This is what happened with the art production in Transvaal: declaring all sorts of critical statements was an empty formalistic gesture in the context of a primary acceptance of the neoliberal logic sustaining the redevelopment. The many artist interventions functioned as a moment of suspension that liberates the public from the need to assume the consequences of the ongoing urban redevelopment and, inversely, prevents them from having to take the criticism seriously and start to counteract the process. Symptomatic of the empty formalist idealism of much art production is the changing point of reference, which conveniently shifts the topic in the narrative from the vicissitudes of the neighbourhood under transition to the often highly personal experiences of the embedded artist. Symptomatic also was the reaction to criticism. In the debate on 'The Undivided City and its Willing Executioners', Wouter Vanstiphout mobilized the spectre of totalitarianism – 'Are you communists or what?' – to counter the idea of a fundamental critique and plea for a radical, pragmatic modus operandi.[11]

In our study of a similar urban development scheme in Rotterdam, presented as part of the exhibition *Neo-Beginners* at *TENT.*, the platform for contemporary arts of Centrum Beeldende Kunst Rotterdam (CBK, Rotterdam centre of visual arts), it became clear that the embedding of artists happened precisely because of this specific way of being-there, not so much because of the content of their work.[12] Again, the redevelopment was about changing the 70/30 property relations in the pre-war housing stock, but the tactics were quite different, less imposing. The project 'De Dichterlijke Vrijheid' (Poetic licence) in the Spangen area was set up to attract young creative people, going beyond the usual temporary and non-committal condition of art production and having them invest their very own life in the disadvantaged neighbourhood.[13] The idea was to save the Wallisblok, an urban block of typical post-war one- or two-storey rental houses, located next to a new development by the Mecanoo architecture office. The project was set up and managed in 2006 by the Rotterdam Development Corporation in cooperation with Steunpunt Wonen, Hulshof Architecten and process managers Urbannerdam. Although the project was officially open to everyone, the idea was to give a free house to young creative people on condition that they organize themselves as a 'collective particular commissioner', renovate the premises and make it their permanent residence. A key element was having creative people invest their personal life in the makeover. The project recognized to some extent that the surplus value of embedded artists was created not so much in the intrinsic qualities of art production, but more by the performative character of the creative subject, call it the being-there. In projects like Dichterlijke Vrijheid, the embedded artist became somehow encapsulated in the discourse of the creative cities, in which being critical (or not) is an issue only insofar as it allows the artist to function as a bohemian, the central figure in Richard Florida's theory of creative cities.[14]

The interesting element of the bohemian is the merging of work and life; it never really is clear at what moment the bohemian is working and at what moment partying. Festivities are often fully part of the work. You might think the party was about fun but actually it was a great moment for networking. The best ideas bubble up during the break, while long working hours count for nothing. The split personality of the bohemian led Gerard Marlet and Clemens van Woerkens to evoke the Calvinist hedonist, a figure that unites 'a Calvinistic work ethic (with hard work as the goal) [...] with a hedonistic lifestyle (with pleasure as the goal)'.[15] Urban development schemes like Dichterlijke Vrijheid tap into the vibrant activities of the Calvinist hedonist and hope to use it to regenerate impoverished neighbourhoods like Spangen. As a result, the figure of the Calvinist hedonist isn't just a biographic feature of creative subjects; the point is that it also fits the cynical reason of the ideology supporting neoliberal urban developments. As Slavoj Žižek wrote: 'the bureaucratic/symbolic institution not only reduces the subject to its mouthpiece, but also wants the subject to disavow the fact that he is merely a mouthpiece and to (pretend to) act as an autonomous agent – a person with a human touch and personality, not just a faceless bureaucrat'.[16] Perhaps none of the new houseowners in Dichterlijke Vrijheid would identify as an instrument of urban regeneration; on the contrary, their involvement was seen as a personal engagement by young people making their living.

The logic of the Calvinist hedonist was perfected in the '169 Klushuizen' (169 DIY houses) project scheme by the City of Rotterdam and local housing corporations, starting in Spangen and soon spreading to other post-war neighbourhoods in Rotterdam. This time, young creatives were embedded on an individual basis, leaving aside the common organization model. It was one of the learnings from the Dichterlijke Vrijheid pilot project: the contradictory goal of 'collective particular ownership' required a lot of negotiation between participants and was thus also considered a cause of frustration. Every single house of the urban block – actually we're talking about the typical Dutch 'etage-woningen', apartments the size of one and a half or two floors – was made available at a bargain price to individuals who committed themselves to the renovation of the premises.[17] The logic underlying the Klushuizen programme was clear as the precarious conditions of the artists were used in a mechanism to change the ownership relations in Rotterdam's post-war housing stock. The logic was clearly that of the superego insofar as the changing of property relations was based on what Žižek calls the imperative of jouissance – who *wouldn't* want to become a houseowner without spending money and by just being who you are.[18] The guarantee of permanent residence was less strict in Klushuizen compared to Dichterlijke Vrijheid, but the director of the housing corporation Woonbron assumed with a wink and a nod that a person who was allowed to design their own personal living environment wouldn't be leaving the area soon.

Politics of Resistance

What interests us, in this retrospective, is not so much the repetition of the argument on neoliberal urban politics and the embedded role of artists as the reception of the critique levelled against the instrumental role of critical art. The critical case studies of Dichterlijke Vrijheid and Klushuizen, part of the essay 'Pleidooi voor een oncreatieve stad' (Plea for an uncreative city), were picked up by many.[19] The magazines *De Groene* and *Metropolis M* asked for articles that continued the debate, radio station RTV Radio Rijnmond asked for an interview, and so on. Interestingly, the criticism of the artists embedded in impoverished areas was usually accepted among politicians, city managers and directors of housing corporations, quite logically as this wasn't so much a dirty secret, at least not for them, but rather the core principle of the development scheme. This was the case with the director of the housing corporation, who suggested it was unlikely the new houseowners would soon be leaving their self-designed spot; the criticism was, to his mind, just an adequate description of the case. However, the same criticism provoked resistance from artists, not necessarily involved in the cases, who weren't at all eager to further discuss the enjoyment of cheap housing, not even to joke about it. The blunt disavowal was again logical; in their situation, the same message started to function as an inconvenient truth about how the creative, allegedly critical way of life was sustained by highly sophisticated urban development schemes. Hajo Doorn, artistic director of the experimental WORM music platform in Rotterdam, sent an intimidating email (we're talking about the pre-Facebook era) in response to a critical passage in the 'Pleidooi', arguing that the criticism was disrespectful of the struggle for the reproduction of the music stage and that we would 'lick his white design shoes' at the next party.[20]

The resistance got echoed in a more civilized way by theorists who jumped into the breach for fellow artists, such as Matteo Pasquinelli in his lecture at the MyCreativity: Convention on International Creative Industries Research (16-18 November 2006), who countered the criticism of the 169 Klushuizen programme as a problematic case of what he called Lacanian paranoia.[21] Usually, criticism is first disqualified by invoking the spectre of communism before a more pragmatist approach is adopted. In this case, the spectre of paranoia was a smokescreen to continue the analysis of artists as passive and innocent victims at the hands of the brutal real-estate market and to heroically call for sabotage of the creative value production.[22] Pasquinelli gave the example of a protest by artists in Barcelona against precarious living conditions under the slogan: 'You will never own a house in your whole fucking life.' In their protest, the artists not only anticipated the cruel, reactionary response of the real-estate market or local government, but also presented themselves as passive victims of abstract market forces that tap into their collective symbolic capital. The protest was thus equally a depoliticization, ignoring the fact that the obstacle to the object of desire (the house) was perhaps a condition of their creative lifestyle. The same entanglement was at stake in the Rotterdam case of the Klushuizen where the real-estate market fully counted on the precarious conditions of the creative class. In the context of creative value production, the demand for housing was perversely answered by the logic of the superego: 'Take this fucking free house, you creative idiot!'[23]

The argument functions as resistance – clinical, not socio-critical – insofar as it opposes the intervention by the critic and offers a theoretical justification to cancel the critical intervention – call it countercriticism to continue business-as-usual, or better: to continue protest-as-usual.[24] Part of the resistance is the misperception of autonomy that characterizes the embedded artist, following Žižek's argument that: 'the bondsman (servant) is all the more a servant, the more he (mis)perceives his position as that of an autonomous agent.'[25] Logic means that for a critical intervention to function as a game changer, one always has to consider the reception by the public and anticipate eventual mechanisms of repression, negation and disavowal. It is one thing to spell out the truth of a certain situation, in our case showcasing the embedded character of critical artists. An equally important challenge is finding ways for the truth to permeate in daily practice and prepare the fertile soil for change to happen.

Labelling the response as clinical resistance is not to be blind to counterarguments which may enrich the debate and even lay bare possible contradictions of our own, but to understand the limits of critique as a motor for social change. Criticism is perhaps not so effective when it immediately provokes negative feelings, falling on deaf ears and resulting in the reinforcement of existing positions. The typical clinical resistance involves reproaching the critic for not being well informed, telling the critic to safely stay on the sidelines, arguing that the critic certainly wouldn't know what to do in their place, that no one can make an omelette without breaking eggs and – once we started to promote the strategy of overidentification, which we'll return to below – that critics should never prescribe the actions of practitioners. Evidently, any resistance betrays a minimum of self-reflection, since the person feels addressed by the criticism and finds it necessary to react; yet the criticism loses its effectiveness when it only provokes people to shoot at the messenger – it is just as lame as criticism that preaches to the converted only. A curious form of resistance is the immediate affirmation of criticism; it happens in applause but also in questions that pretend to share the same analysis. Appreciative comments received after a lecture render a true intellectual encounter impossible and are often a prelude to continuing business as usual. The function is identical to that of the canned laughter used in TV series to express emotions of fear or laughter while the viewer is allowed to do or think something totally different.[26] Slavoj Žižek, referring to statements by Gilles Deleuze, argues that the only real exchange lies in an encounter, the confrontation of ideas, not in the setting up of yet another critical debate.[27] The challenge for criticism lies not only in understanding and expressing the ideological fundaments of a certain situation or project, stating its hidden truth, but also in finding the anchor points to reconceptualize, reformulate and even redesign the project at stake. In the end, the risk for the critic is to find him/herself in exactly the same position we started with, i.e. the critical artist acting as the last idealist on the block, allowed to criticize everything and everybody as long as it doesn't undermine the overall state of affairs. Put differently: the critic is welcome and is even paid to level criticism, but the moment he/she does so, the critique is cancelled for all sorts of good reasons, the fundamental belief being that radical change isn't possible and in fact isn't even desired.

Unanalysable Architects

Resistance reached its peak in dealing with architects – our own field and discipline, note – who simply disidentified from any discussion on the embedded character of cultural actors, which is strange given that architecture mostly comes into being as part of a commission. Quite understandably, discussions on the use-value of art lead to allergic reactions in a context where the supposed autonomy of art is held high, but in architecture a large part of the discourse is typically about what Étienne Balibar has called the heteronomy.[28] Architects will discuss in full detail how specific designs are informed through negotiation with the genius loci in its different guises, i.e. the natural or urban topography, local traditions, socio-economic atmosphere, project brief, needs and desires by the user, and whatnot. Perhaps no cultural activity is better placed than architecture to discuss the embedded role of its subject, and yet still the architect demands a specific treatment, in which you deal with the typical topics of architecture, such as form, typology and material – not forgetting to pay respect to the canon of architecture, in terms of both theoretical bodies and established oeuvres. The disavowal of anything beyond the object is prominent in the work of Geert Bekaert, the founding father of architecture culture in Belgium, for example in his commentary on BAVO's proposal for the '1907' invited competition organized by the VAi for the 2008 Venice Biennale, comparing it with the installation by Office KGDVS in the Belgian Pavilion. Bekaert wrote: 'Those looking for information [in the installation by Office KGDVS] will be disappointed. They will learn nothing specific about architecture in Belgium, but a great deal about the way in which some architects see architecture. There is no sign of national trends, as in BAVO's project. This is all about contemplating architecture and its potential, its necessity and its redundancy.'[29]

Christophe Van Gerrewey, a loyal pupil of Geert Bekaert, even disqualified the BAVO article on architecture and administrative modernization in the *Flanders Architectural Yearbook* published by the VAi because it borrowed notions from Slavoj Žižek, an author 'who never deals with architecture' and 'whose philosophy can only be applied with great reserve to architecture, the most paradoxical of all human pursuits'.[30] Although the claim that Žižek has never written about architecture is false, the point is that Van Gerrewey considers the use of psychoanalytical terms an infringement on the autonomy of architecture. The fun fact is that Žižek has written about the wider political implications of autonomous architecture, not only about Guiseppe Terragni but also about the cultural variations in the design of water closets. The analysis of the French, German and British toilet pot makes it possible to differentiate ways of dealing with the social excrement.[31] The holy mission to defend autonomous architecture somehow fits the traditional French version of the toilet pot with the black hole in the middle, immediately discharging anything that smells like politics. The attempt to demarcate a pure discipline translates in the difficult relation with the commission as a condition of possibility for the architecture object and easily leads to phantasies of architecture without content.

The depoliticization of architecture, necessary to professionalize the process of public tendering and contracting, has taken on epic proportions in the tendency within Flemish architecture culture to present architecture as part of the everyday. Slavoj Žižek has described five ways to disavow the political conflict: by translating it in terms of a surgical operation (arche-politics), a game (para-politics), scientific-technological instrumental procedures (meta-politics), warfare of us vs them (ultra-politics), and, finally, rational business negotiation (post-politics).[32] The reference to the everyday in Flemish architecture fits the first insofar as it presents the political conflict as part of an archaic trend that is part of human nature, it is simply the way people live their life. The best example is Geert Bekaert presenting Victor Horta's art nouveau masterpiece Hôtel Solvay as nothing but a place for the everyday commonplace living of the Solvay family, neglecting the obvious representational function of the extreme luxury.[33] Certainly, the constant emphasis that architecture isn't political is a resistance formation, and still the form of negation, the Freudian *Verneinung*, betrays the opposite: Why bother politics? Why the need to affirm that architecture is *not* political? What is the sense of repeating the pleonasm that architecture is architecture? The permanent bothering acknowledges implicitly that the one can't do without the other, that the commission is framework, platform and backdrop for design. The entanglement means that architectural criticism can't be narrowed down to the study of the sublime object, but must at least take into account, as Balibar argues, that any autonomy of politics immediately comes with the other scenes of heteronomy.[34] First, there is the heteronomy of architecture insofar as every design project is an answer to commissions, the cornerstone of policies, the vehicle for social and economic programmes and whatnot. Second, architecture is defined by the heteronomy of heteronomy: the ideologies, myths and desires that might go far beyond the architectural product while at the same time traversing its core functioning.

The complex that envelops architecture means that we shouldn't only consider the enunciated content in a certain statement but also the place of enunciation, i.e. the place from where the architectural statement is made.[35] Geert Bekaert – who can't be suspected of uncritical handling of architectural production – called his work 'a form of freelance journalism [...] pure journalism',[36] adding: 'Even though these [his published articles] were commissioned – I never actually write without being asked – these were an exploration of the field. I didn't know anything about it.' The exploratory nature of Bekaert's texts was trendsetting for architectural culture in Flanders and still resonates for example in the VAi's *Architectural Review*, previously called *Architectural Yearbook*. The *Yearbook* traditionally makes a strict distinction between, on the one hand, texts with critical analyses about everything that is wrong in urban production in relation to troublesome social events and/or political decision-making and, on the other hand, case studies of best practices that applaud the countless blessings of architecture for the living environment. In this dichotomy, architectural quality is always considered characteristic of best practices, positioned on the side of the solution for social issues, never part of the problem. At the same time, criticism is mobilized as a means to prepare the field for architectural production, which explains the missionary zeal in the work of most architecture critics, spreading the good news of architectural quality. For example, the Pilot Projects programme launched by Flemish Government Architect Peter Swinnen (2010-15), explicitly aimed at prospectively situating architecture in fields of policy (housing, brownfields, care, student housing, etc.). This brings us to the question that has haunted us ever since we started to deal with architecture criticism from the perspective of political philosophy: how to escape the role of critic as acolyte of architecture practice and use criticism to repoliticize architecture? It is one thing to sing the praises of best practices and venture onto unexploited terrains, but quite another to critically reflect on the conditions of (im)possibility of architecture production and use this knowledge to intervene in design processes.

Emetica, Digestiva and Other Critical Agents

The strategy of overidentification opens a line of flight for other ways of doing in architectural criticism.[37] First of all, it entails that architects cease the pretention of autonomous architecture, the safe haven for all their frustration, and instead work through the many complexities and contradictions present in architecture. It is here that the real trouble starts with architecture. The strategy of overidentification fits the critical roles naturally claimed by artists, such as the jester speaking truth to power, the outsider able to take all the blame, the one assuming power, etc. Also, the performative character of art makes it easier for artists to fully subject themselves to the values and standards of the situation they would naturally criticize and take it one step further than everyone is willing to do. Conceptualizations of the strategy of overidentification therefore usually refer to cultural practices, such as Laibach and the wider movement of NSK especially, Christoph Schlingensief and other artists.[38] But how could we apply the strategy of overidentification in the field of architecture? How could we assume that 'all architecture is subject to political manipulation except for that which speaks the language of the same manipulation', to paraphrase the old Laibach dictum about art.[39] The architect might be considered an independent actor (in Belgium enforced by law since 1939), but after all, the service-oriented discipline demands that any criticism needs at least to be negotiated with the interests of the client. Architecture likes to stress that it is one of the seven arts, but it still involves investments by clients, approval by governments, contracts with entrepreneurs and inventories of the client's needs, not to mention all the legal responsibilities it entails. And let's not forget the impact of architecture on the environment in terms of land use, natural resources, pollution, emissions and waste. Taking the wishes of the client one step further and doing away with critical distance – the basic lesson of overidentification – might risk ruining the architectural project or at least might run havoc in the process of architectural production. As a result, the claim for critical proximity in the field of architecture towards the forces one usually opposes might prove difficult to reconcile with design practice, necessarily leading to a rethink of practice, as happened with Forensic Architecture.[40]

Once we tried to apply the strategy of overidentification in architecture, we were confronted with many questions: How can we go beyond the performative aspect of overidentification in the field of art and make it real in the field of architecture? Is there such thing as architecture of overidentification? Taking into account the service-oriented nature of the architectural discipline and lacking positive architectural examples that explicitly refer to the strategy of overidentification, our exploration was in danger of ending up being a speculative proposal without consequences for design practice.[41] Alternatively, we could expand architecture discipline and look at other ways of doing. Again, however, this ran the risk of drifting away from the field of architecture as we know it, enabling architects to disidentify.[42] The impossible desire in our research meant that the strategy of overidentification started to sneak into our own work as architecture critic. Instead of teaching theoretical lessons to fellow architects, we ruthlessly applied the concept of overidentification to our own doings. We started to experiment with the typical dispositifs of a critic, using articles, lectures, debates and exhibitions to overidentify with the topic of discussion, resulting in a sort of critical performance. Later, the strategy of overidentification started to function as the methodological programme for research workshops and participative vision development, again using all the dispositifs of critical practice. The changing tactics were driven by the need to further develop the strategy of overidentification from an ideology criticism performed on the sidelines of architecture practice to critical intervention at the heart of a design process. The context of architectural production forced us not only to act out the perverse logics of urban development among friends in the safe haven of cultural debates and exhibition spaces, but first of all to put in motion the fundamental concepts that underpin architectural practice as the first preparation of the field for change to happen.

The next chapters sketch the changing use of the strategy of overidentification through different works of BAVO, initially navigating between architecture and art and later taking up post in the discursive interstices of architectural practice.[43] Isabelle Doucet talks about interstitial activism in reference to activist practices situated in the rupture lines of the city, for example in the case of the non-profit Recyclart both literally (the centre was housed in an abandoned train station) and metaphorically (the practice is a mix of top-down and bottom-up initiatives). We applied different strategies of overidentification conceptualized in earlier theoretical work, first the merging of the law and its obscene supplement, as practised by the artist duo Yes Men, for example, and later the hyperidealism which takes the law deadly seriously, excluding the obscene supplement, as practised by film-maker Michael Moore, for example.[44] In the first works, we shift between these two strategies of overidentification and either close off alternative options (which Soren Kierkegaard called the emetic agent) or joyfully accept the repressed ideal without compromise (which would inversely function as a sort of digestive agent).[45] The two variations on the theme of overidentification open up an analytic space for full speech that could provoke, tickle and inspire architectural production, taking the conceptual framework of psychoanalysis as a starting point, in particular the so-called analytic discourse defined by Jacques Lacan.[46] The defining characteristic in the analytic discourse is the Objet a – 'the discourse's reject producing effect' – that takes the position of the agent and addresses the split subject. The result is a discursive practice that positions itself in the inherent criticism latent in a certain situation and starts from there a critical labour that engages with ongoing design processes. The chapters sketch a more or less logical chain in the works of BAVO, without pretending either to be exhaustive in the narration of the work or to write an ultimate theory of overidentification.[47]

Notes
1. 'De Stad, de Kloof en de Regels', Feb.-Apr. 2003, Stroom Den Haag arts centre.
2. BAVO, 'Kunst in de Grote Verbouwing: voorbij de collectieve conditie van interpassiviteit' (The Hague: Stroom, 2007).
3. Veronica Hekking, Sabrina Lindemann and Annechien Meier, *Op-Trek in Transvaal: On the Role of Public Art in Urban Development. Interventions and Research* (Heijningen: Jap Sam, 2010). Also: Wim Cuyvers, *Beograd – The Hague: About the Impossibility of Planning* (The Hague: Stroom, 2003).
4. Žižek, *Indivisible Remainder*, 166.
5. BAVO, *De onverdeelde stad en haar gewillige beulen* (The Hague: Stroom, 2003).
6. BAVO, 'Neoliberalism with Dutch Characteristics: The Big Fix-Up of the Netherlands and the Practice of Embedded Cultural Activism', in *Citizens and Subjects: The Netherlands for Example*, eds. Rosi Braidotti et al. (Zürich: JRP-Ringier, 2007), 51-63.
7. BAVO, 'The Dutch Neoliberal City and the Cultural Activist as the Last of the Idealists', in *Highrise: Common Ground, Art and the Amsterdam Zuidas Area*, ed. Jeroen Boomgaard (Amsterdam: Valiz, 2008), 217-52.
8. Francis Fukuyama, *The End of History and the Last Man* (New York: Free Press, 1992), 321. BAVO, *Too Active to Act*, 8-11.
9. Žižek, *Pleidooi voor intolerantie*, 101-09.
10. Žižek, *Repeating Lenin*, 12.
11. Debate with BAVO, Adri Duivesteijn, Wouter Vanstiphout and Wim Cuyvers; conversation led by moderator Piet Vollaard in the programme 'Debates on Transvaal, Urban Development-Related Issues' organized by Stroom Den Haag Arts Centre in Dans Theater Den Haag, 31 Mar. 2003. See the review by Klaske Havik and Sebas Veldhuisen, 'Communisten, jongleurs en cliniclowns', *Archined*, 8 Apr. 2003.
12. BAVO, 'Pleidooi voor een oncreatieve stad' (Plea for an uncreative city), an essay that was part of the exhibition *Neo-Beginners* curated by Reinaart Vanhoe in *TENT.* CBK Rotterdam, Sep., 2006. The paper was reworked as an article: BAVO, 'On Behalf of the Uncreative City', *Metropolis M* 28, no. 1 (Feb. 2007), 27-31. Another version: Gideon Boie and Matthias Pauwels, 'De creatieve stad – Stadsontwikkeling is politiek', *De Groene Amsterdammer* 7 (2007). The research continued in the research project 'Retrosocialism in the European City' with Lukasz Stanek supported by the Stimuleringsfonds for Architectuur, 2006.
13. Ineke Hulshof, *Poetic Freedom: Report on a Regeneration Project in*

the *Neighbourhood of Spangen in Rotterdam* (Delft, 2008).
14. Richard Florida, *The Rise of the Creative Class: And How it's Transforming Work, Leisure, Community and Everyday Life* (New York: Basic, 2004), xiv.
15. Gerard Marlet and Clemens van Woerkens, 'Het economisch belang van de creatieve klasse', *Economisch Statistische Berichten* 89, no. 445 (11 Jun. 2004), 280-83.
16. Žižek, *The Ticklish Subject*, 258.
17. Annemie Sour, *169 klushuizen: van experiment naar instrument* (Heijningen: Jap Sam, 2009).
18. Slavoj Žižek, *How to Read Lacan* (London: Granta, 2006), 79-90.
19. BAVO, 'Pleidooi voor een oncreatieve stad', essay part of the exhibition *Neo-Beginners* curated by Reinaart Vanhoe in *TENT.* CBK Rotterdam, Sep. 2006.
20. BAVO, 'Pleidooi voor een oncreatieve stad'.
21. BAVO, 'The Murder of Creativity in Rotterdam: From Total Creative Environments to Gentripunctural Injections', in *MyCreativity Reader: A Critique of Creative Industries*, eds. Geert Lovink and Ned Rossiter (Amsterdam: Institute of Network Cultures, 2007), 153-64. *MyCreativity: Convention on International Creative Industries Research* was held on 16-18 Nov. 2006 at Stedelijk CS in Amsterdam and organized by the Institute of Network Cultures, HvA Interactive Media, and University of Ulster Centre for Media Research.
22. Matteo Pasquinelli, 'Immaterial Civil War: Prototypes of Conflict within Cognitive Capitalism' (Barcelona, Sep. 2006). The argument is also part of Matteo Pasquinelli, 'Beyond the Ruins of the Creative City: Berlin's Factory of Culture and the Sabotage of Rent', in *Skulpturenpark Berlin_Zentrum*, ed. KUNSTrePUBLIK (Berlin: Verlag der Buchhandlung Walther König, 2010).
23. BAVO, 'Take This Fucking Free House, You Creative Idiot!', *Architecture& Magazine 1: Architecture & Property* (Winter 2008), 15-16.
24. Žižek, *The Ticklish Subject*, 262.
25. Žižek, *The Ticklish Subject*, 262.
26. Žižek, *The Plague of Fantasies*, 109.
27. Slavoj Žižek, *Organs without Bodies: Deleuze and Consequences* (London: Routledge, 2004), xi.
28. Balibar, 'Three Concepts of Politics'.
29. Geert Bekaert, 'Happy Anniversary: Office Kersten Geers David Van Severen at the 11th Venice Architecture Biennale', in *Rooted in the Real: Writings on Architecture by Geert Bekaert*, ed. Christophe Van Gerrewey (Ghent: WZW Editions & Productions, 2011), 230-40.
30. Christophe Van Gerrewey, 'Jaarboek Architectuur Vlaanderen 06-07, editie 2008', *De Witte Raaf* 135 (Sep.-Oct. 2008), review.
31. Žižek, *The Plague of Fantasies*, 3-7.
32. Žižek, *The Ticklish Subject*, 187-91.
33. Geert Bekaert, 'Belgian Architecture as Common Place: The Absence of Architectonic Culture as a Challenge', in *Rooted in the Real*, 90-96.
34. Balibar, 'Three Concepts of Politics'.
35. Žižek, *Looking Awry*, 3.
36. Geert Bekaert in conversation with Johan Thielemans in the VRT documentary *Eiland*, Nov. 1985, on the occasion of the publication of *Verzamelde opstellen*.

37. BAVO, 'The Spectre of the Avant-Garde'. BAVO, 'From Political Games to Absolute Architecture ... and Back: The Architectural Avant-Garde Today', *Andere Sinema AS* 176 (Sep.-Oct. 2006), 42-61.
38. Žižek, 'Why Are Laibach and NSK Not Fascists?'. Inke Arns and Sylvia Sasse, 'Subversive Affirmation: On Mimesis as a Strategy of Resistance', in *East Art Map. Contemporary Art and Eastern Europe*, ed. IRWIN (London: Afterall /MIT Press, 2006), 444-55. BAVO, 'Always Choose the Worst Option', 18-39.
39. Laibach, '10 Items of the Convenant', *Nova Revija* 13-14 (1983). Originally created in 1982.
40. Eyal Weizman, 'Matters of Calculation: The Evidence of the Anthropocene. Eyal Weizman in Conversation with Heather Davis and Etienne Turpin', in *Architecture in the Antropocene*, eds. Heather Davies and Etienne Turpin (London: Open Humanities Press, 2013), 66-82.
41. BAVO, 'From Political Games to Absolute Architecture ... And Back'.
42. Expanding architecture is the subject of the elective master's course 'Architecture and Activism' offered by Lieven De Cauter and the author at the Faculty of Architecture KU Leuven, Campus Sint-Lucas. See: Lieven De Cauter, 'Expanding Architecture', ETH Zürich, lecture, 22 Apr. 2015. Also: Nishat Awan, Tatjana Schneider and Jeremy Till, eds., *Spatial Agency: Other Ways of Doing Architecture* (London: Routledge, 2011).
43. Isabelle Doucet, *The Practice Turn in Architecture: Brussels after 1968* (New York: Routledge, 2015), 79-110.
44. BAVO, 'Always Choose the Worst Option', 29-32 and 37-39.
45. The strategy of overidentification as emetic agent was presented in BAVO, 'Always Choose the Worst Option', 32. In discussing the long waves of activism in Brussels, Isabelle Doucet stresses to need for activism to produce practices that digest the temporal thickness of cities. See Doucet, *The Practice Turn in Architecture*, 94-101.
46. Lacan, *The Seminar of Jacques Lacan, Book XVII*, 42-45.
47. For the sake of argument, the following chapters omit some experimental interventions that may not always have been successful but were certainly fundamental as game changers in BAVO's work when it comes to applying the strategy of overidentification, such as the lecture performance 'Een wereldstad benut haar creatief kapitaal: zeven aanbevelingen van de Rijksadviseurs voor de creatieve Schaalsprong van Rotterdam en omstreken' in the exhibition *Rondom* (31 Jan. 2008) curated by Jack Segbars at DCR in The Hague; the formal intervention within the public hearing procedure (22 Jun. 2009) for the Oosterweel motorway link and bridge construction ('Lange Wapper') in Antwerp; the lecture 'Bouwen aan Creatieve Allianties in Metropool Amsterdam: aanbevelingsbrief' in the programme RED A.I.R. Red Light Amsterdam (26 Sep. 2009) curated by Angela Serino and moderated by Huib Haye van der Werf; the lecture 'Five Theses on the Neoliberal City' at the Civic City Conference (12-13 Mar. 2010) at the Zürich University of the Arts Institute Design2context; the 'Dutch Design Lobby' contribution to the exhibition *Tricksters Tricked* (Oct. 2010) curated by Freek Lomme and Hadas Zemer Ben-Ari at Van Abbe Museum Eindhoven; and perhaps most importantly the 'Euregional Forum', a long-running debate programme at the Jan

van Eyck Academie Maastricht (2006-10) in collaboration with the Province of Limburg (NL) and diverse cultural centres in the Meuse-Rhine Euroregion.

Hystericize the Subject

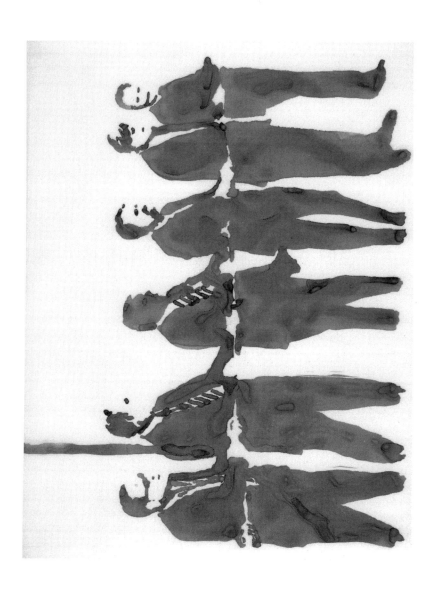

Chapter 5

Tien dingen die je gewoon moet doen voor het ruimtelijk ontwikkelen van een topregio (2007) (Ten must-dos for the spatial development of a leading region) was the result of a study into the fundamental concepts driving the spatial development of the so-called Zuidvleugel (South wing). The study was commissioned by Atelier Zuidvleugel, a special think tank set up by Maxwan Architects + Urbanists and embedded in the provincial administration of the Zuid-Holland province.[1] Atelier Zuidvleugel operated from September 2005 until December 2007, having its base in the administrative building of the Zuid-Holland Province in The Hague. Atelier Zuidvleugel was considering a new planning unit that included the cities of The Hague, Rotterdam, Gouda and Dordrecht. The composition of the Zuidvleugel was unusual in the world of planning and its custom talk about the 'Randstad', focusing on the metropolitan region composed by the four big cities in the Netherlands, namely Amsterdam, Rotterdam, Utrecht and The Hague. The Randstad was looking for business opportunities by mainly integrating the provinces of North and South Holland and opposing it to the rest of the Netherlands.[2] Beyond the socio-economic reality of the Randstad, the notion was a convenient fiction that made it possible to compare the four big cities on an equal footing with metropolitan developments around the globe, especially in popular publications like *Metacity / Datatown* by MVRDV.[3] In contrast, the Zuidvleugel roughly followed the administrative dividing line between the Provinces of North Holland and South Holland, but also included strategic parts of the Provinces of Utrecht and North Brabant. In short, the Zuidvleugel was a narrative that gathered several decisive economic infrastructures, i.e. the seaport, administrative capital, international city of peace and justice, waterways, etc. The horizontal development of the Zuidvleugel was presented as the counterpart of the 'North wing' – never named as such – where the entire region was conceived in function of the metropolis of Amsterdam and the trickle-down effects of its creative sector, top business location, tourism and other beneficial characteristics.[4] Instead of answering the request for a critical analysis of the fundamental concepts active in the Zuidvleugel development, we listed the '10 must-dos for the spatial development of a leading region'. The list merged all the complex and contradictory tendencies found in policy notes and business reports circulating in the Zuidvleugel process. The critical effect of the study was situated not so much in the study of the conceptual roots of regional development, but precisely in sticking to the consensus on the issue and presenting it as the thing to do, including every possible criticism as a reason more.

Say Yes to Competition

In studying the conceptual drivers of the Zuidvleugel, we applied the strategy of overidentification in its classical form, pretty much inspired by the Yes Men.[5] The artist duo Yes Men gained fame by pulling various hoaxes in which they assume the identity of the actors they wish to criticize and make all kinds of public statements on their behalf, a tactic they called 'identity correction'. Most famous is the hoax in which the Yes Men acted on behalf of Dow Chemical, stating they were willing to take responsibility for the disaster in Bhopal (India). After the report was broadcast in a live interview on BBC World, the multinational was forced to issue an official message making unambiguously clear that, after years of false promises, it wasn't going to assume any responsibility. The reaction by Dow Chemical proved the success of the tactic of 'finding out the truth through a lie'. We adopted the tactic in dealing with Atelier Zuidvleugel, not so much including dirty truths, but rather exposing the inherent nature of criticism against it. After studying relevant policy documents and planning notes dealing with the Zuidvleugel, we formulated recommendations in which we fully affirmed the central concepts and iconic projects, carefully turning every critical thought into its positive form. The 10 Must-Dos merely repeated the typical lingo found in policy documents and planning notes, adopting the key terms and projects, and spinning typical criticism (think about the typical reflex to warn about green and social values, etc.) as a reason why you cannot oppose. The set of must-dos started with the inevitable international competitive position ('Don't allow any interest to stand in the way of the international competitive position of your region!'), presented social and green concerns as beneficial for business climate ('Develop spatial quality, quality of life and social cohesion [...]'), described the strategy used to manipulate counterforces into doing the right thing ('Stimulate entrepreneurship, show ambition, forge alliances [...]'), embraced entrepreneurial government and corporate governance ('Always strive for tailor-made solutions, an area-specific approach and project-specific arrangements [...]'), and so on. Every must-do was scripted in a short power text phrased in typical business language capable of naturalizing even the most rigid neoliberal doxa into post-political values that every reasonable person spontaneously understands. Post-politics is the special mode in the disavowal of politics. Discussed by Slavoj Žižek, it turns the political conflict into a rational business negotiation between enlightened technocrats and liberal multiculturalists – which is exactly what we did with the ten must-dos.[6]

The final document was a classic example of overidentification, in which the official narrative on the spatial development of the Zuidvleugel was strictly repeated, but this time including its implicit assumptions, consequential ulterior motives and obscene undertones – thus refraining from the compulsion to level criticism against it. The formula of the intervention was provided by Slavoj Žižek: 'Obscene unwritten rules sustain Power as long as they remain in the shadows; the moment they are publicly recognized, the edifice of Power is thrown into disarray.'[7] Although power's obscene counterpart might seem to hinder the proper functioning of the system, the obscene actually optimizes power and makes it function. Žižek: 'This obscene dimension does not simply hinder the 'normal' functioning of Power, it functions as a kind of Derridean supplement, as an obstacle which is simultaneously the 'condition of possibility' of the exercise of Power.'[8]

The strategy of overidentification intervenes in this nexus by merging the two levels of communication usually kept separate to function properly. Any ideology becomes unbearable when it is spelled out by explicitly including all of its assumptions, ulterior motives and/or consequences. The latter functions as the unwritten manual for the first, limiting in a second move the field of options opened up at first and forcing interpretation in one way or another. At the same time, the obscene message disturbs the smooth functioning of the official ideology once it becomes transparent and public, raising doubt and even disgust by tainting things considered good in general. The strategy of overidentification brings the two levels of communication together and presents a new, transparent text that leaves the public without the comfort of free interpretation. The point is that ideology only functions when it leaves the subject the freedom of critical distance, even allowing the subject to have a totally different understanding, while an orthodox reading runs the danger of confusion and difficult digestion. In its daily operation, ideology depends classically on a certain naivety, argues Slavoj Žižek: 'the misrecognition of its own presuppositions, of its own effective conditions, a distance, a divergence between so-called social reality and distorted representation, our false consciousness about it'.[9] In the cynical reasoning of today, however, ideological distance is anticipated, we assume the divergence between reality and representation and we are experts at deconstructing ideologies, and yet the formula still holds: 'one knows the falsehood very well, [...] but still one does not renounce it.' As a result, the worst possible thing for ideology isn't so much critical investigation, but its translation into orthodox fashion.[10]

The ten must-dos didn't merely repeat the usual management talk in policy notes on the Zuidvleugel – that would just be an identification – but introduced a difference by overdoing the standard procedures of identification. A first difference was introduced by explicitly twisting counter-arguments by the opposition and proudly presenting them as part of the official programme for the development of a leading region. The typical criticism would state that spatial development isn't only about strengthening the competitive position on the hitlist of regions and suggest that there is still something outside the competitive context. Next comes the usual strategy of compromise, to seek a balance between conflicting desires and needs, in this case the ideology of leading regions with social and ecological values. While the leading-region story wages a competition between cities, the social and ecological values suggest a certain degree of equity, degrowth and sustainability. Accordingly, policy notes can't but incorporate objections as a sign of self-awareness about its neoliberal belief, although it remains unclear how the internal critique would correct or at least limit the competition. In writing the 'ten must-dos' we did choose the worst option, meaning we presented the social and ecological concerns as a contribution to the ambition of the spatial development of a leading region, something that would make the difference in the rat race of regions. The instrumentalization was presented as a matter of honesty, leaving aside euphemisms and straightforwardly explaining how green and social desires were inherent to the cause of regional development. In this way, critical reservations weren't so much brushed aside on the basis of one-sided economic thinking, but rather made useful under the header of the leading region, using it as the unique selling points. The customary oppositions were spun as unique success factors in the realization of the ultimate ambition to become a leading region.

A second difference introduced by overidentification was the integration of ideological power arguments that one usually only reads between the lines of a text but are necessary to convince the reader. Therefore, the title of the document wasn't just a power diktat, not an application of scientific models, not even raising an argument, it was a suggestion of ten things you had better do if you want to take yourself seriously. A list of ten commandments would play the power card a little too emphatically and turn a policy document into propaganda material that could easily be dismissed as a bad joke. The '10 things you simply must do' played much more on the fact that spatial development was a matter of common sense, not a strict scientific theory, but knowledge supported by friends and foes. No region wants to lag behind in the competition of regions! No region wants to compromise its social and ecological values! The set of must-dos presented itself as a truth beyond good and evil, embodying the post-politics that merges even the biggest opposition into a rational business negotiation.[11] Remember the five ways to depoliticize a conflict, i.e. by translating the political conflict in terms of surgical operation (arche-politics), a game (para-politics), scientific-technological instrumental procedures (meta-politics), warfare of us vs them (ultra-politics), and, finally, rational business negotiation (post-politics). Going far beyond the old imposing modes of power (hierarchy, order, diktats, etc.), post-politics mobilizes discipline, a form of soft power that rests on professional arrangements, mutual agreements, competitive classification and, perhaps most importantly, mere repetition. Discipline is usually understood as a professional field defined by knowledge and skill without noticing how it coincides with the punitive power of disciplinary methods, as described by Michel Foucault.[12] The power of discipline thus coincides with the figure of the expert – in our case, spatial planner, urbanist and/or architect – who has deep insights into the desire of the Zuidvleugel to become a leading region and knows how to realize it. The ten must-dos repeated the same catchwords over and over to convey the bottom line that regional development is key to strengthening the competitive position and business climate of the catch words.[13] Finally, the repetition of words, empty as they may be, is how ideology functions. To explain this, Slavoj Žižek refers to the function of the voice – the 'foreign intruder' – in the film *The Great Dictator* (1940), directed by Charlie Chaplin. Obviously the loudspeakers in the Jewish ghetto are an element to transmit the voice of ideology; the message makes the barber (played by Chaplin), his girlfriend and family very concerned, even though the overall message isn't clear at all. The same logic is strongest in the nonsensical speech of dictator Hynkel (also played by Chaplin) who addresses the crowd at something that resembles a Nazi gathering. Nobody understands anything from the speech by the dictator, the people on stage even look very concerned, and yet a few repeated catchwords – *Mädchen! Sauerkraut! Juten! Hunden! Strafen!* – brings the crowd in ecstasy. The great dictator cannot utter the word '*Juten*' without a spasmodic contraction. The hilarious scene shows how ideology functions thanks to the voice introducing signifiers that are easily recognized and repeated, regardless the clear meaning and the coherence of the overall story.

There is No Such Thing as Criticism

The reception of the study by the people working in the Atelier Zuidvleugel was a difficult one, for understandable reasons. Although we were invited to critically assess the fundamental concepts of regional development policies, we took upon ourselves a different, seemingly uncritical role, acting as critics that affirmed fully the desirability of a thriving Zuidvleugel. Instead of warning against the negative side-effects of regional development, we advocated going all the way in the competition with other regions and making better use of social and ecological ambitions as spearhead. Instead of highlighting the obvious contradictions in the Zuidvleugel narrative, we supported an even stronger application of the development strategies by including traditional checks and balances. Playing on the double character of a discourse, we acted as a mouthpiece for the official ideology, not without including its complex and contradictory nature. In the introduction to the ten must-dos, we explicitly admitted the lack of coherence in the constructed narrative on spatial development and we invited the reader – the commissioner of our study in the first place – to join the loose ends and fill in the gaps. The position of non-criticizing critic ran against the logic of the Atelier Zuidvleugel, as it positioned itself as an embedded critic in the heart of the provincial government administration. Actually, overidentification was criticizing not only the corporate governance of the Province of South Holland obsessed with regional competition, but also the function of Atelier Zuidvleugel embedding critical architects and planners in the bureaucratic context. Instead of presenting deep philosophical insights, the overidentification generated another kind of critique that confirmed the main narrative and rendered any critique futile by including it as part of the game.

Logically, the embedded project team of Atelier Zuidvleugel were the first to resist – in the clinical understanding of the term – the results. The study was seen by the project team as a confirmation of what they already knew and therefore set aside as a document that lacked critical value. However, the project team ignored the logic that criticism is more often than not the obscene supplement to a master's discourse, providing the space for free thinking that avoids the power of becoming total. Traditionally, the master rules the game through the superimposition of the ideal sustained by an attitude to keep doubt and criticism part of the private sphere. Jacques Lacan has defined the distortion as the capitalist master who publicly plays out doubt, weakness and fear while dealing with ideals as a dirty truth.[14] Slavoj Žižek describes the reversal of the capitalist master discourse as follows: 'This passage can also be conceived in more general terms, as the passage from the pre-revolutionary *ancien régime* to the post-revolutionary new Master who does not want to admit that he is one, but puts himself forward as a mere "servant" of the People[.]'[15] This explains why the project team couldn't accept the integration of critique in the public discourse as it dissolves their own position as embedded critic. Raising all kinds of questions, remarks and doubts is the best way to digest an ideology, unwittingly identifying with ideas you naturally disagree with, since the subject can continue to believe that it doesn't fully coincide with it. The non-critical approach was diametrically opposed to the logic of Atelier Zuidvleugel, set up as an embedded critical agency in the heart of provincial government administration. The idea of Atelier Zuidvleugel was that a good dose of out-of-the-box thinking by creative-minded experts would expand the always narrow-minded context of a public administration tied up in its own policy ambitions and its implementation on the ground. Instead of opening new vistas, our study closed off every breathing room, every hope for thinking differently, by including critique as asset, and inviting the reader to work out the loose ends in the story.

The overidentification in the ten must-dos made clear that the ambition to expand the narrow focus on international competition between regions easily ends up presenting the critical objections as a unique factor for the business climate of the region. We should therefore apply also to criticism the P.T. Barnum wisdom that 'There's no such thing as bad publicity': even the critique of a certain development brings the ideological set under public attention, just as negative media coverage still helps to build the brand. Atelier Zuidvleugel may want to broaden the one-sided corporate view of regional development and supplement it with fresher social and ecological points of interest, but it can only do so by incorporating these into the prevailing logic and repeat the main signifiers. In the ten must-dos, a well-intended argument to take into account the living environment in the spatial development of a region was twisted into an argument that present the green element as an interesting attraction that adds to the regional business climate. The gain is clearly ideological, the fantasy that green space is also important in the future development of the Zuidvleugel helping to maintain a critical distance from the ideological text of spatial development and its focus on the international competitive position between regions. At the same time, in the injunction of green development, the focus remains on the adjective and can be seen as the final victory of the neoliberal doxa to develop everything, even an urban region. What happens is defined by Slavoj Žižek as 'the superego displacement of the prohibitive injunction of the symbolic law'.[16] The finest example was provided in the discussion of Krzysztof Kieslowski's famous *Decalogue*, in which the commandment 'Thou shall not kill' should be understood as an obscene injunction insofar as it anticipates the human tendency to kill, thus silently hints at the obscene joy of it, as opposed to the Christian invocation to 'Love they neighbour as thyself'.[17] Years of progressive politics may have added green awareness to regional development, but the ecological twist can't escape repeating the capitalist signifiers and consequently helps to spread interest in the keyword they officially oppose.

The reproductive function of criticism within an ideological complex thus urges to change strategy and forget about the obvious resistance against the neoliberal logic of regional development; what should be countered in the first place is the noble struggle to make that development more social, green and just. In that sense, criticism should be located not so much in the direct negation of a certain process, but rather in the negation of the negation, the subversion of critical statements that remain inherent to the things they object. Žižek argues that the 'negation of the negation' is 'not a kind of "superseding" of negativity but the experience of the fact that the negativity as such has a positive function, enables and structures our positive consistency'.[18] In scripting the ten must-dos, we negated the supposedly critical role of Atelier Zuidvleugel by showing how their primary negation of the neoliberal ideology was part of its reproduction. Strikingly, the project team of Atelier Zuidvleugel wrote a critical afterword that summarized some of the most important contradictions in regional development, using the right academic references, and presenting it as proof of the 'funny caricature' of the ten must-dos.[19] Absent from the afterword is any reflection on the role of Atelier Zuidvleugel itself, rather confirming the strange position of the embedded critic who poses a fundamental critique of the neoliberal logic of regional development without feeling the necessity to cancel its own role in the same process.

Have the Debate Where It Should Be

A critical aspect of the ten must-dos came as a surprise after the presentation of the final document before a limited group with a few higher bureaucrats working in the planning agencies of the administration of South Holland.[20] In the discussion with our distinguished guests, we remained faithful to the ten must-dos. The presentation, like the text, didn't leave any free interpretation to the reader, but functioned as a memorandum mixing the ruling neoliberal logic of regional development with social and ecological values. An important element in the presentation was the twisting of every question into evidence that our storyline needed further precision and answering the critique as an open invitation to connect the loose ends. Ending a debate with a call for questions is a typical move for academic discourse, Jacques Lacan defining it as the University Discourse: admitting there is always something unclear that needs greater precision and additional study is a way not only to extend operation but also to avoid a master position.[21] Playing the academic was not at stake in the performance of the ten must-dos; instead, we, the critics, were acting out the capitalist discourse that introduces a new style of power by showing doubt and weakness, the ultimate blackmail that answers every critical question with an invitation to join forces.[22] The gesture turned the table in terms of criticism and invited the programme directors to provide constructive feedback, which is a trick to lure the addressee into accepting the fundamental concepts and set hierarchy.

Interestingly, the presentation of the ten must-dos led to two totally different reactions. One man excused himself in a friendly manner – the reader understands that these were well-dressed administrators wearing business suits – arguing that our words were untenable and even unacceptable in light of what the Province of South Holland was striving for. He argued against the strict hierarchy of the ten must-dos, as the top position for the international competition position and 'settlement factors' means that all sorts of genuine social and ecological targets are perverted from a profit-driven perspective. After these friendly objections and rational arguments, he made the bottom line clear: the ten must-dos are neoliberal bullshit and go against everything that he as a professional had been working on for years. The reproach made clear that the overidentification had had its expected effect insofar as the criticism was no longer treated as something to be discussed in the reception, but something to be corrected immediately.

Breaking the respectful silence of the public is an important moment in overidentification, it is the basis of many performances by the Yes Men. For example, in the presentation of the 'Post Consumer Waste Recycling Programme (WTO)', the Yes Men explain how faeces of McDonald's customers could be recycled in a programme to end starvation in the 'developing' world.[23] Although the academic public is clearly shocked, the speaker is somehow given the benefit of the doubt, even though he is clearly talking the most scandalous and nonsensical bullshit. The point is that criticism remains worthless as long as it is thought and discussed privately; it only functions in public: it demands from the individual the courage to speak up, break the silence of the mute audience, disrespect the power position of the speaker and make oneself equally vulnerable to scrutinization. It is the moment that happened in the debate of the ten must-dos for Zuidvleugel: the person was brought to the point where he skipped the convention to answer every critical study with a second round of critical questions, making unambiguously explicit the position he was working from.

Equally surprising was the reproach by a second director, who began to contradict the first. In the experience of the second person, the ten must-dos were not neoliberal bullshit, but a clear view on the challenges the regional Zuidvleugel development faces, properly balancing contradictory targets in an overall synthesis. Moreover, he experienced the ten must-dos as a living reality in which he recognizes the exact words, phrases and logics from the policy documents he was working with on daily basis. He said he had worked on the regional development of the province for years, the Zuidvleugel in particular. Having now heard its programme explained for the first time in such a clear way, he said he would gather his office on the next occasion to announce and explain the ten must-dos. He even considered hanging the summary as a billboard on the wall in his office.

In the ensuing debate, both persons argued fiercely with one another. This made clear that the overidentification not only sorted out the individual positions of the two persons, but had even more effect in creating a dispute among two persons that had been working together for years on the same programme. Apparently, both found it necessary, perhaps for the first time, to openly discuss their different stakes and opinions on the same policies defining a project. The discussion that unfolded opened up a crack in the seeming consensus sustaining the discourse on spatial planning in the Zuidvleugel, or better: it made clear that the official discourse was actually supported by an underlying but neglected dissensus.[24] Again, this reminds us that power doesn't function by demanding people to walk strictly in line with the ruling ideology, but only becomes functionable and liveable thanks to the openings that allow for different opinions and interests among the protagonists involved.

The Comfort of Escape

The opposite reproaches by the two colleagues forced us to reconsider the impact of critique on a certain social dynamic, and equally our role as critic towards it. The starting point of the study was the traditional request by Atelier Zuidvleugel to the critic supposed to act as a neutral outsider, an expert at detecting blindspots, paradoxes and deadlocks which protagonists aren't even aware of. At stake is a transferential relationship, defined as believing through the other. In the case of Atelier Zuidvleugel, the main actors could pretend to be professionals who were conscious about the many pitfalls of neoliberal logic while positioning the people in the administration as the sort of people who are fully submerged in it.[25] Actually, the easy affirmation of criticism is part of the logic; for instance, applause after a lecture is meant to avoid critical discussion and annul the criticism by acting as ally. The result is interpassivity: we all agree on the criticism and are happy to list complaints about the bastards out there, as long as everything stays the same on a more fundamental level.[26] The transferential relationship means that criticism gets locked in a perverse loop in which the critic is first invited to speak up freely and the moment s/he does so, the critical comments run the danger of being immediately contextualized, nuanced and contradicted – or worse, applauded. In the writing and presentation of the ten must-dos, we managed to change the position of the critic as expert into that of analyst addressing the split subjectivities underpinning the discourse on Zuidvleugel, neither solving blockades nor raising difficult questions, but actually rather acting as remainder.

The ten must-dos were shifting the discourse to activate another critical capacity. While the university discourse (academia and expertocracy) is critical insofar as it silently accepts the ruling figure of power (in the scheme by Lacan symbolized by S1 in the repressed position) and will always arrive at new problems/ enigmas yet to be researched, the discourse of the analyst, on the contrary, takes the remainder of the discourse in the place of the agent and confronts the split subject with it.[27] As a result, in the debate following the presentation of the ten must-dos, the critical effect was transposed to the public itself, having two directors reflecting the discourse to their daily practice and feeling the urge to make clear their totally different understanding of the very same signifiers. As a critic, we could leave the room without ruining the critical debate, or better: the challenge was to keep the talk going between the two gentlemen. The discussion of the two directors gave a clear view of the stakes of regional development in the Zuidvleugel and the different subject positions that support the narrative. In the end, the roles were reversed: the invited public – the two directors – became the protagonist in the critical discussions, fighting over the right interpretation of the programme, and the critic was somehow present to register the disagreement and avoid it being covered with the mantle of love.

At the same time, our critical intervention failed insofar as our own position as critic was left outside the picture of overidentification. We reserved for ourselves the privilege to withdraw from the overidentification after the presentation to the public and enjoy the confusion stirred among the two directors and the project team. Also, outsiders present in the discussion were provided with the luxury and comfort of neutrally observing the spectacle, including our sociologist friend Merijn Oudenampsen, who fiercely criticized the strategy of overidentification as a case of cynical idealism, but apparently never felt the urge to save the two poor directors from the cruelly manipulating mind of the critic.[28] The setup respected a comfortable position for the enlightened outsider, who could pretend to look through the game of the ten must-dos and see how the two poor directors were dragged into the venomous game of assimilation – in the words of Merijn Oudenampsen – with the neoliberal logic of spatial development without believing in fundamental change. The outsider position is comfortable but also untenable, as we saw how the narrative of the regional development includes counter-voices, even allowing for fundamental criticism, and drifts upon the belief of doing something totally different. The back cover of the final publication on Atelier Zuidvleugel summarizes the process as an 'intense discovery of the network-city phenomenon' and claims it has 'no patent on a solution'. Against the leftist myth of disaster capitalism, we should affirm the argument by Immanuel Wallerstein that historically, capitalism is most successful in social democratic countries: the mediation and softening of capitalism helps it to survive.[29]

After all, even the ten must-dos were included as a chapter in the proceedings of Atelier Zuidvleugel, though with editorial commentary, and the embedded critics in the Zuidvleugel narrative stayed committed to the cause, despite the clear disagreements over the neoliberal logic of regional competition. Ending the hoax is a defensive mechanism that was clearly at stake in the interventions of the Yes Men, although their performances certainly did have a critical impact on the public; the weakness is located precisely in the aftermath. Especially in the film *The Yes Men*, the protagonists comment on the set-up and the reactions they provoked, having fun with the excitement and misunderstandings.[30] The gesture reserves a place of heroic opposition against the powers that be and nurtures the belief that one is totally part of the ruling ideology. Having reached this point, we realized how Alexei Monroe has argued against the Yes Men that 'any stance claiming to be situated outside and diametrically opposed to a regime is committing the same kind of unhealthy falsification practiced by the regime it ostensibly opposes'.[31] In our case, the hoax might have been an act of overidentification, but it was sustained by the belief that it is possible to stay outside the picture and oppose the hegemonical ideas that run regional development in the Netherlands. Stepping aside and abandoning the set-up doesn't only let the genie out of the bottle, it also shows how the application of overidentification wasn't total enough, somewhat criticizing market and political forces while leaving the engagement of the critical actors – including ourselves – out of the picture.

Notes

1. The symposium 'Het Regionale Ontwerp in Actie' held at the Dutch Architecture Institute (NAi) on 1 Nov. 2007 was considered the finale. The outcomes were collected in: Verena Balz et al., eds., *Netwerken in Zuidelijk Holland: 1000 dagen Atelier Zuidvleugel* (The Hague: Provincie Zuid-Holland, 2008).
2. Ries van der Wouden et al., *Ex Antetoets Startnotitie Randstad 2040* (The Hague: PBL Netherlands Environmental Assessment Agency, May 2008).
3. MVRDV, *Metacity / Datatown* (Rotterdam: 010, 1999).
4. BAVO, 'Building Creative Alliances in Metropolitan Amsterdam: Letter of Recommendation', lecture in the programme RED A.I.R. Red Light Amsterdam, 26 Sep. 2009, curated by Angela Serino and moderated by Huib Haye van der Werf.
5. *The Yes Men*, film starring Mike Bonanno and Andy Bichlbaum, MGM Distribution, 2003. See the discussion of the Yes Men in terms of overidentification in BAVO, 'Always Choose the Worst Option', 29-32.
6. Žižek, *The Ticklish Subject*, 198-205.

7. Žižek, *The Plague of Fantasies*, 73.
8. Žižek, *The Plague of Fantasies*, 73.
9. Žižek, *The Sublime Object of Ideology*, 24-27.
10. Žižek, *The Puppet and the Dwarf*, 7.
11. Žižek, *The Ticklish Subject*, 187-205.
12. Michel Foucault, *Discipline and Punish: The Birth of the Prison* (1975; New York: Vintage, 1977), 235-236.
13. Slavoj Žižek, *Enjoy Your Symptom! Jacques Lacan in Hollywood and Out* (London: Verso, 2001), 2-3. The film is also interpreted by Slavoj Žižek in: Sophie Fiennes, *The Pervert's Guide to Cinema: Presented by Slavoj Žižek*, documentary film, 2006.
14. Jacques Lacan, 'Du Discours Psychanalytique'. BAVO, *Too Active to Act*, 63-70.
15. Slavoj Žižek, *Iraq: The Borrowed Kettle* (London: Verso, 2004), 131-32.
16. Žižek, *The Puppet and the Dwarf*, 24-25.
17. Slavoj Žižek, *The Fright of Real Tears: Krzystof Kieslowski between Theory and Post-Theory* (London: British Film Institute, 2001), 114-15.
18. Žižek, *The Sublime Object of Ideology*, 176.
19. Nadia Casabella, 'Nawoord', in *Netwerken in Zuidelijk Holland: 1000 dagen Atelier Zuidvleugel*, ed. Verena Balz et al. (The Hague: Provincie Zuid-Holland, 2008).
20. BAVO, '10 dingen die je gewoon moet doen', lecture organized by Atelier Zuidvleugel at the Natuurhistorisch Museum Rotterdam, 5 Jul. 2007.
21. Lacan, *The Seminar of Jacques Lacan, Book XVII*, 34. Žižek, *Iraq: The Borrowed Kettle*, 131-32.
22. Lacan, 'Du Discours Psychanalytique'. Žižek, *Iraq: The Borrowed Kettle*, 131-32. BAVO, *Too Active to Act*, 63-70.
23. *The Yes Men* (2003), film.
24. Jacques Rancière, *Disagreement: Politics and Philosophy* (Minneapolis: University of Minnesota Press, 2004), 51.
25. Žižek, *The Plague of Fantasies*, 113.
26. Žižek, *The Plague of Fantasies*, 109.
27. Žižek, *Iraq: The Borrowed Kettle*, 131-32.
28. Merijn Oudenampsen, 'De pijnlijke scherpte van het cynisch idealisme', *Archined*, 25 Jan. 2011. English version: Merijn Oudenampsen, 'Too Active to Act: Review', *Open! Platform for Art, Culture & the Public Domain* 21 (2011), 164-65.
29. Immanuel Wallerstein, *Historical Capitalism with Capitalist Civilization* (1983; London: Verso, 1995).
30. *The Yes Men* (2003), film.
31. Monroe, 'Full Spectrum Provocation'. The argument is further developed in: Alexei Monroe, 'The Myth of the Slovene Stag: Neue Slowenische Kunst and the Reprocessing of Traditional Symbolism', in BAVO, *Cultural Activism Today*, 49-57.

Provoke Full Spectrum

Chapter 6

Adopting the name of the then popular and charismatic mayor of Antwerp, the 'De Janssens Werken' (The Janssens works) campaign allowed us to go a step further in the strategy of overidentification by closing off any safe harbour from where one could oversee the spectacle. The project was part of the *35m³ Young Architecture* exhibition series, organized by the Flanders Architecture Institute (VAi) and the arts centre De Singel from 10 April to 18 May 2008. Curators Katrien Vandermarliere and Moritz Küng invited BAVO to present their work in the exhibition series on emerging practices in Flemish architecture. The series was a format to present young Flemish architecture practices, such as Office KGDVS, Jan De Vylder, Jo Taillieu, BARAK, URA and noAarchitecten, giving each team the opportunity to fill in the 35m³ black cube placed in the main corridor of De Singel, the cube itself being an artwork by Richard Venlet. The invitation to BAVO was odd given the tradition in Flemish architecture to focus on best practices. Since an exhibition with critical analyses and location-specific interventions produced in the Dutch context was not that relevant to the Flemish public, we proposed to make an exhibition showing contemporary architecture in Antwerp to itself. The underlying ambition was to translate our study on urban politics in the Netherlands to the Flemish context and to situate architecture in Antwerp as the ideal case of the winning combination of neoliberal development and post-political governmentality.[1] Post-politics is 'the perverse mode of administering social affairs, the mode deprived of the "hystericized" universal/out-of-joint dimension', Slavoj Žižek argues.[2] The definition definitely fits architecture in Flanders as politics is usually delegated to the other scene, i.e. the world of (public) commissioners and government agencies that define the architects' field of action, put constraints on experiment and innovation, and even manipulate design practice to steer it this way or that. Antwerp was somehow different as there was a general consensus about the positive climate for architecture in city, thanks to its mayor, Patrick Janssens. Following the strategy of overidentification, the exhibition was developed as a promotion campaign highlighting the many benefits of architectural quality for the public good and mobilizing our colleagues for the acclaimed reconquest of the City of Antwerp launched by Janssens. In preparation we conducted a series of interviews with stakeholders and shareholders to gain insight into the many existing forms of co-operation between politics and architecture, the role of architectural quality in urban marketing, the added value of architectural quality and so on. The exhibition was designed as a propaganda booth that presents material designed in the PR format of the City of Antwerp but still follows the language and imaginary of Flemish architecture culture. The main tactic of De Janssens Werken was to practise full-spectrum provocation, addressing all parties involved, politicians and architects equally and leaving no one the possibility of escaping easily.

The Janssens Effect

A key element in De Janssens Werken was obviously the overidentification with the city's charismatic mayor, Patrick Janssens, the former leader of the Flemish social democratic party SP.a (since 2021 renamed Vooruit), who was very outspoken about the use and value of architecture in reconquering the city. The work was directly inspired by 'The Geert Wilders Works' by Jonas Staal, in which the artist honoured the Dutch public enemy no. 1 as a living martyr of the Dutch people.[3] The work led to a lawsuit filed by Wilders against Staal, during which the court hearings were announced by the artist as public debates and the defence was published as a manifesto on art and politics. Contrary to the oppositional work of Jonas Staal, typical for artists, we took Mayor Janssens as the hero of architecture culture in Flanders, fetishizing his role publicly, not just part of corridor discussions in an architecture institute. De Janssens Werken adopted the highly recognizable PR format used by the city for brochures, posters and signage, something that was generally considered the work of the mayor, who had a background in the world of advertising. Part of the house style was the radiant 'A' logo, also used as a pin on his suit, and progressive messages wrapped in a language easily understood by the layman. For example, the official slogan ''t Stad is van Iedereen' (The city belongs to everyone) – including the (grammatically incorrect) local dialect expression of 'het Stad' – and 'Zot van A' (Crazy about A) – a pun in which the abbreviation of Antwerp with capital A sounds like the local dialect expression of 'you'. De Janssens Werken introduced the house style in the atmosphere of architecture and produced the same writing of bite-sized chunks of text to talk about architecture and architects. The imitation was total, up to the point that the public mistook the campaign documents of De Janssens Werken for official city communications.

The overidentification with the person of Patrick Janssens was most explicit in the poster series in which mainly interiors of high-profile architectural projects, all originating from the archives of the *Flanders Architectural Yearbook*, were tagged with a handwritten 'Patrick'. It was a direct imitation of Patrick Janssens' personal campaign for the local elections of 2006, in which the obligatory attributes of an election poster – i.e. party logo, list number and slogan – were replaced by a photogenic portrait of a well-known cultural inhabitant of Antwerp and a simple handwritten inscription 'Patrick'. The posters with well-known Antwerp citizens were a fairly literal expression of the common front formed by all democratic forces against Vlaams Belang, the far-right party whom everybody feared would become *incontournable* in the next coalition for the local government. The apolitical poster with the simple inscription 'Patrick' shows how one person managed to rise above all political parties to avert the imminent disaster over the city.

In the poster series of De Janssens Werken, architectural quality was instrumentalized as an apolitical force to support the incumbent mayor. Mainly interior images of single-family houses developed within the Land and Property Policy by AG Vespa (Autonomous City Company for Real Estate and Urban Projects) were used, for specific reasons. Firstly, the images played out the intimate character of a living room as a seduction strategy in the PR, rather than the more usual representative quality of a façade. In an interview, Jan Verhaert, architect and adviser in the mayor's cabinet, referred to the wisdom of Patrick Janssens who claimed that a city shouldn't so much seduce outsiders as first and foremost conquer the hearts of the inhabitants of Antwerp, which would radiate to the non-resident public. Herewith the mayor explicitly distanced himself from the notorious Bilbao effect, the holy grail of urban politics, in which one striking building designed by a starchitect features as the central element of city marketing.[4] The Bilbao effect is perhaps most succinctly described by Deyan Sudjic: 'With its puckered titanium-skinned roof, swooping and soaring through bridges and embankments that line Bilbao's river, the Guggenheim was more like a train crash than a building, a home-made mutant version of the Sydney Opera House. Its biggest achievement was seen as its part in the transformation of Bilbao from a grimy and run-down industrial backwater plagued by terrorism, with just a couple of international flights a day, into the sort of place where affluent Americans might spend a weekend, and which could figure in the opening sequences of a Bond movie – not, it has to be said, universally regarded as the essential measure of urban civilisation.' The effect Antwerp was looking for was the contrary, call it a campaign addressing its own citizens and mobilizing an aesthetics that fits the middle-class dream in Flanders. Exemplary are the single-family houses produced by AG Vespa in the context of the Land and Property Policy, designed by emerging Flemish architects: the façade width is just a few metres, the architecture fits the messy aesthetics of a typical Belgian streetscape, and the homely atmosphere was a central issue in an aesthetics that taps into the phantasy of good living, necessary to keep the middle class in Antwerp.

Janssens' vision could therefore be defined as an internal

city marketing of Antwerp, an inward-looking form of campaigning, which can help us to assess the function of an iconic building in a city differently. Following this logic, even an eye-catcher like Museum aan de Stroom (MAS) designed by Neutelings Riedijk Architects was not only meant to attract the attention of day tourists, but was first and foremost intented to create a feeling of pride and chauvinism among the people of Antwerp. With the urban politics of chauvinism playing in the background, it is not surprising that the spearhead of AG Vespa's Land and Property Policy was the refurbishment of modal city dwellings. Here, too, we see city marketing aimed at the city's own inhabitants, seducing them to reverse the classic movement of suburbanization and resettle the impoverished nineteenth-century belt. The images of cosy interiors (designed by Huiswerk Architecten, Mys-Bomans, URA, etc.) that AG Vespa brought into circulation appealed to the desire for homeliness, security and intimacy. In the poster series, we mixed the images of cosy public interiors, such as the reception desk of the Sint-Felixpakhuis (a warehouse turned into city archive, designed by Robbrecht en Daem architecten) and the bus station at Kiel (widely labelled an engineering gem, designed by B-architecten with Ney & Partners). The inclusion of the Palace of Justice in the poster series was intended as a provocation, because the building designed by Richard Rogers was highly contested, not only because of the overrun budget, but especially because of the dramatic setting at the end of the Leien with the spectacular hi-tech supporting structure plus the name of the starchitect – all elements taken straight from the handbook of city marketing after Bilbao. The Palace of Justice in Antwerp, built by the Federal Buildings Agency, was nicknamed the Butterfly Palace and the roof was referred to as the pointy bags used to hold chips. Despite the criticism, the building nevertheless appeared on the posters for the 2007 Architecture Day under the tagline: 'Looking into extraordinary buildings', but only for trivial reasons: the VAi wanted to make up for the absence of the building on the cover of the *Flanders Architectural Yearbook 2006-07* (edition 2008), which was somehow expected for the most spectacular building (the UGent Faculty of Economy building designed by Stéphane Beel and Xaveer De Geyter was chosen instead).[5]

The mechanism of internal city marketing helps us to understand the political dimension of architecture better with respect to the philosophical difference between politics and the political.[6] The standard narrative on the depoliticization of architecture misses the philosophical difference between politics and the political. Chantal Mouffe wrote: '[...] by "the political" I mean the dimension of antagonism which I take to be constitutive of human societies, while by "politics" I mean the set of practices and institutions through which an order is created, organizing human coexistence in the context of conflictuality provided by the political.' Now, some people misunderstood the message of De Janssens Werken as a critique of the privileged relationship they had with the mayor's project – the thing defined by Chantal Mouffe as politics – and claimed for themselves a terrain of pure architecture. However, the campaign wasn't so much intended to suggest that architecture is subject to manipulation by daily politics, nor that there are internal ties between architects and particular parties, not even that some architects have privileged relations with politicians. The point was that architecture is always permeated by the antagonisms constitutive of human society, which was obviously present in the ambition to hold on to the citizens of Antwerp through the building of exemplary one-family housing against the far-right discourse. Architecture is perhaps the ultimate extra-ideological referent in public relations and political campaigning, precisely because of its supposed neutrality (buildings aren't understood as ideological messages by certain political parties) and its objective functioning (buildings aren't just cultural phenomena, but actually play a part in the everyday life of citizens). The architectural quality of the environment seems to function for Janssens' political project in Antwerp as the extra-ideological kernel in the same way the inner greatness of the community featured in Nazi ideology, although both ideological formations have, certainly, nothing to do with each other.[7] Although architects may produce architecture on the basis of an inner pursuit of beauty, keeping far from party politics, the display of sublime beauty does generate political added value depending on the context in which it appears. To avoid the idea that architecture is manipulated for personal gain (for instance, as status symbol for a person or city, which is the main narrative of Deyan Sudjic), we should hold that every object of architecture has the potential to be politicized. In the case of Patrick Janssens, the notion of architectural quality was an apolitical element that was uplifted for aesthetic reasons and the higher goal of good architecture and still it produced meaning in the political urban project to keep the community together against the forces of the far right.

The dynamic reflects on what is generally understood as architecture criticism in Flanders, especially in the context of architecture culture as defined by the VAi. Since the first edition of the *Flanders Architectural Review* (first published as *Flanders Architectural Yearbook*), we have seen a curious dichotomy between, on the one hand, case studies of good architecture, presented as an apolitical entity, and, on the other, essays that critically elaborate on building production in Flanders.[8] The critical analysis seems to function as the phantasmatic support of good architectural practice, since the publications never subjected the best practices to equal scrutinization, most probably because it seemed contradictory to criticize architecture products that were first identified as best practices. Against this opportunistic disidentification with politics, it is important to understand how good architectural practice is never free of urban politics, for better or worse. Here we follow Slavoj Žižek's response to the petty-bourgeois reaction of feigned innocence after the riots in the Paris banlieues in 2008: the riots are senseless only insofar as general politics are kept out of the discussion.[9] In this context, Žižek argues, ideology criticism should be about including oneself in the picture, referring to the statement of Jacques Lacan: 'Sure, the picture is in my eye, but me, I am also in the picture.'[10] The challenge is not to regard the conceptualization as subjective in contrast to the true objective state of affairs, but rather to recognize how the subject itself is part of the imaginary.

Architectural Surplus

There was a second layer in the overidentification going beyond the personal figure of the mayor of Antwerp and focusing on the construction of the narrative and image of 'a city doing a good job'. In De Janssens Werken, we confirmed the myth, true or not, that the city of Antwerp had finally turned the fate of history. In the early 1990s, Antwerp made the news as a city that was falling apart after years of suffering social disintegration, widespread corruption and failing governance. There were multicultural conflicts in notorious neighbourhoods situated in the so-called nineteenth-century belt, Borgerhout most particularly. There was the so-called VISA scandal, in which corrupt politicians and administrators used public credit cards for personal gain and enjoyment. There was the 30 per cent landslide victory for the far-right party Vlaams Blok in the 1994 local elections, becoming the biggest party in town. In 2008, almost twenty years later, everybody was somehow convinced that the city was simply 'doing a good job' ('goed bezig') and had managed to do away with all evil in town. Patrick Janssens became the protagonist of the makeover, leading a coalition of the willing in which all democratic parties pulled together against the far right. Part of the political programme enforced by Janssens was the reorganization of the city administration as a business, comparing the governance of the city with a (public) holding in which the city council functioned as the parent company and semi-private administrations as daughter companies.[11] Running the city like a business was less visible in the political front against the far right, but at least as important as it set the institutional choreography for the new post-political narrative of everyone pulling together, leaving differences behind.

When it comes to urbanism, the post-political coalition of the willing against the far right found its double in the joining of all civil and market forces in the so-called 'Werf van de Eeuw' (Construction site of the century), interestingly combining large scale development projects with urban renovation projects. The Werf involved a whole series of landmark projects by starchitects, such as Museum aan de Stroom (Neutelings Riedijk Architects), Park Spoor Noord (Secchi Vigano) and the redevelopment of the Military Hospital into a residential complex (Stéphane Beel Architects). The city of Antwerp published a promotional brochure collecting all major urban works.[12] Equally important were the single-family dwellings within AG Vespa's Property Policy, with the aim of positively influencing the image of the neighbourhoods in the nineteenth-century belt by strategically intervening on street corners and tackling dilapidated housing.[13] In the debate on urban governance, most criticism focuses on large-scale urban developments, most often criticizing public-private partnerships, its capitalist logic, profit-driven commodification, elite circle decision-making, and so on.[14] The case of Antwerp, however, shows that urban renovation projects ('stadsvernieuwingsprojecten') might appear as a true counterpart to large-scale urban development – small-scale, classic government initiative, one-on-one with architect, etc. – but still follow the same post-political logic.[15] The small-scale urban renovation projects repeated the new urban governance model insofar as it was supported by a market logic, most visible in the privatization of several municipal departments into autonomous city corporations (AG Vespa for real-estate operations and later also AG Stan for urban planning), but also present in the use of smart public-private partnerships for urban development, as in the former Military Hospital in Berchem. Part of the entrepreneurial culture was the strengthening of the role of the Antwerp City Architect, a position held at the time by Kristiaan Borret, as an element for the further depoliticization and professionalization of public commissions. One of the most visible functions of the City Architect was the organization of the so-called pool of architects working for AG Vespa, within which a number of young architectural firms could be quickly deployed via blanket orders in the redesign of dilapidated houses.[16]

The underlying model of urban governance strengthened once again the relation of architecture and politics, not directly, but in the form of a Möbius strip, in which you start at one point of the paper strip and end up at the other side without noticing. In the striving for a professionalization of design practice, the architecture culture in Flanders held high the idea of autonomy, in which architecture follows an internal dynamic defined by its values and expressed in its own language. In line with this ambition, the entrepreneurial climate in Antwerp was particularly nourished as a unique opportunity to achieve architectural quality. Architecture culture was thriving on the pool of architects at AG Vespa, as it allowed for an enlightened design negotiation between public government and private partners. The same went for the launch of public-private partnerships in which architectural quality featured as a key requirement and in which the Antwerp City Architect appeared as a professional actor in the jury, thus gently forcing the building market to subcontract architects with a good reputation.[17] The success of the following best practices built in Antwerp began to function retroactively as the tangible justification for the new governance model set in place by Janssens.[18] The result is a seeming paradox in which the depoliticization of architecture in the city, i.e. cutting the link between design or building contracts and party politics and making it part of a professional negotiation process, played an important role in the creation of the political image of the city 'doing a good job', i.e. the idea that the city was beyond party political divisions and as such was the most effective electoral weapon against the far right.

De Janssens Werken complemented the official communication of the City of Antwerp with a campaign in which architecture was presented as a reliable investment in the political makeover. The 'Architect's Guide' was an imitation of the 'Werf van de Eeuw' brochure and contained an extensive argumentation on the use of architectural quality in city marketing and explicit praise of best practices with a detailed description of the political, social, financial and electoral added value architectural quality generates. In the spirit of urban governance, we presented architecture as a highly performant element with guaranteed return on investment, massive power for mobilization and great impact. Landmark architecture projects such as Park Spoor Noord (Secchi Vigano), MAS (Neutelings Riedijk Architects) and others thus created an enormous return upon investment, as it creates the image of a city 'doing a good job', chasing away the VISA ghost from the past and providing the opportunity for Janssens to conveniently rise above all parties.

Architects active in Antwerp also benefited, as they were now able to cast off the shadows of nepotism and clientelism and make room for an enlightened architectural culture where design intelligence and technical expertise prevailed. Crucial moments in the architectural production process, such as the project brief, choice of architect and design phase, were no longer influenced by party politics and clientelist relations, but were subject to professional consultation between enlightened technocrats. The architect was no longer the joker of urban developments, a figure to make fun of; on the contrary, his/her name became a sign of authenticity and a promise of the future. De Janssens Werken thus provocatively affirmed the key function of architecture by turning the official slogan 'The city belongs to everybody' into 'The city belongs to the architect'. The adapted slogan put the architect even more centre stage in the political project for the city, not only using architecture as a physical indicator for the wind of change in urban developments, but suggesting the architect him/herself was the main political author of that project. Later, the slogan 'The city belongs to everybody' became the focal point of the election campaign in 2012, when the new right-wing populist Bart De Wever competed against Janssens. Discussing troubles after a demonstration by Muslim youngsters, De Wever referred to the official city slogan in claiming: 'Iets wat van iedereen is, is niets waard' (Something that belongs to everybody is worth nothing). Removing the slogan was the first act when the right-wing mayor took office in 2012.[19]

We included two highly contested projects in the Architect's Guide: Kievitplein, the corporate office development at the back of Antwerp Central Station, and the Oosterweel highway link and bridge construction. The two mentions were meant as provocations. The main actors of stRaten-generaal (Estates/Streets-General), Manu Claeys and Peter Verhaeghe, were preparing a legal procedure to organize a referendum against the Oosterweel bridge, designed by Laurent Ney & Partners and Robbrecht en Daem architecten. The challengers won the referendum easily. Although the VAi internally decided only to publish on best practices, not giving a platform to opposition voices, it was clear that, on a personal level, people at the institute supported the brave fight against the multi-billion-euro building project. The only possibility to include the Oosterweel development in the *Architectural Review* was casually adding a chapter that included newspaper headlines and which I edited.[20] The mention of the Kievitplein was digging up an urban trauma, the corporate office environment was somehow erased from official architecture culture, while the popular protest failed miserably. Still, it had a positive effect in giving birth to the citizen movement stRaten-generaal.

Discipline and Profit

A third part of the overidentification concerns the engagement of the architect within the urban politics of Antwerp. It would be too easy to consider architectural quality as an innocent unity crudely capitalized upon by external actors. No doubt the mediation of the Antwerp City Architect led to a necessary depoliticization of the choice of architect, meaning that the choice is no longer the result of political favouritism and clientelism, but of a transparent negotiation process led by professional juries. However, the depoliticization of the choice of architect in design competitions doesn't exclude the existence of such a thing as a politics of architecture. On the contrary, the depoliticization of architecture in Antwerp was pregnant with many political effects. The general image of Antwerp as a 'Construction site of the century' was at least a good thing for the architects themselves, who thus had an unprecedented opportunity to expand their portfolio with all kinds of exciting projects. Also, the presentation of an individual project as part of the general project for Antwerp was an unprecedented opportunity for the architect to gain legitimacy and credibility. The city's business model tapped into the opportunism of architects and presented AG Vespa's small-scale housing projects as a mechanism for putting young (and not so young) emerging architects to work. Many of the architects involved complained about the limited resources in relation to the demanding attitude that was enforced by AG Vespa in terms of availability and workload, but the frustration was always rationalized by the opportunity to gain visibility in the city's extensive communication.

In order to redirect the question of politics to our community of peer architects, De Janssens Werken was in the first place set up as an awareness-raising campaign, especially addressing architects, though wrapped in a promotion campaign for the general public. City Architect Kristiaan Borret taught us the strategic triad necessary in negotiations with public and private partners: first you try to convince the other through argumentation; if that doesn't work, you try to seduce the other; and if all that doesn't work, you have to bluff your way in.[21] In our campaign, we applied the three techniques at once. The exhibition design was conceptualized as a disciplinary tool of multiple formats (guide, posters, video conferences, advertisements, etc.) to seduce the architect and make him/her enlist in the makeover of Antwerp. The underlying message was that architects were already participating in Janssens' political project, most often for opportunistic reasons. They didn't have to change anything, just come out of the box and continue their way of doing in a more explicit way.

Much against the will of curator Moritz Küng, we didn't want to start from the exhibition space as white cube, provided with the artwork of Richard Venlet, and asked noAarchitecten for permission to reuse their installation – we argued that the quality of the installation was such that we'd never do any better. We added a red carpet (the main colour in the city's PR material), reused a poster rack from earlier exhibits to showcase the brochure, and installed a couple of TV screens to show the press conferences. The outside of the box was used to support the propaganda, even making cutouts with the shining 'A' logo of Antwerp. The idea was that the cultural public going to concerts at De Singel would perhaps have little time to take a look inside the box. Therefore, it made more sense to use the outside of the black box as a publicity board. The posters, brochure and press conference registrations suggested that the box was nothing but a booth for a public campaign running out there and concocted by the city services. A voice-over repeated ad infinitum the necessity of De Janssens Werken, announcing the long-awaited meeting of architecture and its political other and the final fulfilment of architectural history.

In crediting architects for all good things happening in Antwerp and blatantly describing the way architects profit from the good climate in the city, De Janssens Werken undermined the fundamental concept of depoliticization active in architecture culture in Flanders. Certainly, the identification of architectural quality with a political figure was a disturbing issue for sensitive souls, but the equally explicit identification of 'The Architect' as the driving force behind the makeover in Antwerp was unacceptable. The crediting of the architect as the main author of architecture could be defined as an 'appropriation of architecture by architects', but something that in the architectural discourse remains implicit.[22] The suggestion that architects played a key role in the reconquering and marketing of the city undermined the most fundamental rule of architecture culture in Flanders, in particular the idea that architectural quality is linked to depoliticization. In the background, the trauma of the all-too-deep interweaving of politics and the building industry slumbered, with architectural firms as the third party in the triangulation, with fees for public contracts flowing back to the party treasury. The illegal financing system of political parties got massive attention with the so-called Augusta affair, a public tender for military equipment in 1988 that led to the fall of several state secretaries in 1994 and gave rise to the call for a new political culture.[23] Instruments such as the City Architect and the Architects Pool of AG Vespa were intended to professionalize design and building processes. Depoliticization, understood as cutting through the relation of dependency between architectural firms and political parties, was undoubtedly an advantage and contributed to better architectural quality. The political dimension of architecture is, however, not so much about the link between architecture and party politics, but far more about the fundamental support of architectural projects, lingering in the intentions and motivations of the different actors, their needs and desires, which, in Chantal Mouffe's terms, are the antagonism constitutive of human society, and the effects it sorts out well beyond the direct, causal result of the built object.[24]

The overidentification with the disciplinary function of architecture culture brings us to the element of institutional critique in De Janssens Werken. We underscored the disciplinary function by using a selection of best practices that strictly followed the canon set by the VAi, fitting the work as *objets trouvés* in the grand narrative of the city 'doing a good job'. The official narrative may be that depoliticized architecture is the basis for quality, but this doesn't alter the fact that politics are always involved in architecture culture, if only because of the implicit considerations steering the selection and programming. Call it the internal politics of an institute, with rules that remain unwritten but manifest themselves in the micro-sociology occurring around decision-making. Clearly, the VAi has to respect all sorts of links with other institutes, most notably the Antwerp City Architect and AG Vespa, but also with preferential oeuvres produced by architects followed over a longer period of time, and also with the different schools operating in the field of architecture. Architecture culture also nourishes institutional ambition that has to remain implicit, such as the communication of best practices only. This explains why the VAi was and still is absent in the debate on contested public works in Flanders. There is also the disciplinary function of architecture culture towards its constituency, with the VAi policing – in the strict Rancièrian sense of the term – what projects should be presented to the public and what projects should remain in the shadow, and also legitimizing the distribution, i.e. what architectural products are made visible. In the case of the Oosterweel highway link, the act of policing was even about what contested project could be debated. In the public hearing for the Oosterweel highway link and bridge construction in Antwerp, an architect-insider approached the VAi with the request to file a complaint against the design. The VAi hastily redirected the person as it would be not done for the institute to engage in criticism. Considering it a sequel to De Janssens Werken, we took the case upon ourselves and filed a complaint addressed to the mayor of Antwerp after listening to the whistle-blower. Unsurprisingly, the VAi was put under pressure to refrain from relaying criticism of the Oosterweel project. Jacques Rancière introduces the term police to go beyond general conceptions of politics that are actually making politics impossible: 'Politics is generally seen as the set of procedures whereby the aggregation and consent of collectivities is achieved, the organization of power, the distribution of places and roles, and the systems for legitimizing this distribution. I propose to give this system of distribution and legitimization another name. I propose to call it *the police.*'[25] In this respect, the proper political struggle is understood not only as the exact opposite of policing, but above all the 'extremely determined activity antagonistic to policing' – this means fighting the actual distribution and legitimization active in the field of architecture.

Enter the Other Scene

An important element in the assessment of the strategy of over-identification with the inherent critique of a certain situation is the deliberate shifting of discourse in De Janssens Werken during the production of the exhibition. Initially, the intention was to discuss political issues in urban development by explicitly referring to best practices in the field of architecture. The idea was to exhibit a critical investigation of architecture production in Antwerp by situating it in all sorts of urban development schemes and conceptualizing it as the *point de capiton* that stabilizes a fluid and constantly changing field of political and economic forces. Case studies of recent architectural practices in Antwerp, such as the Military Hospital in Berchem designed by Stéphane Beel Architects and the corner house in Borgerhout by URA, showed how architecture is not a neutral element in eventually questionable urban developments. These cases show how architecture constitutes the very building stones of the urban development allowing the negotiation of public and private interests and also distributing (equally or not) the economic, social and political profits generated in the operation. By highlighting how neoliberal logics continue to work in the body of building production, we wanted to criticize the recurrent ideology of an autonomous, depoliticized architecture in Flanders and its standard trick of uncoupling architecture from urban development.

Soon we shifted attention from the general public to the architectural field itself, directing all the propaganda of De Janssens Werken to the architects themselves and thus using architectural critique as a sort of pedagogy. The change in perspective and choice of another public are particularly visible in the visitor guide published by De Singel with an interview by Caroline Goossens, written on the basis of an interview made in the preproduction phase and published in the exhibition brochure even before the exhibition material was produced.[26] During the preparation, we carried out an information round in which we interviewed numerous actors in Antwerp on the role of architecture within urban development. We soon stumbled on a strange mindset among the architects we interviewed: often the analysis of the interviewee confirmed that architecture played a decisive role in bigger social, economic and political trends, and still they held the suspicion about numerous dubious interests as a legitimization of their own striving for architectural quality. So-called good architecture became the fetish for a design discussion cleared of political games, though never able to arrive at a clear definition of what it meant for architecture to be good, for who and for what purpose.[27] We considered the separation of design and (urban) politics as a resistance, in psychoanalytical terms, as it immediately transfers inherent critique to the manipulations in the other scene, securing the image of pure architecture. Architectural quality is presented as a panacea for any social issue while any critique that linked architecture with the object of criticism was considered political, or at least unable to understand architecture's inner striving for beauty.

The strategy of overidentification was redirected from not

only showing the unity of architecture and politics, but also taking away the breathing space that architects use to differentiate between murky urban politics and pure architectural design. Therefore, we had to undertake two steps: identifying the key role of architecture in urban developments while at the same time reflecting back all the major social and economic dilemmas – subjects about which common sense is usually spontaneously critical or at least suspicious – in the matter of architecture itself. The double gesture would have no critical effect if we had directed the exhibition to the general public alone; on the contrary, it would have helped the architect to sustain the fictional distance. In strategically realigning the exhibition concept, we chose the side of Mayor Patrick Janssens and called upon architects to follow his political project without any reservation. We turned every possible critique into a positive message and elevated the mayor's popularity as a symbol of the good architectural climate in Antwerp. The challenge was to carefully avoid the typical critical reflex of depoliticization active in the architecture culture of Flanders and overidentify with its unacknowledged truth and assume that architecture culture would be non-existent without the other scene of politics and economy.

The change of strategy in De Janssens Werken forced us to rethink our own role and position as critic, this time fully leaving the typical position of watchdog on the sidelines and stepping into the scene of overidentification, assuming a vital role in the play. The tactic functioned the same way Alfred Hitchcock's cameo appearances do. He appears in most of the starting scenes of his own films, sometimes offering a short explanation, sometimes just appearing among the actors silently. Referring to Hitchcock's cameos, Slavoj Žižek presents the inclusion of oneself in the picture as a '[...] reflexive twist by means of which I myself am included into the picture constituted by me[...]'.[28] In De Janssens Werken we stepped into the image, presenting our own critical role as the missing link in the great unity of architecture and urban politics in Antwerp and calling on fellow architects to join Janssens's political project. We even rationalized the U-turn vis-à-vis the visitor guide by stating that in-depth study had helped to overcome previous reluctance and we were now convinced about the unique possibilities for architecture in Antwerp. The campaign on the good collaboration of architecture and politics was a public declaration of things usually kept discreet, not worth bragging about, not even considered part of architecture culture. The change of perspective from critical to affirmation was rationalized by spinning an argument about the necessity of doing away with paranoid and all-too-critical reflexes against urban politics. Remember how the critical paranoid method was used by Rem Koolhaas in his study in *Delirious New York*, referring to Salvador Dali as source, but later functioned strangely as the manifesto for the highly productive Office for Metropolitan Architecture (OMA), building anything from embassies to hotels and shops.[29] In the overidentification of De Janssens Werken, the other scene of architecture was embodied as a friendly, good-natured and social-democratic father figure whose smart communication functions as common-sense intelligence of architecture and urban development. In the same line of criticism, the political dimension of architecture appeared as something light, far from political manipulation, far from Lacanian paranoia and conspiracy, but something that is part of the everyday discipline of good architects, nothing new under the sun, nothing to write home about.[30]

The reference to the everyday discipline caused an ambiguous reception of De Janssens Werken among architects. Stéphane Beel asked why only his personal name was mentioned in the documents and not all the names of people working in his office, thus implicitly subscribing to the message of De Janssens Werken. META Architectuurbureau reacted by saying they didn't want to feature in a programme that mixes architecture and politics, unwittingly affirming the necessity of pure architecture. Only Willem-Jan Neutelings wrote that the straightforward communication of De Janssens Werken was something he had been dreaming about for years. Strikingly, the reactions dealt with the form of De Janssens Werken, not so much the content. The campaign was particularly scandalous because architecture criticism in Flanders usually pretends to write from an objective or at least non-partisan standpoint, not only disavowing the political currents traversing the architectural object, but also hiding personal relations. In reality, writings on architecture aren't free from politics, if only because critics often entertain friendly relations with architects, articles are commissioned, and/or works are written to favour this or that ambition.[31] We hinted at the community element at the heart of the architectural culture in Flanders in De Janssens Werken campaign material by mockingly crediting the architects one by one, only using their personal names, while skipping any affiliation with an office. Addressing architects by their first name is common practice in the architecture community, somehow expressing familiarity and appreciation and also establishing a common sphere of peers.[32]

The irony of the situation was that Mayor Patrick Janssens himself reacted with surprise, admitting that that the municipal services had been beaten by critics who knew how to use the proper desktop publishing software.[33] Although architects were somehow not ready to assume collaboration within urban politics, there was no moment of doubt for the mayor about the key role of architecture in the city's PR. A similar affirmation came surprisingly in a debate organized by Dirk Pültau, editor of the art magazine *De Witte Raaf*, with eminent figures such as Prof. Pieter Uyttenhove, former The Hague Government Architect Maarten Schmidt, and the first Flemish Government Architect b0b Van Reeth.[34] As the debate moderator, Pültau longed to go beyond what he considered as the cynical play of De Janssens Werken and hear the final truth about architecture's political dimension. The moderator was surprised to hear that b0b Van Reeth didn't contradict the statements made in the framework of De Janssens Werken. Moreover, b0b accused us of selling old news, using age to overpower us. His argument was that architecture is indeed the key to starting the process of gentrification needed for urban development, while referring to the pivotal role of his design for Huis Van Roosmalen in the redevelopment of the Scheldt quays in Antwerp. The editor didn't realize that the everyday reality of architecture practice is perhaps far more cynical than a poor performance – a theme we'll return to in the next chapter, when we discuss the 'Bureau Kunstenaarsparticipatie' (Office for artist participation) set up in Rotterdam.

Notes

1. BAVO, *Urban Politics Now*.
2. Žižek, *The Ticklish Subject*, 248.
3. Jonas Staal, *The Geert Wilders Works* (2005-08), artwork.
4. Deyan Sudjic, *The Edifice Complex* (London: Penguin, 2006), 278.
5. Lars Kwakkenbos, 'Glass Under Siege: Two New Court Buildings in Flanders', in *Flanders Architectural Yearbook 2006-2007*, 9-14. Lionel Devlieger, 'Law Court, Antwerp', in *Flanders Architectural Yearbook 2006-2007*, 50-57.
6. Chantal Mouffe, *On the Political* (New York: Routledge, 2005), 9-14.
7. Žižek, *The Plague of Fantasies*, 21.
8. *Flanders Architectural Yearbook 1990-1993* (Brussels: Ministry of the Flemish Community, 1994).
9. Slavoj Žižek, 'Some Politically Incorrect Reflections on Urban Violence in Paris and New Orleans and Related Matters', in BAVO, *Urban Politics Now*, 12-29.
10. Žižek, *The Parallax View*, 16.
11. Erik Swyngedouw, 'A New Urbanity? The Ambiguous Politics of Large-scale Urban Development Projects in European Cities', in *Amsterdam Zuidas: European Space*, eds. Willem Salet and Stan Majoor (Rotterdam: 010, 2005).
12. Wim Cassiers, ed., *Antwerpen, Werf van de Eeuw: Een nieuwe fase* (Antwerp: Stad Antwerpen, 2007).
13. André Loeckx, 'Labo Vespa', 217-48.
14. Swyngedouw, 'A New Urbanity?'.
15. André Loeckx, ed., *Stadsvernieuwingsprojecten In Vlaanderen: ontwerpend onderzoek en capacity building* (Nijmegen: SUN, 2009).
16. André Loeckx, 'Labo Vespa', in *Flanders Architectural Yearbook 2008-2009* (Antwerp: VAi, 2010), 217-48.
17. Kristiaan Borret, *Beleidsnota 2006-2011* (Antwerp: Stad Antwerpen,

18. Gideon Boie, 'Architectural Asymmetries', in *Is There (Anti-)neoliberal Architecture?*, eds. Ana Jeinić and Anselm Wagner (Berlin: Jovis, 2013), 104-17.
19. Kristof Windels, 'De Wever gooit stadsslogan in de kiesstrijd', *De Morgen,* 17 Sep. 2012.
20. 'Selection of Newspaper Cuttings 2006-2007', in *Flanders Architectural Yearbook 2006-2007,* I-X.
21. Stefan Devoldere, 'Een stadsbouwmeester moet durven bluffen: interview met Kristiaan Borret', *A+ Belgisch tijdschrift voor architectuur* 209 (2008), 50-55.
22. Gideon Boie, 'The Only Good Architect Is a Dead Architect', *OASE* 96 (2016), 44-50.
23. Jeroen Maesschalck et al., 'De evolutie naar een nieuwe politieke cultuur in België: een beleidswetenschappelijke analyse', *Beleidswetenschap: kwartaalschrift voor beleidsonderzoek en beleidspraktijk* 16, no. 4 (2002), 295-317.
24. Mouffe, *On the Political*, 9.
25. Jacques Rancière, *Disagreement: Politics and Philosophy* (Minneapolis: University of Minnesota Press, 2004), 28-29.
26. Caroline Goossens, 'De Janssens Werken', in *35m³ BAVO*, eds. Katrien Vandermarliere and Moritz Küng (Antwerp: De Singel/VAi, 2008), exhibition brochure.
27. Hans Teerds, Christophe Van Gerrewey and Véronique Patteeuw, eds., 'What Is Good Architecture?', *OASE* 90 (May 2013), 4-6.
28. Žižek, *The Parallax View*, 17.
29. Rem Koolhaas, *Delirious New York: A Retroactive Manifesto for Manhattan* (1978; New York: Monacelli, 1994).
30. See the criticism by Matteo Pasquinelli of what he called 'Lacanian paranoia' in the work of BAVO in Chapter 4.
31. Geert Bekaert in conversation with Johan Thielemans in the programme *Eiland*, VRT, Nov. 1985, television documentary, on the occasion of the publication of *Verzamelde opstellen*.
32. Gideon Boie, 'Architectuur in de naam van de vader', *Architect: Vakblad voor de Architect* 49, no. 1 (2018), 122-24. The argument was reworked in the essay: Gideon Boie, 'Seven Questions on the Fundaments of Flemish Architecture', in *7 Questions – ETH Studio Jan De Vylder: Universum Carrousel Journey*, eds. Jan De Vylder and Annamaria Prandi (Berlin: Ruby, 2022), 241-46.
33. Geert Van der Speeten, 'Gezocht: architecten voor 't Stad', *De Standaard,* 14 Apr. 2008.
34. Pieter Uyttenhove, 'De Janssens Werken (BAVO) en architectuur in Antwerpen – een paneldiscussie', *De Witte Raaf* 119 (May-Jun. 2009, 1-4).

Shoot at Your Own People

Chapter 7

Launched by artist Jonas Staal, discussions on the post-propaganda condition of art within the wider context of continuing (neo-) liberalization and rising populist politics in the Netherlands in the 2000s allowed us to create a platform for the suppressed complicity between artists and the forces they struggle with. In the previous chapter, we discussed how architecture is able to present itself as post-political by delegating political responsibilities to the other scene, a world of machination and manipulation in which the architectural subject appears as passive victim. The same reflex was clearly present in the response by artists to the ongoing liberalization in local politics in Rotterdam and later budget cuts in the arts sector launched by the populist right-wing government in the Netherlands. Subverting the easy process of transference was the topic of 'Bureau Kunstenaarsparticipatie' (Office for artist participation), BAVO's contribution to the exhibition *The People United Will Never Be Defeated* (2010), curated by Jonas Staal and organized by the arts centre TENT in Rotterdam.[1] The strategy of overidentification was used here to embrace the ongoing liberalization and the budget cuts as something matching the intimate desires of the arts sector and thus to call upon artists to leave aside their natural impulse to resist. An action programme to boost the social return of art was scripted in close consultation with the main local art institutions in Rotterdam, such as CBK, TENT, Fonds BKVB and the Dienst Kunst en Cultuur. The programme was supported by the best practices of renowned local artists that could hardly be suspected of dealing uncritically with the social and political dimension of their practice, such as Jeanne van Heeswijk, Jonas Staal and Kamiel Verschuren. In this chapter we will show how the critical impact of the Bureau was situated in the spinning of a metanarrative in which the obscene truth of the specific situation was propagated as the official doctrine: the liberalization of the arts announced by the new government had actually been an accepted part (whether accepted consciously or not) of art practice for many years. Boris Groys defined the subversive power of a curator in writing a metanarrative in which individual artworks figure as accidental examples. Groys writes: 'Thus modern artists began to condemn curators, because the figure of the curator was perceived as the embodiment of the dark, dangerous, iconoclastic side of exhibiting practice, as the dark doppelgänger of the artist who creates art by exhibiting it.'[2] In the case of the Bureau, the exhibition was even more dangerous as it aimed to turn the discourse on the cultural actor him/herself, excluding any reference to external political figures. The visualization of the inherent paradox of art practice was certainly a strong critical strategy and yet it brought us to the limits of criticism as it was simply too scandalous to accept: the obscene truth of a situation must remain hidden for the symbolic order to function.

Strike at Oneself

Bureau Kunstenaarsparticipatie was preceded by the publication of the 'Rotterdam Code' for artist participation, a set of rules prescribing how artists should relate to the challenges the city of Rotterdam faces and gathered in a book, edited by artist Jonas Staal, on the political, even propagandist dimension of art.[3] In the text, we put into practice the rule formulated by Slavoj Žižek that any true critique should consist of the 'radical gesture of striking at oneself', which he presents as the constitutive act of subjectivity because it cuts the obsessional links with 'the object through whose possession the enemy kept him in check'.[4] The Bureau text didn't follow the classic protest of artists criticizing the other scene, i.e. the scene populated by mayors, state secretaries and other manipulative figures that function as a condition of (im-)possibility for artists. On the contrary, the text dealt a blow to the mythical figure of the artist as the last of the idealists by sketching a programme that shows the political usefulness of critical art.[5] The gesture was inspired by Slavoj Žižek's interpretation of the Medea myth, arguing that the critical act is situated in the breaking of overt ties with the evil other: Medea cuts any bond with her unfaithful husband Jason by sacrificing the precious object through which Jason controlled her, i.e. by murdering her most precious children. 'By cutting himself loose from the precious object through whose possession the enemy kept him in check, the subject gains the space of free action', Žižek writes. The crazy Medea-like choice of killing that which is 'in you more than yourself' has far-reaching effects: 'This act, far from amounting to a case of impotent aggressivity towards oneself, rather changes the coordinates of the situation in which the subject finds himself.'[6] In this light, the text of the Rotterdam Code deconstructed the figure of the idealist artist by building an argument around the use and value of critical art as a lubricant for public-private partnerships of any kind.[7] In a mix of bureaucratic language and art theory, the text explicitly instrumentalized the dirty little secret of artists collaborating with the powers they openly protest against and also anticipating the natural resistance of artists against voluntary cooperation within urban politics. Smart techniques to lure artists into cooperation with governments and market actors in urban developments were suggested, using methods of open negotiation, seduction and bluff, and repeating over and over that the feelings of autonomy in artists is perhaps the most useful of all.

The presentation of the Rotterdam Code took the form of an official briefing of the 'Stedelijk Protocol Kunstenaarsparticipatie' (Urban protocol artist participation) during a Corillos meeting at the TENT arts centre in Rotterdam.[8] The evening was set up as a first public debate on the draft version of Jonas Staal's *Post-Propaganda* essay.[9] Although the presentation had a certain critical effect, it confronted us with a weakness of Yes Men-like interventions, which consist of assuming all sorts of obscene truths about a certain situation and presenting these as common sense.[10] Instead of having a fundamental discussion on the role of artists in the challenges that Rotterdam faces and on the question of whether it is advisable to collaborate or not in that context, the topic shifted towards our own role as critics. The overidentification didn't reach its target as it didn't take into account the self-reflexive nature of art culture in Rotterdam, with artists immediately starting to deconstruct the performance itself, thus keeping themselves out of the picture.[11] The public was adopting an easy outsider perspective and their reactions were aimed at unmasking the manipulative discourse, questioning our position as a critic playing tricks on the public, etc. Still, the transference opened a window for criticism; even more, Slavoj Žižek described the critical role of the rock band Laibach in the very manipulation of transference through their seemingly totalitarian performances: 'The ultimate expedient of Laibach is their deft manipulation of transference: their public (especially intellectuals) is obsessed with the "desire of the Other" – what is Laibach's actual position, are they truly totalitarians or not? – i.e., they address Laibach with a question and expect from them an answer, failing to notice that Laibach itself does not function as an answer but a question.'[12] The same misrecognition was at play in the presentation of the Rotterdam Code: in the obsessive focus on the critic's desire, the public could again easily disidentify and play the passive victim, this time the victim of cynical intentions by the critic, failing to see how our poor performance was only a reflection of a much bigger cynicism supporting the everyday of artists working in Rotterdam.

The Rotterdam Code was relaunched on a larger scale one year later at Bureau Kunstenaarsparticipatie, BAVO's contribution to the exhibition *The People United Will Never Be Defeated* curated by Jonas Staal at TENT.[13] Instead of giving in to the counter-criticism, we took the overidentification even more seriously by explicitly self-instrumentalizing our role as critic, leaving no doubt about our role as institutional reformist. The Bureau was an announcement for a full reform of the arts sector in Rotterdam and communicated in the city's standard PR formats. The role of the critic was to function as a herald of good news. The installation was set up in the exhibition space of TENT and mimicked a sort of booth at a job fair. The exhibition material consisted mainly of paper works (with posters, flyers, brochures printed in large numbers) and a website. The Bureau was designed as a typical bureaucratic initiative using a language that blends right-wing populist honesty – it was the period when a third of votes were going to Leefbaar Rotterdam, the party founded by Pim Fortuyn, who was murdered in 2002 – with progressive art theory – most notably the conceptualization of relational aesthetics by Nicolas Bourriaud.[14] The *pièce de resistance* was the policy note called 'Actieprogramma Kunstenaarsparticipatie' (Action programme artist participation) that explained the reform at length with detailed arguments inspired by the idea of 'relational aesthetics' and documented with best practices from celebrated artists in Rotterdam, such as Jeanne van Heeswijk, Jonas Staal and Kamiel Verschuren.[15] The installation in the exhibition space was supplemented with a booth set up in the main hall of the town hall, with the former intended to spread information and the latter inviting everybody to enrol in the programme.

The programme consisted of three strategic reforms, each aimed at specific targets. The first reform was the transformation of all art centres into 'Kunstenaarsuitzendkantoren' (Temp agencies for artists), making an explicit exception for the top art institutes with a strong international competitive position. The temp agencies would employ artists as problem solvers for the genuine needs and desires of people and businesses alike. The reform was a response to the budget cuts in the arts sector that were hanging in the air and was inspired by the way the CBK municipal centre for visual arts actually operated (which I will return to below). The second target was the launch of 'Stedelijk Protocol Kunstenaarsparticipatie' (Urban protocol for artist participation) to streamline the engagement of artists in dealing with urban challenges. The premature 'Rotterdam Code' was recycled and reframed as a set that defines the rules of engagement that would inspire artists to spontaneously do what everybody expects them to do. The document was a mimesis of the 'urban protocols' drafted by the City of Rotterdam to solve, or at least manage, all sorts of issues by scripting certain procedures to be followed step by step. The third reform was the installation of the 'Kunstmarinier' (Art marine), a figure that closely follows art production in Rotterdam, monitors the use value of art and eventually enforces the participation of artists vis-à-vis the city's challenges. The reform was inspired by the 'stadsmarinier' (Urban marine), another populist right-wing project that was soon adopted by social-democrats as a go-between of soft discipline and control society.

Staging the Obscene Truth

The Bureau was no longer a walk in the park of overidentification. We were well prepared to avoid the same mistake of having a somewhat misplaced lecture in a gathering of critical artists. In preparation, we had held interviews on the uses and disadvantages of art in urban development with numerous stake- and shareholders in both the public and private sectors. The direct trigger for the Bureau started in a conversation with Ove Lucas, director of the CBK Rotterdam. As the local elections were upcoming (3 March 2010), we were discussing the general concern in the arts sector about the possibility of a right-wing populist coalition in the local government. Everybody expected a backlash on the local arts sector. Budget cuts and liberal reforms were in the air. Artists feared the further precarization of their living/working conditions and had already started thinking about how to find new ways to sustain their art practice.

Surprisingly enough, the director of CBK reacted to the imminent threat in a relaxed, even laconic way, suggesting that the new coalition of populists and liberals would only be a change in discourse but wouldn't change anything fundamentally for artists. The director suggested that the much-discussed new coalitions in which artists sought other sources of funding besides government subsidies and grants would merely represent a change in discourse and that otherwise little new could be expected within a liberal arts policy. He said, with a touch of irony, that the CBK had *de facto* always been working as a 'temp agency for artists'. The liberalization of the arts sector may lead to a downsizing of the cultural infrastructure, but wouldn't change the fundamental ways of doing among artists. The remark showed that the accusation of the 'Rotterdam Code' being cynical was only possible by forgetting that it was nothing but a mirror for a structural cynicism underpinning the arts sector in the Netherlands, a cynicism so pervasive that it is not even recognized as such.

The inherent cynicism in the Rotterdam arts sector became the starting point for the Bureau, set up as a platform to act out the repressed liberal infrastructural support of the arts sector and take it more literally than artists were prepared to do themselves. The exhibition built a whole campaign around the idea of a temp agency for artists, totalizing the dirty little secret by the director and presenting it as the long-awaited liberation for all artists in Rotterdam. The campaign blended the progressive values of artists (legitimizing their production by talking about artistic freedom, participation and engagement) with business governance jargon (targets to reach, tapping into surplus values, trickle-down benefits) and populist rhetoric (good for the people, good for artists, good for the city). The action programme was continued under the title 'Kunstenaarsparticipatie en hoe het leven en werk in Rotterdam verandert' (Artist participation and how it changes life and work in Rotterdam). To test its reality character, it was submitted as a paper to the Hans Baaij Essay Prize (2010 edition), where it received a special award.

A logical step in the overidentification was the self-chosen withdrawal from the art world in order to activate the work of the Bureau where it belonged, in the sphere of politics, an ambition that was latent in the overall exhibition, although in the end the political effect remained limited to the art world. The idea of the Bureau was to install a booth in the central hall of the town hall at the Coolsingel and to discuss art in the nexus of (local) politics, instead of pretending to be political within the white cube of the arts centre. The walk-out from the exhibition space to the town hall appeared not to be evident, as permission to present work in the lobby needed special approval in a meeting of all presidents of the local political parties. In the end, the Bureau was allowed to install a booth in the main reception of the town hall at the Coolsingel from 22 to 25 February 2010. We used the opportunity to invite artists to come over for further information, which they actually did, some even with the request to enrol in the programme. Though we made clear that there was no defined programme running for the moment, some wanted to enrol anyway, awaiting future opportunities. The presence at the town hall was also helpful in reaching out to politicians. Separate talks with all factions were held, explaining our ideas, gathering feedback and distributing summaries in newsletters through the communication channels of CBK. Talks about the action programme with Hamit Karakus, alderman for culture, and with presidents of the local political parties were used to show how the action programme was closer to reality than most of the art world was ready to accept. In the same intent, the action programme was handed over to Stef Oosterlo, director of the local arts and culture department of Rotterdam (Dienst Kunst en Cultuur) and images of the meeting were immediately capitalized upon.

More Real than Reality

The Bureau Kunstenaarsparticipatie equally showed how the selling of a political narrative – the thing called propaganda – can easily absorb criticism as it not only adds to the truthful character of the action programme, but also supports the dissemination of the main ideas, like the old PR logic that there's no such thing as bad publicity. Although taken seriously by most, the Bureau also caused confusion among the public, with some people hoping for an escape route that ended the overidentification. At the exhibition opening, Mariko Peters, at the time a member of the Tweede Kamer (Chamber of Representatives) for the GroenLinks party, admitted not knowing whether she should laugh or cry, while eagerly looking for a moment of doubt in our discourse. Such a reaction is a very common resistance – in clinical terms, not socio-critical – by the public trying to sneak out of the overidentification and avoid an engagement in the tough critical labour.[16] The public is eager to be released from the burden of critical reflection on an artwork that comes too close to their own position and they eagerly wait to see an ironic grin on the face of the critic that admits it's all but a colossal joke. The public waiting to be released from the performance is exactly why the genre of stand-up comedy misses the critical effect, even when it does unmask dirty details: the discourse loses critical effect because the public expects an entertaining evening. Theatre is the spatial context of performance that makes it possible to openly address all sorts of obscene truths while at the same time having a good laugh, thus ensuring that nobody takes it seriously after leaving the show. The theatre space has the same effect as the canned laughter in TV series: it is the other space that 'relieves us from the duty to laugh', or better put: in the theatre, the public is freed from the duty to take the joke seriously.[17] The anticipation on the performative character of criticism can be considered blackmail by the public towards critical art, since the critic was invited in the first place. Against the blackmail, the challenge is to 'stay true to the pose', not for art's sake, but from the firm conviction that the pose is more real than everyday reality or, in the Lacanian formula: 'reality masks the Real'. Discussing the 'abstract-virtual movement of Capital', Slavoj Žižek argued: 'Here we encounter the Lacanian difference between reality and the Real: the former is social reality of actual people involved in interaction and in the productive process, while the Real is the inexorable, "abstract", spectral logic of Capital that determines what goes on in social reality.'[18]

The same dynamics of resistance was played out in the final debate held at the Arminius centre, located in the former Remonstrant Church of Rotterdam, with a panel consisting of curator-artist Jonas Staal, artist Kamiel Verschuren, cartoonist Joep Bertrams and myself.[19] The debate was announced as a general discussion about art and activism on the occasion of the exhibition *The People United Will Never Be Defeated* in TENT, but ultimately resulted more or less in a final hearing on the Bureau. Many saw the debate as an opportunity to find out the truth about the programme put forward by the Bureau. The impression was enhanced by the fact that artist Kamiel Verschuren wasn't part of the exhibition, but involuntarily used as a best practice in the propaganda material of the Bureau, now having the chance to react publicly to the (mis)interpretation of his work. Staying true to the Bureau's programme, the debate was used for my part as an opportunity to continue the discourse, twisting all counter-criticism as proof of doing the right thing. Engaging in the debate as if it were just a routine PR moment of the Bureau was crucial, although this created massive frustration among panellists and the public. The criticality of the debate was located in the very frustration among panellists and public, who were hoping, consciously or not, for a radical but abstract discussion on art and activism and thus avoiding a discussion on how artists in Rotterdam participate daily in urban politics. The reflection was possible only by spinning every doubt or counterargument as an open invitation to join forces with the Bureau, as it is a programme that is open for critical minds certainly, up for fine-tuning and perfection.

Halfway through the discussion, artist/critic Sander Zweerts de Jong suddenly stood up at the back of the former church, saying (I paraphrase), 'When will you stop assuming the role of the Bureau? We want an explanation to our questions'. Later he wrote in an article published in the CBK magazine that, to the great surprise of the public, BAVO continued the performance undisturbed, not giving in to demands for clarity, not willing to put an end to the alienating enterprise.[20] Zweerts de Jong assumed that our criticism was a pose, a temporary occupation of a role it was possible to step out of again when the show was over, missing out on the real character of the performance. After all, the Bureau was taken seriously by many people asking for more information and even ready to enrol in the programme. More importantly, we constantly underscored the reality effect of the performance, presenting the reform as something we had really started to believe in after doing extensive research on the subject. Actually, we didn't even have to lie, pretend, act or perform, as the starting point of the Bureau was undoubtedly more real than reality itself. The whole fictionalized campaign touched upon the truth of the Rotterdam art scene following the Lacanian dictum: the truth is structured as a fiction. We, the critics, were transparent in the fact that the Bureau was just a performance set up in the context of an art exhibition in Rotterdam but touching upon the real role of artists in the urban politics of Rotterdam. On the contrary, it was the normal state of affairs in the Rotterdam arts sector that was living in denial, with directors of arts centres not able to make explicit their own functioning in the ongoing liberalization of the arts and artists spontaneously fighting their own conditions of possibility.

In maintaining the pose of the Bureau, the motivation wasn't so much that the 'analyst is always right', but the Lacanian logic that 'the analysand is always wrong', assuming the a priori guilt in the therapeutical relationship.[21] Slavoj Žižek wrote about the David Lynch film *Mulholland Drive* (2001): 'For a short moment, part of reality was (mis)perceived as a nightmarish apparition –

and, in a way, this apparition was "more real than reality itself" [...] one should discern which part of reality is transfunctionalized through fantasy, so that, although it is part of reality, it is perceived in a fictional mode.'[22] The Bureau was played out as a fundamental fantasy, the nightmare of artists that at the same time supports their daily engagement with the many challenges in Rotterdam. The perception of the programme as fiction, a sort of artwork that ends with a simple push on a button, shows how the fantasy functions as a construction that can't be subjectivized as it would imply the disintegration of the social discourse. Talking about the 2011 Occupy Wall Street protests and their use of the Guy Fawkes mask, taken from the dystopian film *V for Vendetta* (2005) directed by James McTeigue, Žižek argues how the mask 'should not be read as a means of simply hiding their identity to the police, since it harbours a much more refined insight: the only way to tell the truth is to wear a mask, or, as Lacan put it, the truth has the structure of fiction'.[23]

We Love to Hate You

Although the Bureau was a work of criticism without end, it was taken over by reality, or rather: the fiction of the artist as the last of the idealists fighting the liberal current got restored in the fight against budget cuts announced by the new liberal right-wing government. Following the fall of Jan-Peter Balkenende's fourth cabinet on 20 February 2010, general elections were held on 9 June 2010. The local coalition in the Rotterdam City Council suddenly turned out to be the precursor to Mark Rutte's infamous minority cabinet (taking office on 14 October 2010), in which a coalition of the liberal party VVD and Christian democratic party CDA received the so-called 'gedoogsteun' (tacit support) of the right-wing populist party PVV. Once the new right-wing populist government came to power, in the autumn of 2010, all critical parties in the arts sector organized themselves against the figure of Halbe Zijlstra, the new state secretary for culture from the liberal VVD party. Once the austerity measures were announced, Zijlstra, nicknamed 'Halbe the butcher', became the focal point of resistance in the arts sector. He seemed to enjoy the criticism levelled at him, even assuming his nickname with certain pleasure, and why not? Being in the position of power, Zijlstra accomplished what all liberals and populists had been dreaming of for years: shaking up the culture sector and applying market logic in the leftist hobby place of art. The fierce reaction of artists – culminating in the organization of the 'Mars voor Beschaving' (March for Civilization) from Museum Boijmans Van Beuningen in Rotterdam to the Malieveld in The Hague (26-27 June 2011) with slogans like 'Aan 130 km/u naar een achterlijke cultuur' (At 130 km/h towards a backward culture) – was taken by Zijlstra as a clear sign that he was on the right track. In a remarkable gesture of political spinning, the state secretary presented the arts protest as proof that it was high time to 'shake the bed' – a suggestive choice of words mobilizing the populist image of the lazy artist who enjoys doing nothing all day while begging the state for money.

Being in full opposition mode, not one artist was ready to admit that the arts sector had for years already been operating according to market logics, i.e. the obscene truth given a platform with the Bureau. Understandably, the obscene truth must be repressed, negated or disavowed at all cost, since its appearance in public would ruin the normal functioning of the arts sector as a force always opposing social wrongs and unfair politics. The barricades erected by the arts sector against Halbe Zijlstra's budget cuts and liberalization plans should be interpreted as a gesture of disavowal in which the internal divide underpinning the arts sector was externalized and projected onto the state secretary. In this context, the continuation of the Bureau had no chance of success. The follow-up plan was that BAVO would itself embody all the functions proposed in the programme, i.e. organizing a temporary employment agency that functions as a match-maker between commissioners and artists, detailing further the protocol that streamlines the engagement and acting as the 'art marine' enforcing compliance with the protocol and monitoring the equal distribution of surplus values among the parties involved. Despite the initial enthusiasm of director Ove Lucas and co-director Siebe Thissen to organize such a Bureau within a programme of the CBK in a housing redevelopment in Rotterdam-Zuid, the plan never materialized.

The later continuation of the Bureau at the Embassy Gallery (Edinburgh) lacked the local engagement and embedding necessary to 'shoot into one's own ranks'.[24] The programme was reconceptualized in the *Dutch Design Lobby* (2010), BAVO's contribution to the exhibition *Tricksters Tricked: (Un)Covering Identity* at Van Abbemuseum in Eindhoven, curated by Freek Lomme and Hadas Zemer Ben-Ari, as part of Dutch Design Week (DDW).[25] After confusion between the management of the Van Abbemuseum and DDW, the contribution was quickly withdrawn from the exhibition hall, since the DDW was one of the sponsors of the Van Abbemuseum.[26] The self-censorship by Van Abbemuseum was senseless as the Dutch Design Lobby was set up from the beginning as an extra-muros activity taking place in the Dialogues House of ABN-AMRO at the Klokgebouw, the venue of the DDW. Ironically enough, the ABN-AMRO bank was acting in turn as a main sponsor of the Van Abbemuseum and DDW. Meanwhile, we continued to discuss the budgets cuts in culture by the new right-wing populist government, strictly following the spirit of the Bureau, but generalizing the discussion. The opinion articles called upon artists to act more liberally than Zijlstra, make the liberal arts agenda liberal, supporting the message with a poster series that used the house style of the election campaign of the liberal party VVD. Again, the criticism necessarily fell on deaf ears.[27] The argument that fighting Halbe Zijlstra was to prove him right and suggesting that artists should better subvert his liberal position from within, accepting the liberal assumptions implicitly active in the arts sector today, was considered even more an insult to the arts sector.

After all, the arts sector was too concerned about their own public appearance while remaining blind to the contradiction in the state secretary's subject position. Wasn't it a very poor gesture for Halbe Zijlstra to brag about the liberalization of the arts but actually be a miser skimping on poor budgets and failing to formulate an ambitious programme for the liberal arts? Equally, the arts sector remained blind to the split in their own subject position. The director of the Rijksmuseum, Wim Pijbes, bragged about the 'boys and girls of the visual arts sector' for who it was time to get real. His statement was an utterly opportunistic attempt to favour the state secretary, but maybe true for one reason alone. How brave could the protesters be, who gathered in their thousands to march from Rotterdam to the Malieveld in The Hague while art institutions and artists started that very week what the state secretary had been asking for: looking for new collaborations and mergers, setting up creative alliances with private parties, looking into new financing models, reaching out to new public groups, etc. In the public hearing of the arts commission (20 June 2011) in the Tweede Kamer (Chamber of Representatives), the artists held onto the radical position while the political parties in the opposition (the representative of PvdA in the first place) were asking the state secretary to soften the blow for the weak segments in the arts market, unconsciously taking over the state secretary's discourse. The figure of Halbe Zijlstra stands not only for the other scene of manipulation and machination but also for the artists' own renunciation of a political will to formulate a common counter-project. In reference to Austrian right-wing populist leader Jörg Haider, Slavoj Žižek argues that progressive critics couldn't accept that the advance of right-wing thought is a consequence of their own renunciation of a radical political project. In that respect, we all 'love to hate' Jörg Haider. Žižek continues: 'The "truth" of Haider's claim does not lie in the identity of New Labour and the New Right, but in the generation of his populism by the zombification of European social democracy at large.'[28] In the same fashion, Zijlstra might behave like a despicable butcher in the arts sector, and yet we must understand that he came at the same time as a petty excuse generated by the artists and signalling their renunciation. Žižek writes:

'One can never experience the symbolic big Other as such [...] The only way to experience the big Other in the real is thus to experience it as superego agency, the horrible obscene Thing.'[29] The Bureau Kunstenaarsparticipatie did away with the external figures like Halbe Zijlstra and performed a superego voice stemming from the arts sector itself, proposing all sorts of scandalous yet familiar and seductive proposals.

Notes
1. BAVO, 'Bureau Kunstenaarsparticipatie', part of the exhibition *The People United Will Never Be Defeated* at TENT Rotterdam, 19 Feb.-28 Apr. 2010, curated by Jonas Staal.
2. Boris Groys, 'On Curatorship', in *Art Power* (Cambridge, MA: MIT Press, 2008), 45.
3. BAVO, 'The Necessity of Enthusiastic Leadership in the Formation and Activation of Creative Coalitions in the Netherlands', in *Power?... To Which People?!*, ed. Jonas Staal (Heijningen: Jap Sam, 2010), 25-34.
4. Slavoj Žižek, *The Fragile Absolute* (London: Verso, 2000), 150.
5. BAVO, 'The Dutch Neoliberal City'.
6. Žižek, *The Fragile Absolute*, 150.
7. BAVO, *Too Active to Act*.
8. BAVO, 'Toelichting bij de startnotitie "De noodzaak van een enthousiast artistiek leiderschap in de formatie en activatie van creatieve coalities in Nederland: de Rotterdam Code"', presentation at the Corillos meetings of artists at TENT/Witte de With, Rotterdam, 16 Jun. 2009, initiated by Marjolijn Dijkman and David Maroto, hosted by Jonas Staal and artist duo Iratxe Jaio and Klaas Gorkum.
9. Jonas Staal, *Post-Propaganda* (Amsterdam: Fonds BKVB, 2010).
10. *The Yes Men* (2003), film.
11. *The Yes Men* (2003), film. See earlier note on ending the strategy of the hoax in the film on the work of the artist duo Mike Bonanno and Andy Bichlbaum in Chapter 5.
12. Žižek, 'Why Are Laibach and NSK not Fascists?'
13. BAVO, 'Bureau Kunstenaarsparticipatie', part of the exhibition *The People United Will Never Be Defeated* at TENT/Witte de With, Rotterdam, 19 Feb.-28 Apr. 2010, curated by Jonas Staal.
14. Nicolas Bourriaud, *Relational Aesthetics* (1998; Dijon: Les presses du réel, 2002).
15. BAVO, 'Actieprogramma Kunstenaarsparticipatie', Bureau Kunstenaarsparticipatie, Rotterdam, exhibition piece, 2010.
16. Žižek, *The Ticklish Subject*, 262.
17. Žižek, *The Sublime Object of Ideology*, 35.
18. Slavoj Žižek, *The Year of Dreaming Dangerously* (London: Verso, 2012), 101-02.
19. The debate 'Protest! Activisme in de Kunst' was organized by TENT, Willem de Kooning Academy and Arminius to conclude the exhibition *The People United Will Never Be Defeated* at the Arminius Church, Rotterdam, 25 Mar. 2010.

20. Sander Zweerts de Jong, 'BAVO en het Bureau Kunstenaarsparticipatie', *CBK Magazine*, Mar. 2010.
21. Žižek, *The Plague of Fantasies*, 35-36 and 107.
22. Žižek, *Organs without Bodies*, 170.
23. Žižek, *The Year of Dreaming Dangerously*, 103, fn. 20.
24. BAVO, *Office for Artist Participation*, Embassy Gallery, Edinburgh, 26 Mar.-10 Apr. 2011, artwork part of the *Going Public* exhibition curated by Erwin Van Doorn and Inge Nabuurs.
25. The programme was reconceptualized in the *Dutch Design Lobby* (2010), BAVO's contribution to the exhibition *Tricksters Tricked: (Un)Covering Identity* at the Van Abbemuseum, Eindhoven, 16 Oct. 2010-06 Feb. 2011, curated by Freek Lomme and Hadas Zemer Ben-Ari, as part of Dutch Design Week. See the short paragraph in Chapter 2 of this book.
26. Marina van der Bergen, 'De Dutch Design Lobby', *Archined*, 28 Oct. 2010.
27. BAVO, 'Maak liberaal kunstbeleid liberaal', *Metropolis M*, 8 Jun. 2011. BAVO, 'Denkverbod op liberale kunst', *Joop.nl,* 18 Jun. 2011 and *Metropolis M*, 23 Jun. 2011. BAVO, 'Een nieuwe culturele elite voor een nieuwe liberale kunst in Nederland', lecture at the symposium *De Nieuwe Elite*, 9-10 Sep. 2011, organized by Stedelijk Museum and De Appel and moderated by Hendrik Folkerts and Ann Demeester. See also Gideon Boie, 'Waarom Bas Heijne een nieuwe baan moet zoeken', *Joop.nl*, 22 Sep. 2011. Gideon Boie, 'Artists Form a New Alliance with Geert Wilders', lecture at the *Cinema Clash Continuum Conference*, 28 Mar.-1 Apr. 2011, organized by the Rietveld Academie.
28. Slavoj Žižek, 'Why Do We All Love to Hate Haider?', *New Left Review* 2 (Mar.-Apr. 2000).
29. Žižek, *The Plague of Fantasies,* 80.

Choose Hyperidealism

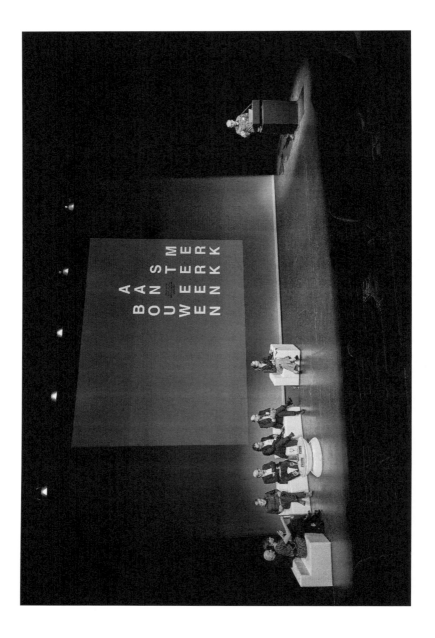

Chapter 8

'Why don't you write a plea for a Provincial Government Architect?', was the direct request made by Tim Vekemans and Dimitri Minten in December 2011 on behalf of Architectuurwijzer, a non-profit cultural organization active in the province of Limburg. The request was in itself already an overidentification with a statement made by b0b Van Reeth, the first Flemish Government Architect, in a debate on architectural quality in Limburg. His suggestion was to establish a Provincial Government Architect for Limburg. It wasn't clear whether this suggestion was made in jest, but nonetheless the audience took it deadly seriously. In our first meeting, we came up with the plan to take the overidentification to the next level and effectively draft the contours of the new function for a Provincial Government Architect, not just writing a plea that brings a good idea but leaves it up to those in power to implement. The strategy was to jump directly into the political game by scripting the constitution of the position and use the writing process as a tool for negotiation with relevant actors in politics and architecture. The critical effect was generated in the overidentification with the official ideal, which we labelled earlier as hyperidealism, in this case with the architecture quality of the living environment in Limburg.[1] It involves that we take all steps necessary to realize the ideal and, already, build a solid consensus around it. With the notion of hyperidealism, we redefine the usual negative hysterical meaning of criticism, meaning an intervention in which the official ideal is unmasked by highlighting its compromises and indicating the weaknesses in the master's position. Referring to orthodox theologist G.K. Chesterton, Slavoj Žižek has argued that the hysterical gesture can also be about the exact opposite: fully embracing the ideal and not accepting any compromise.[2] In the background of hyperidealism plays a mutation in Jacques Lacan's definition of the Master Discourse to the so-called Capitalist Discourse: while in the first the Master Signifier in supported by the repressed split subject the terms are exchanged in the second, the master signifier is in in the repressed position of the split subject.[3] The capitalist master no longer pretends to embody an ideal, but embraces his subjective doubt and powerlessness. Slavoj Žižek describes the mutation of the master as follows: 'This passage can also be conceived in more general terms, as the passage from the pre-revolutionairy *ancien régime* to the post-revolutionary new Master who does not want to admit that he is one, but puts himself forward as a mere 'servant' of the People[.]'[4] In this chapter; we will discuss how a three-year discursive programme of discreet talks and public programmes engaged different stakeholders and shareholders to articulate their interest in the architectural quality of the living environment in Limburg. In the hyperidealist version of the strategy of overidentification, provocation was given a positive twist: no longer showing the official ideal as compromised by clandestine interests, no longer hinting at inconvenient truths or dirty little secrets, but on the contrary staying true to the noble ideal, understanding how the empty signifier can be filled with meaning through a collective process of negotiation and rearticulation.

Shaping an Idea

In preparing the plea for the Provincial Government Architect, we started a round of discrete talks with the province's governor and deputies, mayors and aldermen, people working in the public administration, the provincial Chamber of Commerce, representatives of the labour union, former Flemish Government Architect bOb Van Reeth and his heirs, the Dean of the Faculty of Architecture and Art at Hasselt University, the president of the Order of Architects, prominent architects, and others. The interviews were a means to collect feedback from all these experts, assuming both affirmative and critical thoughts, little by little giving concrete form to an idea of a Provincial Government Architect, gradually scripting its programme and enriching its magnitude. Although names were kept discreet during the work, they were disclosed in the acknowledgements in the publication. As the interviews were, for some of the interlocutors, the first time they were hearing about architectural quality, the talks were not only gathering feedback but also preparing the terrain and the guarantee that the idea of such a Government Architect would not fall on rocky soil during the presentation. As such, the intense round of interviews, harvesting ideas and scripting of a programme itself embodied the diplomatic work on the ground necessary for any ambition on architectural quality to become a reality.

The slogan 'Art is fanaticism that demands diplomacy' was used by NSK to frame its various diplomatic elements necessary to organize the first virtual state in time, such as the establishment of temporary embassies and consulates, the issuing of passports, and the like. Miran Mohar (IRWIN) situated the subversive value of NSK's diplomatic tools in the fact that fiction largely caught up with reality when it turned out that many demands for the passport came from Nigeria.[5] Although the NSK embassy made clear the passports were of no 'official' use, the applicants claimed it could become useful at a later moment. The same happened allegedly during the fall of the former Yugoslavia, when the NSK passports really were used to cross borders, since the proliferation of former Yugoslav states meant that the border police often didn't know anymore whether or not a state still existed; the same holds for the foundation of new states. As a result, the NSK passports functioned as what they defined as state-cultural documents, suggesting that political constructions as states primarily take form with lightweight and easily replicable cultural documents.[6]

The round of interviews resulted in a start note titled 'Building Up a Stronger Brand: Initial Memo Limburg Government Architect', with a declaration and programme for the Provincial Government Architect as an essential yet missing piece in the apparatus for architecture culture in Flanders.[7] The document referred explicitly the stereotypical PR phrases about Limburg Province being a strong brand, in contrast to other Belgian provinces, mainly dominated by cities, and used this as the frame for architectural production. In listing the benefits of architectural quality for the living environment, we played the card of chauvinistic Limburg rhetoric explicitly. The profile of the province as a 'sterk merk' (strong brand), the horizontal network of forty-four cities and communes and the role of Hasselt-Genk as the first ever 'bipool' in the Spatial Structure Plan for Flanders were put forward as the firm building stones for a future architecture culture. The ambition was to embed architectural quality in the existing professional discourse and practice and in the province's wider social and economic structures. The explicit argument that 'architecture culture always grows outside culture' subverted the traditional tendency of architectural culture in Flanders to define itself in the form of a tautology, i.e. architecture as something that finds a value in itself. For example, the autonomy of architecture was defended by Christophe Van Gerrewey as 'a necessary precondition for [architecture's] social role' in reference to the work of Office KGDVS, which exempts architecture from any outside interference by means of the tautology 'architecture is itself'.[8] Three functions were scripted as the core agenda of the Provincial Government Architect: first, the negotiation of interests and desires in specific local projects (which we defined as 'design mediation'); second, the implementation of supralocal spatial management around common design challenges ('liaison officer'); and, third, the promotion of projects and realizations with provincial appeal and acquisition of talent ('public relations').

The start note 'Building Up a Stronger Brand' was presented at the first Staten-Generaal (C-mine, 21 November 2012), to which we invited all parties active in the field of architecture culture in Limburg and surroundings.[9] The afternoon session was introduced by Wim Dries, the mayor of Genk, and gathered academics, architects and administrators in parallel debate sessions on the future Provincial Government Architect. The plenary evening debate was introduced by Herman Reynders, Governor of Limburg Province, and followed by a panel with distinguished guests such as Christoph Grafe (newly appointed director of the VAi), Véronique Claessens (board member of the Vlaamse Vereniging Ruimte en Planning, VRP, head of department Spatial Development for the city of Genk), Jo Coenen (former Rijksbouwmeester in the Netherlands), Peter Bongaerts (professor at UHasselt and co-author of the Spatial Structure Plan Limburg), Roland Dûchatelet (captain of industry, former Senator and Alderman for the City of Sint-Truiden) and Wilfried Vandeghinste (programme director at Winvorm). The debate was moderated by media personality Ianka Fleerackers.[10] The set-up invited the most diverse figures in an attempt to both broaden the base for architecture culture, not reserving the issue of architectural quality for architects alone, and construct in live action the consent for the Provincial Government Architect. It proved how varying interests, and the complexity and contradiction arising from them, are not necessarily a compromise to the ideal, in our case the architectural quality of the living environment. Complexity and contradiction can equally be considered as the necessary friction needed to trigger moments of subjectification, a lesson learned from Giorgio Agamben's theory on the apparatus. Apparatuses are not effective when they count on dumb subjects that operate as machines, but only when they leave ample room for manoeuvring and interpretation by free subjects involved in a relentless fight with the apparatus. 'I call a subject that what results from the relation and, so to speak, from the relentless fight between living being and apparatuses', argues Giorgio Agamben.[11] The 'relentless fight' suggests that the birth of the subject doesn't follow from a disciplined follower of a certain apparatus, but on the contrary, that the apparatus allows for a certain individuality and even stubbornness.Individuality and stubbornness add to the openness necessary to find a convergence of parties with totally different agendas, in our case politicians, businesspeople, architects and other stakeholders in the regional development of Limburg.

The challenge in pushing the issue of a Provincial Government Architect was to remain faithful to noble ideal of architectural quality and spin the usual pragmatic reservations and obstacles as a possible cliffhanger. Despite b0b Van Reeth's explicit support, acting Flemish Government Architect at the time Peter Swinnen reacted dismissively, as he saw the provincial position as a further weakening of his own position, which was under heavy pressure under the new right-wing populist coalition. Swinnen's response also meant that the VAi never really supported the initiatives of Architectuurwijzer wholeheartedly, although director Christoph Grafe did join the public debate at the Festival of Architecture. In fact, only the VRP provided a platform in *Ruimte*, its magazine with the report I wrote under the title 'Het werk moet nog beginnen' (The work is yet to begin).[12] A delicate element in the discussion was the voluntarily participation of local authorities, also in Limburg, as a key success factor in the Open Call, the main instrument of the Flemish Government Architect to assist public commissioners in the project definition and choice of architect.¹³ Clearly, the position of Flemish Government Architect would be weaker without the local support, even though strictly speaking it is a function on a regional level. In response to this sensitivity, we scripted the provincial functions as a complement to the regional ones, with the three functions of design mediation, space management and PR not interfering in any way with the instrument of the Open Call. Still, we touched a sore spot with the invitation of Jo Coenen, former Chief Government Architect of the Netherlands and himself from the Dutch province of Limburg. When the lingering dispute between the Flemish Government Architect and his yet-to-exist provincial counterpart became a topic of debate, Jo Coenen reacted furiously, officially announcing that Swinnen had tried to convince him not to join the initiatives by Architectuurwijzer. In the debate, Coenen stressed how important it was to transcend the eventual feelings of competition, referring to his own experience as Chief Government Architect in the Netherlands, where he also had to deal with political pressure and cutbacks. His argument was that a strong local architectural culture would not only be beneficial for the province of Limburg, but also serve as the perfect support base for the Flemish Government Architect. The personal experience was that, at the moment of severe cutbacks to the Chief Government Architect in the Netherlands, the architecture centres in faraway provincial cities functioned as local strongholds. Coenen's words turned out to be a prophecy as far as Swinnen's resignation of as Flemish Government Architect happened not much later (mid July 2014) and support appeared to be very thin and weak. The dismissal was challenged with a petition 'Geen Kwaliteit Zonder Bouwmeester' (No quality without a government architect) and a series of strong statements, but without much avail.¹⁴

In the same vein of staying true to the ideal whatever it takes, it was equally important to provide a platform for the voices that might support the Provincial Government Architect for perhaps the wrong reason and try to integrate contradictory interests, knowing that these frictions are necessary in the functioning of an apparatus. Giorgio Agamben refers to Martin Heidegger in defining the apparatus as a challenge ('Gestell') and as the 'triumph of the oikonomia, that is to say, of a pure activity of government that aims at nothing other than its own replication'.¹⁵ As a result, we also provided a platform for sentiments (rightfully or not) that 'Heimat' architecture got fewer opportunities within the working of the Flemish Government Architect and the VAi. The implicit criticism often heard in Limburg was that the focus in Flemish architecture culture was mainly on architectural production in cities such as Antwerp, Ghent and Brussels. In the same line, there was the sentiment in Limburg that the Open Call launched by the Flemish Government Architect played a role in promoting architects who were already part of the Flemish canon, often located in the main cities, while discriminating against local architectural offices. On top of that, there was the sense that the VAi was monopolizing the field of architecture culture and reducing local partners like Architectuurwijzer to the level of content provider for the Day of Architecture. The criticism was capitalized upon by G30, a lobbying association of the thirty largest architecture and engineering firms in Belgium that opposed the institutions created to depoliticize architecture and was planning an alternative procurement procedure against the apparent monopoly of the Flemish Government Architect. Few big architecture and engineering offices from Limburg were part of the G30 and its actions consist of filing policy recommendations for procurement and suchlike, often presented as good corporate governance against public actors like the Government Architect.[16] Instead of debunking, we twisted the sentiment as an argument in favour of the Provincial Government Architect and even politicized it in terms of the third PR function that capitalizes upon architecture to build Limburg as a strong brand, not without suggesting that the opening up of the local field would be a win-win for local architects. Doing so, the internal critique was integrated in a professional discussion, instead of being downplayed as a false sentiment and leaving it to the wolves only.

The Politics of Quilting

The outspoken interest in the local field of architecture culture, and equally outspoken disinterest among others, strengthened us to turn the table even more. The strategy was to take over the discourse by appropriating the empty signifiers that function as quilting points in the discourse on Limburg's regional development and complete them with a meaning relevant for the debate on architectural and spatial quality in the province. In French, Jacques Lacan was using the word 'point de capiton', referring to the pin that fixes the fabric on the sofa. Discussing the notion, Slavoj Žižek wrote: 'In Lacanese, in every set of signifiers, there is always "at least one" which functions as the signifier of the very lack of the signifier. This signifier is the Master Signifier: the "empty" signifier which totalizes ("quilts") the field – in it, the infinite chain of causes ("knowledge") is interrupted with an abyssal, non-founded, founding act of violence.'[17] The quilting point was provided by Herman Reynders, Governor of the Limburg Province at the time, who referred in the opening speech at the Staten-Generaal (21 November 2012) to an old political ambition to create a single Limburg City by joining the forces of the forty-four cities and communes. The future Limburg City would have a number of inhabitants equal to Antwerp City and would thus considerably strengthen its competitive position. The renewed interest in the scenario of a united Limburg City was due to the possible abolition of the provincial government as part of a state reform in Belgium, later reduced to the transfer of person-related affairs to the regional and local level.[18] The governor's argument was that once you do away with the provincial level of management in Limburg, it will always return for necessary reasons. In the first place, there was the absence of a strong single metropolitan orientation, as is the case in Antwerp where the functioning of the local government outweighs the provincial government. More important was the weak power of the local government structure resulting from the small size of the forty-four cities and communes in Limburg and the need for an intermediary layer of governance.

We took a full year to work through the idea of Limburg City, borrowing the notion brought up by the governor, again starting a 'long march through the institutions' and having discreet talks with stakeholders. Considering the earlier rejection of the Flemish Government Architect, we reached out directly to Ruimte Vlaanderen, the Flemish government department responsible for spatial planning and at that moment busy developing the 'Territoriaal Ontwikkelingsplan' or T.OP (Territorial development plan) for Limburg.[19] Expressing doubt over the Provincial Government Architect as yet another administrative body (which could be seen as going against the reduction of the provincial administration envisioned by the Flemish Government), still the secretary-general Peter Cabus saw potential in the idea of Limburg City as a lever for 'supralocal' cooperation between cities and communes, a necessity for territorial development.[20]

The closure of the Ford factory at Genk, announced on 24 October 2012 and effective from 18 December 2014, causing huge unemployment in the region, added drama to the renewed interest in the narrative on Limburg City. The subsequent launch of the 'Strategisch Actieplan Limburg in het Kwadraat' or SALK (Strategic action plan for Limburg squared) by the Flemish Government proved the sense of urgency to think about Limburg as a unified entity. The president of the SALK committee, Prof. Herman Daems, also president of BNP Paribas Fortis Bank, was unambiguously in favour of the idea of a Limburg City as it could provide the framework for cooperation and community building in the province, the two fundamental principles for the SALK plan that are easily forgotten in the rush for quick wins.[21]

Surprisingly, the vision of Limburg City was even supported by Johann Leten, president of VOKA Limburg Chamber of Commerce, who saw it as an answer to the undoing of the provincial government and the province's economic challenges. He was very critical of the transfer of provincial responsibilities to lower or higher government levels, as it amounted to a downsizing of human resources and financial means and thus would affect the opportunities for local entrepreneurs and businesses. In the argument, Johann Leten contradicted, consciously and explicitly, the official position of the national council of the VOKA Chamber of Commerce, which strictly followed the classical liberal point of view in Belgium, saying the province was a redundant layer of governance. Keeping the provincial government in Limburg was important in the perspective of Limburg, argued Johann Leten, as it has always been an important driver for the economic development of the remote border area, first in the creation of the mining industry, later the automobile industry and today the post-industrial economy.

The support for supralocal cooperation among the stakeholders somehow contradicted the official policy of the Flemish Government heralding the so-called 'ontvoogding' (emancipation) of local government as part of a subsidiarity principle that is about organizing affairs at the lowest possible government level. The emancipation of the local government level is an age-old party line defended by the populist right-wing party N-VA, the biggest party in Flanders, which was part of Flemish government agreements and especially present in the Beleidsplan Ruimte Vlaanderen (Spatial Policy Plan for Flanders), the framework for the Territorial Development Plan for Limburg. The contradictions of so-called spatial emancipation by the local government level gave a twist to the much-discussed shift from 'spatial planning' to 'spatial development' which runs parallel to the shift in thinking from redistributive to entrepreneurial city.[22] The point is that everyone knew very well that the forty-four cities and communes in Limburg were relatively small scale and lacked the institutional capacity to tackle the economic and social crisis triggered by the closure of the Ford factory. Exemplary is that Ruimte Vlaanderen was setting up all sorts of instruments, as part of T.OP Limburg, through which local governments, organizations and businesses were encouraged to tap into the many spatial challenges that could potentially lead to new industries, such as upcycling or leisure, through studies by architecture offices operating internationally like ZUS, MAAT, 51N4E and others.[23] The result is a paradoxical relationship in which the hand of the regional government that bypasses the provincial government in the idea of capacity-building on the local level immediately strengthens the interdependency as there are no intermediary actors anymore. We called it the Bono effect: no fixed or heavy 'structure' is imposed on the cities and municipalities in

Limburg, but they are provided with investment funds, awareness campaigns and pilot projects that easily reaffirm the traditional dependency between central government and local administration – if only through the transfer of know-how necessary to understand the difficult phraseologies underpinning the programmes.[24]

The narrative of Limburg City functioned as a sort of watchword, provoking the stakeholders to take a clear position vis-à-vis the agenda we put forward for the Provincial Government Architect earlier. While the programme of strengthening architectural quality, spatial management and PR raised interesting discussions, suddenly the stakes of the very same programme became clear once discussed in relation to Limburg City. It felt like hitting an open nerve, making clear that the spatial structure was a crucial component in the ongoing dismantling of the provincial government level and the dismantling of the industrial complex. Improving the living environment was not just a feel-good item anymore, but appeared to be in the first place a transversal key to impact territorial development, state reform and post-industrialization in Limburg all at once.

Negotiating the notion of Limburg City with diverse actors allowed us to intertwine architecture culture with ongoing political and economic processes, such as the dismantling of the provincial government and the dismantling of the Fordist industrial complex, not without subverting the message in many ways. The notion of emancipation was filled out with a content inspired by theories of self-organization, making clear emancipation means nothing as long as the Bono effect is in place, meaning it is vertically sustained by bodies of know-how that assist local parties in doing the right thing. A case in point here is the notion of productive city as a lever to think about the necessity of industry and commerce for a healthy urban infrastructure, originally promoted in programmes by the Flemish Government Architect, Brussels Government Architect and Architecture Workroom Brussels (AWB), but also very present in T.OP Limburg.[25] Adopting the notion of the productive city enabled us to discuss how welfare, according to Michael Hardt and Toni Negri, is always created in the cohesion between productivity, community and conflict.[26] The challenge was to avoid the narrow focus on the entrepreneurial logic in the SALK and expand the scope on life in the post-industrial city more generally, discussing how the changing jobs in the post-industrial age necessarily relate to ways of living together and also social conflicts. Certainly, new jobs were needed in Limburg, but the search felt as if it didn't imply these urban questions. Hardt and Negri draw a strict parallel between the hegemonic role of the factory in the industrial period and the city in the post-industrial period following the central logic: 'the metropolis is to the multitude what the factory was for the industrial working class'. The resulting second note entitled

'Limburg City: Memorandum on the Limburg Europe Workshop' explicitly introduced the Hardt and Negri argument and aimed to sketch the contours of Limburg as a post-industrial metropolis. The title referred explicitly to the old concept of Limburg City, an urban conglomeration that replaced Limburg Province, favoured by Governor Reynders and his predecessor Steve Stevaert. The document was presented at the second Staten-Generaal (9 October 2013). Mayor Wim Dries, Deputy Inge Moors and Secretary-General Peter Cabus discussed another spatial development in Limburg. The Limburg City document was also an announcement of local workshops, for which the notion of a Limburg City would be the framework, to be set up later. The idea was that the workshops would be the test case for another design practice in Limburg. For this reason, inspirational lectures on spatial interventions were presented by Freek Persyn (51N4E), Ronald Rietveld (Rietveld Architecture-Art-Affordances) and Ekim Tan (TU Delft/Play the City). The evening programme was opened by Governor Reynders and focused, with a lecture by Constantin Petcou (AAA) and debate with Christoph Grafe (VAi), on how another spatial development should be paralleled by another design practice.

The Working Is the Work

The strategy of hyperidealism was caught up by reality again, this time in a surprisingly positive way. The whole process boiled down to a stealth operation in which we subtracted an empty signifier from the public domain, loosened its ideological function, gave it a material base in reference to the living environment, engaging actors from the architecture field, constructed new meaning in a common negotiation process, thought through the consequences and re-embedded it in political programmes and planning processes. The strategy was successful if only because the idea of 'Stad Limburg' was adopted by T.OP as a name for its strategic target 'Spoor 03: RE-Mine Stad Limburg' to develop a healthy urban dynamic by 2020. The special target claimed to acknowledge the importance of a local human perspective in their effort to stimulate regional development in Limburg by setting up large new industrial conglomerates that tap into territorial opportunities.[27] On top of that, Governor Reynders took over our new interpretation of Limburg City in his yearly inaugural speech to the Provincial Council (23 October 2013), explicitly addressing the topic of space, also in the title: 'Plea for more urbanity and cooperation in Limburg'.[28] The governor's annual speech was closing a circle, after we first were criticized for adopting an old worn-out and disputed concept from the governor, misused in so many political jousting games. Now it appeared that the governor proudly took over the reinterpretation, including the architectural focus. In the following year, the governor took over the initiative by gathering prominent figures at his residence to discuss the idea of 'Stad Limburg', among them communication adviser Noël Slangen, artist Koen Vanmechelen, Prof. Willy Miermans and many others. In the talks, the scope of 'Stad Limburg' was enlarged once more from administrative cooperation and spatial issues to discussions on entrepreneurship, social resilience, culture, nature, mobility and other relevant topics in the management of the province, resulting in the book *De Stad Limburg II* published under the authorship of the governor.[29]

Bending a discourse is one thing; the actual setting-up of workshops, announced in the second note, proved to be quite another challenge. The issue was first of all the choice of extremely local and particular design challenges that could function as a stand-in for the universal issue of architectural quality in Limburg, which implies a political fight over what exactly would symbolize the spatial wrong and potential change. The dialectic of the particular functioning as a stand-in for the universal is a Žižekian logic, meaning that politics is basically the struggle about what particular will take the place of the universal.[30] Change the specific case and the whole understanding of the universal notion will shift. And don't forget the equally important question of which content is lost in the choice of a particular. In the words of Žižek, 'which specific content has to be excluded so that the very *empty form* of universality emerges as the "battlefield" for hegemony?'[31] The choice of a particular case forced us to dig deep in the functioning of local governments, administrations and associations, opening up a totally different political struggle: engaging the agencies that could function as local support for the more general interest, while preventing other agencies from dropping out or being neglected. The short lines in the provincial area didn't make the job easier, on the contrary. Asked about how the periphery relates to urban activism, Doina Petrescu answered that perhaps one of the most interesting benefits of the province was the proximity with actors as it provides short communication lines.[32] The answer was surprising because the local is often presented as conservative in terms of activism, precisely because everybody knows everybody and every choice runs the danger of entering a micro-sociological minefield.

For the N75/N702 Workshop, a call for ideas was launched to rethink the green area languishing as in-between land of Hasselt and Genk.[33] The call resulted in an exhibition, *N75 / N702: Inspirerende antwoorden op de oproep tot grensoverschrijdend denken* (N75/N702: Inspiring responses to the call for cross-border thinking) organized by Architectuurwijzer at the CIAP arts centre in Hasselt.[34] The Reigersvliet Workshop was devoted to the construction of the new prison in Leopoldsburg, tapping into the Prison

Gear research.³⁵ The other workshops that were announced failed to arrive at the point of a public programme and resulted in writing ambition notes, sketching programmes, newspaper articles and other public statements fuelling the negotiations and/or triggering new contacts. The workshops on the Blondeswinning farm (Bilzen), Alberthaven (Hasselt) and Sint Barbara Mining Cathedral (Maasmechelen) failed as they never turned real, remaining on the level of statement by different authors. In the case of the Blondeswinning farm, the article 'Geef Blondeswinning terug aan de natuur' (Give Blondeswinning back to nature) was published in *Het Belang van Limburg* and suggested to turn the historical site into a monumental landscape.³⁶ The same strategy of combining statements with artwork was used to start the negotiations on the Alberthaven (with artwork from BuroBill) and Church of Sint Barbara (with artwork from Ruben Janssens, Sibe Duijsters and Jeroen Bohnen). Although the workshops failed in terms of direct outcome, the process was nonetheless useful in the underlying ambition to broaden architecture culture in Limburg and build up personal relations. Significantly, both Frieda Brepoels (mayor of Bilzen) and Raf Terwingen (mayor of Maasmechelen) were present on the panel at the third Staten-Generaal (22 October 2014) to discuss the future of 'spatial management' (for which we used the Dutch neologism 'ruimteregie') in Limburg with representatives of the civil society: Kris Claes (VOKA Chamber of Commerce), Peter Govaerts (provincial development company Limgrond) and Habib El-Ouakili (platform for ethnic-cultural minorities Minderhedenforum). The programme was introduced by Inge Moors, the deputy for Spatial Planning at Limburg Province, and closed with a lecture by Indy Johar from 00:/ architecture + research and a debate moderated by Jo Berben (A2O and UHasselt).³⁷

In the end we came to realize that the focus on output (in our case, the workshops) is perhaps contradictory to the idea of building up an architecture culture. The main labour was about diplomatic talks with so many actors, discussing the value of architectural quality, dreaming of eventual programmes and expressing the desire to come back to it at a later point, in short: the working is the work.³⁸ The realization was often postponed, as things appeared to be not that easily organized or the person in charge changed job, demanding a new round of talks. There was no production except for some people sitting at the table fantasizing about something that could eventually happen. Still, seen from a meta-perspective, we were doing the very thing we had dreamed of at the start of the project: expanding architecture culture in Limburg. In the process, the idea of a Provincial Government Architect appeared to be nothing but a MacGuffin, the famous device used in Alfred Hitchcock's films to trigger a dynamic, before unwittingly disappearing from view but still providing meaning to the ensuing narrative. Žižek writes: 'The famous MacGuffin, the Hitchcockian object, the pure pretext whose sole role is to set the story in motion but which is "nothing at all" [...] that it must seem to be of vital importance to them.' A good example is the film *Psycho* (directed by Alfred Hitchcock, 1960), that opens with the search for a lady who took money from her employer, but while the money disappears, the murdered lady is drowned with the car and money in a swamp, bringing people together in a narrative that continues with all sorts of thrills and climaxes.[39] The Provincial Government Architect in itself was just a triggering element for a reflective process on how a region could take the issue of architectural quality of the living environments into its own hands. In the start note, we proposed three tasks for the Provincial Government Architect, one of them being the neologism 'ruimteregie' (spatial management), and this is what we detailed in the following years. In the subsequent process, we drifted away from the initial fetish of a 'Government Architect' and still we were brought to the core of the desire expressed around the table in the winter of 2011. The idea of 'spatial management' was out there, scripted in a programme, discussed by so many different actors and ready to be taken up by anyone.

At one point, we organized round-table discussions to talk directly about how to set up the Government Architect in Limburg with two powerful politicians that have been supportive throughout the years.[40] The first discussion was a duo talk with Wim Dries, the mayor of Genk, and b0b Van Reeth, the first Flemish Government Architect (1 April 2014). The second was a duo talk with Herman Reynders, governor of the Limburg Province, and Kristiaan Borret, former Antwerp City Architect (3 April 2014). The discussions were publicly announced and joined by a professional public. One of the scenarios discussed was the question why Architectuurwijzer didn't take itself seriously and start to act itself as Provincial Government Architect. Certainly, this gesture would be the ultimate politics of self-affirmation. At the same time, it would run the danger of being a grotesque pose and lose credibility – bringing us back to the artistic pose of the Yes Men discussed earlier. Also, the whole programme, which was considered a critical action, had to remain cultural for the fairly good reason of keeping culture free of actual politics and guarding the neutrality of the cultural operator.[41] The paradox is that the cultural free space needed as a fertile breeding ground to develop critical ideas and animate a professional debate would close upon itself the moment it started to act as a professional player itself, losing the possibility to integrate competences, shortcut power hierarchies, subvert *idées fixes*, freely self-criticize, etc. Mayor Dries said in one of his opening speeches, 'Where logic reaches its limit is where politics start'.[42] We gave it another turn of the screw, saying, 'Where politics gets stuck in endless debates is where culture takes the stage.'[43] In culture it is possible to remain faithful to an ideal, not compromising a desire, and still maintain the openness to disagree or connect with opposite viewpoints. In this perspective, culture goes beyond daily politics, and yet we learned that the cultural intervention cannot cross the threshold of political action. Jacques Lacan limits the task of psychoanalysis by saying: '[...] psychoanalysis may accompany the patient to the ecstatic limit of the *Thou art that*, [...], but it is not in our mere power as practitioners to bring him to that point where the real journey begins'.[44]

Steps of Criticality

Over the course of three years, the role of the media played a key role in preparing the ground for the Provincial Government Architect and, more generally, the ambition for an increase in architectural quality for the living environment in Limburg. We don't mean the opinion articles we wrote, but very short and selective articles appearing in the popular newspaper *Het Belang van Limburg*, picking up just one element from the booklet. The reduction of the content might seem trivial and an infringement of the general programme, but only if you neglect the inverse proportionality of the media scoop and media attention. Let's look at three anecdotes in the programme and take them as the starting point for a reflection on the role of the media in activism.

On the occasion of the start note published in 2012, an article appeared in *Het Belang van Limburg* with the obvious blunt title 'Architecten vragen eigen Limburgse Bouwmeester' (Architects request their own Limburg government architect), discussing the ambition of the Provincial Government Architect in general terms.[45] In the article published in *De Standaard* and *Het Nieuwsblad* newspapers, however, the headline was twisted and referred to the particular example of 60,000 new dwellings, simply headlining: '60.000 woningen naar Limburg' (60,000 homes coming to Limburg).[46] The reference to the housing programme was taken from a press release by Architectuurwijzer that referred to a recent news item about the housing need in Flanders and plans by the Flemish Government to tackle it. Although the housing need in Limburg wasn't directly discussed in the start note, it was mentioned in the press release by Architectuurwijzer to underscore the importance of the Provincial Government Architect and spatial management more generally. Flemish Government Architect Peter Swinnen reacted furiously, as he experienced the announcement as a threat to his ambitions to create a programme dealing with the Flemish housing policy. The article touched an open nerve and brought out slumbering tensions. The success story of the Flemish Government Architect was the participation with local authorities, also in Limburg province, and these good relationships were clearly cherished. Another element was the pressure by the populist right-wing government on the position of the Flemish Government Architect, leading to his resignation later in February 2015, after accusations that years later appeared to be false and ungrounded.[47]

The next year, on the occasion of the Limburg City memorandum, an article appeared in *Het Belang van Limburg* with the provocative headline 'Ikea beter in Genk?' (Ikea better in Genk?).[48] The article presenting the five workshops of the Limburg Europe workshops caused great concern among the public by linking the issue with the political fights over the new IKEA branch in the headline. The article took a minor discussion from a chapter about the need for spatial management in Limburg and used it to throw fuel on the existing competition between Hasselt and Genk, the province's two main cities. The opening of a new IKEA store was one of the spearheads in the SALK revival programme and the ambition to create alternative employment in Limburg, after the closure of the Ford factory in Genk. The suggestion that the future IKEA megastore wouldn't be located in Hasselt caused great concern with Governor Reynders, who had supported the work on the Provincial Government Architect from the beginning. The governor called early on the morning of publication with the urgent advice to ask the newspaper for a rectification, as he thought the utterly populist framing could possibly ruin our project. The rectification opened a window of opportunity to publish a short but highly ambitious declaration on spatial management in Limburg under the title 'Ikea is coming to ... Limburg City' (19 October 2013).[49]

In the third year, the newspaper *Het Belang van Limburg* published a full page on the occasion of the 'Spatial Management in Limburg' note, focusing on the Reigersvliet Workshop under the screaming headline: 'Denktank pleit voor kleinschalige aanpak gevangenis Leopoldsburg' (Think-tank pleads for small-scale approach to Leopoldsburg prison).[50] The article detailed the alternative vision for the spatial planning of the future Leopoldsburg prison, following our argument that a humane design of a prison would depend on the very abstract lines of the territorial zoning plans, which were under investigation by the government at the time of writing. The day before publication in the newspaper, we received a call from the secretary of Wouter Beke, mayor of Leopoldsburg and president of the Flemish Christian democratic party CD&V, asking for an urgent meeting. It was one of the more awkward meetings, in which the mayor wanted to know about what he sneeringly called a thought experiment, suggesting it was a premature intervention as the design process would come much later and at the same time refuting all arguments, asking for proof that the vision model would be financially and politically achievable. The mayor had forgotten the basic lesson of spatial management that early decisions in urban planning procedures have great impact on the end result of design processes happening years later; decisions that might look rather bureaucratic define the playing field for architecture, long before the project definition.

The lesson drawn from this threefold moment of media confusion is that neither of the three notes, a text with page-long arguments, were taken seriously before they made the papers. The short newspaper articles with provocative titles and easy-to-digest arguments had the power to draw the attention of the public. Journalism appeared to function on the basis of an overidentification or at least overstatement, i.e. creating an alarming atmosphere around everyday concerns. The critical moment occurred not so much in the misunderstanding among readers who took the announcements a little too seriously, but among people in power afraid that the announcements would confuse readers. The newspaper articles meant that actors who usually remain silent, having no fear of ideas floating in the air, sure that even the most fundamental criticism would blow away with the wind, showed themselves to be ticklish subjects. In these three moments, it was the people in power that put the game on the bandwagon by displaying either their unwillingness to listen, their fear of having a true debate, or their own confusion. This brings us to what we could call the steps of criticality, paraphrasing again the words of Ernest Mandel: the ruling order can live very well with criticism floating in the air; what they fear most are organized attempts to make sure that these words are taken seriously beyond the limited professional circle and that internal contradictions are made public.[51] The newspaper is perhaps the best place to put words into action, the cabinets of mayor or governor second.

In the steps of criticality, the problem of reception runs parallel with the intention of the critics. Most criticism is written not to be taken seriously, especially when the cutting-edge analyses are wrapped in eloquent and lengthy essays, draping radical arguments with introductions, questions, methods and conclusions. The labour of criticism can't be left to corridor discussions on the right interpretation of this or that concept and its applicability when analysing a certain situation. Of course the impact of criticism depends on the precise and well-targeted intervention, but the collateral damage and confusion are still part of the show. It should be understood as a cluster bomb with shrapnel flying in all directions hitting as many people as possible. Similarly, the role of the critic is not only in the construction of thoughtful arguments, but also in unpacking the message, making sure the letter reaches its destination, even if in a fragmented or distorted form. The point is that in such a viral dynamic, the critical intervention will not only be supported by natural followers, but even the attempts to tone down and contain the impact of the criticism will have an amplifying effect and spread the message.

Notes
1. BAVO, 'Always Choose the Worst Option', 37-39.
2. Žižek, *The Fragile Absolute*. Žižek, *The Puppet and the Dwarf*.
3. Lacan, 'Du Discours Psychanalytique'.
4. Žižek, *Iraq: The Borrowed Kettle*, 131-32.
5. Miran Mohar, lecture at the Euregional Forum in the Glaspaleis Heerlen, organized by the Jan van Eyck Academie, 14 Jun. 2007.
6. Alexei Monroe, *Interrogation Machine: Laibach and NSK* (Cambridge, MA: MIT, 2005), 254-57.
7. Gideon Boie, *Bouwen aan een sterk merk: startnota Provinciaal Bouwmeester Limburg / Building Up a Stronger Brand: Initial Memo Limburg Government Architect* (Hasselt: Architectuurwijzer, 2012).
8. Christophe Van Gerrewey, 'Architecture Is Itself: Een gesprek tussen Joachim Declerck, Kersten Geers & David Van Severen', in *35m³ Office Kersten Geers David Van Severen*, eds. Katrien Vandermarliere and Moritz Küng (Antwerp: De Singel/VAi, 2005), exhibition brochure. Van Gerrewey, 'Jaarboek Architectuur Vlaanderen 06-07'.
9. See 'Staten-Generaal – aankondiging', announcement on the website of Architectuurwijzer, http://architectuurwijzer.be/staten-generaal-aankondiging/.
10. NN., 'Terugblik op de eerste Staten-Generaal van de Limburgse architectuur', report on the website of Architectuurwijzer, https://architectuurwijzer.be/staten-generaal-vd-limburgse-architectuur/ and https://www.facebook.com/pg/Architectuurwijzer/photos/?tab=album&album_id=10151488354544758.
11. Giorgio Agamben, *What Is an Apparatus? And Other Essays* (2006; Stanford: Stanford University Press, 2009), 14 and 22.
12. Gideon Boie, 'Het werk moet nog beginnen', *Ruimte* 17 (Mar. 2013), 28-29.
13. Marc Santens and Jan De Zutter, *Het Vlaams Bouwmeesterschap 1999-2005: Een zoektocht naar kwaliteit in de publieke ruimte* (Antwerp: Houtekiet, 2008).
14. For an overview of the public statements in the press on the reform of the Flemish Government Architect, see https://www.vai.be/nieuws/persoverzicht-hervorming-vlaams-bouwmeester. See also Gideon Boie, 'De Bouwmeester en de onheilsprofeten', *De Standaard*, 14 Aug. 2014.
15. Agamben, *What Is an Apparatus?*, 14 and 22.
16. Geert Sels, 'Eén of vijf Bouwmeesters?', *De Standaard*, 14 Aug. 2014.
17. Slavoj Žižek, *Enjoy Your Symptom* (New York: Verso, 2001), 102-03.
18. The redistribution of power was part of the Provincial Decree, 9 Dec. 2005, drafted by the Flemish Government.
19. Liesl Vanautgaerden, programme director of the 'Territoriaal Ontwikkelingsplan' for Limburg, part of the Flemish Government

Department for the Environment, https://omgeving.vlaanderen.be/nl/top-limburg.
20. Peter Cabus, interview with the author, 10 Jun. 2013.
21. Herman Daems, interview with the author, 4 Sep. 2013. Gideon Boie, 'Stad Limburg: baanbreker in de ruimtelijke ontwikkeling van Vlaanderen', *Ruimte* 19 (Sep. 2013), 64-67.
22. Swyngedouw, 'A New Urbanity?'.
23. ZUS and MAAT, *Ontwerpend Onderzoek Territoriaal Ontwikkelingsplan Centraal-Limburg*, commissioned by Ruimte Vlaanderen (Brussels: Vlaamse Overheid, Jun.-Dec. 2013).
24. Gideon Boie, *Stad Limburg Projectnota Atelier Limburg Europa* (Hasselt: Architectuurwijzer, 2012), 46-47.
25. Liesl Vanautgaerden, 'Het Kolenspoor', *Ruimte* 31 (Sep.-Nov. 2016), 48-51. Elke Vanempten, *Manifesto for a productive landscape – Manifest voor een productief landschap* (Brussels: ILVO, Team Bouwmeester, Departement Landbouw en Visserij and Departement Omgeving, 2018).
26. Michael Hardt and Toni Negri, *Commonwealth* (Cambridge: Belknap Press, 2009), 249-62. Gideon Boie, *Stad Limburg Projectnota*, 18-21.
27. Liesl Vanautgaerden, *T.OP Limburg: Ruimte voor groei. Nr. 1* (Brussels: Ruimte Vlaanderen, 2015), 7.
28. Herman Reynders, *Rede van de Gouverneur 2013: De Stad Limburg Pleidooi voor meer stedelijkheid en samenwerking* (Hasselt: Provincie Limburg, 2013).
29. Herman Reynders, *De Stad Limburg II* (Hasselt: Provincie Limburg, 2014).
30. Žižek, *The Parallax View*, 30.
31. Slavoj Žižek, 'Class Struggle or Postmodernism? Yes, please!' in *Contingency, Hegemony, Universality: Contemporary Dialogues on the Left*, Judith Butler, Ernesto Laclau and Slavoj Žižek (London/New York: Verso, 2000), 109-10.
32. Doina Petrescu, lecture at De Oude Molen, organized by ASRO, KU Leuven, 28 Oct. 2014.
33. Gideon Boie, ed., *Ruimteregie in Limburg: Atelier Limburg Europa* (Hasselt: Architectuurwijzer, 2014).
34. 'N75/N702: Inspirerende antwoorden op de oproep tot grensoverschrijdend denken', organized by Architectuurwijzer at the CIAP arts centre, Hasselt (5 Sep.-5 Oct. 2014), http://architectuurwijzer.be/tentoonstelling-n75n702/.
35. Gideon Boie and Fie Vandamme, 'Gevangenis van de nabijheid', in *Ruimteregie in Limburg: Atelier Limburg Europa*, ed. Gideon Boie (Hasselt: Architectuurwijzer, 2014), 59-79. See also Chapter 9 in this book.
36. Gideon Boie and Roel De Ridder, 'Geef Blondeswinning terug aan de natuur', *Het Belang van Limburg*, 22-23 Mar. 2014, 14.
37. De Staten-Generaal was organized by Architectuurwijzer on 22 Oct. 2014 at C-mine, Genk, http://architectuurwijzer.be/staten-generaal-ruimteregie-in-limburg/.
38. Mierle Laderman Ukeles, *Manifesto! Maintenance – Proposal for an Exhibition*, 1969, artwork.
39. Žižek, *The Sublime Object of Ideology*, 163.
40. The 'Ruimteregie in Limburg?' debates were organized by Architec-

tuurwijzer on 1 and 3 Apr. 2014 at C-mine, Genk, http://architectuurwijzer.be/ruimteregie-in-limburg-drie-dialogen/.
41. Roeland Dudal in a lecture on the practice of AWB within the elective master's course Architecture and Activism at the Faculty of Architecture KU Leuven, 15 Apr. 2016. See also the mission statement on the website of AWB, of which Dudal is a co-founder: https://www.architectureworkroom.eu/en/about.
42. Wim Dries, lecture at the 'Avond van de Architectuur' organized by the VAi at C-mine, Genk, 12 Oct. 2013.
43. Boie, *Ruimteregie in Limburg*, 12.
44. Lacan, 'The Mirror Stage', 8.
45. Chris Nelis, 'Architecten vragen eigen Limburgse Bouwmeester', *Het Belang van Limburg*, 22 Nov. 2012, 46.
46. Ralph Gregoor, 'Limburg heeft 60.000 nieuwe woningen nodig', *De Standaard,* 22 Nov. 2012. Also published in *Het Nieuwsblad*, 22 Nov. 2022.
47. Walter Pauli and Ewald Pironet, 'Voormalig Vlaams bouwmeester Peter Swinnen: Hoeveel visuele rommel kan een mens aan?', *Knack*, 13 Jun. 2018.
48. Liliana Casagrande, 'Ikea beter in Genk?', *Het Belang van Limburg*, 10 Oct. 2013, 8.
49. Gideon Boie, 'Ikea komt naar... Stad Limburg', *Het Belang van Limburg*, 19 Oct. 2013, 16.
50. Jan Bex, 'Denktank pleit voor kleinschalige aanpak gevangenis Leopoldsburg', *Het Belang van Limburg*, 22 Oct. 2014, 12.
51. Frans Buyens, 'Een mens genaamd Ernest Mandel (1972)'. See Chapter 3 in this book.

Keep the Paradox Alive

Chapter 9

Although architecture acquired a prominent place in the modernization of the prison system in Belgium, it appeared to be a non-topic, not just absent from the professional media, but also not thought about among stakeholders and shareholders. The building programme for new prisons was laid out by the 2008-12 Master Plan of the Federal Public Service Justice (FPS Justice) against the background of the new 2005 Prison Act, defining the prisoner's internal rights for the first time in history. In this context, public-private partnerships appeared as a saving grace to modernize the prison system in a short time and with external financial resources. A novelty in the tender for four new prisons included architectural and spatial quality as an assessment criterion, the assumption being that market forces would achieve what the Belgian Buildings Agency could not: modernize and humanize the prison infrastructure. Strikingly, the designs for the first new prisons in Beveren, Dendermonde, Leuze-en-Hainaut and Marche-en-Famenne all followed the Ducpétiaux typology, merely focusing on capacity replacement while repeating the ancient logic of solitary confinement, this time in a suburban setting and contemporary form. The disconnect of architecture from the main principle in the 2005 Prison Act – which understands the modernization of the prison system in the first place as a humanization – brought us to the inherent paradox of the operation: how do you humanize infrastructure whose very essence is the inhuman act of depriving someone of his/her freedom? The Prison Gear Knowledge Platform Humane Prison Architecture research project was set up to critically understand the role of architecture in the ongoing building programme and constructed an architectural discourse that starts from the basic paradox of 'humane imprisonment'. The project was initiated as part of my research at the KU Leuven Faculty of Architecture, adopting Prison Gear as office name. The research started with a critical reconstruction of the 2008-12 master plan in discreet interviews with government officials, prison management, professionals and (government) architects. The consultation was used to build up knowledge around the inherent paradox of humane imprisonment and critically intervene in the ongoing design process by constantly emphasizing the nearly impossible but still ethically just maxim. In the second phase, the research ambition was expanded to formulating a counter-design intelligence on humane prison architecture in common consultation with management, staff and prisoners before infusing it in the ongoing design processes. The workshops with prisoners in Dendermonde Prison (2015) and Hasselt Women's Prison (2015) were limited in terms of output and impact for distinct reasons but functioned as experiments in the run-up to an elaborated participative process in the prisons of Merksplas and Hoogstraten. The context of UNESCO world heritage was the anchor point to critically intervene in the debate on the future of Merksplas Prison, part of the 'Kolonies van Rijksweldadigheid' (Colonies of Benevolence), in collaboration with the cultural organization AR-TUR and the Opleidingscentrum voor Penitentiair Personeel or OCPP (Prison staff training centre) of the FPS Justice. The critical moment was generated through the creation of a cultural scene gathering government officials, managers, staff, professionals, volunteers, civilians and prisoners and using this as a parallel platform to work through the central paradox of prison reform: humane imprisonment.

Absence of Architecture Culture

From the start of the research into the architecture of mental healthcare, the issue of the architectural renewal of prisons in Belgium was present in the background, more specifically in the very first interview with architect Patrick Lefebure (ArchiPL) in 2010 on his design for the Lumen admissions department at Sint-Jan-Baptist Zelzate psychiatric hospital.[1] While talking about the general absence of innovative care architecture in the field of psychiatry, Lefebure pointed to what he called the other scandal of psychiatry. He referred to the inadequate living conditions of internees in prison, a situation that persisted despite the fact that the Belgian state has been condemned several times by the European Court of Human Rights. At the time of speaking, the first forensic psychiatric centre (FPC) in Ghent, designed by Abscis Architects, was still in its planning phase, as part of the 2008-12 Master Plan for the modernization of prisons, drawn up by the FPS Justice and implemented by the Belgian Buildings Agency. The public debate surrounding the FPC mainly concerned the search for an operator. No living soul seemed to cast doubt over the use and value of the design for the FPC. The planning process of the first FPC was long overdue and construction thus started while awaiting the selection of an operator. The fact that the expert group that advised Minister for Public Health Laurette Onkelinx about the establishment of the first FPC was first asked to sidestep and enter the tender as a potential operator and later lost the bid to a joint venture of commercial players was a delicate issue only known to insiders.[2] Likewise, the design of the FPC, despite the architect's good intentions, was based on modified requirements for prisons and the project brief contradicted on crucial points the original intentions of the expert group. Once the operation was awarded to the joint venture of Parnassia and Sodexo and the FPC facility was up and running in

2015, the user didn't want to communicate about unsuitable infrastructure to protect its private interests in the tender for FPC Antwerp. Management did admit infrastructural issues in the operation of the FPC during a guided tour for members of the non-profit organization De Huizen, but didn't want to raise the issue publicly. Around the same period, the documentary *Weg van de waanzin* was broadcast on national television, praising the success of the operation of FPC.[3] Much to the distress of FPC management, parts of the unpublished article 'FPC Gent: geen markt, geen gevangenis' (FPC Ghent: no market, no prison) was used by the journalist of the newspaper *De Standaard*. Their argument to stay discreet about internal criticism was about the candidacy of FPC Gent in the tendering procedure for the operation of FPC Antwerpen, then a facility under construction.[4]

The absence of an architectural debate about the FPC turned out to be small beer compared to the so-called 4Gs, the first four new prisons elaborated within the 2008-12 Master Plan, with two prisons in the Flemish region (to be located in the town of Dendermonde and the municipality of Beveren) and two prisons in the Walloon region (in the towns of Marche-en-Famenne and Leuze-en-Hainaut).[5] The inclusion of architectural quality as a selection criterion in the tender for a public-private partnership dealing with the construction for the first four new prisons in Belgium testifies to the high level of ambition of the FPS Justice and the Belgian Buildings Agency to drastically renew the penitentiary infrastructure following the definition of the internal legal status described in the 2005 Basic Law. Architects were also on the jury, in particular Marc Dubois (KU Leuven) and b0b Van Reeth (representing the Flemish Government Architect). The acting Flemish Government Architect, Peter Swinnen, was replaced in the jury by his predecessor, because his office 51N4E was also a candidate in the tendering process for the new prison of Dendermonde, part of the 4Gs. In any case, the stress on architectural innovation was clearly having an effect. Unsurprisingly, the winning bid on the Flemish side of the 4Gs was based on a design made by the established architectural firm Jaspers Eyers Architects in an unusual collaboration with Stéphane Beel Architects. The consortium around the Jan De Nul Group submitted a bid for the new Dendermonde prison based on a design drawn up by architecture office 51N4E. The engagement of two renowned architecture offices as part of the innovative architecture culture promoted by the VAi shows the ambition of the programme. Strikingly, all design proposals followed the Ducpétiaux typology, a hybrid of the panopticon and rectangular cellular complexes visible in almost all prison complexes in Belgium since the nineteenth century. It was precisely the Ducpétiaux typology that the federal government agencies had hoped to leave behind by mobilizing the building market in a public-private partnership and somehow forcing the bidding contractors to engage with high-level architecture offices. That didn't happen.⁶

The hope for innovative prison architecture was renewed in the planning process for the new prison in Haren (Brussels) that had to replace the existing prisons in the Brussels-Capital Region and expand it with other facilities. The prisons of Sint-Gillis and Vorst were exemplary for the physical dilapidation of the prison system in Belgium with a nineteenth-century infrastructure still in use and with entire cellular wings closed for reasons of sanitation and stability. On top of that, the two prisons (one of them a house of detention) were heavily overcrowded with individual cells used by two prisoners sleeping in a bunk bed and a ground-sleeper added on a mattress. Berkendaal Prison, which housed the female department, was relatively more recent but was included in the new building programme as it was institutionally part of Vorst Prison. The complex was envisaged as a prison village, concentrating all sorts of delinquencies, even adding a juvenile prison and forensic psychiatric centre on the same terrain, though the plans changed over the years.

In preparation for the public tender, round-table discussions were held at the cabinet of the then Minister of Justice Stefaan De Clerck, with architectural input from Olivier Bastin (Brussels Government Architect), Peter Swinnen (Flemish Government Architect), Joachim Declerck (AWB) and professors Marc Dubois (KU Leuven), Bart Verschaffel (UGent), David Vandenburgh (UC Louvain) and others.⁷ All hope was placed in the drafting of the so-called 'smart specifications' by law firm Stibbe in collaboration with AWB as architecture consultants. The smart element was about leaving the opening to the contractor in the public-private partnership to produce a design that would leave behind the old Ducpétiaux logic for once. Although the use of the term 'prison village' suggested a rupture with the past, the strategy of the smart specification succeeded only in a formal way. At first sight, the prison complex differed largely from the Ducpétiaux typology, showing cubicle buildings randomly dispersed over the rolling terrain and enclosed by an irregular perimeter. The building design, with complexes of three times thirty places, tapped into the innovative ideas of De Huizen, the non-profit organization advocating prison reform. Nevertheless, the design of the prison village did fit in what we know as prison, as it translated progressive ideas into an environment that is fully indebted to the nineteenth-century logics of the total institute, solitary confinement and geographical segregation.⁸

Curiously, the involvement of many tenors from the Flemish architectural culture scene didn't result in a rich architectural debate on prison design, quite the contrary. In an interview with Marc Dubois on the jury for the 4Gs, he remembered a discussion with fellow juror bOb Van Reeth, standing in for the Flemish Government Architect, about what the late Geert Bekaert once called the 'tantalizing clarity' in the designs by Stéphane Beel and their mutual entertainment around the use of the term 'cour d'honneur' for the courtyard in the French design offers.⁹ In an interview with Joachim Declerck, founding partner of AWB, he had little recollection of his role in the drafting of the specifications for the future Haren Prison in team with law firm Stibbe, which had ended without remarkable success and was admittedly limited to the compilation of a book of references.¹⁰ The architecture of the Haren prison village was discussed in the final overview of the published compilation at the end of the term of Brussels Government Architect Olivier Bastin.¹¹ The short note was extremely sparse in providing information, mainly focusing on the redevelopment of the prison sites of Sint-Gillis and Vorst, and was rather intended to tick off the involvement of the Brussels Government Architect in the dossier. The only publicly available information about the Haren prison village were the press releases issued by the FPS Justice and the Belgian Buildings Agency and was therefore endlessly reproduced in the newspapers. Apart from the above, the only available critical discourse on the prison construction was all about the discontent of local residents and action committees fighting the building projects, mostly circulating online.

The federal government's discreet communication strategy is understandable if one takes into account the heavily loaded business interests in public tendering processes for a public-private partnership dealing with the design, construction, financing and management of the prison. The 4Gs are an actual privatization of the prison infrastructure, creating an industry with contracts spanning a period of more than twenty years, only leaving the daily operation of the prison in the hands of the federal state. Similarly, the discreet communication is understandable in the light of the volatile public opinion that threatens to jeopardize the construction of a humane prison by confusing deprivation of liberty as punishment with all too human feelings of retaliation and revenge. And yet leaving the public debate on humane prison architecture to the wolves turned out to be of little benefit to exactly the thing it wanted to protect: the ethical maxim set out by the Basic Law of 2005 and the prospect of humane imprisonment. In the non-debate, the subject of humane prison architecture was gridlocked in a technical consultation between experts, each of whom had a good reason to remain silent at the time when the ambitions and expectations were drastically lowered throughout the long design process.

In the case of the prison in Haren, the position of the Brussels Government Architect in the first term was extremely unstable and Olivier Bastin had to fight for credibility and seemed to concentrate design research on the reuse of the old prison heritage, which was a regional competence, not so much the new prison, which was a federal competence.[12] At that time, the Flemish Government Architect Peter Swinnen was fighting other demons, as his position was under pressure from the new right-wing government, and he would in any case only get a voice in the Haren prison village dossier because of the car park located on Flemish territory.[13] Architectural consultancy AWB seemed to be happy after establishing good relations with the federal government agencies, the Buildings Agency and FPS Justice, launching a design competition on the Palace of Justice in Brussels for that matter.[14] Architect Rita Agneessens (B2ai) stressed good intentions but admitted how the business interests of architects operating in a consortium, i.e. the special purpose vehicle Cafasso NV, limited the window for innovation in the final design.[15] In the case of the prison in Beveren, Marc Dubois and the other members of the jury seemed happy with the choice of architect Stéphane Beel, at least on one side of the language frontier. In good old Belgian tradition, the choice of architect was left in the hands of the jury members representing their own language community.[16]

The Pervert's Guide to Democracy

All the actors involved in the prison design were somehow diminished in their roles, not to say humiliated, and yet none came to the idea that a critical debate on humane prison architecture could also strengthen their ambitions. Criticism was either kept as a private consideration internal to the design process or delegated to actors that saw no good in the government's building plans. In the case of Haren, the only criticism was levelled by organizations claiming to fight for abolition, defend nature and protect the local area against urbanization; they were therefore labelled 'radical' and not considered a legitimate conversation partner when it came to prison design.[17] Also, the radical oppositional criticism in the case of the new Haren Prison was considered a benefit as it would be easier to deal with by the federal state in contrast with the new penitentiary vision by the non-profit organization De Huizen, which demanded a more plural answer.[18] The Knowledge Platform Humane Prison Architecture was set up in an attempt to escape the deadlock by radically affirming the belief that architecture can contribute to the humanization of imprisonment.[19] It was an overidentification with the letter of the Basic Law of 2005 defining the prisoner's internal rights which functioned as the fundamental concept for the building programme laid out in the initial Master Plan 2008-12. It was also an overidentification with the belief that architectural quality is able to fulfil the dream of humane imprisonment, a belief confirmed by the federal agencies as this was a formal evaluation criterion in the tender for the 4Gs and Haren prison village.

The Knowledge Platform and perhaps also the KU Leuven business card were essential attributes to enter the discussion on humane prison architecture, raise issues on abolitionism, environmentalism and local embedding, and still ensure that the criticism was taken seriously. Acting in the role of architect expert in this case, and not as direct opponent, fit the belief that architectural quality is a post-political value dealt with by technocrats who know that it must always be weighed in terms of political feasibility, financial liability and security considerations. Slavoj Žižek argues that post-politics is about 'the perverse mode of administering social affairs, the mode deprived of the "hystericized" universal/out-of-joint dimension'.[20] In such an atmosphere of enlightened negotiation, criticism is only considered relevant insofar as it translates into a specific interest and balanced with the others interests. Radical criticism is quickly brushed aside as a voice that has put itself in a place outside the negotiation, i.e. what happened with the criticism by the action groups in Haren who presented themselves as abolitionist and environmentalist. The radicality in the criticism of the Knowledge Platform was situated in assuming the role of expert and adopting the existing discourse, following the official ambition of humane imprisonment, and using that position to translate subversive ideas into that discourse.[21] An early result was the publication and exhibition of design projects by master's students Maarten Moonens and Fie Vandamme together with critical articles on FPC Gent, the 4Gs and the use of art in prisons. The material was published in the context of the Conflict & Design Triennial at C-mine Genk (15 December 2013-9 March 2014), curated by Kurt Van Belleghem. The status of expert meant that preliminary conclusions in articles and even student projects were immediately taken seriously in sharp contrast to the often-elaborated arguments by the protest groups.

The results of the interviews were published in professional magazines and the popular press in the hope of collecting a new round of critical comments. Persons interviewed often started to spontaneously explain their position and contradict specific critical arguments in articles I had published, showing how the critical articles always reached their destination. Following the interpretation of Jacques Lacan, Slavoj Žižek has used Edgar Allen Poe's 'The Purloined Letter' to argue that the addressee only becomes the addressee when the letter has arrived and s/he recognizes her/himself as such.[22] Part of the logic is the transferential relationship in which the critic is immediately perceived as the subject supposed to know about the little secret, thus assuming a priori guilt over the discussion. The critic takes the position of the 'subject supposed to know', a function Žižek describes as follows: 'when the analysand enters into a transferential relationship with the analyst, he has the same absolute certainty that the analyst knows his secret (which only means that the patient is a priori "guilty", that there is a secret meaning to be drawn from his acts)'.[23] In an interview, Jo Demuynck, the director of Antwerp Prison, suddenly conjured an article published in *Ruimte* from his desk drawer and began to carefully deconstruct the argument, among others by arguing with the help of a calculator that the transfer of Belgian detainees to prisons in Tilburg (the Netherlands) was not an expensive undertaking.[24] Rita Agneessens (B2ai), architect of the Haren prison village, spontaneously reacted in a first, unexpected encounter: 'Your reputation precedes you', before excusing herself for being part of a business context that forces you to compromise personal beliefs, more specifically her beliefs in the vision of non-profit De Huizen.[25] In the first meeting with Jurgen Van Poucke, director of the prisons in Brussels, he also introduced himself as project manager of the new Haren Prison with the words 'You most probably know', suggesting the critic somehow knows all sorts of details from the internal organization of FPS Justice.[26] Next he countered the criticism of Haren Prison by arguing that changes to the prison design weren't welcome in the context of the public-private partnership once the book of specifications is closed, literally saying: 'Haren prison village has already been built, even though no stones have been stacked on top of each other'. In an interview years later, the director refuted criticism with the argument that a 'reallocation of the plans' was ongoing for the new Haren Prison since some buildings were without object as a result of the state reform that had happened in the meantime.[27] The fact that modest articles in professional magazines were followed attentively shows how the disclosure of information on the actual prison design processes, merging official discourse with internal critique, functioned as a modest democratic gesture that broke open the elite circle of the prison system.

The informal yet direct feedback by individuals stood in sharp contrast to the cynical rejection of the written complaints officially filed in the public hearing for the Haren prison village organized by the City of Brussels. Among many complaints by citizen movements and action groups, I filed a complaint (8 May 2015) linking the issue of prisoners' rights with the code of conduct of architects in Belgium and requesting the Order of Architects to check any possible conflict of interest in the operation of the architect within the public-private partnership.[28] Although the public hearing, held on 20 May 2015, was announced by Minister-President Rudi Vervoort as the place to be for democratic debate on the prison of Haren, the jury neither interacted with the public nor reacted to the complaints put forward. The setting of the public hearing in the auditorium of the Viage Grand Casino Brussels with the mute jury sitting in the dark on stage, allegedly on safety grounds, was perceived by many of the protesters as a mockery of democracy, a symbol of the formalist state of democracy when it comes to urban planning.[29] Talking about another major public building project in Antwerp, Peter Verhaeghe, an activist fighting the Oosterweel bridge and tunnel construction in Antwerp as part of the citizen movement stRaten-generaal, claimed: 'Governments are legally forced to launch a public hearing, but not forced to read the complaints and suggestions by citizens.'[30] Even if the complaint had been taken seriously by the commission in charge of the public hearing, there was no guarantee the government agencies would have followed the arguments. In the report of the public hearing, the complaint was mentioned but the specific objections were shown to have been misinterpreted, most probably due to language confusion between Dutch and French.[31] There was, however, one party that took the complaint deadly seriously: the architecture firm B2ai operating as part of Cafasso NV and responsible for the design of Haren Prison answered with a written complaint for slander and defamation and disavowing the words of architect Rita Agneessens.[32] The firm's fierce reaction brings us to what we could call the steps of criticality: publishing criticism in the written media is tolerated and will be corrected in private, or commented upon if necessary, but it is only when criticism is actually acted upon in the reality of professional practice that it meets a swift formal response, in this case by shooting the messenger.

Apart from the unwillingness to take a complaint seriously, the public hearing commission was the perfect trap to cancel all critique for another structural reason. At a certain moment in the design process of the Haren prison village, anonymous protesters vandalized the headquarters of the FPS Justice as well as the private residency of the Minister-President of the Brussels regional government and demolished the prison model exhibited in the main hall of the Belgian Buildings Agency.[33] In the same news item, it was announced that the private home of the architect had also been attacked a few months earlier. In the media, Minister-President Rudi Vervoort called upon the protesters to use the existing democratic channels to voice their discontent, referring to the forthcoming public inquiry set up by the City of Brussels in relation to the request for an urban building permission by development company Cafasso NV. The cynicism of the minister-president's words became clear in the first public hearing organized to allow citizens to motivate verbally their complaints against the design for Haren Prison. In his introduction, chairman Geoffroy Coomans de Brachène, Alderman for Spatial Planning of the City of Brussels, said that only objections relating to competences of the local authority – i.e. spatial planning – would be considered.[34]

Next, the alderman made crystal clear that citizens who had prepared complaints relating to the issues of justice or land use were redirected to the specific government levels dealing with the issues, respectively the federal and regional government. The cynical truth is that neither the federal nor the regional government organized any participative procedures and the critique against Haren Prison was thus caught in a perverse loop once they opted to enter the channels of legitimate democratic debate. Violence is not justifiable and it actually never became clear who committed the violence, the action groups distancing themselves from it, but the violence should at least be understood as a result of the zero level of democracy in urban planning in Brussels. At play is a logic similar to that of the 2005 French riots in which the destruction and rage of youngsters should be understood, according to Slavoj Žižek, not as a senseless act of violence, but as the result of everyday liberal politics in France.[35]

Professionals with a Human Face

In the attempt to construct a critical debate on the architecture of the humane prison, we faced a second formation of resistance: besides the opposition of neighbourhood committees and action groups, there was strong internal opposition among the professionals involved in the building operation. In interviews, we encountered a subjective modus of people who fully endorse the need for a humane imprisonment but who explain in the same breath how they are somehow professionally bound to compromise that desire, for one or another reason. Rita Agneessens, CEO of the firm responsible for the design of Haren prison village, made a distinction between personal opinions – she was active in the non-profit organization De Huizen advocating an alternative vision for imprisonment (we will return to this below) – and business relationships (her function within a special purpose vehicle).[36] Herman Reynders, at the time governor of Limburg involved in the planning of the future prison in Leopoldsburg, stated that as a human being he understood the advantages of other prison typologies, but that his function as a politician forced him to take into account the notion that the man in the street is not ready for change.[37] Servais Verherstraeten, then secretary of state for the Federal Buildings Agency, argued that the new prisons would indeed not humanize so much the conditions of detainees in the future Haren prison village, but that the current inhumane overpopulation forced him to start the new building project as soon as possible.[38]

There is no need for external opposition when you have the oxymoron of humane imprisonment, an ideal with two irreconcilable parts, functioning as the subversive core of the law causing a split in the subject. The subject position is ambiguous: they are aware that the new prison repeats the old penitentiary logic, they show a great deal of empathy with the vicissitudes of the detainees, they are familiar with the new visions on humane prison architecture, they are eager to spend hours discussing it, and still they continue the work. Slavoj Žižek argues that every ethics is founded on some sort of fetishist disavowal in the form of 'I know very well, but nonetheless...', as it shows how the subject may have personal doubts, believing only through the symbolic order.[39] The invocation of self-doubt and disidentification with the ruling ideology smartly twists the discussion about humane imprisonment to one's own fate as a professional with do-good intentions. Was it an attempt to arouse pity for the forced compromise of ideals? An attempt to act as robust decision-makers or reliable business partners? Sentimentalism (whether sincere or not) should be understood as a transference aimed at rejecting any critique as something that takes no account of practical feasibility in terms of the functioning of the prison system, the political decision-making and the process of prison design. In any case, the result is that any critique is cancelled as something that doesn't fit in with practice and is a mere consequence of an abstract academic thought experiment. The recourse to reality turned out to be the very form of a post-ideological construction since, to put it mildly, the professionals involved were generally little informed themselves about life in prison. Rather the opposite was true: the pragmatic professionals showed themselves to be masters in abstraction, pushing through decisions and finalizing the design for the prison village based on business calculations, unverified statistics and political assumptions. The invocation of a split subjectivity was perhaps most cynical in the case of the architect as it discharged her from the design challenge to fundamentally rethink the prison village on the basis of the design intelligence provided by the non-profit she herself was part of.

The presentation of personal belief vs professional ethics raised a mental wall against even the most constructive critique, such as that of the alternative vision on humane imprisonment formulated by De Huizen.[40] This non-profit think tank was initiated by prison director Hans Claus. It gathered professionals, academics and civil servants around the issue of prison reform. Although the dismantling of the large institutional prison as we know it was certainly the final goal, De Huizen didn't so much critically oppose the federal government's master plan as aim at imposing an alternative discourse. It introduced an alternative vision for the so-called detention houses, based on three fundamental principles: first, small scale, each detention house having a capacity for thirty persons maximum; second, regime diversification, breaking up the one-size-fits-all for whatever offender; and, third, local embedding, often also labelled as proximity, allowing the detention house to use and contribute to the local social-services system. The activities of the non-profit organization consist not only of constructing an alternative prison model, but also of developing a business case with interested actors that proved how a detention house is feasible. The strategy was to disseminate the ideas by any means necessary: reaching out to the popular press, consistently expanding the network of volunteers and intensely lobbying political authorities.

De Huizen held a position that escaped the antagonism between government and action groups, who mutually rejected each other's position and opinion, and its critique was therefore far more difficult to cancel out. After all, it was quite easy for the federal government agencies to ignore radical positions by activists, but the split subject showed the difficulty in contradicting a vision put forward by an initiative that takes the official policy line deadly seriously. Strikingly, the government found a strange bed partner in the opposition groups active in the struggle against the Haren prison village who ridiculed De Huizen as mere prison reform, swearing by the abolitionist doxa. This prompted Hans Claus, initiator of De Huizen, to make the bold statement: 'Forty years of abolitionism have not been able to change anything in the prison system, but in the meantime De Huizen is sawing the foundations of the existing order.'[41] De Huizen confronted the federal government with an impossible response dilemma that they would lose either way: by ridiculing the alternative vision of detention houses, the government would admit to being unwilling to realize a humane imprisonment and by accepting the alternative vision it would admit that the prison designs were not in tune with humane imprisonment. Referring to historical examples like the 1963 Children's Crusade by the Civil Rights Movement in the US, Roger Hallam argues that the impossible choice is something to be organized by activists in what he calls dilemma action design.[42] As a result, through every reaction by the federal government, positive or negative, the alternative vision of De Huizen seeped into the public discourse. The criticism formulated by De Huizen could only be cancelled by subsuming it into the power position: by accepting it as a personal belief and accompanying it with a deeper-lying passivity towards the matter. This confronts us with a reversal of the traditional subject position described by Michel Foucault: 'We know that prison is useless, if not dangerous, but we can't imagine what could replace it.'[43] Today one knows very well there is an alternative detention model that potentially could replace the current useless if not dangerous prison typology, and yet we can't imagine how to make it real.

Stirring the political debate around prison reform is one thing De Huizen does successfully, but still the (mis)use of their innovative ideas in the design for the Haren prison village shows the cunning of the professional with a human face. One way to undermine the sentimental humanity expressed by the do-good professionals was to expand the critical reconstruction of the master-plan platform with the construction of design proposals informed by life in prison. The idea was to invite detainees to the design table, work together on concrete design improvements in the prison infrastructure and then present these counterproposals in the boardrooms, council chambers and ministerial cabinets. Although to many the ambition came across as a joke, we were strengthened by the spirit of the 2005 Basic Law, whose author, emeritus professor Lieven Dupont, demanded the primary responsibility of all those involved in the prison system when presenting the draft text to the Parliamentary Committee.[44] Prof. Dupont, author of the Basic Law, spoke before the Chamber's Justice Commission on 2 February 2001, saying, 'If people [he was talking about detainees] are to be empowered, they must be respected and involved in the decision-making process with respect to the decisions that affect them.' It took a lot of energy to convince prison directors to open up the cell doors and allow us to discuss with prisoners the topic of humane prison architecture. But in the end it became possible to organize design workshops with long-term inmates at Leuven Central Prison (as part of the master's thesis project of Fie Vandamme).[45] The same participative set-up with detainees was relaunched at Dendermonde Prison, discussing with detainees the architectural aspects in the business case for the organization of a detention house in a former church in a non-disclosed city in Flanders, set-up by De Huizen in cooperation with local non-profits.[46] The booklet with results of the workshop was never published upon request of prison director Hans Claus, who feared that the ideas would backlash on the work of De Huizen at the moment Minister of Justice Koen Geens was receptive to the idea of detention houses, an understandable act of self-censorship that still counts in the series of 'I know very well, but nonetheless...'. In contrast, the later workshop series with female detainees at Berkendaal Prison (Brussels), organized by Heleen Verheyden as part of her master's thesis, was easier to digest and still it was critical in its smart ambition to translate the generic model of the detention house towards the needs and desires of imprisoned mothers.[47]

Enter the Sphere of Culture

The introduction of the figure of the prisoner in the vision development proved to be key in going beyond the cunning figure of the professional with a human face and generating an architectural debate on prison architecture. In the context of Atelier Reigersvliet, organized by the cultural organization Architectuurwijzer (see Chapter 8), a number of unsolicited proposals were drawn up for the spatial planning of the future prison at the former military site in Leopoldsburg. The aim was to critically intervene in the study for the demarcation and zoning in the Provincial Spatial Implementation Plan (PRUP) and thus have an impact long before the design of a building came up for discussion. Starting from the key ideas of De Huizen – differentiation, small scale, proximity – a series of alternative spatial structure plans were drawn up in order to engage with shareholders and stakeholders. The result was an alternative vision for a 'Prison Up Close' and a 'Penitentiary Spatial Structure for Leopoldsburg' published by Architectuurwijzer in the book *Ruimteregie in Limburg / Spatial Management in Limburg*.[48] The project ended in a rather difficult conversation with Mayor Wouter Beke (at the time also chairman of the Flemish Christian democratic party CD&V), after he was somehow made aware of an article on the vision development that was to appear in the newspaper *Het Belang van Limburg*.[49] One day before publication, the mayor summoned us for an urgent meeting at his office in Leopoldsburg. The meeting turned into an uncomfortable interrogation about what he called a thought experiment while at the same time dismissing all arguments based on the requirement that even the noblest ideas should be financially viable. The mayor also argued that the discussion was premature as nothing was decided yet and government agencies were actually only dealing with technical elements in the layout of zoning plans. In doing so, he failed to understand that the aim of the project was precisely to show that the architecture of the prison always follows the zoning, which was a common reason brought up by architects when asked why changes in the design of the prisons for Beveren and Haren weren't possible. This brought us to the paradoxical conclusion that the architect was only allowed to speak up at the moment that the design of the building complex was on the table and therefore always comes too late when it comes to innovation, since the fundamental design decisions were set out in the zoning plans.

The failure to put the spatial planning of Leopoldsburg Prison on the political agenda led us to resume all the work in conversation with the prisoners and introduce their voice in the discussion. The strategy was to give a human touch to the abstract discussion about the impact of delimitations and zoning in spatial implementation plans on the later construction of a humane prison, following the guidelines of De Huizen. The request to discuss this with female prisoners received the full support of Paul Dauwe, director of Hasselt Prison, actually the only prison in the province of Limburg.[50] The workshop series 'Ontwerp je eigen detentiehuis' (Design your own detention house) began in the spring of 2015 and continued at the request of the detainees into the autumn of 2015.

Although some prisoners knew about the scheme of De Huizen, it wasn't so easy to reflect with them on a future prison on a site in Leopoldsburg unknown to them. The relatively new Hasselt Prison, built by the Belgian Buildings Agency in 2005, was a much more direct occasion to discuss the spatial perception and user experience of female prisoners in a very concrete way. The plan was adjusted. We started from the needs and desires of the women to formulate some targeted adjustments within the spatial planning of Hasselt Prison, assuming that these were generic for the plans in Leopoldsburg. The appointment with the women was to discuss the conclusions with prison management and to invite Mayor Beke on this occasion. After a series of about ten workshops we sent the invitation to the mayor with the bluff that we were willing to let the briefing take place in his office in the town hall of Leopoldsburg or party headquarters in Brussels, but that it would be better if he would come to Hasselt Prison as it would allow the female detainees to join the talk.

The briefing with Mayor Beke took a while to organize, but finally took place on 5 February 2016 in the presence of no fewer than thirty female detainees, two prison directors and a few guards. The booklet *Vrouwen ontwerpen hun eigen detentie* (Women design their own detention) was prepared with the detainees and summarized the discussions from the workshop series. The final material was also relatively new for the prison directors. What followed was an unusual interaction, without faint arguments about feasibility and false excuses about premature suggestions. Numerous problems were discussed: from clandestine lesbian sexuality in prison and the dream of organizing children's visits in a green, secure zone around the prison to the inconvenience of being in a remote location on a business park, which makes one prefer to walk to the station on foot rather than wait an hour for the bus. The prison management and custody officers confirmed and/or commented on the stories on the spot. The mayor also shared his amazement, doubts and dreams. The meeting was set at one o'clock but ended up being a long work session including a reception with non-alcoholic sparkling wine and cocktail crackers. The relaxed atmosphere proved to be the best way to ensure that critical design knowledge wasn't immediately swept off the table but was taken seriously and thought through. The series of workshops in the female section of Hasselt Prison opened up a sanctuary of thought in which people with often conflicting interests discussed an architecture that fits the ambition of humane imprisonment.

We relaunched the initiative to engage with prisoners on a bigger scale in a project within Merksplas Prison, this time in close collaboration with AR-TUR, the organization for architecture culture located in Turnhout, and the OCPP prison staff training centre.⁵¹ The fire in Merksplas Prison on 7 May 2016, happening in parallel to a five-week strike of prison staff in Brussels and Wallonia, was the trigger to publish the article 'Toiletemmers in werelderfgoed' (Toilet pots in world heritage) that discusses the riots in Merksplas Prison against the background of the nomination of the site as UNESCO world heritage.⁵² Merksplas Prison is part of the Colonies of Benevolence built in 1824 under the short rule of King Willem I van Oranje-Nassau, with a prison still in full use, but not considered part of the heritage plans. The workshops series 'Gevangen in Beschermd Landschap' (Imprisoned in a listed landscape) was held as part of the public programme by AR-TUR and the MOOOV film festival organized by De Warande in Turnhout. Once again, the aim was to build a platform on which the paradox of humane deprivation of liberty could be pursued in an open and generous atmosphere engaging prison management, prison staff, politicians, professionals, volunteers, civilians and prisoners. Having the support of the OCPP, it became possible to set up workshops with the voluntary participation of prison managers, prison staff, politicians, academics, professionals and prisoners. The workshops were wrapped in a cultural programme that included prison visits, film evenings and the like, both inside and outside the prisons of Merkplas and Hoogstraten. The enthusiastic cooperation of Serge Rooman, director of the OCPP of the FPS Justice, turned out to be crucial in opening (prison) doors. The key was the parallel sphere of culture as it made possible the engagement of actors within various policy domains and levels and starting to function for them as a sanctuary to set the thinking on humane prison architecture in motion.

The cultural programme focusing on the current penitentiary programme within UNESCO world heritage enabled us to develop a critique of prison architecture that was formulated by the participants in the workshops and was enriched by site visits, film screenings and debates. It goes without saying that inmates were frustrated about prison architecture when asked about their perceptions of space and user experiences. It turned out that almost all of the other attendees in the workshops had similar frustrations. The prison directors shared their frustration at not being able to humanize life in prison for distinct reasons, and so did the politician, the social worker, the architect and others. All appeared to be searching for anchor points to connect their noble dreams with everyday reality in prison. In this case, we can speak of an internal criticism that didn't even need provocation to be articulated but hadn't yet found a way to express itself for one reason or another. In this context, the challenge was to capture the internal critique in words and images and allow it to circulate in public in the hope of finding ways to transform it into a design intelligence that can steer actual planning processes in a positive direction.

The cultural programme provided the parallel universe to the monopoly of state when it comes to prison architecture and allowed creative thinking free from political negotiation, decision-making, business interest and ideological adherence. Of course, the programme had no power to decide the future plans of the prison, but at the least the thinking on humane prison architecture was temporarily freed from the limit that defines knowledge on the topic and produces its inherent contradictions. Interestingly, the workshops didn't so much come with a brand-new alternative vision on humane prison architecture, no dirty details or smoking guns. On the contrary, everything was already known in terms of both problem and solution. The point is that, throughout the new relations built up in the cultural programme, the 'same knowledge as before starts to function in a different mode'.[53] The workshops functioned as analytical setting, built up in the parallel world of culture, enabling the actors involved to collectively work through the many contradictions of the humane deprivation of liberty and bring the impossible ends together in a meaningful way. Inherent criticism was neither shamed nor blamed from a radically external position, which could be called hysterical insofar as it aimed at the impotence of the policymaker or architect. The hysteric discourse is defined by the split subject always addressing the figure of power and hinting at his/her fraud, weakness or doubts.[54] Inherent criticism was also used as a stepping stone in the construction of design intelligence that breaks with the closed expertocracy governing the prison system today. In the discourse theory of Jacques Lacan, the University discourse is defined by knowledge always addressing the remainders while being underpinned by the repressed figure of power.[55] In political terms, the University discourse will always lead to expertocracy.[56] Equally importantly, there was not one politician who channelled the inherent criticism away into the proper democratic procedures that earlier proved to be a perverse loop immobilizing any engagement by action groups and citizen movements. Even more, in the closing debate the participants expanded the scope by including the closed Centre for Illegal Migrants in Merksplas Colony, also part of the UNESCO world heritage site and expressing the hope that the discursive programme would be repeated at the appropriate moment. In the constructive atmosphere of the workshops, inherent criticism appeared as the inability to respond to a desire for change that still can be realized once it finds the proper articulation. Those involved in the workshop programme didn't solicit criticism to dismiss it a little later, but now started to confront the inherent criticism openly and commonly, searching for opportunities to give it a place in the professional practice and, in the words of the prison director, 'pave the path upon which others can walk'.[57]

Notes

1. Patrick Lefebure, interview with the author, Feb. 2010, part of the publication on Lumen admissions department as part of the *Flanders Architectural Yearbook*. Gideon Boie, 'Plea for Care Architecture', *Flanders Architectural Yearbook 2008-2009* (Antwerp: VAi, 2010), 249-66. Jan Braet, 'Bouwen voor de broeders' (interview with Patrick Lefebure), *Knack*, 18 Feb. 2009, 38-41.
2. Martin Vanden Hende, member of the advisory group to the Minister of Public Health and director of the non-profit OBRA, interview with the author, 19 May 2012. See Gideon Boie, 'Een slakkengang voor internering', *Psyche* 24, no. 3 (Sep. 2012), 20-21. Trans. and pub. by Prison Gear as 'The Twists and Turns of Internment' on the occasion of the Conflict & Design Triennial at C-mine Genk, 15 Dec. 2013-9 Mar. 2014.
3. *Weg van de waanzin*, Koppen, VRT, 25 Nov. 2015, television documentary.
4. Nicholas Vanhecke, 'Gebouw centrum geïnterneerden kampt met kinderziektes', *De Standaard*, 4 Dec. 2015. The newspaper article was based on: Gideon Boie, 'FPC Gent: geen markt, geen gevangenis', 4. Dec. 2015, https://www.bavo.biz/fpc-gent-geen-markt-geen-gevangenis.
5. Gideon Boie, "'t Stad is ook aan de gevangenen', *Ruimte* 15 (Sep.-Nov. 2012), 58-62. Trans. and pub. by Prison Gear under the title 'The City also Belongs to the Prisoners' on the occasion of the Conflict & Design Triennial at C-mine Genk, 15 Dec. 2013-9 Mar. 2014.
6. Antoon Demuynck, managing director of the Belgian Buildings Agency, interview with the author, Belgian Buildings Agency, 15 Nov. 2011.
7. Stefaan Declerck, 'PV Workshop nieuw penitentiair complex te Haren', minutes of the meeting with architects and criminologists made by the cabinet of the Minster of Justice, 22 Apr. 2011.
8. Gideon Boie, 'De gevangenis als oplossing voor internering', *Psyche* 26, no. 2 (Jun. 2014). Gideon Boie and Fie Vandamme, 'Gevangenissen in België: de fabel van marktinnovatie', *De Architect* 25, no. 10 (Dec. 2015).
9. Marc Dubois, KU Leuven Faculty of Architecture, interview with the author, 13 Oct. 2012.
10. Joachim Declerck, AWB, interview with the author, 21 Dec. 2012.
11. Ward Verbakel and Joeri De Bruyn, *bMa: Man of Thoughts* (Mechelen: Public Space, 2014), 116-19 and 136-39.
12. Olivier Bastin, Brussels Government Architect, interview with the author, 9 Nov. 2011.
13. Peter Swinnen, Flemish Government Architect, interview with the author, 7 Apr. 2012.
14. Roeland Dudal in a lecture on the practice of AWB within the elective master's course Architecture and Activism at the KU Leuven Faculty of Architecture, 15 Apr. 2016.
15. Rita Agneessens, B2ai, lecture at the UHasselt Faculty of Architecture and Arts, 27 Feb. 2014.
16. Marc Dubois, KU Leuven Faculty of Architecture, interview with the

author, 13 Oct. 2012.
17. Antoon Demuynck, Belgian Buildings Agency, interview with the author, 15 Nov. 2011.
18. Jurgen Van Poecke, director of Bruges Prison, interview with the author, 19 Oct. 2015. Gideon Boie, 'Het Penitentiair Verdriet van België', *De Standaard*, 27 Oct. 2015, 37.
19. See www.prisongear.be.
20. Žižek, *The Ticklish Subject*, 248.
21. Gideon Boie and Fie Vandamme, 'Prison Gear', in *Conflict & Design: 7de Triënnale voor Vormgeving / 7th Design Triennial*, ed. Kurt Van Belleghem (Leuven: Lannoo, 2014), 152-53.
22. Žižek, *Enjoy Your Symptom*, 1-28.
23. Žižek, *The Plague of Fantasies*, 107.
24. Jo Demuynck, director of Antwerp Prison, interview with the author, 07 Jan. 2013.
25. Rita Agneessens, principal architect B2ai, lecture at the UHasselt Faculty of Architecture and Arts, 27 Feb. 2014.
26. Jurgen Van Poecke, director of Bruges Prison, interview with the author, 19 Oct. 2015.
27. Jurgen Van Poecke, director of Sint Gillis-Vorst Prison, interview with the author, 24 Mar. 2017.
28. Gideon Boie, complaint about the Haren prison village design addressed to the mayor of Brussels in the context of the public enquiry part of the urban building permit procedure, 08 May 2015, https://www.bavo.biz/bezwaarschrift-stedenbouwkundige-vergunning-gevangenis-haren.
29. NN, 'Protest tegen megagevangenis Haren: Gespannen sfeer tijdens overlegcommissie', *BRUZZ*, 20 May, 2015.
30. Peter Verhaeghe, 'Introduction to Co-Productive Architecture', lecture in the elective master's course Architecture and Activism, KU Leuven Faculty of Architecture, Brussels, 12 May 2017.
31. Th. Van Ro, 'Official Report of the Public Enquiry Commission by the City of Brussels', Urbanism Department, Permit Section, meeting 20 May 2015. Ref. W14/2014 – W131/2015.
32. Eubelius attorneys, Registered letter sent to Gideon Boie and Dag Boutsen, dean of the KU Leuven Faculty of Architecture, 16 Dec. 2015.
33. NN, 'Tegenstanders megagevangenis bekladden huis Vervoort: Geen normale democratie', *BRUZZ*, 19 May 2015.
34. Gideon Boie, 'Welke democratie zal Haren redden?', *BRUZZ*, 10 Jun. 2015.
35. Žižek, 'Some Politically Incorrect Reflections'.
36. Rita Agneessens, B2ai lecture at the UHasselt Faculty of Architecture and Arts, 27 Feb. 2014.
37. Herman Reynders, governor of Limburg Province, interview with the author, 13 Feb. 2014.
38. Servais Verherstraeten, state secretary for the Belgian Buildings Agency, interview with the author, 07 Apr. 2014.
39. Slavoj Žižek, *Violence: Six Sideways Reflections* (London: Profile, 2009), 45-46.
40. Hans Claus et al., *Huizen naar een duurzame penitentiaire aanpak* (Brussels: ASP, 2013).

41. Hans Claus, interview with the author, 5 Mar. 2014. The same argument is implicitly present in the history line from abolitionism to reintegrative approaches of today: Hans Claus, 'De re-integratiegerichte gevangenisdirecteur. Een wedervaren', *FATIK* 147 (2015), 24-30. Hans Claus and Ronny De Meyer, 'In een of ander huis. detentie op een keerpunt?, *A+ Architecture in Belgium* 261 (Aug.-Sep. 2016), 81-85.
42. Roger Hallam, *Common Sense for the 21st Century: Only Nonviolent Rebellion Can Now Stop Climate Breakdown And Social Collapse* (London: Chelsea Green, 2019), 7-8 and 41.
43. Michel Foucault, *Discipline and Punish*, 231.
44. Belgian Chamber of Representatives, notes of the first presentation of the Prison Act in the Committee on Justice, 24 Nov. 2004.
45. Fie Vandamme, 'Recycle the Prisoners' (master's studio project, Brussels, KU Leuven Faculty of Architecture, 2013). See also Gideon Boie and Fie Vandamme, 'Fit In, Stand Out! From Adjacencies to Agencies in Prison Architecture', in *Creative Adjacencies: New Challenges for Architecture, Design and Urbanism. Proceedings of the Conference 'Creative Adjacencies'*, eds. Yves Schoonjans et al. (Santiago de Chile and Brussels/Ghent, 2014), 455-63.
46. Gideon Boie and Fie Vandamme, *Ontwerp je eigen detentiehuis: Prison Gear* (Ghent: Faculteit Architectuur KU Leuven, 2016).
47. Heleen Verheyden, 'Een detentiehuis in my backyard' (A detention house in my backyard) (master's thesis, Brussels, KU Leuven Faculty of Architecture, 2017).
48. Gideon Boie and Fie Vandamme, 'Atelier Reigersvliet', in *Ruimteregie in Limburg: Atelier Limburg Europa,* ed. Gideon Boie (Hasselt: Architectuurwijzer, 2014), 59-80.
49. Jan Bex, 'Denktank pleit voor kleinschalige aanpak gevangenis Leopoldsburg', *Het Belang van Limburg*, 22 Oct. 2014. See also Chapter 8 in this book.
50. Gideon Boie and Fie Vandamme, *Vrouwen ontwerpen hun eigen detentie: Prison Gear* (Ghent: Faculteit Architectuur KU Leuven, 2016).
51. Gideon Boie, *Gevangen in open landschap: Kempenlab Cahier 7* (Turnhout: AR-TUR, 2017).
52. Gideon Boie, 'Toiletemmers in werelderfgoed', *De Standaard*, 3 Jun. 2016, 38-39.
53. Žižek, *The Parallax View*, 304.
54. Lacan, *The Seminar of Jacques Lacan, Book XVII*, 31-38. Žižek, *Tarrying with the Negative*, 165-99.
55. Žižek, *Tarrying with the Negative*, 165-99.
56. BAVO, 'Democracy & the Neoliberal City: The Dutch Case', in BAVO, *Urban Politics Now,* 212-33.
57. Serge Rooman, 'Voorwoord', in *Gevangen in open landschap: Kempenlab Cahier 7,* ed. Gideon Boie (Turnhout: AR-TUR, 2017), 7.

Design Your Symptom

Chapter 10

The critical strategy of surgically cutting loose an empty signifier, deconstructing its meaning through collective negotiation and putting the enriched result back into circulation got further developed in the research on architecture for mental healthcare. One of the results of the research project is Kanunnik Petrus Jozef Triest Plein, a monumental outdoor space at the KARUS psychiatric centre in Melle, designed by architecten de vylder vinck taillieu, a project that received massive attention after winning several international prizes. The project was, however, part of long-running research that started with critical case studies on the architecture of mental healthcare in Flanders, published in the *Flanders Architectural Review* and the *Psyche* quarterly. The case studies employed a discourse analysis to pinpoint recurrent topics, logics and hopes that drive everyday design practice in the perspective of both designer and commissioner. The aim was to subtract a design intelligence from specific local situations and use it, following the logic of Michael Speaks, as a prototheory on care architecture instead of leaning back on generic typologies, categories and concepts.[1] In a second phase, the series of case studies flipped over in a prospective research for the spatial master plan of the Caritas psychiatric centre (since 2018 renamed KARUS), which could function as a blueprint for an ongoing demolition and new-build programme. The ambition was expanded by starting to common the clinic, highly inspired by Doina Petrescu, and construct design intelligence in different work groups of psychiatrists, management, staff *and* patients discussing the uses and advantages of architectural quality in the daily operations of specific treatment programmes.[2] A third phase was defined by a recursive moment in the research, opening up the possibility of intervening in the architectural production process at the psychiatric centre and set in motion fixed concepts on hospital design and the decision approved by the board earlier. The enthusiasm released through the commoning of the spatial master plan made it possible to rethink the framework of the research (i.e. the demolition plan) and dream up an alternative project definition to turn the abandoned Sint Jozef pavilion into a monumental outdoor space. A limited tender was launched, leading to the design of the Triest Plein by architecten de vylder vinck taillieu. The critical intervention didn't end with the prizewinning project but was scaled up in relation to urgent issues at the clinic. The after-phase concerns in the first place the ongoing discussion of the use, deterioration and patient safety of the Triest Plein, questions that were present even before the opening. Another important legacy is the reuse of another abandoned pavilion, part of the initial demolition plan, and its organization as a new residence for the Dageraad psychosis department. The renovation of Dageraad can be seen as an emancipatory moment insofar as the technical service of the psychiatric clinic took matters into their own hands and the process thus overtook the work of the architect and ourselves as mediators. Another follow-up was the work focusing on the seclusion room in crisis psychiatry, a topic that led to the next chapter. In this chapter, I will cover the full story of the research into the architecture for mental healthcare, from the very first steps to the ongoing discussions and legacy.

Silence in the Reflection Room

The research on architecture for mental healthcare started with the year-long wish at the VAi to impact building production in the field of care and hospitals. The sector was and still is a closed world monopolized by a few big architectural and engineering firms. In the absence of best practices, the discourse on care architecture was very general and conveniently flipped over into the general value of architects to 'care' for the commission they were dealing with. The twist was clear in the slogan used by Flemish Government Architect Marcel Smets in the organization of a symposium on elderly care homes: 'Architecture for care, care for architecture'.[3] The slogan was the guiding idea for the chapter on care in the 'Architecture Note 2009-2014', a non-binding policy note published by the VAi and the Flemish Government Architect in the wake of the 2009 regional elections.[4] It was only in the production of the 2010 edition of the *Flanders Architectural Review* that the selection committee, of which I was a part, had selected, for contingent reasons, two architecture projects from the field of psychiatry: the Lumen admissions unit at the Sint-Jan Baptist psychiatric hospital in Zelzate (designed by ArchiPL) and the psychiatric 'PAAZ' department of the Imelda general hospital in Bonheiden (designed by Hans Verstuyft Architecten).[5] Once we had reached the editing phase of the *Flanders Architectural Review*, surprisingly, nobody in the committee seemed prepared to write an essay on the two projects to clarify the reasons and motivations leading to their selection. Silence fell in the reflection room like a heavy, weighted blanket. The distinguished members of the committee – Kristiaan Borret, Maarten Delbeke, André Loeckx, Katrien Vandermarliere and Koen Van Synghel, among others – started to list names of experts on the architecture of care active in neighbouring countries, the Netherlands in particular. The unease was not incomprehensible as the selection committee, myself included, had to admit that, although we might favour the idea of care architecture and wish to put the topic on the political agenda, our knowledge about the subject was next to nothing. The 'absence of architecture culture' was present in the room, the very challenge diagnosed by Geert Bekaert back in 1987, the prehistory of the later VAi, now in relation to hospitals and care.[6] Even worse, we could use the argument by Christophe Van Gerrewey as to how the challenge for architecture culture today was its presence, not its absence.[7] The peak of architecture culture, embodied in architectural reviews, festivals, publications, international recognition, competitions and other media scoops coincided with an eclipse of critical understanding on the meaning of architectural quality, painfully present in the case of care. Taking weakness for a strength, I jumped on the occasion, assuming that it couldn't be that difficult to do case studies on the two selected projects and write something that could make sense in the year-long search for care architecture.

The result was a 'Plea for Care Architecture' based on the two case studies selected in the process of the *Flanders Architectural Review*, call it an overidentification with the dream of the VAi and Flemish Government Architect.[8] The hunch was that the case studies could provide design intelligence on care architecture which could be used to form a concrete and useful discourse on the topic. We followed Michael Speaks, who argued that innovative knowledge is constructed on an operative level, part of action and counteraction. Speaks uses the example of the Iraq War, where the terrorist networks always have an advantage because they don't follow handbooks but learn on the back of their opponents: the terrorist network 'goes to school on you'.[9] Following this operational logic, Speaks was locating design intelligence in everyday chatter, even using the term bullshitting, doing away with any stereotype that tends to absorb all creativity and flexibility. A healing environment functions as such a concept that totalizes the discourse on care architecture; although it may not yet be clear in what way the spatial context could help the healing process, still the idea covered the whole field and matched the most corporate building developments. Even the great Charles Jencks felt shame when asked in an interview for BBC Radio whether a healing environment existed: he was unable to answer the question.[10] The giant in the history of postmodern architecture and initiator of more than thirty Maggie's centres (designed by famous architects such as Richard Rogers, Zaha Hadid, Rem Koolhaas, Frank O. Gehry, Snøhetta and many more), he was shying away, knowing full well that architecture is certainly not fit to heal cancer-suffering patients in any way. Interestingly, Jencks described how he was saved by an NHS doctor claiming that architecture may not heal persons from cancer, but it will affect the work atmosphere in Maggie's centres and allow staff to provide better care. In our search for care architecture, the idea was to include interviews with clients and users –

perspectives often considered bullshit, certainly from the perspective of architecture – to analyse the different stakes in architecture and understand how it functions as discursive envelope of the architectural object.

We merged the notion of design intelligence with the ignorant master, a pedagogical method conceptualized by Jacques Rancière.[11] He situates the historical figure of the ignorant master in Prof. Joseph Jacotot, who taught a subject to students without knowing the subject and without even using the same language as his students. Jacotot was going far beyond the new methods for open learning that, according to Rancière, merely reproduce the old hierarchy between teacher and pupil in a more horizontal disciplinary fashion, ditto for the old modes of knowledge transference. A crucial distinction in Jacotot's ignorant learning method is monitoring, not the transference of knowledge from teacher to student, but the efforts of a student to learn about the topic, fathom its depths, follow the consequences, etc. The pedagogical method of ignorance is the basis for intellectual emancipation, argues Rancière, as the pupil can no longer merely repeat the wisecracks from the canonical handbooks. Applied to criticism, I assumed the critic doesn't even have to know anything about a certain topic in order to critically intervene in the debate, not because of intellectual laziness, but for emancipatory reasons: allow the actors to explain how they see the connection of architecture and care. The critical intervention was thus about the formation of discourse on care architecture starting from specific cases and equally about the inclusion of other actors in the discourse, the commissioner in the first place. In the context of care, the main challenge was to go beyond intrinsic qualities of the architectural object – form, proportion, material, etc. – and identify how these relate to the specific treatment programme, how specific spatial arrangements are informed by specific care service, how the design hopes to innovate usual hospital design, etc.

Presenting design choices as acts of pure invention by the architect is one of the typical fantasies in architecture culture – it is only undone with a good dose of ignorance. Going beyond the often short-lived engagement by architects, the initial motivations by commissioners can be seen as the prehistory in the creative moment and, at the other end of the line, the (mis)use by staff or patients as the actualization of the design. In sketching the full picture of architectural objects, the most difficult part is defining how design decisions are often impacted through choices made by actors usually regarded as mere consumers of architecture.[12] The general aesthetics of the architectural object is interpreted by Alain Findeli and Rabah Bousbaci in the Bremen Model as having two corresponding windows, first the production (the act of design) and second the consumption (the act of use). The problem starts when the model is interpreted as a linear process. It then fails to conceptualize how the user is (often) also the commissioner, and the latter's intentions are as fundamental, even preceding the creative moment of the architect. The impact of commissioners and users on the architectural project isn't only about the negotiations in the design process but more fundamentally about prescribing or even predestining the design through the project definition. Also missing in the scheme of production/consumption of architecture is the role of mediators, responsible for the moment of distribution in architecture. The Flemish Government Architect is such a mediating actor, organizing the choice of architect through the limited 'Open Call' competitions and supporting the professionalization of the prior project definition. There is also the mediation by the VAi, which brings certain design projects into circulation through the *Flanders Architectural Review*, identifying theses as nothing more than best practices in Flanders and showcasing these as examples for others. Taking the distributive moment into account means understanding how certain design projects are more likely to function as a fetish for the non-existent discourse on care architecture, such as the PAAZ of Imelda hospital in Bonheiden.

The explorative essay for the *Flanders Architectural Review* got a sequel in a still ongoing series of articles appeared in *Psyche*, a quarterly magazine published by the Flemish Association for Mental Health (VVGG, since 2022 the non-profit operates under the name Psyche). The series started with a report on the conference 'Het Huis van de Psychiatrie' (The house of psychiatry), underlining the importance of so-called commissionership in the architectural production process, using the operations of the Flemish Government Architect to hint at the project definition and the choice of architect as two fundamental pillars of good architecture.[13] The general issue of commissionership came into focus as the conference missed out on best practices in the field of mental healthcare, apart from the Lumen admissions department presented by architect Patrick Lefebure and the spatial master plan of the Duffel university psychiatric hospital presented by technical director Luc Pelgrims. The keynote speech by UR Architects, the office that took the initiative for the conference, was a speculative study on the redevelopment of psychiatric clinics in the Netherlands, studying spatial logics of mixed use to avoid merely abandoning psychiatric campuses often located in remote areas.[14] The speech by Anne Malliet, project leader for the Flemish Government Architect, discussed architectural projects realized within the context of the Open Call and some international reference projects, mainly inclusive housing projects from Switzerland. The focus on commissionership made it possible to expand the understanding of care architecture and recognize the creative moment in the project definition, following the slogan once put forward by b0b Van Reeth, first Flemish Government Architect, that 'one shouldn't leave architecture to the architect alone'.[15] Still, the focus on commissionership could be seen as an element of institutional bluff as only a few of the best practices presented were actually situated in the field of psychiatry and care in general.

Psyche magazine provided the platform for the further exploration of architecture in the psychiatric field and with a series of case studies used these reference projects to construct design intelligence from the different perspectives involved.[16] The articles included concrete design projects such as the Kasteelplus centre for addiction care, part of Sint-Camillus (today part of KARUS) in Sint-Denijs-Westrem, the Hotel MIN home for forensic psychiatric care, the spatial master plan for PZ Duffel, the psychiatric care home PVT De Lorkenstraat, the forensic psychiatric centre FPC Ghent, and more. The case studies also included critical reviews of a debate about organizing regular housing as part of psychiatric hospitals organized by UR Architects, the Pilot Projects Invisible Care programme organized by the Flemish Government Architect, the Open Call for Sint-Kamillus university psychiatric centre in Bierbeek, and even on the art triennial organized at Duffel university psychiatry hospital. The case studies consisted of extensive fieldwork including interviews with actors such as the architect but also the client and users. Integrating different actors was important in going beyond the official ambitions and intentions, often monopolized by the figure of the architect, and enriching the discourse by including the inherent criticism heard in private interviews. It was a way of subverting the necessary split between the symbolic law and its obscene supplement active in any discourse, as Slavoj Žižek argued, not through orthodoxy – ruthlessly sticking to the official rules – but through full speech that incorporates in public speech that which is supposed to remain implicit.[17] The operation of incorporating implicit uses and values in the discourse on care architecture coincided with the inclusion of other voices as commissioners or users often provide different motivations for certain design decisions and thus unwittingly subvert the official message. This explains how criticism remains in the eye of the beholder; the same thing that might be obvious for commissioners and users might well be indigestible for architects and their weak-hearted patrons; this is something we learned from writing the article on 'Wet89', the headquarters of the Flemish Christian democratic party CD&V designed by 51N4E, that merges the discourse of the architect (focused on aesthetic and urban values) and the commissioner (focusing on the value of the design in terms of political PR). Although at first the editorial team of the *Flanders Architectural Yearbook* assumed the text would never be accepted by the architect (because of the clear interweaving of the architectural and political motivations), architect Peter Swinnen did affirm its message and even reproduced the article later in the oeuvre book of 51N4E.[18]

Commoning the Clinic

The director of the Caritas psychiatric centre in Melle (since 2018 operating under the name KARUS) referred to the *Psyche* article series, asking in the summer of 2014 to study the future spatial master plan for the campus. The invitation confirmed how the criticism developed in the article series was perhaps difficult to digest by weak-hearted architects while others were reading it as a useful introduction to architecture in the field of care. Still, the invitation by the clinic was based on what could be called a lucky miscast, as the director actually expected the design of a spatial master plan, while the research focused clearly on architecture criticism. Although having no prior experience in drawing spatial master plans and no ambition to do so, I eagerly accepted the invitation as a way to continue the research on care architecture with other means and complement it with an embedded vision development. The proposal was to come up with a master plan through a process of commoning, setting up a series of workshops with psychiatrists, management, staff *and* patients, and involving the different treatment programmes at the psychiatric clinic. The proposal was motivated by a theory course on the commons taught with Lieven De Cauter at the KU Leuven Faculty of Architecture in which we attempted to bridge philosophical works on the topic with architectural practice today.[19] Again, the ambition was to introduce an element of ignorance in the research, this time giving it a relational twist in a setting of design workshops that invites psychiatrists, management, staff *and* patients to articulate and visualize the spatial future of the institute on the basis of their needs and desires. In particular, the hybrid work of Atelier d'Architecture Autogérée, headed by Doina Petrescu and Constantin Petcou, provided the conceptual tools to envision how the commons lead to other ways of doing architecture.[20] The master's thesis project of Fie Vandamme (2014) in Leuven Central Prison, which I participated in as supervisor, was used as proof that it makes sense to engage users, in this case a group of long-term detainees, in deepening an architectural debate.[21]

In the first meeting of the Master Plan Committee at Caritas, the former head psychiatrist Philippe Van Petegem contradicted the director and claimed he was the one who brought the *Psyche* article series to the attention of the board of directors. It never became clear who actually was first and it is indeed irrelevant, but the anecdote shows again how criticism doesn't necessarily undermine the architect's professional practice. The VAi's unwritten rule is that only best practices are communicated in its programmes, such as the *Flanders Architectural Review* and the Festival of Architecture. The same goes for the exhibition programme focused mainly on exemplary oeuvres. This means that, for example, the VAi never communicated on the highly contested tunnel and bridge construction Lange Wapper, part of the Oosterweel project to close the Antwerp Ring, a project designed by Ney + Partners and Robbrecht en Daem architecten. The social protest with referendum and daily scandal in the newspapers simply didn't fit the good-news format of the VAi – the only way to communicate about it was sneaking in the special press dossier part of the *Flanders Architectural Review*.[22] The fact that the case studies published in *Psyche* did serve a reflection on the use of architecture for mental healthcare gives a twist to the common PR wisdom, usually associated with Phineas T. Barnum, that 'there's no such thing as bad publicity'. In the conventional interpretation, it goes that even a negative backlash on a certain article is helpful in spreading the message, as perhaps most of the public will never fathom the critical reach of the message and will only remember the main signifiers (brand name, author, etc.). In our case, the case studies on care architecture in Flanders might have disclosed inconvenient truths – the criticism on FPC Gent designed by Abscis is difficult to misunderstand – and yet these were read as constructive contributions that make it possible to navigate the still unknown field of architecture and understand how it intersects with mental healthcare.[23]

Dealing with best practices only, architecture culture in Flanders proves to be quite paternalistic, somehow believing the reader is not competent to judge architecture for him/herself and understanding criticism as a means for capacity-building directed at government administrations and potential commissioners. Capacity-building was the fundamental concept of the programme for urban renewal set up in the context of the Flemish urban policy and organizing design research around specific local projects in cities and communes, more precisely targeting the local administrations and supporting them in raising the ambition.[24] The request by the Caritas psychiatric centre shows, on the contrary, how the general manager and head psychiatrist were receptive to criticism and even solicited an in-depth study in the hope of arriving at an alternative spatial master plan. At stake was not so much the absence of an architecture culture in the clinic and criticism more generally, but rather its presence of it. To rephrase the words of Christophe Van Gerrewey, the criticism was present in the daily functioning of the psychiatric centre, at least latently, on the work floor and in the boardrooms.[25] The psychiatric clinic fostered plenty of institutional platforms and moments in which staff could come up with constructive ideas to improve the care services, but somehow the feedback didn't get translated into operational plans, especially when it comes to demolition and building plans. The challenge for the vision development was to define – in psychoanalytical terms – the so-called *point de capiton* (quilting point) that makes it possible to grasp the latent criticism, give it meaning, and understand its structural implications. Slavoj Žižek wrote about the quilting point: 'Let us imagine a confused situation of social disintegration, in which the cohesive power of ideology loses its efficiency: in such a situation, the Master is the one who invents a new signifier, the famous "quilting point", which again stabilizes the situation and makes it readable; the university discourse which then elaborates the network of Knowledge which sustains this readability by definition presupposes and relies on the initial gesture of the Master.'[26] In the participative process, different workshops were set up for different treatment programmes, allowing psychiatrists, managers, staff *and* patients to articulate their ideas on the architecture and spatial setting of the psychiatric care in Caritas in the future. The series of workshops with psychiatrists, management, staff *and* patients organized an informal atmosphere in which it became possible to articulate and visualize the inherent criticism lingering in the psychiatric institute and use these as the quilting points.

The layout of the asylum built in 1904 was modern insofar as it organized separate buildings for different treatment programmes, originally only for women, in sharp contrast to the more monastery-like, even military-like setting of the psychiatric centre Dr. Guislain for men in Ghent. During the workshopks, the layout proved to initiate a whole symptomatology. One of the learnings was what we called hospital psychasthenia, the feeling of losing yourself in the clinical environment, especially newly arrived patients, but also when entering the many buildings and navigating the campus.[27] Edward Soja used the term psychasthenia to indicate the lack of coordination in metropolitan areas and the associated loss of the ability to navigate independently through space. In the absence of possibilities to demarcate one's own boundaries, the subject is forced to adapt and even surrender to the situation in which they find themselves.[28] The imminent vanishing of the subject causes the ambivalent appreciation of the hospital as something that, on the one hand, creates a safe haven in times of mental crisis and, on the other, poses a threat to the fragile peace of mind. Interestingly, the feeling of psychasthenia was shared by fresh staff arriving at the clinic. Specifically problematic were the 'bed houses', the neologism being a contraction of the bed (the financing unit in the care sector) and the hospital. The pejorative term raised the question of what to do with all the buildings that are the mere sum of a number of beds and how these can be fitted into contemporary conceptions of mental healthcare. No one denied that the bed has a place in psychiatry today, but still the question was about the dominance of the bed in living and working in a ward.[29] Strikingly, patients are usually seated on a row of chairs in the two entrance halls (i.e. the place where they are seen) or at the terrace door (i.e. the place where smoking is permitted). The positioning of patients near the terrace door related to the feeling of what was called the 'ocean of empty green' when talking about the gardens in the psychiatric clinic. In the freestanding disposition of the buildings, we recognize what Wim Cuyvers defined as the 'unfolding of the façade' up to the plot boundary with the sole purpose of keeping people out.[30] The result is that 'the garden is no longer an outdoor space, but a strange atrium around the interior' and fear gradually increases with the approach of the different pavilions, which offer no destination except if you have a reason to knock on the door. However, it is important not to reduce the function of the shallow spatial setting to an 'architecture of fear' in which users can only 'freeze, flee and fight'.[31] Ultimately, the spatial setting fulfils a therapeutic function. Michel Foucault attributed two functions to the institution in terms of a religious institution without religion, on the one hand, a representation of a 'moral uniformity' and, on the other, an instrument for 'social unmasking'.[32] In the end, the spatial setting at Caritas differs little from the villa subdivisions typical of Flemish suburbia, and at the same time it is here in this open area that the patient shows him/herself being a patient.

    Soon it became clear that the creation of a common platform to articulate and visualize the inherent criticism operating in the psychiatric clinic doesn't so much frustrate the decision-making processes, but rather functions as the necessary first step of a professional design debate on the architectural qualities required in mental healthcare facilities. A key element in the process of commoning was the side-stepping of the already existing consultation platforms active in the clinic; the step was necessary to actively undermine the institutional culture in which participation was organized. The parallel platform created the necessary atmosphere of the commons needed to activate a process of commoning, a term coined by Susanne Hofmann to stress the importance of the corporeal experience in participative design processes.[33] The focus by Hofmann on atmosphere could be considered an addition to the three elements classically considered essential in the theory of the commons: the common pool of resources, the community of commoners taking care of it, and the active self-management of the latter defining their own rules (summarized in the verb 'to common').[34] An important gesture was to voluntarily leave the boardroom behind and organize the workshops in a meeting room part of the main entrance of the hospital restaurant. This meeting room was not only a symbolical invitation for the managers and staff to leave the boardrooms and close the door behind them; the location was actually the true hotspot in the clinic's daily operations. The location thus forced managers and staff outside their comfort zone and turned the vision development into a (quasi) public debate, at least publicly visible.

The location was but a feature in the ambition to make the vision development a public affair in the psychiatric clinic. Of course, welcoming patients in the workshops with psychiatrists, managers and staff was not evident, but at least the location allowed them to catch up with the proceedings easily on their way to the restaurant. Other ways of involving patients in the vision development process happened in our visits to patients in various departments; distributing posters and leaflets with preliminary results from the workshops was a good alibi to start informal talks and gather personal experiences. Creative therapist Myrthe Vandendriessche, also a photographer, took patients from the Acquired Brain Injuries and Mental Handicap programme on a tour of the clinic to register the ongoing demolition of the Ghislaine and Sint Jozef pavilions. Also, architectural photographer Stijn Bollaert was asked to register the different phases of the demolition work at the Ghislaine and Sint Jozef pavilions. The photography project was abandoned after the demolition work was halted, but the images were certainly helpful in discussing the built environment in the psychiatric clinic, even triggering fantasies of reusing the ruined buildings – dreams that would later become a reality.

In the same vein, the reports of the gatherings were made public as soon as possible, distributing the minutes of meetings, premature notes on findings and using the incompleteness as an invitation to speak up. Also, the publication of the workshop proceedings in the *Psyche* article series helped in this regard, making it possible to further define and immediately spread critical visions and thoughts formulated earlier in the workshops, such as articles on the issues of hospital psychasthenia, in-between space and demolition of care heritage, including the vision for reuse of the abandoned Jozef pavilion (an idea that later took over the process).[35] Later, the vision for the reuse was even presented and discussed at the Vlaamse Hersteldagen (Flemish recovery days) organized by Vlaams Herstelplatform (Flemish recovery platform) at the Vooruit arts centre.[36] Clearly, the publication of articles impacted the vision development process by creating other feedback loops, beyond the workshops and even outside the clinic. Still another function of the publications was to prove to workshop participants that the talks were taken deadly seriously. It's one thing for a workshop participant to provide critical input on the spatial development of the clinic and have it noted down in an institutional report, quite another to reread your critique as part of a theoretical reflection published in an established journal in the field.

The pinpointing of floating issues was only half the job. Next came the translation into design intelligence and the use of this body of knowledge on the psychiatric centre of the future as relevant building stones for the master plan. Different plans were drawn up, most importantly the activity plan and silence plan, respectively defining the zones in the clinic where programmes could be added and other zones that should be actively preserved from building. Part of the master plan was the decision to ban all cars from parking on the campus (which still happened at the door of many facilities) and create a large green car park on the other side of the street, perhaps the easiest decision. The translation of ideas into the master plan appeared to be extremely difficult as such documents are the result and part of an extremely volatile process of decision-making. Plans to move one or another department were permanently shifting, depending on mergers or collaborations with other hospitals and the ensuing horse-trading with subsidized beds. Given the unstable nature of master plan, again the dissemination of knowledge became important, not so much in terms of publication to a wider public, but in the first place having it embedded in the bookkeeping of the institution and ensuring it was acted upon in the final moment of decision. The discursive nature of master planning is certainly a weakness, at least an uncertainty, compared to architecture that always finds its finality in the physical building and the necessary breakthrough moments of budget calculation and closure of contracts. In our case, however, the element of commoning in the vision development provided a staunch support for the master plan; the proposals might change here or there, the timing of the process might still be unknown, but the ground for action was prepared through the enthusiasm of the different actors in the clinic.

The process of commoning helped to overcome two gaps that are usually embedded in the heart of design projects and potentially function as its main obstacle: first, the hierarchical divide (experts on one side, users on the other) and second, the disciplinary divide (architects and nursing staff encountering an epistemological discord). The first divide was overcome by getting rid of the expertocracy and acknowledging the user experiences in the design and planning process, thus functioning as a genuine democratic moment that challenged the accepted framework of discussion in the clinic.[37] The problem wasn't just a democratic deficit with staff being unaware of decisions taken at management level (or vice versa, managers unaware of the daily reality on the work floor), but also an epistemological deficit, with psychiatrists, managers and staff admitting to be illiterate in architecture and vice versa. Thinking in terms of capacity-building would be too easy to overcome the divide, since it's not about a cognitive deficit but foremost an epistemological conflict of parties unable to understand each other – as Bruno Latour pointed out in the context of the new climate regime.[38] Instead of educating one part or the other, the challenge was to accept what Herman Roose, general director of Caritas, defined as mutual illiteracy by finding a common space that allows differences in knowledge and, most importantly, makes it possible to use it as a strength rather than a weakness.[39] In retrospect, the director argued that the language confusion made it possible to overcome the typical linear way of thinking in building process: first the staff defines the requirements based on their vision on care, next the architect translates it into space and form. Instead, we came to a dialectical process of architecture and care being reflected upon each other, since it is only by thinking in terms of space that the staff at the clinic may redefine its care services and vice versa, the architect understanding the functioning of the hospital better through thinking through the desires of staff and patients. Once it became part of commoning the clinic, the obstacle in the vision development process – i.e. mutual illiteracy – thus turned into the motor of change.

The element of architectural emancipation was evoked by head psychiatrist Philippe Van Petegem in his answer to my neurotic complaint about the difficulty of realizing facts on the ground. He answered dramatically: 'Hey, look around! Nothing has been built in a year, but still everything in Caritas looks so different today – everybody is discussing architecture and everybody is dreaming out loud about the psychiatric centre of the future.' The process of master planning found a moment of what you could call realization, not visible in physical interventions in the terrain, but more in the fact that the architectural and spatial qualities of the psychiatric centre had become the talk of the town, with psychiatrists, directors, staff *and* patients suddenly looking differently at the same world they'd been working and living in for years. In other words, the discursive result is the moment of capacity-building, people gaining critical knowledge that allows for deeper insight in the spatial surrounding in which they take part. The master-signifier in the first place produces critical understanding that allows the old knowledge to function differently, argues Slavoj Žižek.[40] The result is at the same time an architectural emancipation that subverts the context of expert rule in hospital management, since the users – psychiatrists, staff and patients – are able to transcend their specific role at the design table and trace lines for the future. The workshops of psychiatrists, directors, staff *and* patients thus resulted in having people with different expertise starting to reflect their specific set of knowledge related to mental healthcare with the architectural setting, and back. As such, a dialectical process was started, in which staff could better understand their visions on care by confronting the spatial setting, and vice versa: the vision on the architecture for mental healthcare was deepened by learning to understand from the perspective of people active in the daily process of mental healthcare. The result was an emancipation of a group of people who were first set aside as mere end users, people who have nothing to do with the design of the hospital and only come into the picture at the end of the chain, now becoming primary actors in the design process.

Recursive Architecture

The vision development in the KARUS psychiatric centre wasn't limited to the mere immaterial, discursive product of undoing illiteracy of how architectural issues could function as a support for the everyday care services and of emancipating the user in that regard. At one point in the process, while drawing up spatial master plans, the vision development did spill over into the organization of the psychiatric centre. I'm not so much talking about the typical issues that relate to the master planning of a psychiatric centre, like the new parking plan, which was one of the early results from the workshops effectively implemented on the terrain. The evacuation of the car from its central position and only reserving automobile movement to services and urgent interventions drastically changed the use and experience at the centre. The most prominent materialization of the architectural emancipation, however, is the project that came to be known under the name of Kanunnik Petrus Jozef Triest Plein, designed by architecten de vylder vinck taillieu, after the demolition of the Sint Jozef pavilion was halted and the ruined space got opened up as a monumental outdoor space.[41] A lot has been written about the Triest Plein after winning prestigious prizes such as the Silver Lion at the Venice Architecture Biennale and mentions by the EU Mies Award and European Prize for Urban Public Space, most often referring to the exceptional design and its supposed healing qualities. The project was often framed as a classic commission, understanding architecture production in a linear process, and eclipsing how it could only come into being as a line of flight. The rare project definition – even including Parsifal's motto: 'The wound can only be healed by the very weapon that inflicts the wound' – was a result of the participatory vision development for the spatial master plan, even a side-result that could only come into being as part of the enthusiasm aroused in the process of commoning.

Although the unique design by architecten de vylder vinck taillieu is certainly a key feature of the success, the formal interventions in the first instance allow the rare function – insofar as you can call it a function – of a building that was conceptualized as a space of pure potentiality. Freezing the former Sint Jozef pavilion in the phase of demolition was possible only because the building had already been deleted from the mental map, but was still there for contingent reasons, such as the delay of the demolition process after asbestos was found and because of the Christmas holidays. If one takes into account the trivial chain of causalities leading up to the project definition, the most important use of the Triest Plein is perhaps to symbolize the unexpected event at which the framework of the vision development, i.e. the demolition programme, somehow got included in the discussion. It is precisely at this point that the idea of opening the half-demolished Sint Jozef pavilion came into being as a piece of unsolicited architecture and opening up a line of flight that overtook the initial vision development process focused on the master plan. The Triest Plein allowed us to go beyond the vision development on the spatial quality of the campus in function of the master plan, but also to transubstantiate the internal criticism into an object that takes a prominent place in the psychiatric centre, if only because people pass by daily on their way to the hospital restaurant. By directly embodying the specific points of debate in the workshops, the Triest Plein is therefore to be considered a symptom of the clinic, more than just an answer to specific needs or desires. The Triest Plein didn't solve anything, but rather embodied all the problems we had discussed in the workshop, in the first place the issues of hospital psychasthenia and in-between space, but also the awkward demolition processes so typical for clinics. It is only by taking into account the symptomatic nature of the design project that one can understand the ongoing frustration about the use, deterioration and safety of the monumental outdoor building.[42]

The general director framed the project as a recursive moment in which the whole vision development process was repeated from the start once a single point in the process had been reached.[43] First, the demolition scheme of the heritage at the psychiatric centre was the framework of discussion about the future of the centre, a final frontier nobody was willing or prepared to discuss, as it provided the scene for the newly built programme without being able to be questioned itself. An aerial view found in the archives shows not only the extension of the clinic on the other side of Heidestraat, but in the first place the common practice of demolishing old buildings to make way for new ones: buildings that were in the waiting line for demolition were literally crossed out with a red X. Once the demolition of the central Sint Jozef pavilion started, all the general ideas concerning the architectural and spatial qualities of the psychiatric centre suddenly got reflected onto that single building. It was a spontaneous inclusion of the research framework in the research and becoming the topic in itself. After the workshops had discussed at length the troubled orientation in the hospital buildings (the thing we called hospital psychasthenia), people could suddenly no longer understand why the heritage had to be demolished blindly, while buildings of the late twentieth century proved to be much more difficult to inhabit. Similarly, after discussing the possibilities of creating addresses in what was called the ocean of green emptiness, the workshops produced the idea of leaving the ruins of Sint Jozef as a landscape element and using the spot to organize the in-between space everybody had been fantasizing about. It was only in discussing a future for Sint Jozef that the initial demolition scheme, the initial trigger for the newly built programme, took centre stage in the workshop discussions. Suddenly, all ideas that people were dreaming about in the workshops, often quite utopian and almost impossible to realize in a lifetime, found an anchoring point in the here and now, suddenly making it possible to fulfil itself. It was the sort of moment of which Doina Petrescu wrote: 'driven by desire, participatory design is a "collective bricolage" in which individuals (clients, users, designers) are able to interrogate the heterogeneity of a situation, to acknowledge their own position and then go beyond it, to open it up to new meanings [...] in order to discover a common project'.[44]

The recursive moment also appeared in terms of method, as the project definition for the Triest Plein provided the opportunity to deepen the dialogue among psychiatrists, managers, staff *and* patients. Something fundamental changed in gathering these people back around the table, this time to discuss a real project and a discussion with direct binding effects in terms of therapeutic setting, aesthetics, budget, planning, daily use and most notably patient safety. Putting the project definition of the Triest Plein together as a bricolage of desire immediately positioned the people around the table as the collective author of the design project, not just an advising body to support the work of management or architect. The collective subjectivation is the result of the process of commoning in the clinic, just as Doina Petrescu argued how the 'participative process [is] a way of assembling a collective economy of desire'.[45] The two elements of desire and subjectivation go hand in hand in Petrescu's conception of participatory design: 'Participation should concern not only the realisation of sustainable spaces but also what Deleuze and Guattari have called *subjectivation processes,* creative understandings of the subjects themselves in relation to their environment and the ways they inhabit it.'

Once the reuse of the Sint Jozef pavilion was an explicit topic of discussion, we went round the clinic to collect ideas among staff and patients. In a meeting with (mostly elderly) people in the day therapy programme, a lady suggested turning the abandoned building into a wailing wall, which led her neighbour to say, as she sipped her coffee, that there was enough wailing at the clinic and she was more in favour of what she called a wishing wall. In a meeting at the young-adults programme (JOVO), the young were dreaming of an activity space they could use in their free time to play paintball, hide-and-seek and such. Also, the general director had been dreaming from the beginning of the vision development about a central meeting place, which he called the Ramblas, that at the same time could function as a fair ground for the clinic's annual open day. Finally, there was the longing expressed in the workshops for an in-between space that provides patients with a place to roam around in, a space that is part of neither the inside nor the outside of the clinic. The idea to use the remnants of the Sint Jozef pavilion raised widespread enthusiasm among psychiatrists, managers, staff *and* patients, and motivated the board of directors to stop the remaining demolition operation – in fact, not only of Sint Jozef, but also of Lente and Wasserij. The agreement with the demolition contractor got renegotiated into a project to use the ruined building as a monumental outdoor space open for public activity in the clinic. In fact, the idea of using the remnants of Sint Jozef as an activity square was published even before it got approved by the board. The publication was criticized by the management as a result, but still it generated a feedback loop that was fruitful in digesting the crazy project definition.[46]

All the fantasies floating around the Sint Jozef pavilion were assembled in the project definition for a monumental outdoor space and was used as the basis in the limited tendering process for architects. A limited design competition was launched with De Smet Vermeulen Architecten, de vylder vinck taillieu architecten, and noAarchitecten, resulting in three unique variations on the idea of a monumental outdoor space.[47] Although the proposal by architecten de vylder vinck taillieu did go beyond the project definition, the basic idea to take the starting point in the building as-found and somehow freeze time awaiting future action was true to the drastic turn around of the process. Also, the method of commoning the clinic was included in the tender to architects, by explicitly demanding that the design process should engage the work groups of psychiatrists, managers, staff *and* patients. The collective subject formed through the workshops had proven to be a vital and active force, as it allowed the board of directors to accept the mad proposal to halt the demolition and turn the ruin into a monumental outdoor space. The collective subject of the workshops proved to be an equally active force in the elaboration of the design for the Kanunnik Petrus Jozef Triest Plein by architecten de vylder vinck taillieu, the most radical proposal in the competition. Logically, central elements in the proposal threatened to disappear throughout the design process for distinct reasons: aesthetic, practical, financial, patient safety, etc. The at times reluctant position of the architect was complemented with the enthusiasm of the work group sticking to initial ideas at the moments when feasibility and economics threatened to downsize the ambitions. Participation thus proved to be a progressive force that pushes to remain faithful to the initial desire, even when things get practical at the design table and decisions have to be argued in the boardroom. The informal and low-pressure atmosphere of the workshop, especially in the meeting in the abandoned Jozef pavilion while rain dripped in, allowed all actors to be open about their stakes: the head psychiatrist discussing his legal responsibility, the general manager the financial implications, and patients the being-there at the clinic. The readiness to negotiate proved, again, the strength of the collective subject, even allowing collective authorship over the work, an issue that was only difficult to manage in media formats focusing on the figure of the architect.[48] The Sint Jozef pavilion finally got renamed Kanunnik Petrus Jozef Triest Plein in honour of the founder of the psychiatric centre and opened during the yearly open-day festival on 16 June 2016, in the presence of the abbess of the Sisters of Charity of Jesus and Mary and the mayors of Merelbeke and Melle.

The Legacy of Architecture

Soon after the opening, the Triest Plein attracted a lot of attention from an international public, especially after the installation *Unless Ever People: Caritas for Freespace* was part of the central exhibition curated by Shelley McNamara and Yvonne Farrell at the 16th Venice Architecture Biennale in 2018. The entry by architecten de vylder vinck taillieu with BAVO and Filip Dujardin was awarded the prestigious Silver Lion. We used the occasion to write the history of the Triest Plein in a book published by the VAi, underscoring the symptomatic character of the project and including the reception by psychiatrists, managers, staff *and* patients. The reception was ambiguous, not surprisingly if one considers the origin history. Soon after the opening of the Triest Plein, discussions arose about use, deterioration and, most notably, patient safety. How to measure use in a project with no function? How to keep a ruin clean and neat? And how to deal with potentially dangerous situations and responsibilities? Again, we published the discussions to show the open-ended character of the Triest Plein and the need to permanently renegotiate its existence.[49] The Triest Plein is a symptom signalling, not just what was wrong in the architectural production at the psychiatric centre, but also the hope for the psychiatric centre of the future, showing how a bricolage of desire can bend the building process and give birth to unexpected events. Imagine the idea of transforming a ruin into a monumental outdoor space to be presented straightaway to the board, it would have been laughed away as a fantasy of a lunatic. In the case of the Triest Plein, the crazy idea gathered so much enthusiasm among so many different actors at the clinic, supported by a collective subject built up across all the previous steps, and including the board of directors. Still, part of the confusion is that, four years after the research had started, nothing had been realized of the initial building programme for a new crisis department and child psychiatry department. The Triest Plein didn't answer the search for an alternative architecture in psychiatry; instead it dodged the question and offered a line of flight. The point is that the real change in the architecture of the psychiatric centre only happened in the aftermath of the Triest Plein. What happened in that aftermath was far more important than the sublime object itself. In the words of Malkit Soshan, the true stakes is the legacy of the design project.[50]

The cancellation of the demolition scheme at KARUS gave way to another future for Wasserij (Wash house) and Lente (Spring). While the first project definitions for the Sint Jozef pavilion also implied the makeover of the Wasserij as *hortus conclusus*, now the Wasserij was given a new roof to save it from further deterioration, awaiting a new programme. The Lente building found a new future as accommodation for the residential psychosis care programme Dageraad and was renamed accordingly. The story of the Lente building is entangled with the Triest Plein as the demolition contracts were signed and budgets reserved accordingly. Only a temporary lease of the Lente building to 'De Heide' (The heath), a centre for people with physical disabilities located in the village of Merelbeke, delayed execution. The Lente building was finally saved in the same contract renegotiation as the Sint-Jozef pavilion. The renovation of Lente was carried out by the technical service of KARUS and should be considered as the true change in the history of the psychiatric centre, going far beyond the allegedly radical design of the Triest Plein. In the makeover of Lente, now functioning as accommodation for the Dageraad psychosis care department, the entire process of vision development initiated in 2014 was finally arriving at the residential programme of the psychiatric centre, not just discussing the outdoor space.

The story of Dageraad liberates us from the doxa that the architect is a key function for every good architecture culture and the belief that architecture finds its moment of glory in the delivery of the building project. The massive media attention tended to forget that the Triest Plein doesn't solve all that much, but rather functions as a symptom for the changing meaning of architecture in psychiatric care. The monumental outdoor space might have turned a symbol of despair into hope, but the discussions on use, deterioration and patient safety were still ongoing, logically because these were the questions raised even before the opening. We should think beyond the sublime object of architecture. In the case of the Triest Plein, the most important result isn't so much located in the monumental outdoor space, but in the empowering of the main actors – psychiatrists, managers, staff *and* patients – to take matters into their own hands.

The moment of emancipation is to be found first in the project definition when the team of the psychosis care department took matters into their own hands. The Dageraad department was located, together with its Siamese twin 'Klimop' (Ivy), in the expansion area of the hospital across 'Heidestraat' (Heath street). In the 2014 workshops with psychiatrists, managers, staff *and* patients, the complex building for Dageraad and Klimop was described as oppressive, claustrophobic, disorienting and worse, despite its suggestive layout as a holiday park in a green, Arcadian landscape. In contrast, the workshop was dreaming of an accommodation with open and bright spaces, short or no corridors, multiple entries and exits, and possibilities for staff to work in the same space where the patients stay. Once it became clear that the heritage could be saved in 2016, the psychosis work group, headed by psychiatrist Celine Matton and psychologist Inge De Paep, immediately produced the vision note to move the psychosis treatment to the Lente building. The argument was that the abandoned building exactly met the spatial needs expressed earlier in the workshops. The team of the psychosis department pursued the ideas put forward in the work group, taking matters into their own hands. In that respect, the Dageraad renovation is not just the aftermath but the ultimate moment of architectural emancipation at the psychiatric centre, call it capacity-building if you want, deepening the abstract visions developed in the workshops, learning from the sublime monumental outdoor space and accelerating its implementation in the residential programme of the clinic.

The second moment of emancipation is to be found in the design process when the architect disappears from the scene. Unlike the collaboration with renowned firm architecten de vylder vinck taillieu in the Triest Plein, the renovation of the Lente building to accommodate the Dageraad psychosis department was in the hands of the technical service of the psychiatric centre.[51] You can describe the moment as an acceleration, the renovation of the Dageraad building starting immediately, not waiting for a vision development on the future nor for slow architectural competition procedures. The clear division of space in the old heritage was used to create different entrances and the former collective bedrooms transformed into open living spaces, while using the old cabinets in the aisles as individual bedrooms. Today, patients and staff praise the building's clear spatial layout, its spacious living rooms, lofty ceilings, short corridors, easy access, comfortable furniture and welcoming atmosphere. This allows us to think beyond the architect, parallel to going beyond the sublime object. The vision development at KARUS started with the ambition to formulate a discourse on the psychiatric centre of the future by expanding the agency of architecture. The workshops with psychiatrists, managers, staff *and* patients were exemplary for the dream of producing a common genius on architecture and a collective subject that supports it. In the end, the renovation of Dageraad shows how the figure of the architect must disappear for architectural emancipation to happen; at the least, the architect should be reduced to an intermediary function, not an end-in-itself. The common genius opposes the discourses on 'other ways of doing architecture' that may present alternative design projects but still refer to the solitary creative work of one or another architect, somehow nurturing the idea of a 'master genius' and disowning the creative role of others.[52]

At some point in the process, the director expressed his frustration about his relation to the architect active in the clinic for a generation: 'How is it possible that the architect always says "Yes!" to any question I ask, as if, as a client, I'm supposed to know everything about architecture?' The truth is that the architect is hired as a problem fixer, whose response is expected to come quick, even though he/she knows nothing about the topic. Call it a relationship of interpassivity set in place to maintain business as usual and prevent inherent paradoxes from coming to the fore. No wonder there is an absence of architectural innovation in the landscape of care, as it is monopolized by a handful of architectural and engineering offices, often operating in framework agreements and mutually subdividing the market, even filling the holes in the market with joint ventures. It is precisely this sort of relationship that was frustrated in the vision development by assuming the role of ignorant architect who knows nothing or at least answers every question in the slowest possible terms. After months spent organizing workshops, general manager Herman Roose got nervous about the slow progress and said, 'You're the creative people, I think about feasibility and smooth process'. It was only by avoiding this push to play the expert that we could leave the floor to local actors and trigger the birth of an architecture culture at the clinic. In the Dageraad, we see how management of the psychiatric centre took the design process into their own hands, no longer waiting for an architect to deliver them from the burden of architecture. This shows how the disappearance of the architect does lead to an expansion of the architecture culture, not only entering the mythical start phase but also the equally mythical end point of delivery.

Notes
1. Michael Speaks, 'Design Intelligence', in *Constructing a New Agenda*, ed. A. Krista Sykes (New York: Princeton Architectural Press, 2010), 204-15.
2. Doina Petrescu, 'Losing Control, Keeping Desire', in *Architecture and*

Participation, eds. Peter Blundell Jones, Doina Petrescu and Jeremy Till (London: Spon Press, 2005), 43-65.
3. Studiedag 'Bouwen aan zorg. Naar geïntegreerde woonzorgcentra in Vlaanderen' organized by the Flemish Government Architect and the Flemish Infrastructure Fund for Person-Related Matters (04 May 2009).
4. Tine Hens et al., *Architectuurnota 2009-2014* (Antwerp/Brussels: VAi/Team Flemish Government Architect, 2009).
5. Boie, 'Plea for Care Architecture'.
6. Geert Bekaert, 'Belgian Architecture as Commonplace: The Absence of Architectonic Culture as a Challenge', in *Rooted in the Real*, 90-96.
7. Van Gerrewey, 'Jaarboek Architectuur Vlaanderen 06-07'.
8. Boie, 'Plea for Care Architecture'.
9. Speaks, 'Design Intelligence'.
10. Charles Jencks, *Can Architecture Affect Your Health?* (Arnhem: ArtEZ Press, 2012).
11. Rancière, *The Ignorant Schoolmaster*.
12. Alain Findeli and Rabah Bousbaci, 'L'éclipse de l'objet dans les théories du projet en design', *The Design Journal* 8, no. 1 (2005), 35-49.
13. Gideon Boie, 'Zorgarchitectuur is een opdracht', *Psyche* 23, no. 1 (Mar. 2011), 4-7. The article was a short report on the seminar 'Het huis van de psychiatrie: over de intieme relatie tussen architectuur en geestelijke gezondheid' (Ghent, Museum Dr. Guislain, 25 Nov. 2010). The seminar was organized by the VAi, Museum Dr. Guislain and the VVGG and was supported by the Flemish Government Architect. Gideon Boie, *Het Huis van de psychiatrie: verslag* (Antwerp: VAi, 2010).
14. Nikolaas Vande Keere and Regis Verplaetse, *De Psychiatrische Kliniek Ontmanteld* (Antwerp: UR Architects, 2009). The research was supported by Stimuleringsfonds voor Architectuur, Fonds Psychische Gezondheid, EFL-Stichting, College Bouw Zorginstellingen and Twynstra Gudde Adviseurs en Managers.
15. André Loeckx, 'Meesterzet in drie bewegingen: gesprek met Peter Swinnen, Marcel Smets en b0b Van Reeth', *A+ Architecture in Belgium* 242 (Jun.-Jul. 2013), 90-94.
16. Speaks, 'Design Intelligence'.
17. Žižek, *The Fragile Absolute*. Žižek, *The Puppet and the Dwarf*. BAVO, 'Always Choose the Worst Option', 18-39.
18. Gideon Boie, 'A Lesson in Added Architectural Value', *Flanders Architectural Yearbook 2008-2009* (Antwerp: VAi, 2010), 175-77. The essay was later republished: Gideon Boie, 'Wet89' in *Double or Nothing*, ed. 51N4E (London: AA Publications, 2011).
19. Lieven De Cauter, 'Utopia Rediscovered: A Redefinition of Utopianism in the Light of the Enclosures of the Commons', in *A Truly Golden Handbook: the Scholarly Quest for Utopia*, eds. Veerle Achten, Erik Schokkaert, and Geert Bouckaert (Leuven: Leuven University Press, 2016), 534-45.
20. Petrescu, 'Losing Control, Keeping Desire'.
21. Fie Vandamme, 'Fit In, Stand Out: Een actieonderzoek naar architectuur als antwoord op mortificatie en recidivisme in de gevangenis' (master's thesis, Brussels, KU Leuven Faculty of Architecture, 2014).

22. 'Selection of Newspaper Cuttings 2006-2007' in *Flanders Architectural Yearbook 2006-2007*, I-X.
23. Gideon Boie, 'Een slakkengang voor internering', *Psyche* 24, no. 3 (Sep. 2012), 20-21.
24. Loeckx, *Stadsvernieuwingsprojecten In Vlaanderen*.
25. Van Gerrewey, 'Jaarboek Architectuur Vlaanderen 06-07'.
26. Žižek, *The Parallax View*, 37. Slavoj Žižek, *For They Know Not What They Do: Enjoyment as a Political Factor* (1991; London: Verso, 2002), 16-20.
27. Gideon Boie and Fie Vandamme, 'Lijdt ook u aan ziekenhuispsychastenie?', *Psyche* 26, no. 4 (Dec. 2014), 20-21.
28. Edward W. Soja, 'Postmetropolitan Psychastenia: A Spatioanalysis', in BAVO, *Urban Politics Now*, 78-93.
29. Gideon Boie and Fie Vandamme, 'Wat gebeurt er tussen paviljoen en schietveld?', *Psyche* 27, no. 2 (Jun. 2015), 20-21.
30. Wim Cuyvers, 'The Belgian House: The Waiting Façade and the Field of Fire', *A+U* 392 (2003).
31. Nan Ellin, ed., *Architecture of Fear* (New York: Princeton Architectural Press, 1997).
32. Michel Foucault, *History of Madness* (1961; London/New York: Routledge, 2006).
33. Susanne Hofmann, *Architecture Is Participation: Die Baupiloten – Methods and Projects* (Berlin: Jovis, 2014), 22-41.
34. Anarchitektur, 'On the Commons: A Public Interview with Massimo De Angelis and Stavros Stavrides', *E-flux Journal* 17 (2010).
35. Boie and Vandamme, 'Lijdt ook u aan ziekenhuispsychastenie?'. Gideon Boie and Fie Vandamme, 'De toekomst is aan het zorgerfgoed', *Psyche* 27, no. 1 (Mar. 2015), 20-21. Boie and Vandamme, 'Wat gebeurt er tussen paviljoen en schietveld?'.
36. The Vlaamse Hersteldagen 2015 were organized by the Vlaams Herstelplatform at Vooruit, 17-18 Nov. 2015. See presentations and reports: https://www.bavo.biz/een-psychiatrisch-centrum-bouwen-we-samen.
37. BAVO, 'Democracy & the Neoliberal City', 212-33.
38. Bruno Latour, *Down to Earth: Politics in the New Climate Regime* (Cambridge: Polity Press, 2018), 21-24. Originally published as *Où atterrir? Comment s'orienter en politique*, 2017.
39. Herman Roose, 'Design Dialogue and Co-Authorship: A Social-Constructionist Approach', in *Unless Ever People*, eds. Gideon Boie and architecten de vylder vinck taillieu (Antwerp: VAi, 2018), 228-45.
40. Žižek, *The Parallax View*, 304.
41. Gideon Boie, 'Design Your Symptom', in *Unless Ever People*, ed. Gideon Boie and architecten de vylder vinck taillieu (Antwerp: VAi, 2018), 186-223.
42. Gideon Boie, 'The Social Mind', *Domus* 1036 (Jun. 2019), 650-57. Gideon Boie, 'Ode aan het Caritas project', *Psyche* 34, no. 2 (Jun. 2022), 18-19.
43. Roose, 'Design Dialogue and Co-Authorship'.
44. Petrescu, 'Losing Control, Keeping Desire', 45 and 54.
45. Petrescu, 'Losing Control, Keeping Desire', 45 and 54.
46. Boie and Vandamme, 'De toekomst is aan het zorgerfgoed'.

47. Gideon Boie, 'Drie variaties op een monumentale buitenruimte', *Psyche* 28, no. 2 (Jun. 2016), 20-21.
48. Gideon Boie, 'Everybody Architect: The Authorship of the Square', in *Unless Ever People*, eds. Gideon Boie and architecten de vylder vinck taillieu (Antwerp: VAi, 2018), 228-45.
49. Gideon Boie, 'La mente sociale – The Social Mind', *Domus* 1036 (Jun. 2019), 650-57.
50. Malkit Soshan, *BLUE: Architecture of UN Peacekeeping Missions* (Barcelona: ACTAR, 2022). The publication presents the exhibition *BLUE: Architecture of UN Peacekeeping Missions* at the Dutch Pavilion at the 15th Venice Architecture Biennale (2016), curated by Malkit Soshan and organized by the Netherlands Architecture Institute.
51. Gideon Boie, 'De nalatenschap van de architectuur', *Psyche* 32, no. 1 (Mar. 2020), 20-21.
52. Awan, Schneider and Till, *Spatial Agency*.

Stay True to Ignorance

Chapter 11

The use of inherent criticism as a catalyst for recursive moments breaks with the linear understanding of architecture production and also repositions the role of the critic from the phase of post-production to that of project definition. Criticism will always come too late if it doesn't acknowledge the basic lesson of the Flemish Government Architect that architecture is better not left to the architect alone, especially in cases where there isn't yet a clear demand or vision. The project brief is the condition of possibility for the innovation to be realized in the later design phase and the lack of ambition in the early phase often results in the reproduction of the same in spite of the known shortcomings. We came across this problem when discussing the seclusion room in crisis psychiatry as part of the vision development at KARUS, discussed in Chapter 10. While the use of coercion and compulsion in psychiatry is a matter of intense debate and new care models are increasingly common in Flanders, the seclusion room somehow miraculously survives. Worse still, everyone knows the problem of the seclusion room in psychiatry, we complain a lot about it and dream up alternatives, but nonetheless, when it comes to building new facilities, that one specific room reappears. Design intelligence is simply lacking at the crucial phase of project definition. As a result, best practices in Flanders are ad hoc interventions situated outside the seclusion room, more specifically in the layout of comfort and low-stimulus rooms of all kinds, even in recently finished buildings. The architecture of the seclusion room could therefore be considered as the final and perhaps greatest challenge of the socialization of mental healthcare, the hard core that resists innovation and embodies the last remnant of the fiercely contested coercive era of psychiatry. After the issue of the seclusion room came up in the work at KARUS, we further explored the topic in a field survey and looked into possibilities to start a comparative research at different psychiatry clinic, first without success. The breakthrough came after publishing a critical article in the newspaper which triggered a direct request to research an alternative design of the seclusion room in the Sint-Jan acute admissions department of the Sint-Annendael psychiatric hospital (Diest) starting from their experience with the 'Prikkelarme Kamer' or Low-Stimulus Room (LSR), a practice commonly recognized as best practice in Flanders. We took the request to expand the effects of the LSR as the starting point to relate the issue of seclusion with the overall functioning of the department and more specifically reconsider its relation to the traditional seclusion room, nursing station and community rooms. The vision development started in the autumn of 2017 again following the relational method, putting the design question into the hands of work groups composed of doctors, directors, staff, experts by experience *and* patients. The work group became the vehicle to undertake a number of methodological steps from the inventory of user experiences and space perceptions, investigation of care models and alternative practices, imagination of alternative scenarios to formulation of a project definition, even setting up test models in the department. Throughout the project we managed to further experiment with the role of the critic as mediator in the building process of an everyday but all the more real concern of acute mental healthcare. The research became part of the *Prikkels* (Stimuli) exhibition at Museum Dr. Guislain, Ghent, 20 October 2018-26 May 2019, and got included in the permanent collection. This chapter describes the successive steps in the vision development for the architecture of the seclusion room, starting with the survey and ending with the test set-up in Room 4 of the Sint-Jan acute admissions department.

The Second Recursion

Although the vision development at KARUS psychiatric centre in Melle managed to put architectural quality at the heart of debate on the master plan and future building projects, it failed to answer the one question that triggered the whole process: the new-build programme for the crisis admissions department and the department for children and youth psychiatry with an attached forensic youth unit. The two treatment programmes have nothing to do with each other, except for the fact that both were considered paradigmatic for the future of the psychiatric clinic, since both are intensive programmes that will never really fit the ideal of resocialization. Questions on the seclusion rooms were many, but the central one was how architectural design and the spatial setting more generally could help to reduce the use of coercion and compulsion in the daily service of crisis care. The work groups with psychiatrists, managers, staff *and* patients answered only indirectly the issue of coercion and compulsion, more specifically in the discussion on the need for in-between space at the campus and the overall atmosphere of hospital psychasthenia. The design of the Kanunnik Jozef Triest Plein by architecten de vylder vinck taillieu did answer to some extent the constraining character of a typical hospital ward and contribute to a hospitable atmosphere in the psychiatric clinic, but it certainly doesn't replace the use of the seclusion room as such. The same holds for the renovation of the Lente building, which offered the Dageraad department for psychosis care an unexpected answer for the desire to deliver care in a building that provides comfort through its clear layout, short corridors and plenty of openings. Still, in its daily functioning, the treatment offered in Dageraad was leaning upon the use of seclusion rooms in the Sint-Elisabeth crisis department, located in the quasi-modernist building just across the lane, easy to reach through the garage door.

Both Triest Plein and Dageraad symbolize a mind shift in the use of heritage for the psychiatric clinic of the future, but the design projects certainly didn't answer the basic need for an architecture specially fit for crisis situations. On the contrary, the projects were the result of a deliberate attempt to dodge the design question for the crisis psychiatry unit and the children and youth psychiatry department and first reflect on the spatial needs and desires in general. In thinking about architecture for the psychiatric centre of the future, so many lines of flight were explored, but one question remained: what to do with the seclusion room itself? After all, it's quite easy to talk about the normalization of psychiatric care and how the spatial setting can contribute to that challenge, while leaving aside the stumbling block of the seclusion room. Even worse, it would be cynical to rethink the space for psychiatry while silently anticipating the continued use of the existing seclusion rooms in the crisis department as happens so often in newly built facilities. This brought us to a point at which we had to do the whole process over again, call it a second recursive moment, accelerating the vision development by returning to the starting point and reflecting the relational method and preliminary findings into that one crampy, stinking and suffocating room.[1] The challenge was to reimagine the psychiatric centre of the future starting from the elementary particle of the seclusion room, but including the new circles of meaning that were produced in the workshops with psychiatrists, manager, staff *and* patients. Although alternative design solutions for the seclusion room were lacking, the urgency of the problem was all the clearer and was becoming part of public debate.

At the time of speaking, in May 2015, the issue of seclusion in times of mental crisis was a trending topic in popular media, after the complaints and dismissal of psychotherapist Tom Verhaeghe about the excessive and improper use of seclusion and medication in Fioretti, the psychiatric youth centre for people with mental disabilities at the Dr. Guislain psychiatric centre, campus De Deyne, in Ghent.[2] In the same period, there was the dramatic case of a young girl (17 March 2015) who ended up in a police cell after not being accepted in a psychiatric hospital, all of which claimed to lack the proper infrastructure. The same situation led to the death of Jonathan Jacob, a case that got mediatized after the Panorama documentary 'De Gestoorde Procedure' (The deranged procedure) was broadcast.[3] Our attempt to frame the highly mediatized and moralized discussion around Fioretti from an architectural perspective was met with great reluctance. We published the article 'Ruimte voor Humane Isolatie' (Room for humane seclusion) in *Psyche* (Dec. 2015), referring to the agitation at Fioretti and suggesting design intelligence that came up in the work groups at KARUS.[4] Soon after publication, both the general director and president of the board formally distanced themselves from the article in a written response (14 January 2016), making clear that KARUS remained loyal to colleagues in the care sector and demanded that all future articles on the vision development first be read before publication. In their view, the complaint by Tom Verhaeghe put the blame on the care sector one-sidedly and kept the political responsibility out of the discussion, i.e. disinvestment by the Flemish Government in terms of staffing and infrastructure. Nevertheless, KARUS agreed to support a comparative research into the design of the seclusion room that would involve other psychiatric clinics and include the legislative side of the story. After publishing a call for engagement in *Zorgwijzer* (the magazine of the umbrella association Zorgnet-Icuro), we organized information sessions to engage other psychiatric hospitals in a joint research proposal and look for government funding at IWT (now Vlaio).[5] Although four psychiatric clinics were ready to invest in the comparative research, we didn't manage to start after some practical miscalculations again opened up internal discussions about unequal investment from the participants. After all, the financial disagreement was symptomatic of an ideological reluctance of clinics when it comes to research on such a difficult and sensitive topic as the seclusion room.

The bottom line, said Herman Roose, the general director who took the initiative, is that hospitals are looking for concrete advice that fixes a clearly defined defect in the local infrastructure and they expect the government to subsidize research into questions of general importance and structural change. This explains why the general interest in undoing the shameful history of the seclusion room and rethinking its function in mental healthcare today didn't necessarily translate into coordinated action, even in a context of widespread professional frustration and public indignation. In the same period, the topic of the seclusion room got massive attention after the leading newspapers *De Standaard* and *De Morgen* published alarming reports by the Flemish Government Agency Zorginspectie (Care inspectorate) on the state of seclusion rooms and their misuse in the clinical treatment.[6] In principle, although the reports were already publicly accessible and the state of affairs was known certainly to professionals and former patients, the newspaper articles still caused a scandal and triggered a series of worrying testimonies and opinions. The disclosure of the reports happened against the background of an ongoing professional debate on the reduction of coercion and compulsion in mental healthcare, leading to the report by the Superior Health Council and civil action by Kollectief Zonder Dwang (Collective against coercion).[7] We intervened in the debate by publishing an article in the newspaper that criticized the generic quality of the seclusion room in contrast with the highly specific categorization of mental illnesses.[8] The day after publication, the head nurse of the Sint-Jan acute admissions department of the Sint-Annendael Diest psychiatric hospital called, asking for help in the redesign of the individual rooms of the Sint-Jan admissions department, learning from their experiences with the LSR. The urgent call from the head nurse confirmed how hospitals did indeed want direct advice on concrete challenges in the first place, having no time to waste on year-long comparative studies preparing for structural change at policy level. Still, the step to the side by the Sint-Annendael Diest psychiatric hospital was a great opportunity to start the research on the design of the seclusion room in relation to the LSR, a practice that had received the status of best practice in Flanders when it comes to the reduction of coercion and compulsion in mental healthcare.[9]

In the daily operation of the Sint-Jan acute admissions department, the LSR was conceptualized as an intermediary step that hopefully rendered the seclusion room obsolete or at least minimized its use. The LSR was nicknamed by staff the 'low-stimulus studio' as it consisted of a setting with two individual bedrooms around a central living room giving access to a small terrace and garden. The idea was that patients in distress or crisis could use this space, which was in no way reminiscent of a seclusion room, but still offered a place for separation from the community of patients. From talks with staff and reading through patient reports, we understood that the LSR turned out to be a brilliant failure in terms of architectural design. The infrastructure of the LSR was such that two patients in crisis were gathered in two bedrooms arranged around a common living space, bathroom and garden.[10] Logically, the second bedroom remained empty as persons in crisis are undoubtedly not apt to share certain facilities, thus by chance providing an extra space for the patient to roam around. After the empty second bedroom was once spontaneously used by a relative of a patient to stay over during the crisis, the team started to further the experiment with the now much acclaimed practice of rooming-in. Again, the question of the seclusion room was answered by taking a step to the side, but still the LSR provided the anchor point to translate the later discussions on the normalization of the architecture for mental healthcare into the topic of the seclusion room. In the first place, patients in crisis were no longer taken to the smallest, barest and securest room of the ward, but on the contrary to the most spacious room with doors they could open anytime. Moreover, the experimental practice of rooming-in allowed us to think beyond the architecture of seclusion and reflect how the spatial setting was helpful in establishing the idea of recovery in crisis care, i.e. the idea that it might be necessary for the patient in crisis that staff take over control immediately, acknowledging the importance to restore self-control as soon as possible. As a result, the question of the seclusion room is directly linked with the bigger challenge of resocialization in mental healthcare, according to chief psychiatrist Wim Simons: 'The driving force behind the socialization of care is the so-called "recovery movement". The aim is to let people with as much self-management as possible regain a meaningful and satisfactory life.'[11] Although the general ambition to (re)socialize mental healthcare is better known for the typical building projects that dismantle hospital complexes in favour of mental healthcare networks that combine psychiatric care homes, centres for mental healthcare, mobile teams and more, the seclusion room might serve as key.

Architect-mediator

The second recursive moment allowed us to further deepen the research methodology for vision development based on the premise of the ignorant master, using the theory by Jacques Rancière. This pedagogical method takes as its starting point the presupposition one can teach a certain topic without necessarily knowing the slightest thing about it and even though teacher and pupils don't share the same language.[12] In the research at KARUS, we adopted the concept of ignorance as the guiding principle for vision development, starting from the assumption that the architect has no original source of knowledge about care architecture and setting up workshops that initiate a conversation among the diverse actors of the clinic about how architecture sustains (or not) the daily work or life in the clinic. The firm belief was that the emancipation of staff and patients in terms of architecture, raising their awareness about the spatial dimension of care services and strengthening the capacity to express spatial needs and desires, would naturally lead to innovative design intelligence. The method merges the theory of Doina Petrescu on architectural design as commoning and the search of Michael Speaks for design intelligence that stems from everyday chatter.[13] The first results of the Triest Plein and the makeover of the Dageraad psychosis department were perhaps answers beside the question but still they showed how orthodox methodological ignorance triggered a lot of enthusiasm among the actors, pushing the vision development into previously forbidden territory and leading to unforeseen results. The methodology was taken up again in the context of the Sint-Jan acute admissions department of Sint-Annendael Diest psychiatric hospital, this time strictly putting the focus on the reimagination of the seclusion room and giving work groups of psychiatrists, managers, staff *and* (former) patients the lead in a five-step research plan.

Assuming ignorance wasn't difficult to maintain in the context of the seclusion room as best practices were lacking in the field of architecture and the LSR in the Sint-Jan acute admissions department was one of the rare positive references in the field of mental healthcare. What is important, however, is not so much the knowledge or expertise the architect carries, but much more the transferential relation usually installed between commissioner and architect. The knowledge situates in a linear sequence between the one identifying the design challenge and the one fixing the issue, the latter finding themselves in the position of subject-supposed-to-know.[14] The transferential relationship became clear during a first site visit (29 March 2017) to the LSR in the Sint-Jan acute admissions department of Sint-Annendael. The visit was concluded in the existing seclusion room, with the care manager, chief psychiatrist, psychologist and head nurse squeezed into a few square metres. Someone in the group raised the ominous question as to 'what's to be done' with this space knowing it runs contrary to the care vision supported by the team at the clinic focusing on the proximity of staff and the patients' recovery of self-control. I didn't have a ready-made answer and returned the question back to sender. Silence was the answer. The refusal to answer the question created unease certainly, no one had an easy solution at hand, and yet I believe the silence in that moment also provided comfort in the recognition that we all share the same problem. Ignorance was the necessary precursor that defines an equal playing field where all actors involved come together in the search for the right words and images that helps to articulate an answer to the most difficult question of seclusion in mental healthcare. Ignorance breaks the transferential relationship with the management team and their obsession to know the desire of the critic. Slavoj Žižek described the critical role of the rock band Laibach in the transferential relationship bestowed upon them by the public: 'The ultimate expedient of Laibach is their deft manipulation of transference: their public (especially intellectuals) is obsessed with the "desire of the Other" – what is Laibach's actual position, are they truly totalitarians or not? – i.e., they address Laibach with a question and expect from them an answer, failing to notice that Laibach itself does not function as an answer but a question.'[15]

The methodology of having work groups of psychiatrists, managers, staff *and* (former) patients leading the vision development was adopted from the work at KARUS and relaunched in the context of the seclusion room, this time following a five-step research plan:

- First, assessment of space perceptions and user experiences in the Sint-Jan department, mixing methods of participative observation, in-depth interviews and biographical cartography.
- Second, environmental analysis discussing new care models in relation to architecture and also studying best practices in other (psychiatric) care practices in relation to the local infrastructure of the Sint-Jan acute admissions department.
- Third, formulation and visualization of spatial scenarios that generically answer the findings in the previous steps, thus negating local specifics, such as the local infrastructure, allocated budgets and/or operational considerations.
- Fourth, the application of the generic visions onto the existing infrastructure of the Sint-Jan acute admissions department, translating the spatial scenarios into concrete interventions at the local facility.
- Fifth, the installation of a mock-up in an existing patients room, trying out the new vision defined in the previous steps and generating yet another feedback loop, this time through (experimental) use.

The research plan was choreographed as workshops that gather psychiatrists, managers, staff and (former) patients at intervals of two (or more) weeks, taking one step at a time and avoiding that discussions were hastily passed over. The ambition was to add slowness to the participative ignorant research method, taking our inspiration from Liza Fior (muf architecture), who introduced slowness as methodological principle, using the slogan: 'spending fast money in the slowest possible terms'.[16] The design logic is to allow for divergences in the procedure by answering the question of the commissioner in the slowest possible terms and hoping that lines of flight will appear by postponing the final design solution as long as possible. A key element was the suspension of personal *idées fixes* carried by one or another actor, readymade conceptions available in the field, or easy gadgets provided by the market, so as to avoid easily saturating the design challenge, in our case the seclusion room. The tactic connects with the argument of Slavoj Žižek that the worst thing that can happen to a protest is the demand being immediately answered, a gesture of depoliticization that, I paraphrase, deprives the protesters from the true aim of their protest.[17] Keeping the question open is the only way to avoid the fetishization of the demand and allows for a political moment in which assumptions are reconsidered in light of the full complexity of the situation before arriving at solutions. The design work was postponed as long as possible by first allowing the people at the table to narrate their experiences and desires, search best practices in the context analysis and discuss theoretical models found in literature. Another way to delay the actual design work was to reframe the topic of the seclusion room in relation to the acute admissions department as a whole, undermining the usual interpretation of the seclusion room as a monad in the clinic ward. The challenge was to reimagine the seclusion room as a positive part of the treatment and fitting the spatial setting at the Sint-Jan acute admissions department, some patients being residential while others were in day therapy. At the same time, the challenge was to connect the design of the seclusion room with the new visions on crisis care and finding meaningful links with care service. The relatively popular High and Intensive Care (HIC) model was clearly defining the importance of the 'first five minutes' for the admissions procedure, reinforcing the proximity of staff up to one-on-one situations in moments of crisis and strengthening recovery by including family and network in the treatment of persons.[18] The HIC model might have a chapter on 'spatial design' but still the guidelines are rather vague in terms of architecture, for example in specifying requirements for the layout of specific rooms but forgetting to translate the overall therapeutic ideas (such as the notorious rule of 'five minutes') and management structure (such as staff ratio).[19]

Still another way of slowing down was to welcome change of participants in the workshop and using every newcomer at the table as a possibility to summarize previous steps over again, thus allowing new feedback loops that help to sharpen the findings. The change in participants also made it possible to reconsider the agenda-setting after each gathering, making sure that the ambitions of the management matched the expectations of the different users, i.e. psychiatrists, staff *and* patients. In the common vision development at the Sint-Jan admissions department, the typical role of the architect as problem solver changed into that of mediator who constructs a bricolage of desire by collaging the one collage onto the other, to paraphrase Doina Petrescu.[20] In the context of the workshops at the Sint-Jan admissions department, to mediate meant to welcome psychiatrists, managers, staff and (former) patients to delve into the seclusion room, express their needs and desires, confront the possible conflicts of interests, work through the complexities and contradictions, define spatial scenarios in which interests converge, answer the design challenge, etc. The work of the mediator is to construct from all that design intelligence that is useful in producing unheard-of answers and, equally importantly, the enthusiasm among all actors involved to turn these ideas into reality. In such a process, foreknowledge is not forbidden – after all, absolute ignorance would require each time entering a new field of action – but should only be used to continue to question assumptions, unfold conceptual models, stimulate imagination, generate feedback, animate discussions, synthesize dreamwork, question interim results time and again, in short: hystericize the design process. To do so, the informal presence at the admissions department was just as important as it generated new feedback loops outside the workshops and opened up the circle of participants to the proverbial unexpected guest. Every week we gathered on the terrace to eat a sandwich, fold the latest documents we had prepared and/or chat with patients in the living room. Interim results, often premature, were posted on walls and spread out on tables. The idea was to enable everyone, also minor voices, to react to the vision development according to their own insight and ability. Our presence meant that patients and staff addressed us as 'the architects' and the resulting trust allowed us to gain knowledge through spontaneous conversations and thus prepare the solid foundation for the project definition of specific interventions. Ultimately, we saw the presentation of the research outcome to the general director and care manager as only a next phase in the research plan, again debriefing the talks at the management meeting to all those working and staying at the Sint-Jan department through posters, leaflets and small talk.

The Patient Takeover

Bringing the different actors and users together around the design of the seclusion room, the weekly workshops functioned as an analytic space that enabled the users to get a grip on the spatial setting in which they stay and work. The idea was to undermine explicitly the set hierarchies at play in the management of psychiatry and create an equal playing field for psychiatrists, managers, staff and (former) patients. In mental healthcare, it has become customary recently to involve former patients as experts by experience in decision-making processes, often combined with a role as confidential contact person for newly arrived patients. The work in the Sint-Jan acute admissions department showed how the creation of a position for the expert by experience is certainly a wonderful gesture, and yet their role was not fully recognized in the usual management functions of the psychiatric clinics, headed by the tripartite function of general manager, care manager and head psychiatrist. Especially when it comes to technical issues (such as design processes, facility management and purchase services), clearly the expert by experience might be heard but still remains in the lowest ranking order. In the set-up of the workshops, we dealt with psychiatrists, managers, staff *and* (former) patients in exactly the same way, i.e. turning the manager equally into expert by experience (or non-expert, that was to be seen), and thus create an equal playing field among the different stakeholders. The transgression of hierarchies was embodied by the symbolic gesture of leaving behind the boardroom and holding meetings in in any room available, forcing managers to leave their comfort zone. The different informal setting did away with the expertocrat atmosphere in which architects usually engage in a direct dialogue with managers and technical departments, only organizing participation as a compulsive moment or, even worse, at the end of the production line.

The focus on the participative character of vision development guarantees not only support by people of all ranks, which is the standard trick of participation, but equally introduces an element of ignorance in the formal set-up, in the first place by doing away with readymade answers and underscoring that we somehow have to learn it anew. In retrospect, Herman Roose, general director at KARUS, considered the language confusion as one of the main obstacles in the design process: care workers and architects may use the same words but they have a totally different understanding.[21] This connects to Bruno Latour, who argued in the context of climate politics that the divide between the climate youth and climate negationists was foremost an epistemological conflict of parties unable to understand each other.[22] Applying the lessons of the ignorant education method as discussed by Jacques Rancière implied a completely different way of acting as architect, traditionally operating as an oracle that always finds the right words and images to solve the problem and anticipates future questions – in Lacanian terminology, it comes close to the University discourse. In the vision development project at the Sint-Annendael Diest hospital, the architect operated in the figure of someone who assumes to know nothing about the subject – given the technicality and complexity of service issues in crisis care, the ignorance was ultimately not so far from reality. The gesture of ignorance suspends not only the standard knowledge but also the limits of what is considered possible or not, such as the typically managerial concerns about the predefined research question, the existing local infrastructure or available budgets for renovation. In contrast to the all-knowingness of the traditional architect, it is about locating oneself as architect in the obstacle in the design process, in our case the seclusion room, and reshaping the discourse from there. The workshops opened up an analytical space in which users – implying psychiatrists, managers, staff *and* patients – were strengthened to confront their own spatial perception and user experience about the architecture of the hospital and take it as the start to construct new design intelligence. The typical university discourse supporting the managerial operations in the clinic was replaced by free speech on spatial obstacles in the treatment programme, doubts in the usual readymade answers and other personal emotions. Free speech was essential in building an atmosphere of commoning that further dissolved the epistemological domains separating the actors and thus created the possibility of a collective understanding. It simply makes no sense to organize participation while respecting the set roles of knowledge by distinguishing the expertise of care workers, the expertise by experience from (former) patients, the meta skills of managers and the creativity of architects. Therefore, the format of participation had to acknowledge that psychiatrists, directors, staff, patients and architects may use different languages and have different imaginations, still they have one common objective in the humanization of the seclusion room.

The role of the architect as mediator is to facilitate the dialectical process in which the needs and desires of the different users are reflected, in the first place between care workers and care recipients, but also with management and even general policies. Of course, the challenge is to ensure that everyone at the table, especially the minor voices, is given a chance to speak out and to tap their capacities in the search for care architecture. The biggest challenge, however, is to keep the conversation going and to expand its scope as much as possible, as Jacques Lacan used to say. The different steps in the methods with assessment of space perceptions and user experiences, environmental analysis with care models and best practices, the generic spatial scenario-scripting, and so on, were meant for that purpose: these were just so many alibis to relaunch the talk each time to greater magnitude. Part of the challenge was to allow the conversation to overflow the workshop room and discuss the issue of architectural quality in times of seclusion beyond the set moments of negotiation. The reports from the meeting, even the final meeting with the general director of the Sint-Annendael psychiatric hospital, were distributed randomly in the hope of sparking corridor discussions on the spatial setting of the treatment programme. In short, the architect-mediator's task was to turn the architecture of the seclusion room and the psychiatric ward more generally from an expert-business into a matter of commoning, turning it into the talk of the town. Besides the three main elements of commoning (a common resource, a practice of commoning and community of commoners), we argued that it is necessary to add the 'atmosphere' of commoning – using a term coined by Susanne Hofmann to stress the importance of the corporeal experience for user engagement in her practice with Die Baupiloten.[23] Obviously, the commoning of the clinic creates a great deal of enthusiasm among the different users of the psychiatric centre, but it is about creating a setting in which design intelligence emerges from the chatter of the different actors present in the situation.[24]

Of course, although the architect-mediator takes a more or less central position in the vision development, the whole process should be regarded as a moment in intellectual emancipation – in the field of architecture, one generally talks about capacity-building.²⁵ The emancipatory effect of the workshop series in Sint-Annendael Diest manifested itself very concretely when, at one point, a patient assumed our own role as project manager. Although everyone could contribute according to their own insights and abilities, it was more than understandable that a lot of patients had other things on their minds or simply recoiled at the idea of brainstorming with staff about architecture. After a while, a patient, enrolled in the day-care programme, took upon himself the responsibility of informing other patients about the weekly results and gathering feedback among them, thus introducing less audible voices in in the vision development. Another patient in admissions care, an elderly lady, took charge of the debriefing by distributing the work documents in the department and sorting the material in the waiting room near the psychiatrist's office. Part of the moment of emancipation of staff *and* patients in the design process is the transformation at management level, not only strengthening the directors in their capacity to deal with architecture quality in the clinic but first enabling them to let the architecture production process be informed by the different minor voices in the clinic.

The Mediator Must Vanish

The architect-mediator defines a new role for criticism within the field of architecture culture in Flanders, for a long time embodied by the VAi. In parallel with the design practice of architecture, the architecture culture consists of discursive practices such as exhibitions, lectures, publications, explorations and much more. Criticism functions traditionally in this field at the end of the production line, most notably in the identification of best practices and the building of an architectural discourse around it – this is in fact the core business of the VAi. Recently, however, architecture culture has gained a more explorative and operational role in light of urgent social challenges, especially present in the Pilot Projects of the Flemish Government Architect and in the work of organizations such as AWB and AR-TUR.²⁶ The work isn't so much about the post-factum identification of best practices in the hope this will inspire future developments, but rather about what Joachim Declerck, co-founder of AWB, called setting the fruitful context in which new practices can potentially emerge.²⁷ The term of cultural operator was used by the other co-founder, Roeland Dudal, to define the job that uses the field of culture to venture into new grounds, understand the new design challenges, harvest visions, define concrete actions, gather stakeholders, force breakthroughs, ensure translation into master plans, etc.²⁸ The new job description of the critic runs close to that of a cultural operator who translates the urgencies of our times into burning design questions and brings the management to the threshold of making it real. Still, the operative element of criticism can be as negative as ever, meaning highlighting inherent contradictions without giving in to the obscene command to be constructive. Moreover, the new operative role of curator or mediator enables the critic to act from the strict ethical perspective of unpacking the paradoxes of a certain situation and next launch a call to the stakeholders to fix the issue as soon as possible. Slavoj Žižek argues that the beauty of Greta Thunberg is her function as pure ethical call. Unable to 'see the complexity' that adult politicians use to water down the emergency, she is not even willing to answer the deadlocks of our current society; on that point, she respects the given labour division in which politicians have the duty to come up with solutions.[29] Embracing the power of autism is the best way to answer the blackmail that argues criticism should be always be constructive, that critical words should always be accompanied with concrete counterproposals.

Another good old function of criticism that remains in the new mode of the cultural operator as we applied it at Sint-Annendael Diest is to steer clear from practice, for different reasons. First, ignorance of the business or political interests in the project at stake is the condition of possibility for including the inherent paradoxes in the discussion and making sure it doesn't disappear from the design table. In the case of the elderly care home Klein Veldekens in Geel, we see how the rethinking of the role of architect, allegedly needed to make room for innovation in hospital architecture, ended up in a very mercantile role of architect-entrepreneur. Although Klein Veldekens was part of the Pilot Projects Invisible Care of the Flemish Government Architect, clearly from the start it contradicted the ambitions set by the programme and thus arrived, unsurprisingly, at innovation that was rather a repetition of the same. There was no way for the Government Architect to correct the innovation process as the architect was also acting as project developer with a commercial interest in the design project.[30] Against this sort of mercantile pseudo-critical operations of architect-entrepreneurs, ignorance relates to the principle of analytical intervention in which the initiative should be kept on the side of the analysand; it is the figure that should become subject through the process and take the initiative from there.[31] Therefore, it was important that we somehow vanished from the scene at the Sint-Annendael Diest hospital soon after the test phase was installed in the room at the Sint-Jan acute admissions department. The test set-up was only used for day use, being not yet approved for night service, but it allowed the project team of psychiatrists, staff, patients and experts by experience to negotiate their respective perspectives once again. The withdrawal of the architect-mediator may risk a failure of the project or end up in a poor compromise; still, leaving the initiative to the main actors was an important sign of belief in the capacity of the collective subject to further deal with it. So it happened that almost a year later the head nurse sent images of the redesign of the room according to the vision defined by the work group, of course altered according to the feedback gathered in the test phase and the input of the architect involved in the execution. A year after that, images were sent of the refurbishment of the room finally realized.

In the overall process of architecture production, the role of the critic is transposed from a function in the post-production phase to that of pre-production, more precisely from singing the praises of final results to triggering early moments of vision development and project definition. The critic extends the role of the architect beyond its mythical point of beginning: the project definition. One of the key tasks of the Flemish Government Architect has been to include the project definition in the overall process of architectural production, meaning the assignment isn't just taken as the pregiven framework of the design job; on the contrary, the framework can be in itself the subject of design thinking. In this sense, the Flemish Government Architect has introduced another way of doing architecture by breaking open the envelope of the assignment, entering the forbidden terrain and changing the programmatic settings. Entering the forbidden terrain means a totally different mindset, much less focused on the direct result, with no sublime image to admire. In fact, the result is only visible years later and even the process may recur in waves, such that 'working is the work'.[32] The thing produced in the process is the ever-growing collective subject, not so much in the numbers of participation, but first of all in the deepening of knowledge and the expanding of the capacity to act as an agent of change.

Part of the working is the spreading of research to other hospitals. At first, the request of Sint-Annendael Diest psychiatric hospital enabled us to bypass the failure of the initial comparative study and start the discussion of the seclusion room in a local facility. The results of the work at Sint-Annendael, however, started to disseminate in the field through personal contacts as well as through publications, lectures and talks. An important moment was the presentation of the work as part of the exhibition *Prikkels* (Stimuli) at Museum Dr. Guislain in Ghent, running from 20 October 2018 to 26 May 2019, after which the work got included in the permanent collection 'History of Psychiatry'. The contribution presented different parts: first, the brilliant failure of the LSR in Sint-Annendael Diest with video documentary by Lieven Vanhove and visual artwork by Rosa Fens; second, the photography series *Null* made in the seclusion room by Kurt Deruyter; and, third, the scale mock-up with the different layout of the patients' room. As a result of all this, the dissemination of research results spontaneously tilted over into the comparative study we once had in mind. The knowledge first gained in Diest was later developed in similar vision development projects in the Sint-Agnes department for psychosis care at the University psychiatric centre KU Leuven in Kortenberg, the acute admissions at psychiatric hospital Bethaniënhuis in Zoersel, the urgency unit 'OA' in psychiatric centre Gent-Sleidinge in Sleidinge, crisis admissions at psychiatric hospital Dr. Guislain in Ghent and the acute admissions department Sint Elisabeth 2 in KARUS, campus Melle. In all the studies we developed a vision that projected limited interventions that anticipated the short lifespan and hoped the ad hoc intervention could trigger learning elements (as in the LSR at the Sint-Annendael Diest hospital).

The final working is the translation of it onto policy level as part of an innovation programme set up by Zorgnet-Icuro, the umbrella organization of many Catholic hospital, dealing with the Ministry of Public Health in implementing the HIC model in Belgium. Being part of the workshops organized by Zorgnet-Icuro, we came the realize the lesson we learned years earlier from Chris Bervoets while setting up the research on humane isolation: he stressed that architecture shouldn't be seen as an additional item to the new regulations for a different care service, but as a special application of the very same service rules.[33] Talking about the new HIC innovation, the architectural and spatial setting was dealt with as a separate chapter, just as the HIC handbook prescribes, forgetting how space is inscribed in the every detail of the care model.[34] Talking about seclusion, space should rather be dealt with as a transversal element that cuts through all other chapters on care service (for example, the so-called five-minute rule), management (the rule of one-on-one counselling), employment (involving professional roles other than nurse or therapist) and other chapters. Dealing with space as a different chapter enabled members of the work group to claim rather opportunistically that they would always have worked as HIC if only they had had the right numbers of staffing. Turning the innovation into a question of staffing, the members of the work groups were looking for possibilities to introduce the new logic of care service within the existing infrastructure, slightly adjusting it here and there. What is symptomatic is that in many cases the topic of attention became again the seclusion room, though in a more innovative fashion, instead of turning to the other spaces required in high and intensive care, such as meeting rooms, coffee tables, rest rooms, outdoor facilities, etc. The cynical result is that once again, most investments are channelled into the space that accommodates the old practice of coercion and compulsion rather than investing in the disclosure of the seclusion room.

Notes
1. Herman Roose, 'Design Dialogue and Co-Authorship'.
2. Barbara Debusschere, 'Therapeut klaagt aan: Jeugdpsychiatrie bezorgt jongeren vaak méér trauma's', *De Morgen*, 30 Mar. 2015.
3. 'De gestoorde procedure', Panorama, VRT, 21 Feb. 2013, television documentary.
4. Gideon Boie and Fie Vandamme, 'Ruimte voor humane isolatie', *Psyche* 27, no. 4 (Dec. 2015), 20-21.
5. Herman Roose, 'Architectuur en zorg samen op zoek naar ruimte voor humane isolatie', *Zorgwijzer* 59 (May 2016), 23-25.
6. The newspaper *De Standaard* started publishing the article series 'De Stoornissen van de psychiatrie' (Psychiatry's disorders) on 27 Jan. 2017 with articles like: Maxie Eckert and Veerle Beel, 'De stoornissen van de Psychiatrie: de inspectieverslagen doorgelicht', *De Standaard*, 27 Jan. 2017. The newspaper *De Morgen* started publishing 'Het Grote Psychiatrierapport' (The major psychiatry report) on 18 Feb. 2017 with articles such as: Femke Van Garderen, Sara Vandekerckhove and Jonas Lampens, 'In een isolatiecel wordt niemand beter', *De Morgen*, 18 Feb. 2017; Femke van Garderen and Sara Vandekerckhove, 'Te snel naar de isoleercel', *De Morgen*, 21 Feb. 2017; Sara Vandekerckhove, 'Psychiatrie moet sociaal zijn', *De Morgen*, 25 Feb. 2017; etc.
7. Hoge Gezondheidsraad (Superior Health Council), *Omgaan met conflict, conflictbeheersing en dwanginterventies in de geestelijke gezondheidszorg* (Dealing with conflict, conflict management and coercion interventions in mental healthcare), *HGR* 9193 (Jun. 2016). The work group of the Hoge Gezondsheidsraad was presided by Dr Chris Bervoets (UPC KU Leuven). Kollectief Zonder Dwang released a press file in the context of the study day 'Jeugdhulpverlening zonder dwang! Op zoek naar alternatieven voor eenzame opsluiting' (Youth services against coercion! In search of alternatives to solitary confinement) in the Flemish Parliament on 4 May 2017 on the initiative of Flemish MP Freya Van den Bossche. Kollectief Zonder Dwang was initiated by psychologist Ariane Bazan, philosopher Ignaas Devisch, therapist Tom Verhaeghe and many others.
8. Gideon Boie, 'De onuitroeibare schaamteplek', *De Standaard*, 31 Jan. 2017, 29.
9. On the occasion of the study evening 'Vrijheidsbeperkende maatregelen in de geestelijke gezondheidszorg' (Restrictive measures in mental healthcare) (2 Oct. 2017), Zorgnet-Icuro published a manifesto and best-practice file with, among others, the rooming-in of the Sint-Annendael psychiatric hospital in Diest. Zorgnet-Icuro nominated (17 Mar. 2017) the rooming-in operation at Sint-Annendael Diest as the 'care story of the year'. Reference is made in both documents to: Kris Pieters, Dominik Renson and Wim Simons, 'Primeur binnen de GGZ: Rooming In', *Similes* 158 (Dec. 2016), 8-10. In the 'Grote Psychiatrierapport' of *De Morgen*, the LSR was described under the heading 'Zo kan het ook' (An alternative is possible); see Femke Van Garderen, 'In Diest mag je man mee in afzondering' (In Diest your husband can join you in the seclusion room), *De Morgen*, 24 Feb. 2017.

10. Gideon Boie, 'De geniale mislukking van de prikkelarme kamer', *Psyche* 30, no. 1 (Mar. 2018), 20-21.
11. Interview by Joris Hendrickx with chief psychiatrist Wim Simons and general director Koen De Meester, 'Geestelijke gezondheidszorg zet voluit in op welzijn en comfort', *Media Planet*, Dec. 2016.
12. Rancière, *The Ignorant Schoolmaster*.
13. Petrescu, 'Losing Control, Keeping Desire'. Speaks, 'Design Intelligence'.
14. Žižek, *The Plague of Fantasies*, 113.
15. Žižek, 'Why Are Laibach and NSK not Fascists?'.
16. Liza Fior, 'The Art of Public Action', lecture in the series 'Common Grounds' organized by the KU Leuven Faculty of Architecture at Novanoïs, Schaarbeek, 17 Feb. 2014.
17. Slavoj Žižek, *The Ticklish Subject*, 204.
18. Tom van Mierlo, Frits Bovenberg, Yolande Voskes and Niels Mulder, eds., *Werkboek HIC: High en intensive care in de psychiatrie* (Utrecht: De Tijdstroom, 2013).
19. Van Mierlo, *Werkboek HIC*, 112-35.
20. Doina Petrescu, 'Losing Control, Keeping Desire'.
21. Roose, 'Design Dialogue and Co-Authorship'.
22. Latour, *Down to Earth*, 33-37.
23. Hofmann, *Architecture Is Participation*, 22-41. Gideon Boie, 'Relational Architecture: Experiences from the Psychiatric Field', in *Urban Living Labs for Public Space: a New Generation of Planning? Proceedings of the Incubators Conference*, ed. Johan Verbeke (Brussels: KU Leuven, 2017), 49-57.
24. Speaks, 'Design Intelligence'.
25. Loeckx, *Stadsvernieuwingsprojecten In Vlaanderen*.
26. Gideon Boie, 'Flemish Architectural Culture for Beginners'.
27. See the report of the sofa-talk with Joachim De Clerck about the role of AWB in the redevelopment of the Northern Quarter in Brussels: Gideon Boie, 'The future is (not) here', in *WTC Tower Teachings* (Brussels: KU Leuven Faculty of Architecture, 2019), 178-80.
28. Roeland Dudal, lecture on the practice of AWB in the framework of the elective master's course Architecture and Activism at the Faculty of Architecture KU Leuven, 15 Apr. 2016.
29. Slavoj Žižek, 'Only Autistic Children Can Save Us', in *A Left that Dares to Speak Its Name* (Cambridge: Polity, 2020), 74-93.
30. Gideon Boie, 'Here Comes the Architect-Entrepreneur', *A+ Architecture in Belgium* 287 (Dec. 2020-Jan. 2021), 84-87.
31. Lacan, 'The Mirror Stage'.
32. Laderman Ukeles, *Manifesto! Maintenance – Proposal for an Exhibition*.
33. Gideon Boie and Fie Vandamme, 'Architectuur zonder dwang: drie ontwerpuitdagingen' in *Psyche* 29, no. 3 (Sep. 2017), 20-21. The text is based on the lecture presented at the study day 'Jeugdhulpverlening zonder dwang: op zoek naar alternatieven voor eenzame opsluiting' (Youth care without coercion: In search of alternatives to solitary seclusion) organized by Kollectief Zonder Dwang in the Flemish Parliament (5 May 2017).
34. Van Mierlo, *Werkboek HIC*.

Make Things Public

Chapter 12

The political dimension of art, architecture and urban planning is an interesting and critical research topic. It has even been BAVO's tag line ever since the start of BAVO as a critical writing collective. However, this political dimension doesn't automatically translate into critical work. Libraries are filled with books and articles full of critical content; critically intervening in a debate is quite another job. In the previous chapters, I have extensively reported on how criticism depends on determination to make sure that the message reaches its target. A lesson learned from my engagement in citizen movements in Brussels is even worse: one can write a piece with a critical message about road safety, urban change, the right to the city and much more, find that everybody immediately adheres to the message and still end up with the awkward feeling that nothing ever really changes. This shows how critical content needs to be complemented, even supplemented by embodied action in order to function as an instigator for moments of change. In the following chapter, I will discuss my different engagements in citizen movements in Brussels such as 1030/0, Heroes for Zero and Filter Café Filtré. Including the work as part of urban activism and teaching assignments in this book doesn't mean that I want to claim it as part of my oeuvre; on the contrary, I want to show how public debate, political engagement and civil action for road safety also inspired my work as a critic in the field of architecture while enriching my academic and professional knowledge. Activism has been a research interest of BAVO's from the beginning, starting with activism in the arts in relation to urban activism; in fact, the study of inspiring practices by the Yes Men and Laibach led me to experiment with the strategy of overidentification in the work of architecture criticism. Later, the topic shifted to the search for the holy grail of activist architecture as part of the joint teaching assignment at the KU Leuven Faculty of Architecture with Lieven De Cauter. A defining moment in my interest in activism was the road accident involving my children in the municipality of Schaarbeek, where we live, on Monday 15 January 2015. The accident was certainly a traumatic event, but it also strengthened me to pull out all stops when it comes to road safety in Brussels, especially in the context of citizen movement 1030/0, founded in November 2017, and put academic and professional knowledge on urban politics, cultural activism and more to use in the fight for the good cause. Under the Covid regime, the struggle for road safety was brought to greater magnitude in seizing the sanitary measures as a window to redesign the city, starting with the streets in the first place. Dealing with sanitary politics from a strictly spatial perspective was a hyperidealist gesture of overidentification, thinking through half-baked measures in the perspective of the years-old dream for a redistribution of public space. The different engagements within citizen movements have been influencing my work of criticism in the field of architecture, looking for ways to discuss design issues as key to the wider debate on urban politics and thus practise architecture criticism as part of the public debate.

From the Penitentiary to the City

A line of flight in my work as architecture critic is situated in the involvement within citizen movements in Brussels, in the first place the struggle for road safety by the 1030/0 action group and its supporting non-profit association Heroes for Zero. The issue of road safety took a lot of interest and energy after being the victim of a road accident with my children on our daily walk from primary school to home. It happened on the pedestrian crossing near the Heliotropen tram stop on Boulevard Lambermont, on Monday 15 January 2015, around 5:30 in the afternoon.[1] My 5-year-old son was hospitalized in intensive care at the Queen Fabiola children's university hospital with several serious injuries. Later in the evening, the Flemish television station VTM announced live on the news that Boulevard Lambermont was closed as part of the anti-terrorism operation in Verviers, which happened that same afternoon, but the journalist forgot that local inhabitants of Schaarbeek had been suffering another sort of terror for decades. Actually, the hit-and-run happened while crossing an urban motorway with three lanes in each direction cutting through a residential area. The monstruous boulevard is part of the Greater Ring, one of those relics of the thing that is professionally known as Brusselization, the mad period of blind demolition and wild development of business districts connected by urban motorways.[2] The development was part of the modernization of the city happening throughout the twentieth century and intensified under the drive to improve the city's competitive position; and the business climate of Brussels as wannabe EU capital made it worse. To this day, Brussels is trying to recover from what Félix Guattari called the 'disastrous legacy of self-congratulatory modern town planning'. He mentioned it as a key question for ecosophy in the same line with racism, phallocentrism and liberation of the artistic expression from market forces.[3] Knowledge of urban politics was suddenly touching my everyday life, even my household, and forcing me to do same with my knowledge of urban activism.

In the aftermath of the accident, I found myself spontaneously doing exactly the same things as in critical interventions by BAVO: research the different stakes by directly reaching out to politicians and publishing the outcomes. The engagement was fuelled by the traumatic event, certainly, but perhaps even more by indignation over the utter passivity following attempts to reach out to the secretaries of state and local aldermen.[4] Again, I was confronted with inherent criticism among the persons responsible for the public space in Brussels: of course the politicians felt pity as regards the accident and, clearly, they were well aware of the dangerous situation on that specific boulevard, they had a full list of improvements awaiting implementation, but there was always a good excuse as to why the public road infrastructure wouldn't change soon. In my case, the only thing that did change at the crime scene was the rhythm of the traffic light, giving pedestrians an extra five seconds to cross *outside* peak hours, the very time when children are supposed to be in school.[5] A bit later, the newspapers announced that more than one third of the ninety-five fixed speed cameras on the regional road hadn't been operating for more than a decade, including the one on the pedestrian crossing at Boulevard Lambermont.[6]

The personal fight reached another level after the citizen movement 1030/0 was founded in November 2017; the name refers to the zip code of the Brussels municipality of Schaarbeek added with the EU's Vision Zero ambition to reach zero traffic fatalities in road transport by 2050. Following the deadly car accident with journalist Stephanie Verbraekel on Chaussée de Haecht in Schaarbeek, the movement formed spontaneously and demanded that the local government immediately implement a 30 km/h maximum speed zone.[7] The movement called upon inhabitants to come and block the main artery for a commemoration of the road victim and thus highlight the urgency and determination. The demand was swiftly followed by the local council installing the speed limit across territory of the municipality, no longer awaiting the regional policy that promised a lowering of speed limits in the future. In fact, the 30 km/h maximum speed zone was an old idea that had been floating in the air for years, while the different government levels where awaiting each other. Typically, the regional government needs confirmation from the different municipalities while the municipalities wait for the region to take the initiative, when not frustrating any initiative. The point is that the action on the street by a spontaneous movement of citizens gave a final push; call it an act of overidentification with the official Vision Zero policy line and also the readymade plan for the general speed limit. Certainly, my own indignation was uplifted once part of common action, but the magic is that my professional interest in urban politics, democracy, cultural activism and strategies of overidentification was suddenly turning extremely real and practical.[8]

The 1030/0 movement started responding to every new car accident with unannounced street blockades, e.g. organizing a human chain at the Heliotropen pedestrian crossing on Boulevard Lambermont, a lie-in at the intersection of Chaussée d'Helmet and Rue de Waelhem, dance parties at the junction of Rue Kessels and Avenue Rogier, and other main roads.[9] Although the actions were certainly provocative, the atmosphere was never oppositional; on the contrary, they were organized as commemorations open to everyone, including to politicians from all parties. Politics would certainly destroy the common action, especially when it comes to party affiliation. This was a lesson I often heard in class from Lieven De Cauter – on politics and religion, in fact. Although the apolitical nature of the actions is key, the blockades were extremely political in the sense that the actions were designed to push the issue of road safety. The actions happened each time without asking for permission, only notifying the authorities and police in advance about the intention, and the media of course. The human chain at Boulevard Lambermont followed the rhythm of the green light, standing shoulder to shoulder and holding stop signs to allow children to safely cross on their way to school. The lie-in at the intersection of Chaussée d'Helmet and Rue de Waelhem, held at peak hour in the morning, was about parents and children passengers lying wounded on the asphalt; passengers from the halted tram came out and joined the action. In the case of the dance party at the intersection of Rue Kessels, mothers and children came out of their houses to join, following the party all the way to Avenue Rogier; remarkably, these locals were mostly of foreign background, disproving the Brussels cliché that road safety is just a bourgeois-bohemian 'bobo' thing. Although the element of civil disobedience was certainly key in the success and joy, the enthusiasm was guaranteed insofar as the action is over-obedient to the letter of the law and holding high the evident moral principles of safety for active road users, children in the first place. The act of civil disobedience breaks the law in an explicitly non-violent way to protest unjust politics, amend the law, alter political decisions, just as for David Thoreau it was a duty to refuse to pay his taxes to protest war and slavery.[10]

The action, however, extends from the street into virtual reality, just as Judith Butler has argued about the dynamic of urban and virtual protest in the Tahrir uprising, part of the Arab Spring.[11] The idea was to put political pressure by flooding the newspapers with mediagenic actions of civil disobedience. The spontaneous refusal to go with the flow, even for a short moment, speaks to the imagination, creates an immediate crisis of the urban system, causing huge traffic jams and chain effects in public transport. The courage needed to block a street – first with human chains, later using the lie-ins and dance party – is of immense appeal to the popular imagination. Media coverage of the street blockade is perhaps even more important than the actual blockade, since the media functions as an amplifier for the action in the street, not only spreading the message, but also delegitimizing the authorities, industries and other stakeholders. No wonder the movement spread across the Brussels region, creating local chapters in other municipalities (1082/0, 1210/0, 1080/0, etc.) as well as founding in 2020 the supporting association Heroes for Zero Brussels. The battle of images has always been a vital part of political activism. The best historical reference is perhaps the Civil Right Movements in the 1960s. Best known is the action of Rosa Parks, who got arrested after refusing to sit at the back of the bus, herewith showing in an embodied action how the formal equality of rights wasn't respected in Montgomery, Alabama, and igniting the marches led by Martin Luther King Jr. The famous sit-ins at local lunch bars were partly staged acts, well prepared and disciplined, performed in order to obtain the visual documentation of the everyday abuse and insults African Americans had to endure and have it published in the main papers.[12] A later example is the uprising at Tahrir Square, part of the Arab Spring in 2011, especially the moment, described by Judith Butler, when the fight for control of the roundabout extended into the fight for control of social media.[13]

The third element in the actions by 1030/0 is advocacy and diplomacy, actively reaching out to state secretaries, mayors and aldermen, at official meetings and through personal contact. Most of these activities happen evidently behind the scenes. Still, the public drama of bodies making alliances in the street paves the way for the advocacy, not just in the idea of the radical flank theory where wild actions by radicals open the door for more moderate approaches, but even more efficiently through the so-called dilemma action design.[14] The blockades for street safety present the authorities with a response dilemma, conceptualized by Hallam as follows: the authorities can negate the activists or support them, but in either case they lose the game.[15] In negating the acts of civil disobedience by the 1030/0 movement, the authorities would be admitting that they don't care about road safety policies and would be showing their unwillingness to assume political responsibility on the issue. In supporting the same actions, the authorities would be admitting they were falling short in realizing the ambitions for road safety, part of EU policy, equally showing themselves as politically irresponsible subjects. The movement thus cornered the regional and local governments to use their political power for an active policy on road safety, going beyond the obligatory awareness-raising campaigns and actively adapting road infrastructure, increase police control, regulate automobile industry, etc.

The presentation of actions by 1030/0 in a book on my professional work as critic is dangerous, since the actions are far from an individual achievement and any success is relative to the engagement of the commons. Admittedly, in my modest engagement within the citizen movement, I often practised tactics that were developed as part of my scholarly work, finding it an academic and professional duty to put knowledge into action as part of the struggle for road safety in my own living environment. Strategies of overidentification, politics of commoning, pedagogics of ignorance, and other tactics I experimented with in the work described in the above chapters proved to be very useful weapons in the fight for road safety. The tactic to open the debate with op-eds in the newspaper *De Standaard* was certainly part of the repertoire. I must say the newspaper was even more receptive when it comes to road safety compared to the issues of the architecture of psychiatry and detention. In the op-eds I adopted the role of commentator, using my academic and professional knowledge to confirm the action or add extra flavour to the main report in the newspaper. In some cases, the impact of the op-ed was to turn the role of critical commentator into that of instigator, such as the article 'Inspraak is geen technisch detail' (Participation is no technical detail) blaming the narrow, technocratic definition of participation in the production of the new regional mobility plan GoodMove.[16] In response, Brussels State Secretary for Mobility Elke Van den Brandt invited different civil organizations to hold a citizen panel within the official participation process. Instead, the joint proposal of Heroes for Zero, BRAL Citizen Action and Filter Café Filtré was a parallel process that could function as a public shadow to the official participation procedure and an open invitation to discuss road safety outside boardrooms. The result was L' Autre Atelier/Het Andere Atelier, a multi-year programme organizing field surveys of so-called black-spots, lectures on best practices, debates on burning road issues and publishing the results – the honour goes to other forces, but the reader will surely recognize the format from previous chapters.[17]

The 1.5 m Paradox

The activism for road safety in Brussels was relaunched on a greater scale in the conjuncture of sanitary politics during the Covid pandemic and the ensuing debate on the redistribution of public space. The first lockdown was a shock in many ways, forcing individual citizens not only to adapt to the quarantine rules limiting our freedom of movement and reorganizing our habits in terms of living and work, but also to find other ways to continue activism and keep up pressure on the urgent issue of road safety. Especially, the lying-down of bodies in the streets – a condition for politics to happen, following the argument of Judith Butler – was simply no longer allowed under Covid and we estimated that civil disobedience on this point would severely backfire on a good cause.[18] In 1030/0 there was an ongoing discussion on Avenue Ambassador Van Vollenhoven, an avenue without addresses that crosses Josaphat Park and is mainly used as a parking place and shortcut.[19] The avenue was a case in point for the dubious road politics in the municipality of Schaarbeek as the status had changed a few times in recent years, swinging from open to closed for cars and back, creating dangerous situations if only because of the unpredictability. The latest move by the municipality was to reopen the avenue for car traffic, cynically at the start of the school year. The 1030/0 movement planned actions, but these were suspended in the first lockdown for fear that any gathering in the public space would backfire on the movement.

Nevertheless, the Covid measures helped in the fight for road safety in Brussels, since the spatial order suddenly appeared key to keeping people safe and securing national health during the raging pandemic. On the one hand, there was the command that people should stay home. In Belgium, Minister of Health Maggie De Block, herself a physician, famously said, in a slight dialect: 'Blijf in uw kot!' (Stay in your shack!). On the other hand, the use of public space was limited to strict necessity: 'outings ought to be fraught with purpose and practicality' – as if Mr Banks was popping in and out of *Mary Poppins* – and strictly following the rules of social distancing. The new command of social distancing was perhaps the most paradoxical, as the rule to keep clear from each other by at least 1.50 m certainly had good reason but was simply impossible as sidewalks are often not even that wide in Brussels or any other city in Belgium. The obvious question was how it was possible for the government to command people to keep clear from each other by 1.50 m – even threatening them with fines – while the actual street layout didn't even allow for that social distance on the pavement. Guess what, unsurprisingly: in the first weeks of the pandemic, local politicians appeared not at all willing to make space so that social distancing could happen. This showed the obscene logic of Covid politics: while the authorities where forcing clinics to rearrange bed capacity in the blink of an eye, supermarkets to organize different flows of clients, even households to accommodate online work and school stations at home, the public space was left as if nothing had happened. Covid politics was using all sorts of emergency rulings to interfere with social organization, even mobilizing the police to enforce the sanitary measures in organizing private parties in back gardens; at same time, it was giving up on the political task of reorganizing the elementary particle of the city: the street.

Exactly one month after the start of the first lockdown, I published the article 'De stad hertekenen, nu kan het' (Now's the time to redesign the city) in the newspaper *De Standaard*, presenting the 1.5 m paradox and connecting this with the old dream for a redistribution of public space.[20] The article was certainly not my personal invention, it was part of the reflection we had in 1030/0 on how to fight for road safety during the Covid regime and written after a discussion by phone with Annekatrien Verdickt of Filter Café Filtré. In the same period also, urban planner Maarten Van Acker published a column in the *Gazet van Antwerpen* presenting the city as what he called a spatial vaccine, turning the pending fear for the city as a place of contamination into a welcoming benefit in times of pandemics.[21] You can call it a return of the repressed: the centuries-old fight against car-oriented politics in Brussels – again part of the complex known as *Brussellization* – reappeared with a vengeance as part of the biopolitical complex under Covid, positively understood in the conception of Lieven De Cauter, now becoming an issue of life and death, something politicians could no longer dodge.[22] The pandemic shed light not only on the need to redistribute public space, but also on the usual political passivity on the issue, road infrastructure always having been just a technical affair, not a key political topic. Politicians have never been shy about considering traffic flow more important than road safety; there was simply no alternative. In contrast, the design of squares and parks has always been of high political interest, I guess part of the principle of compensation mentioned by Michel Foucault in his discussion of heterotopias.[23] While narrowing down the definition of public space to squares and parks, the layout of streets remains part the urban unconscious, everybody complains about it, but it is what it is – in Brussels, maintenance budgets typically make that streets are renovated *à l'identique*, it doesn't require the political hassle of building permits. Imagine the miracle during the Covid regime: suddenly, with the new sanitary measure of social distancing, the street had become a key domain in watching over the health of the social body by regulating the movement of people.

The initial hesitation and reluctance regarding street actions present in the citizen movements during the first lockdown appeared to be superfluous and unnecessary. No need to be Covid-sceptic to see through the inherent contradictions supporting the urban politics of the pandemic. In the Covid regime it was enough to highlight the many inherent contradictions of the sanitary politics, which were present in almost any new spatial directive and political statement to defend these. Remember the call of Prime Minister Sophie Wilmès, when announcing the new directive for the famous lifting of the first lockdown, as she called on people to avoid public transport and use their private means of transport. In response, Jens Aerts, Annekatrien Verdickt and I published the article 'Naar de exit zonder auto' (Towards the exit without a car), arguing that the use of private cars would put even more stress on cities and push people on ridiculously narrow pavements.²⁴ In the article we called on the national security council to take up the spatial question. The argument was an act of hyper-idealism insofar as it didn't want to cast doubt over Covid measures, as Covid sceptics did (one of them being Giorgio Agamben), but demanded that the sanitary measures be more rigorous, social and just.²⁵ The article was published simultaneously in three languages by *De Standaard*, *Le Soir* and *The Bulletin* and signed by all present and former Flemish, Brussels and Walloon Government Architects and many figures active in academia and civil society.

Remember also the low level of enthusiasm among the municipalities of Brussels to free parking places in streets and make space for waiting lines at shop entrances or turn lanes for cars into cycle lanes – the famous Covid cycle lanes in Brussels were only created on regional roads and even in those cases, local authorities often showed much resistance. Symptomatically, the use of parking places as terraces for bars and restaurants was first opposed by local authorities. For example, the proposal by citizen collective Imagine Colignon, supported by local commerce, to organize outdoor bars on the square in front of the town hall, actually used as huge parking lot, was professionally smothered by the municipality, which imposed an extra financial fee on the terraces and then argued there was little interest among bar owners.²⁶ Later, when the Covid terraces effectively became a huge success in cities all over the world, the local authorities wanted to keep the terraces on parking places as an exceptional measure only, demanding the terraces be dismantled in winter, arguing people wouldn't use the outdoor facility in harsh weather conditions. When epidemiologist Pierre Van Damme pleaded in favour of winter terraces in a prime-time news show on national television (for God's sake, he said), Annekatrien Verdickt and I wrote an article to shame the politicians heroically fighting temporary Covid measures.²⁷ The success of the Summer Streets organized by Filter Café Filtré was used to argue how the redesign of the Covid city can't be discussed in terms of mobility alone, but should integrate social welfare, cultural exchange, youth activities and more, even making it an issue of life and death. The criticism by weak-hearted politicians opposed to changing one of the five one-directional car lanes on Rue de la Loi into a Covid cycle lane, even crying a river over the city being blockaded, shows that resistance had nothing to do with the pandemic, but more with the primitive ideological resistance against any redistribution of public space.²⁸ The banning of cars from Bois de la Cambre, the green lung in the south of Brussels used as an easy highway entry, was even counteracted through court procedures by the local mayor of Uccle. Unsurprisingly, he won the case and managed to reopen one side of the park for cars.²⁹

Another typical spatial issue that surfaced during the Covid period was the mayor of Schaarbeek prohibiting a family in Rue

Godefroid Devreese from using the parking space in front of their house as a community garden, baptised 'Citizen Garden', even though the family had no car and the presence of the garage made it legally impossible for the neighbourhood to use the spot for parking. The case made the news after the citizen refused to compromise and put the garden on two wheels, using a vaguely known exception in the law for carts.[30] Registered letters by the municipality demanding the removal of the garden and later imposing huge fines were put aside and answered with extensive argumentation, the whole conversation taking place on a special Twitter account. The game continued when the local administration removed the garden on the sly and brought it to the waste disposal site – where the garden was picked up again by loyal supporters and brought home in a strange sort of Covid procession.[31] The surrealist fate of the Citizen Garden was symptomatic of the unwillingness of the Schaarbeek authorities to change their car-oriented politics, even in a pandemic. Still, the stakes of the garden/cart also touched upon the brave measures by regional Minister for Mobility Elke van den Brandt who announced the change of car lanes into cycle lanes and her call to local governments to allow car-free streets, at least to reduce car traffic in neighbourhoods – it was a seed falling on rocky soil. The drama around the garden/cart also shows the Achilles heel of tactical urbanism that became popular under Covid, since any temporary intervention depends on ad hoc political agreements and hocus-pocus judicial interpretations, meaning that any installation may disappear, depending on the mood of the day.

The beauty of the Covid regime – in retrospect – is the extreme transparency of the inherent paradoxes underpinning the sanitary measures; these were discussed endlessly in the media and every time further breaking down into additional issues. The main spatial issue of the Covid regime was public space, but soon it started to trickle down into the most diverse aspects of social life, spreading even into the intimate parts, effectively urging us to redesign the city as a whole. The suspension of everyday life in the Covid regime, the thing Lieven De Cauter had baptised 'corona limbo', was especially tangible in the great seclusion of elderly care homes.[32] In the sanitary crisis, the individual resident no longer counted for a while, the focus being on the health of the whole body, that of the elderly care home as a whole. Residents had to stay inside, visitors outside. Although visits weren't necessarily the main cause of contamination, the goal was to exclude at least one risk factor. The staff could just as easily bring the virus inside the elderly home, but the idea was to control the movements of visitors with intensive registration. The logic of the 'beddenhuis' (bed houses) was detected in our work in psychiatry (Chapter 10), ground plans of facilities literally translating the calculating unit in the world of care, but this appeared key in understanding the awful fate of elderly care homes in the Covid regime.[33] This shows how the separation of generations was not only a sanitary measure during the crisis, it was already present before, although less visible and problematic. No wonder that during lockdown, things shifted quickly and the elderly care home effectively got detached from reality, the facility being reduced to its bed function. Another spatial discontent in the Covid regime was present in the educational complex; so-called Zoom education was realizing the fantasy of moral education in the panopticon-like auditorium in the prison of Fresnes; the image was used by Michel Foucault in his book on discipline and punishment, suggesting a direct knowledge transfer from teacher to pupils sitting in what look like vertical coffins.[34] And still the paradox is that schools weren't closed because the school is the prime site of contamination, schools could be organized safely, the point was that for sanitary reasons it was better to turn to Zoom education to shut down the social dynamic generated by schools.[35] Not to forget the Covid experience realizing the Playboy fantasy of Hugh Hefner living and working from his bed, an argument developed by Beatriz Colomina – it turned out to be an agony rather than a pleasure.[36]

Reporting From the Front Door

The urban activism in Brussels before and under Covid made it possible to put academic and professional knowledge into action, but the reverse also happened: the fight for the redistribution of public space had a serious backflow into the academic and professional work, in the first place teaching me how even the most precise, justified and urgent criticism needs embodiment in order to start operating in politics. Let me take you back to Avenue Ambassador Van Vollenhoven, the street without addresses that runs through Parc Josaphat in Schaarbeek and is mainly used as a parking lot and shortcut. Although the protest was suspended in the first lockdown period, the discussions reappeared at the end of the first Covid year, December 2020, when it appeared that the municipality had stubbornly consolidated the use of the park avenue as a public car park. The new parking signs were painted on the asphalt without public notice. Clearly, the installation was a political compromise as the street was opened only halfway for cars, blocking through-traffic, but still maintaining the parking places in half the street. Opening the street for cars was bad, but the compromise was worse, since cars would only be able to leave the street by making a U-turn halfway and slaloming back. Indignation prompted the citizen movement 1030/0 to intervene with a stealth action that closed the road for cars and used the parking signs to paint children's games on the asphalt, such as a hopscotch, labyrinth, running track and more. In defence of the act of civil disobedience, the citizen movement spun the compromised situation by saying that children's games should never be mistaken for a parking place, shifting the disobedience to the side of the authorities and showing how the municipality was violating its ambitions on road safety.[37] The second lockdown didn't prevent people from showing up in support of the action in relatively large numbers. Only a few days after the protest action, Avenue Ambassador Van Vollenhoven was made permanently car-free and was open for children to play.

A striking element in the whole history of Avenue Van Vollenhoven was the role of Alderwoman Adelheid Byttebier, part of the progressive party Groen, who was interviewed at the site of the action by local television news channel BRUZZ.[38] The alderwoman claimed that, although personally in favour of a car-free park, she was obliged to consider the high demand for parking places in the area. Clearly, the alderwoman was split between her convictions as a politician of the green party Groen and her loyalty to the decisions made in the council, creating the impossible Antigone-like dilemma so typical for politicians in positions of power. More important is the lesson in activism: the split discourse of the alderwoman shows how advocacy for a car-free vision of parks in populated areas, as mobility researcher Jesse Pappers – also active in 1030/0 – did in the newspaper, is justified and at the same time far from enough.[39] The problem is that the alderwoman would certainly be the first to endorse the wonderful vision, and this was my response in the same newspaper a few days later.[40] The point is that it took civil disobedience to reveal the local authorities as part of the problem. The so-called high demand for parking places in a street without addresses was only possible thanks to the parking policies of the municipality keeping the demand artificially high, not only by selling parking permits for next to nothing, even for the second car per household, but also distributing more permits than there were places actually available. The vision of car-free parks in Brussels remains a beautiful dream for the future, moreover one easy to adopt, as long as we don't touch the entire policy infrastructure that prioritizes the car as 'King of the Road'. Schaarbeek's car-oriented policies were kept untouched even after they had heroically declared a climate urgency a year earlier. In such a complex and contradictory situation, criticism only becomes operative after it unfolds the full envelope of political moments defined by Judith Butler, i.e. allied action on the street, appearance of the body, turning the street into the object of the struggle, transposition of the fight to media platforms, etc.[41] The Van Vollenhoven action enabled us even to go beyond the typical oppositional logic of pro vs contra cars and to turn the daily strategic discussions about

road safety in the WhatsApp groups of 1030/0 into a public debate.
Another crucial element in the entanglement of architecture criticism and activism for road safety in Brussels was the possibility to fight the case as a quasi-professional affair, not reducing the issue to a personal affair, but on the contrary advocating the EU's Vision Zero ambition in what you could call an act of hyper-idealism. In my engagement within 1030/0, I usually presented myself as a researcher at the KU Leuven Faculty of Architecture, avoiding the personal traumatic history from taking over the debate. The standard trick of depoliticization is fetishization, argues Slavoj Žižek, it reduces the demand of a certain protest movement as something personal that can be answered as such, while refusing to see how the specific demand may function as a metaphor for a much bigger wrong in the system. Žižek's definition of politics does exactly the opposite when he writes: 'This is politics proper: the moment in which a particular demand is not simply part of the negotiation of interests but aims at something more and starts to function as the metaphoric condensation of the global restructuring of the entire social space.'[42] In that sense, we can describe the spontaneous actions of 1030/0 as the politicization of individual road accidents in Schaarbeek, presenting these as so many calls to make streets safer for active road users, not just the one street of the crime scene, but as part of a more general redistribution of public space and redesign of the city as a whole. On this point, the definition of civil disobedience might be somewhat misleading, since the street actions might violate the traffic code and parking regulations, but still comply with other laws and regulatory policies, such as the European Zero Vision guideline on road safety.

The reverse move was equally important when it comes to countering depoliticization, namely activism bringing academic research to a higher level by giving flesh and bones to the abstract theoretical knowledge that floats in the air of the university building. Facing the everyday issue of road safety in Brussels and the passivity of even the most progressive politicians, I have often wondered: Where have all the theorists gone? Where are the historians of *Brusselization* when you need them? The political passivity that haunts urban development in Brussels is nothing new and not even a public secret, it is common knowledge inscribed in many a history book. How brave to critically reconstruct detailed histories, theorize upon them with peers in annual symposia and next hide all that information the moment you go out the front door. You could call it academic fetishization in line with Žižek's definition mentioned earlier: one knows all the juicy details of urban malpractices and yet one keeps quiet when history repeats itself. The same goes for professional practice obsessed by the agency of architecture and that even devoted the whole Venice Architecture Biennale 2016 to 'reports from the front' (the main theme) and next forgetting about all that design intelligence in the daily fight on the way to school with the children.⁴³

Losing What Deserves to Be Lost

The repression of academic and professional knowledge in relation to everyday politics is part of a larger fetishization of architecture culture, the role of architecture in political struggles being discussed but kept within the safe walls of an architecture biennial; mimicking the logic of the white cube, one highlights the individual creativity of the maker (never mind the project definition by the commissioner), compares work within the boundaries of the oeuvre (forget about the urgency that gave rise to it), etc. The cynical logic of 'we know very well, but nonetheless' makes it possible to both critically analyse the problems *and* continue operating in the world as we know it.⁴⁴ Critical knowledge doesn't necessarily lead to critical engagement in architecture, the latter depending more on moral indignation and the personal involvement and political courage that responds to it.⁴⁵ The case of Avenue Van Vollenhoven functioned for many as the unique moment when indignation shortcircuited with politicization: people were pulled out onto the street, even while in lockdown, mobilizing their knowledge in a creative way and presenting their particular desire as symbol for the redesign of the city as a whole. The public character of urban activism stands in sharp contrast to the usual secretive logic of architecture criticism; it usually remains well hidden in eloquently written papers published in high-profile journals functioning as a gremial veil for a debate that arrives much too late to answer the urgencies at stake, if it ever reaches the design practice at all. In that specific sense, the presence of critical architecture culture is a problem, but for another reason than suggested by Christophe Van Gerrewey in an update of Geert Bekaert's famous dictum, it engages in the most radical statements not without first evacuating the slightest possibility of becoming contemporary to design practice.⁴⁶

Symptomatic for the state of criticism in Flanders is the fact that on the few occasions that leading figures in architecture culture did discuss architecture as part of the public debate, the topic was only about the choice of architect in a certain competition. Recently, there were two heated moments in the written press. In Chapter 1 we already referred to the critique of the Design Museum competition by Christophe Van Gerrewey, who regretted the choice of the dullest design over his favourite. Another heated moment concerned the shortlist of international offices only in the Open Call design competition for the Flemish Opera in Ghent; it was discussed by Sofie De Caigny, director of the VAi.⁴⁷ Her defence of the local scene of architects against international companies found support in an article by architecture critic Marc Dubois but got a furious response from Flemish Government Architect Leo Van Broeck. He stressed that only quality matters in design competitions by the Government Architect and explained how the engagement of international offices has always benefited the local architectural scene.[48] The different position in the debate made sense, but my point is that the debate was about the choice of architect, not about the definition of architecture quality and what it means for the Opera in this case. Flemish architecture culture would be blessed if criticism didn't spend so much time discussing the selection of architect-friends for this or that commission, but would also remember the Benjaminian logic and dare look into the uncanny shadow of barbarism that accompanies the self-proclaimed golden generation.[49]

The debate about the Beer Temple in the former Brussels Stock Exchange, a building that occupies a prominent place in the heart of the city, shows how criticism that does discuss fundamental design choices, not just the choice of architect, meets immediate resistance. My article 'Bier, wafels en architectuur' (Beer, waffles and architecture) published in the *BRUZZ* newspaper was an act of friendly fire on the work of Robbrecht en Daem Architecten. It discussed the work as key in the makeover of the city centre as a terrain for tourist attractions and festivals.[50] The debate was launched in tandem with Lieven De Cauter in an attempt to steer away from the petition to stop the Beer Temple project and explicitly address the political dimension of the architecture project. Lieven De Cauter's article 'Biertempel? Over our dead bodies!' defended the use of the building, the steps in particular, as a platform for political manifestations.[51] The critical interventions were immediately answered in an article by Flemish Culture Minister Sven Gatz and later also Brussels Government Architect Kristiaan Borret; logically, they defended the choices made.[52] Interestingly, the criticism was also answered by loud resistance in the community of architects who were closing ranks in defence of the Beer Temple as a sublime work by renowned office Robbrecht en Daem architecten. 'I get the measles from this toxic cocktail of cultural-political correctness and from the way in which self-proclaimed high culture looks down on so-called low culture', wrote Flemish Government Architect Leo Van Broeck on social media.[53] 'Then put on your penance, Flagellants, this petition is more an act of self-flagellation than a constructive debate', wrote architecture critic Koen Van Synghel.[54] Criticism of the Beer Temple was most inappropriate now that for the first time a quality architect was at work on an important building in Brussels, architecture critic Marc Dubois argued in a private message.

Critical intervention must face countercriticism as it provides the anchor points to work through what Judith Butler calls the passionate attachments towards the sublime thing and, following the paraphrasing of her work by Slavoj Žižek, try to 'undermine the most fundamental level of subjection'.[55] The loud resistance was directly addressed in follow-up articles in which we criticized how the professional reflex to defend the architect is addictive insofar as it will accept everything in return for architectural quality – beer and architecture match well on that point.[56] It was only a year and a half later that Brussels Government Architect Kristiaan Borret admitted that the criticism of the Beer Temple did have a positive effect indeed, since the final advice from the expert committee, closing the period of public inquiry as part of the request for an urban building permit, officially asked for the beer theme to be limited to the upper levels of the building. The statement about the programme in an advice was exceptional and unique in its sort, said Borret, since the urban planning department usually limits its verdict to the composition of the façade, the construction of the pavement, the number of parking spaces, etc.[57] The paradoxical conclusion is that the increased ambition in the renovation of a certain building was only possible by putting at risk what is most dear to us, in this case the high quality design by Robbrecht en Daem architecten. The architecture-lover in me recognizes that the oeuvre of Robbrecht en Daem architecten is outstanding; still, satisfying a desire should be no reason to sell the soul of architecture in an urban marketing scheme.[58]

The gesture of putting at risk the thing dear to us follows the Žižekian formula of the ethical-political act as the willingness to give up the object of desire in order to avoid it becoming the subject of shadowy power games and, on the contrary, to preserve its sublime status. Žižek wrote about the disputed status of Jerusalem in the context of the Middle East conflict: 'For both Arabs and Jews, [the true ethical-political act] would consist in the gesture of renouncing (political) control of Jerusalem – that is, of endorsing the transformation of the Old Town of Jerusalem into an extra-statal place of religious worship controlled by some neutral international force. [...] By renouncing political control of Jerusalem, they would, in effect, be renouncing nothing – they would be *gaining* the elevation of Jerusalem into a genuinely extra-political, sacred site. What they would lose is, precisely and only, what already, in itself deserves to be lost: the reduction of religion to a bargaining chip in political power politics.'[59] The same holds for the golden generation of Flemish architecture culture. Going along uncritically with the questionable programme of the Beer Temple as a strategy to save Robbrecht en Daem architecten's sublime design was perhaps the worst form of self-flagellation, i.e. the betrayal of the canon of contemporary architecture, in particular Michael Sorkin's criticism of the inner-city theme park and post-politics as the architectural logic of capitalism.[60] Putting the object of desire at risk made it possible to undermine the political machination and lose, or at least reduce, the use of architecture quality as a tourist trap as much as possible.

Notes
1. GDC, 'Vijfjarige jongen zwaargewond na ongeval met vluchtmisdrijf', *BRUZZ* (16 Jan. 2015). Steven Van Garsse, 'Ongeval op Lambermontlaan roept vragen op', *Brussel Deze Week* 1459 (28 Jan. 2015), 2.
2. Doucet, *The Practice Turn in Architecture*, 12 and 175-78.
3. Félix Guattari, *The Three Ecologies* (London: Continuum, 2008), 23-24. Originally published as *Les trois écologies*, 1989.
4. Stéphane Hessel, *Time For Outrage!* (London: Quartet, 2011). Originally published as *Indignez-vous!*, 2010.
5. Gideon Boie, 'Francorchamps aan de Maalbeek', *BRUZZ*, 1600 (24 Jan. 2018), 22-23.
6. Kevin Van den Panhuyzen, 'Flitspaal Lambermontlaan al tien jaar defect', *BRUZZ*, 13 Feb. 2019. Kris Hendrickx, '27 van de 95 Brusselse flitspalen defect', *BRUZZ*, 2 Apr. 2019. TDN, 'Flitspalen op Lambermontlaan nog steeds defect', *BRUZZ*, 8 Oct. 2019.
7. GR, 'Wake voor in Schaarbeek verongelukte journaliste', *BRUZZ*, 09 Nov. 2017. Laurent Vermeersch and Sara De Sloovere, 'Beloftes zijn er, nu moeten ze worden waargemaakt', *BRUZZ*, 1637 (07 Nov. 2018), 12-15.
8. Gideon Boie, 'Beste Brusselse politici: het hondsbrutale rijgedrag dat alledaags lijkt, is jullie gedeelde verantwoordelijkheid', *VRT NWS* (2 Apr. 2019). Gideon Boie, 'Het gebrek aan politieke verbeelding houdt de Brusselse verkeersellende in stand', *VRT NWS* (20 May 2019). Gideon Boie, 'Verkeersagressie los je niet op met een likje verf', *De Standaard* (21 Jun. 2019), 34-35. Gideon Boie, 'Hardnekkige hardrijders mogen geen goedkoop alibi zijn voor de verkeersonveiligheid in Schaarbeek', *VRT NWS* (24 Jun. 2019). Gideon Boie, 'Weg met de fietssuggestiestrook', *De Standaard* (27 Oct. 2019), 30.
9. TDN, 'Burgercollectief vormt mensenketting voor veiligere Lambermontlaan', *BRUZZ* (5 Feb. 2019). Gideon Boie, 'Werken aan de Brusselse verkeersveiligheid is een boulevard van gebroken beloftes', *VRT NWS* (16 Jan. 2020). Frank Hoornaert, 'Buurtbewoners komen na ongeval op straat in Schaarbeek', *BRUZZ* (1 Jun. 2020). Wouter Hertogs, 'Honderdtal mensen voeren actie voor veiliger verkeer na aanrijding kind (2)', *Het Laatste Nieuws*, 30 May 2020.
10. Henry David Thoreau, *On the Duty of Civil Disobedience* (1849; New York: Open Road, 2015).
11. Judith Butler, 'Bodies in Alliance and the Politics of the Street', in *Notes Towards a Performative Theory of Assembly* (Cambridge, MA: Harvard University Press, 2015), 66-98.
12. Martin Luther King, *Where Do We Go From Here: Chaos or Community?* (Boston: Beacon, 1967).
13. Butler, 'Bodies in Alliance and the Politics of the Street'.
14. The radical flank theory was discussed in relation to the action of Extinction Rebellion: Dirk Holemans, 'Radicale klimaatactivisten effenen het pad', *De Standaard*, 10 Nov. 2022.

15. Hallam, *Common Sense for the 21st Century*, 7-8 and 41.
16. Gideon Boie, 'Inspraak is geen technisch detail', *De Standaard*, 28 Dec. 2019, 41.
17. Marlies Lenaerts, ed., *L'Autre Atelier / Het Andere Atelier* (Brussels: BRAL, 2021).
18. Butler, 'Bodies in Alliance and the Politics of the Street'.
19. Sara De Sloovere, 'Josaphatpark kreunt onder wildparkeerders: Schaarbeek ontkent gedoogbeleid', *BRUZZ*, 24 Apr. 2019. SN, 'Straat door Josaphatpark wordt weer autoweg', *BRUZZ*, 21 Aug. 2019.
20. Gideon Boie, 'De stad hertekenen, nu kan het', *De Standaard*, 15 Apr. 2020, 26-27.
21. Maarten Van Acker, ''t Stad als vaccin, onze buurt als medicijn', *Gazet van Antwerpen*, 15 Apr. 2020.
22. Lieven De Cauter, *Ending the Antropocene: Essays on Activism in the Age of Collapse* (Rotterdam: nai010, 2021).
23. Michel Foucault, 'Of Other Spaces', *Diacritics* 16, no. 1 (Spring 1986), 22-27.
24. Jens Aerts, Gideon Boie, and Annekatrien Verdickt, 'Naar de exit zonder auto', *De Standaard*, 12 May 2020, 33. Jens Aerts, Gideon Boie, Annekatrien Verdickt, 'Une nouvelle feuille de route pour une nouvelle mobilité', *Le Soir* (12 May 2020). Jens Aerts, Gideon Boie, Annekatrien Verdickt, 'It is not desirable for our streets to be dominated by cars again', *The Bulletin* (12 May 2020).
25. Giorgio Agamben, *Where Are We Now?: The Epidemic as Politics* (Lanham, LD: Rowman & Littlefield, 2021).
26. ADD, 'Maak van Colignonplein een terras', *BRUZZ*, 31 May 2020. NLS, 'Geen uitgebreide terrassen op het Colignonplein', *BRUZZ*, 3 Jul. 2020.
27. Gideon Boie and Annekatrien Verdickt, 'Een winterterras kan levens redden', *De Standaard*, 21 Oct. 2020, 35.
28. EVG, 'Fietspad verdeelt de Wetstraat', *De Standaard*, 5 May 2020.
29. Kris Hendrickx, 'Ukkelse burgemeester: Test Ter Kamerenbos veel te radicaal', *BRUZZ*, 2 Sep. 2020.
30. Jef Poppelmonde, 'Een auto is oké, maar een tuintje dat mensen samenbrengt? Ho maar', *De Standaard*, 17 Jun. 2020. Gideon Boie, 'De huis-keuken-en-tuin-besognes van een stad', *De Standaard*, 18 Jun. 2020, 26-27.
31. Sara De Sloovere, 'Bescheiden steunactie 1030/0 en Gracq aan "stadstuintje" Schaarbeek', *BRUZZ*, 20 Jun. 2020. Kevin Van den Panhuyzen, 'Stadstuintje staat weer op parkeerplaats in Schaarbeek zonder toestemming gemeente', *BRUZZ*, 8 Jul. 2020.
32. Lieven De Cauter, 'Coronalimbo', *De Wereld Morgen*, 27 Apr. 2020.
33. Gideon Boie, 'De onverschillige logica van het beddenhuis', *De Standaard*, 8 Jul. 2020, 28.
34. Foucault, *Discipline and Punish*, plates between pages 169 and 170.
35. Gideon Boie, 'De fantasie van het Zoomonderwijs', *De Standaard*, 19 Feb. 2021, 25.
36. Beatriz Colomina, 'The Bed in the Age of Corona', *Vitra Magazine*, 19 Jun. 2020. Gideon Boie, 'Playboy-fantasie valt tegen', *De Standaard*, 18 Dec. 2020, 33. Also published in English: Gideon Boie, 'We're all playboys', *Domus* (29 Mar. 2021).

37. Gideon Boie, 'Een hinkelspel is geen parkeerplaats', *De Standaard*, 2 Dec. 2020, 36.
38. *BRUZZ*, 29 Nov. 2020, television news item.
39. Jesse Pappers, 'Voor wie zijn de parken?', *De Standaard*, 30 Nov. 2020.
40. Boie, 'Een hinkelspel is geen parkeerplaats'.
41. Butler, 'Bodies in Alliance and the Politics of the Streets'.
42. Žižek, *The Ticklish Subject*, 208.
43. Alejandro Aravena, ed., *Reporting from the Front: 15th International Architecture Exhibition* (Venice: Marsilio Editori, 2016).
44. Žižek, *The Puppet and the Dwarf*, 2003.
45. Hessel, *Time For Outrage!*
46. Geert Bekaert, 'Belgische architectuur als gemeenplaats. De afwezigheid van een architectonische cultuur als uitdaging', *Archis* 9 (1987). Van Gerrewey, 'Jaarboek Architectuur Vlaanderen 06-07'.
47. Sofie De Caigny, 'Het glazen plafond van de Vlaamse architectuur', *De Standaard*, 28 Nov. 2018.
48. Marc Dubois, 'Het spook van de Gentse opera', *De Standaard* (3 Dec. 2018). Leo Van Broeck, 'Het gaat om kwaliteit, en kwaliteit alleen', *De Standaard*, 4 Dec. 2018.
49. Walter Benjamin, 'On the Concept of History'.
50. Gideon Boie, 'Wafels, bier en architectuur', *BRUZZ*, 1586 (4 Oct. 2017), 18-19. Gideon Boie, 'Moet de beurs een biertempel worden?' *BRUZZ*, 3 Oct. 2017.
51. Lieven De Cauter, 'Biertempel? Over our dead bodies!', *BRUZZ*, 11 Oct. 2017.
52. Sven Gatz, 'We geven Beursgebouw terug aan de mensen', *BRUZZ*, 10 Oct. 2017. Kristiaan Borret, 'Tijd om alternatieven voor Disneyficatie concreet te maken', *BRUZZ*, 25 Oct. 2017. Yannick Schandené, 'Biertempel en activisten: mag het debat gematigder?' *BRUZZ*, 25 Oct. 2017.
53. Leo Van Broeck, comment on the post by Lieven De Cauter on Facebook (10 Oct. 2017).
54. Koen Van Synghel, comment on the post by Lieven De Cauter on Facebook (10 Oct. 2017).
55. Žižek, *The Ticklish Subject*, 265.
56. Gideon Boie, 'Verslaafd aan architectuur', *A+Architecture in Belgium*, 16 Oct. 2017. Lieven De Cauter, 'Waarom een verwaterde biertempel? Een antwoord aan Sven Gatz', *De Wereld Morgen*, 26 Oct. 2017.
57. Kristiaan Borret, statement in the sofa-talk, part of the elective master's course Architecture and Activism, KU Leuven Faculty of Architecture, co-organized by CIVA at Kanal-Centre Pompidou, 4 Apr. 2019.
58. *Goudvis*, Season 1, Episode 2, VRT, 2009, documentary.
59. Žižek, *Iraq: The Borrowed Kettle*, 42.
60. Michael Sorkin, *Variations on a Theme Park: The New American City and the End of Public Space* (New York: Farrar, Straus and Giroux, 1992).

Conclusion

The previous chapters provide a more or less theoretical retrospective on twenty years of critical practice by the BAVO collective within the field of architecture, taking the changing use of the strategy of overidentification as a starting point to articulate different tactics for critical intervention. The chapters are written – in the spirit of Félix Guattari – as narrative accounts of a politico-aesthetic praxis articulating the origin of the intervention, understanding the process, evaluating the critical impact and tracing lines of flight for future practice.[1] The retrospective is not about checking structures or references; we have rid ourselves of what Guattari called the scientific superego and use theoretical reflection to forge tactics for critical intervention on the basis of the different applications of the strategy of overidentification in different domains. After using the strategy of overidentification in relation to art after the end of history, including the publication *Cultural Activism Today: The Art of Overidentification* (2007), BAVO began to apply the strategy in the performance as critic. The strategy was adopted from the philosophical work of Slavoj Žižek in relation to NSK, the art movement he was involved in in the former Yugoslavia and his later theories on the subversive character of orthodoxy and autism. The strategy of overidentification generates a critical moment by engaging with the inherent paradoxes of a given situation either by assuming all the consequences that stem from it or excluding any complexity in full adherence to the letter of the law. The application of overidentification enabled BAVO to establish an idiosyncratic practice that expands critical labour from articles and lectures (the usual weaponry of the critic) with formats that are typically part of the cultural sphere, such as exhibitions and performances, and later even entering design methods such as participative workshops and project definition. More importantly, the critical interventions in diverse contexts and engagements with different actors made it possible to experiment with the strategy of overidentification and go far beyond the classical interpretation *à la* Yes Men. The strategy of overidentification was enriched with techniques borrowed from the politics of commoning and pedagogy of ignorance. In this conclusion, we will use the outcomes, first, to articulate a handbook of tactics for critical interventions and, second, to reconsider the role of criticism in the field of architecture today.

Tactics Is the Answer

The main corpus of the book (Chapters 5 to 11) is a retrospective of seven critical interventions by BAVO in the expanded field of architecture, playing the card of overidentification to stir the inherent paradoxes of a certain situation and use it as catalyst for processes of awareness and change. Various social issues were on the table, ranging from regional development, city marketing and art in the public space to spatial management, humane detention and mental healthcare. The critical interventions were set up in close collaboration with different actors in the field of architecture culture. Also, other, unusual partners were engaged in architecture culture. The critical interventions made it possible to define different tactics based on the strategy of overidentification but depending on the specific context, network of actors, overall choreography and, last but not least, lessons learned from previous actions. The resulting practice may have turned into physical results at certain points, but the outcome is still first situated at the discursive level. This enables us to frame BAVO's critical interventions as a work without end; the constant changing of one's tactics is the answer in the search for maximum critical impact, turning the nullifying effect of inherent criticism into a window of change.

The first critical tactic, 'Hystericize the Subject' (Chapter 5), originates from the project 'Tien dingen die je gewoon moet doen voor het ruimtelijk ontwikkelen van een topregio' (Ten must-dos for the spatial development of a leading region) commissioned by Atelier Zuidvleugel. The study blindly repeated the neoliberal presumptions when it comes to regional development (the first act of identification), even presenting countervalues as perfect arguments for development (the second step of overdoing it).The critical tactic functioned well in articulating divisions among colleagues from the provincial government, thus staging the lingering dissensus on the topic of regional development. Still, the act of hystericizing failed to include the embedded critics of Atelier Zuidvleugel and the invited public, who all chose to keep the safe distance of academic objectivity. Keeping the focus too strongly on the policy texts and administrative actors, we left open the possibility for bystanders to disappear into the bushes. In fact, and perhaps most importantly, our own position as critic was not included in the game either. The lesson learned was that the act of total surrender to an opposing force – in this case, neoliberal policy on regional development – and abandoning the false hope of turning it towards social and green values is far from comprehensive enough as long as it leaves open the possibility for embedded critical forces to escape the scene.

The second tactic, 'Provoke Full Spectrum' (Chapter 6), was developed in the context of the exhibition 'De Janssens Werken' (The Janssens works). The exhibition project wanted to underscore how the architect is often unwittingly (or not) implied in the 'evil' policies s/he ostensibly bemoans. The celebration of the greater unity of politics and architecture in Antwerp was a subversion of the good/bad opposition of architecture and politics supporting Flemish architecture culture. Thanks to the tactic of full spectrum provocation, the exhibition was able to show how the obscene truth is part of the material externality, visible for everyone to see, thus shifting the critical gesture: there is no need to uncover anything, it is enough just to spell out the public secrets on the basis of what we see. In the case of Antwerp, the challenge was to show architecture as part of all sorts of programmes for urban regeneration, social reconquest and corporate governance thanks to features usually considered as the autonomy of architecture: form, proportion and materiality. Still, the reference to the figure of the mayor functioned as the last excuse for weak-hearted architects who could not accept that 'there is no easy escape, no position free of political manipulation except for those that speak the same language of manipulation'.[2]

The following tactic, 'Shoot at Your Own People' (Chapter 7), aimed at a critical intervention by launching friendly fire, i.e. willingly directing criticism at natural allies in the struggle instead of targeting the usual suspects. The strategy was applied in 'Bureau Kunstenaarsparticipatie' (Office for artist participation). The blend of liberal and populist language with the progressive hobby horses of art was an overidentification with confessions by the director of the arts centre in Rotterdam. He argued that the new liberal policies would not change so much under the new liberal government since the arts scene had been operating according to market logics already for a long time. The statement was subversive in light of the heroic protests by the cultural sector against state secretary Halbe Zijlstra, nicknamed 'Halbe the butcher'. The resistance provoked by the exhibition was logical insofar as it staged the horrible obscene voice as coming from within and demanding to innovate by doing the same things artists had been doing for years. The tactic subverted the liberal agenda by separating the artist from the 'object through whose possession the enemy kept him in check', i.e. giving up the precious (but fake) autonomy of art.[3] Understandably, the discomfort was such that artists chose to continue the oppositional modus against the evil state secretary and thus prove how they 'love to hate' the butcher.[4]

The fourth tactic, 'Choose Hyperidealism' (Chapter 8), twists the strategy of overidentification by prioritizing the ideal over the obscene and ignoring all petty excuses, personal interests and dirty secrets. The hyperidealist form of overidentification was practised in writing the programme for a 'Provincial Government Architect'. This was once suggested – perhaps in jest – by the first Flemish Government Architect, b0b Van Reeth, in a debate on the issue of architecture quality in Limburg. The tactic was nonetheless to enthusiastically appropriate the empty signifier, rearticulate it through a collective negotiation process and reintroduce it in the system of power and knowledge. The subversive gesture lies in orthodoxy, i.e. taking the ideal more seriously than anyone is prepared to and defending it by any means necessary. The procedure of identifying and filling the empty signifier was done over three times, each time getting closer to the loaded question, What is architectural quality? In the process, the role of the media as echo chamber proved to be crucial in opening doors to parties that usually lack any interest in architecture. Still, the role of criticism was limited to bringing the stakeholders to the threshold of taking action, in this case acknowledging the importance of architectural quality in the spatial management of the province, while it can never accomplish the act itself.

The fifth tactic, 'Keep the Paradox Alive' (Chapter 9), exploits the logic of commoning as a means to transform the inherent criticism in a certain development into design intelligence. The question was how to stay faithful to the complexities and contradictions of a certain situation – in this case, the paradoxical principle of humane imprisonment part of the Prison Act 2005. Strikingly, administrators, prison directors, architects and even the state secretary confirmed the critique of humane prison architecture. More so still, these actors affirmed the need for an alternative. And yet nobody was ready to activate these critical ideas. Another, more critical moment was generated when we took the idea of participation absolutely seriously, especially in relation to the future renovation of a prison facility that is part of the nineteenth-century Colonies of Benevolence recognized as UNESCO world heritage. A cultural programme was set up as a vehicle to common the prison with officials, administrators, directors, guards, civil society and detainees. The programme functioned as an analytical setting allowing the stakeholders to explore the mutual interests and desires. The outcome was located at the level of knowledge, the way we see and experience reality, accepting, in the words of Slavoj Žižek, that 'even if nothing has changed on the level of knowledge, the same knowledge as before starts to function in a different mode'.[5]

The sixth tactic, 'Design Your Symptom' (Chapter 10), continued the hyperidealist version of overidentification, this time using the pedagogies of ignorance as key for vision development on the meaning of architecture in the context of mental healthcare. Ignorant mastery – a pedagogy developed by Jacques Rancière – was used as a means to subtract design intelligence from the daily functioning of the psychiatric clinic. The research results became a body of criticism that acts in itself as a vehicle for vision development and even bends the ongoing design process. The enthusiasm released through the commoning of the clinic made it possible to include the framework of the research, i.e. the pregiven demolition scheme. It brought the research to a recursive moment, meaning that in a singular moment the whole process was done over again in fast-forward mode, this time starting from totally different principles and with the explicit aim of changing course. This is what happened in the alternative project definition for the abandoned Sint-Jozef pavilion, leading to the design of the Kanunnik Petrus Jozef Triest Plein by architecten de vylder vinck taillieu, a project that became famous after winning several international prizes. The project does not solve anything, but functions as a symptom for the creative destruction that has been driving the architecture production process in the clinic.

The seventh tactic, 'Stay True to Ignorance' (Chapter 11), continued the combined strategies of overidentification, commoning and ignorance, developing them into a methodological framework for vision development. The tactic was developed in the context of the most difficult design challenge in mental healthcare: the re-imagining of the seclusion room. The commoning of the seclusion room was a way to create an analytical setting in which the design solution is postponed as long as possible and the meantime is used to work through the inherent criticism lingering in the clinic. The process made it possible to articulate a design intelligence that goes beyond the standard knowledge and also the limits of what is considered possible or not. Key in the function of the architect-mediator is to give way to the stakeholders – in this case, psychiatrists, managers, staff, experts-by-experience and patients – when it comes to project definitions. Vanishing from the scene implies that there is no final product of criticism; the challenge is to enable the working to continue, to broaden the scope of the debate, expand the collective subject, reconsider the first outcome, and so on. The dream labour was not just about finding a solution for the local situation, but also, conversely, using the local situation to redefine the general framework in which we think the architecture of the seclusion room.

The Para-Praxis of Criticism

The retrospective on the work of BAVO allows us to draw general conclusions on the role of critical practice in the field of architecture, taking inspiration from the Freudo-Marxism of Slavoj Žižek (described in Chapters 1 to 4). A defining turn in BAVO's work occurred from the moment we employed concepts and techniques taken from Lacanian psychoanalysis within our critical practice. The strategy of overidentification became the main tool to work through the inherent criticism that lingers in a certain situation and turn its nullifying effect into a window of change. Understanding criticism as a psychoanalysis of the architecture field not only enabled us to develop different tactics based on the art of overidentification, it also made the action platform shift organically over the course of the seven critical interventions. First, the actions took place in the temples of culture, such as museums, art spaces, architecture institutes and other locations where critical debates are always welcome as part of a discursive side programme. The parallel sphere of culture was used to critically reflect on the political dimension of architecture, and writings, artworks, performances and exhibitions became the means for the joyful overidentification with all sorts of obscenities and repressed ideals.

At this point, we were strictly acting in the cultural sphere as a third domain that makes it possible to slip between public and private, as Lieven De Cauter argued.[6] The sphere of culture was the perfect free space for critical reflection, making it possible to add an element of performativity and embodiment to the traditional written and contemplative labour of criticism, and not forgetting the surplus of enjoyment that gets released in mimetic subversion. The act of mimesis is the perfect antidote for the resistance (in its psychoanalytical understanding, not political) evoked by criticism that aims to debunk arguments, deconstruct ideologies and lay bare passionate attachments. Still, the strength and beauty of the parallel universe of culture is at the same time a weakness when it accompanies daily design practice but never really touches it; typically, the cultural sphere neutralizes criticism even when it lashes out with critical data sets and historical fact-checks. Although the interventions by BAVO certainly did have a critical effect from its parallel position, they always ran the risk of being discarded as an interesting thought experiment, the best delegitimization of its relevance for daily design practice.

Later, the actions were held in the professional field itself, such as the architecture of detention and psychiatry, and overidentifications of all sorts were set up by mobilizing the typical tool box of the architect, such as workshops, case studies, benchmarks, site visits, etc. The public we interacted with was not the enlightened art and architecture lover, but directors, corrections officers, social workers and detainees in the case of the prison system, and managers, psychiatrists, staff *and* patients in the case of mental healthcare. Architecture was the topic of discussion and the ambition was to gather design intelligence from talks with the users of the facilities we were talking about, although that ideological term wrongly suggests an end-of-the-chain function – best to use the term 'user-architect' coined by Doina Petrescu.[7] Part of the ambition was to indirectly address the field of architecture with alternative design intelligence and unsolicited visions on detention and care. Leaving the white cube in the latter phase was not a retreat from the cultural sphere; on the contrary, we were still claiming cultural agency while operating in the professional field. The criticism made use of the usual architect toolbox but stayed clear of the job of design.

In the case of Prison Gear, the knowledge platform was set up first as a website with publications and exhibits, still using cultural subsidies and platforms, and later as workshops in the prison, i.e. the place where the issue is rooted. The final project in Merksplas was set up as a sort of cultural festival with workshops, site visits, a film screening, photography exhibition and debate, co-organized by architecture organization AR-TUR and FPS Justice, taking place in and outside the prison. Certainly, commissionership in the prison system is monopolized by the federal state. Nevertheless, the idea was to claim the design debate and drag the main actors in the debate by playing on their own field. In the case of the Caritas project and the following work on the seclusion room in different psychiatric hospitals, we strictly undertook the work as a creative service in knowledge production on the architecture of care. The critical study might be commissioned, but our role remained that of a critic, actively sidestepping the boardroom, organizing workshops as a sort of cultural festival in the clinic – hence, the working title of the project was at first POP-UP Caritas, a name that remains visible on some materials. The project was also actively looking at how to go beyond the pregiven framework of discussion and even postponing conclusions as long as possible in order to include as many feedback loops as possible.

In the latter phase, the cultural element shifted from the white cube of the museum to architecture culture as such, engaging in the sensitizing and promotional work usually done by the so-called architectural civil society, including the architecture institute, government architects, architecture faculties and even individual architect offices insofar as they contribute to the general architecture debate.[8] The comparison with the usual suspects within civil society, such as trade unions and nature organizations, seems rather exaggerated but the idea is similarly to form a non-governmental third force that advocates quality in the physical living environment.[9] However, we found the architectural civil society failing when it comes to the design of prisons and psychiatric hospitals, and this for different reasons. The VAi usually promotes architecture quality through best practices, but these were simply lacking, especially in the case of prisons, and the result was their absence in the public debate. The Flemish Government Architect was equally absent in the prison debate because of conflicting policy levels, the ministry of justice being a competency of the federal state while the government architect resides under the general competences of the regional minister-president. BAVO's critical interventions took on the vacant sites and started raising awareness among the public about the need for and value of architecture quality. The work was in line with the function of AWB as a cultural operator.[10] They chose their name to stress the work of architecture culture as not just being about promoting best practices, but in the first place about creating the fertile ground for innovative projects to come into being and about gathering stake- and shareholders in an attempt to organize breakthroughs.[11] A similar practice is employed by Peter Swinnen who, after his tenure as Flemish Government Architect, took the Pilot Projects – a format that prepares the field by exploring new design challenges and engaging in capacity-building – as a model for a new projective practice which he called 'policy whispering'.[12]

The critical interventions in the prison system and in mental healthcare, discussed in Chapters 9, 10 and 11, were both an exodus from practice to the sphere of culture and a subversion of the design practice from within, transposing the function of criticism to the heart of architectural production. Architect and writer Paul Vermeulen once confided in me that in his view, writing criticism was an evening practice; he called it a free-time activity in which the architect devotes time to reflection after a tiresome day of hard work at the office. Interestingly, the role of after-work critic was combined with a micropolitical design practice, Paul Vermeulen using the term to discuss how small strategic interventions can stretch the building envelope while still accepting the overall framework of the commission.[13] The problem starts when we isolate the idea of criticism as free night work. Most often, architectural criticism in Flanders has a function in identifying, describing and commenting on good architectural practices. This means that criticism is indeed considered part of the post-production of architecture, i.e. the moment when the photographer is called in to do the visualization. The focus on best practices splits the architecture discourse in two with, on the one hand, a highly critical consciousness of all sorts of alarming political and economic processes and, on the other, a celebratory culture singing the praises of immaculate design concepts and shining oeuvres by the self-acclaimed golden generation. The danger of architecture discourse is when only the second half remains and ends up as just another variation of the self-congratulatory modern town planning criticized by Félix Guattari in line with racism, phallocentrism and the commodification of art.[14]

The discursive practice developed by BAVO turned the above tradition upside down; it situates itself in the sphere of culture, not to keep clear from urban politics but to explicitly intervene in it and transform the meaningful context of architecture production. To understand the political dimension of paper architecture, Lieven De Cauter and Michiel Dehaene wrote: 'Today, the act of spending time for the making of paper architecture is in itself an act of resistance by locating itself in the parallel world [...] in the safe haven of *scholè*, free time, the time-space of stubborn devotion.'[15] They called the result 'para-architecture', emancipating the paper output in terms of an architecture product worth just as much as the usual physical object, even qualifying it with the political potential that got lost in other instances of what they call 'hyper-architecture' and 'infra-architecture'. The result of BAVO's performances is equally the construction of a platform for para-architecture that uses the cultural sphere for critical intervention in the process of building production, producing an awful lot of paper work as a catalyst for processes of awareness and change. In the operation as architect-mediator, the role of architectural criticism goes beyond preproduction (embodied in AWB's 'building of meaningful contexts') or post-production (Paul Vermeulen's reflection in the evening hours), but takes on the crucial task of discourse formation, animating the debate, organizing feedback loops, making premature results public, reaching out to different actors, introducing minor voices, in short: re-politicizing architecture at every moment of the design process.

Curator of Anarchic Passages

The last tactic, 'Make Things Public' (Chapter 12), derives from the author's involvement in recent moments of urban activism in my home town, Brussels, organized by citizen movements Heroes for Zero and Filter Café Filtré. The direct activist engagement with urban development in Brussels, especially on road safety in Brussels, was triggered after being victim of a road accident with my children on the way to school. The event was certainly traumatic and cause for indignation. However, the trauma was doubled in the confrontation with the inherent criticism that supported the position of state secretaries and the alderman in charge of public space, mobility and road safety. All these persons were moved by the situation, even sharing the indignation, but at the same they claimed that not much could be done to change the dangerous situation rapidly. The confrontation with the unbearable lightness of urban politics in Brussels functioned as a sort of second trauma – it is a recurring phenomenon in psychiatry: the first trauma is part of the pathology and relates to prior events, the second trauma is inflicted at the moment of hospitalization. Once becoming active in the spontaneous citizen movement 1030/0, later organizing regional activities under the name of Heroes for Zero, the personal pain got uplifted in the common struggle for road safety. The citizen movement organized street actions to stress the issue of road safety, first in Schaarbeek – informally often referred to as *mille trente* after the postcode – and later spreading to other municipalities in Brussels. The activism started to function in parallel to BAVO's work. On the one hand, architectural knowledge was used to somehow professionalize the activism and not allow the issue to be depoliticized as an individual issue. On the other hand, the street actions taught me lessons on how criticism relates to the gathering of bodies in the public space and how to use the media as an extension of the street.

The accidental conjuncture of the work as architecture critic and activism within citizen movements helps to redefine the agency of architecture. Thinking architecture and spatial quality in connection with social and political dynamics has been a thread throughout BAVO's work, the inspiration definitely being the defiling of architecture by political philosophy of Freudo-Marxist tradition mostly. It was often understood as the profanation of architecture by weakhearted colleagues, even as a blasphemy. In response, stricter architectural colleagues often reacted by stressing that they preferred to start from architecture and see how it enables to articulate answers for the urgent issues of our times. The ambition functions as the theoretical counterpart of the tendency to define the field of architecture practice as autonomous; symptomatic is the attempt by Office KGDVS to define architecture within the confines of architecture by means of tautologies like 'architecture is architecture'. The definition of 'architecture without content' – a reduction of architecture to nothing but the 'mediation between inside and outside' – is impossible without the repression of the many complexities and contradictions that architecture shares with other socio-economic processes.[16] The discourse misses the point that philosophical concepts are directly relevant for spatial discipline, not after a difficult process of translation and speculation, but on the contrary, because the particular perspective of architecture and space makes it possible to shed another light on our general understanding of the world. This is the case in so many theoretical arguments by diverse authors, such as Judith Butler discussing performativity on the basis of the occupation of Tahrir Square during the Arab Spring or Achille Mbembe discussing necropolitics on the basis of the spatial organization of South African apartheid and the Israeli occupation of Palestine.[17]

In the Žižekian logic, the particularity of architecture makes it possible to 'look awry' at urgent social issues, not as an example of the abstract theory, but as way to redefine the ideological framework through which we see the issue and highlight forgotten dimensions.[18] In the case of Brussels, the particularity of road safety made it possible to untangle the ideological complexes that support urban politics and define other ways of intervening in it. The same holds for the redistribution of public space during the Covid lockdowns. The engagements in the activist commons taught us how the methodological use of architecture becomes vital as a critical instrument in combination with collective intelligence, bodies in alliance and media politics. The starting point was to locate criticism in the internal contradictions of the situation and invite the actors to confront these through processes of common negotiation at the design table, using different tactics to make the overidentification as total as possible. In sharp contrast to the more traditional critical position that denounces this or that trend from a moral high ground, the new role for the critic comes much closer to that of a mediator. We talked about the architect-mediator in parallel with the notion of architect-curator that comes along with the practice of Doina Petrescu and Constantin Petcou with AAA.[19] However, in the sphere of criticism the term of curator could wrongly suggest a certain hierarchical relationship that does not fit the classic relationship of client and architect. Boris Groys has argued that the curator is not a neutral actor superseding individual artists but, on the contrary, the artist par excellence who sketches the meta-narrative in which individual artworks are reduced to mere example – although he still admits only the artist possesses the mythical creative power to turn even a urinal into a sublime object of contemplation.[20]

The function of mediator is better suited to signify the critical labour necessary to bring the people around the table to the point of digesting and assuming the internal contradictions present in a certain context. The role of architect-mediator also helps to differentiate from the user who is part of the conceptual couple of architect-user and user-architect that both engage in a dialectical relation within design procedures, again conceptualized by Doina Petrescu.[21] The pair of terms is difficult to translate when it comes to criticism, especially in the context of mental healthcare and detention. In the critical interventions, we did mobilize an awful lot of spatial perceptions and user experiences from people living and working in psychiatric hospitals and prison facilities. Certainly, the aim was to present the patient or prisoner as user-architect, provide them with equal aesthetic rights and have them articulate a body of design intelligence. The important dynamic in the critical labour of the architect-mediator is the introduction of an emancipatory element in architecture culture, breaking open the prevailing expertocracy among managers, technical services and architects and introducing minor voices, such as patients and prisoners in the first place.[22] Still, it would be pretentious to present the critic as architect-user in these contexts. The many visits we made to psychiatric hospitals and prison facilities will never match the experience of, respectively, undergoing treatment and 'doing time'.

Street blockades are certainly clearer as interruptions of everyday traffic flows in the city, and yet the critical interventions described in this book were deliberately set up equally as anarchic passages, or moments, in the architectural production process.[23] Although Judith Butler uses the notion of anarchist passages in the discussion of performative politics, especially in the occupation of Tahrir Square during the Arab Spring, the term anarchic might be better suited to define the temporary suspension of power by a singular event. The horizon of activism is not necessarily a government without hierarchy, but rather regime change or at least the bending of decision-making procedures managed by the powers that be. The term anarchic was used by Jacques Rancière to discuss the undermining role of the ignorant master in the panecastic method of education used by Joseph Jacotot; his aim was not a schooling without hierarchy, but radical emancipation by turning upside down the scenography of schooling.[24] In the context of this book, we are talking about capacity-building, the holy grail of architecture culture in Flanders, turning it away from the idea of educating dumb users by organizing an apparatus that mobilizes the passive knowledge that users already possess. This follows the conviction that there is sufficient capacity among psychiatrists, management, staff *and* patients and that it is primarily a matter of combining and activating this knowledge within the decision-making procedures. The hyperidealist version of overidentification consisted in taking spatial perceptions and user experiences deadly seriously in the dream labour of the design process. Emancipation thus runs parallel to a collective subjectification in which the actors in a certain context start to have a grip – in terms of critical understanding and eventual agency – on the spatial setting they operate in on an everyday basis.[25] The term user-architect is helpful in making clear that we are talking about a group of people first set aside as mere users, without a valuable voice in the design process, now becoming primary actors from the very start of the process, not just at the end of chain.

Although the discursive practice led to physical results in some cases, especially in the Caritas project (Chapter 10), the outcome is first situated at the discursive level, putting energy into the articulation of design intelligence on the challenge at stake and thus building an architecture culture more generally. The different projects did experiment with different tactics to mobilize the internal contradictions, first by taking a little too seriously either the obscene content or the lost ideal. The impact of the critical intervention depends on the different contexts. In the case of the KARUS psychiatric clinic, it was possible to organize a recursive moment in the ongoing process and realize with the Triest Plein, designed by architecten de vylder vinck taillieu, an unsolicited outcome that functioned as a pars pro toto for the psychiatric centre of the future. In the case of the seclusion room of the Sint-Jan admissions department of the Sint-Annendael psychiatric hospital (Chapter 11), the change was about developing a vision and organizing a test set-up in Room 4, not having an impact on the decisions made later. In the case of the Merksplas Prison programme (Chapter 9), the change was limited to the discourse that functions as an envelope for the renovation; clearly, the state's monopoly of power leaves no opening for direct impact on the design and building production of prisons. However, the physical result or test model within the mental healthcare context is not necessarily a sign of a better critical impact, compared to the research on the prison that led merely to a change in critical understanding without direct visible and tangible result on the ground. It is important to recognize how the impact of the critical intervention is located at the level of knowledge; whatever the outcome, the result might congeal in the physical reality of a building just as it might end in failure or frustration; still, ideas do trickle down in the process, often after a long delay and in compromised form. This dynamic was particularly the case in urban activism opening the window for change, perhaps speeding up the visions of the future through anarchic passages, but also recognizing the limited agency of the critical agent in the often unbearably longue durée of urban production.[26] Similarly, the result of the critical interventions is the production of knowledge that allows for deeper insight and awakens earlier unthought-of visions from there – to paraphrase Slavoj Žižek: it is about the production of critical understanding that allows the old knowledge to function in unexpected ways.[27]

Exit Through the Massage Room

Turning the screw of overidentification allowed us to develop architecture criticism as a discursive practice that critically intervenes in the process of architectural production, undermining the fundamental concepts and aiming at the redirection of its course. The discursive practice was not an invention ex nihilo but rather an outcome of the continuous ambition in my work as critic, using BAVO as an alter ego, to watch over the impact of criticism in a certain context by any means necessary. This means that the critical practice differs strongly from other traditions in criticism, such as the contemplative criticism of standard academic discourse and also the comfort of cultural hypercriticism. In earlier chapters, we referred to the Lacanian structures of, respectively, the discourse of the university and the hysteric. Although these discourses might be highly critical, we discussed how they are often implied in the inherent criticism of a system and allow the subject to keep a healthy distance from the situation they complain about and continue to operate in it. Inherent criticism can also be understood as a failure to put knowledge and insight in a certain worrisome situation to use in processes that initiate change, or at least raise awareness, also about personal complicity. The strategy of overidentification operates in the different discourse of the analyst, taking the inherent contradictions as an anchoring point to instigate processes of awareness about troubles in the past, envision lines of flight of an alternative future and, most importantly, bring the subject to the brink of taking action.[28] Providing historical perspective, alternative sets of data and deconstructions of fundamental concepts is only half the job of criticism; it demands another breath to ensure that criticism reaches its destination without imposing outcomes or taking over initiatives.

Unpacking criticism also means finding the right platform of intervention, if necessary pulling out all the stops and playing on different registers at once. The efficiency of critical arguments to dynamize a certain context and reach out to the public is relative to the form in which it is presented. It was Marshall McLuhan who cunningly argued that the message always needs massage.[29] In our critical interventions we tried out different formats, exploiting the visual aspect of architecture to support the content and also switching between types of writing and publishing platforms. First, architecture criticism published in an academic magazine certainly adds to the deep understanding of a certain topic, but the heated debate is kept safe among peers and somehow historical per definition, if only because of the long waiting times in review procedures. Second, architecture criticism published in the format of professional magazines potentially interferes with the set of ideas and best practices in the design practice. Still, critical content easily disappears in the celebratory culture in the field of architecture which feeds upon the power of the image. Third, architecture criticism published in newspaper articles provokes immediate resistance in the form of counter-criticism, factual correction and requests for clarification. No doubt shortcuts are taken in newspaper columns, but the critical efficacy of an argument comes from a symptomatic feature much more than from full coverage of data; it is only the former that starts the conversation, the latter will most likely kill it.

Besides traditional publication platforms, I also expanded architecture criticism into new terrains, such as public hearing procedures, something that proved to be quite effective as it forced stakeholders to react in registered legal correspondence. One can consider immediate resistance as proof that the criticism certainly did reach its destination. Another alternative platform for architecture criticism was the open invitation sent by email, combined with self-publications; the free and unbound action appeals to the enthusiasm of the public to become critics in their own right, voice critical thoughts kept private, join a public debate and so on. Joining forces with action groups and citizen movements is still another useful platform to activate architecture criticism in the struggle for a more just, social and sustainable city; in this case, WhatsApp groups and social media channels functioned as the main platform. The daily struggle by citizen movements is not about losing objective academic distance in fight for the good cause, it is on the contrary about using the objective distance to deepen the analysis of the situation and widen the scope of critical intervention. Joining forces with urban struggles also makes it possible to embed architecture criticism in the long waves of urban activism – often spanning decades if not centuries – that define the way we see the future of the city and, even more importantly, how we will remember the past.

The permanent 'massage' necessary to politicize architecture might seem to run contrary to the fundamental principle of depoliticization in Flemish architecture culture, especially as embodied in the so-called architecture civil society.[30] An initiative like 'Architectuur als Buur' (Architecture as neighbour) organized by Stichting Architectuurmuseum (S/AM) in 1988 rebelled against the close ties between party politics and architecture production in Ghent and located architecture in the authentic one-on-one between client and architect.[31] In the same tradition, architecture critic Geert Bekaert used the metaphor of the commonplace – the literary topos, not the common places in a city – to understand architecture as part of the everyday activities of individuals making the earth inhabitable and meaningful, even when talking about the outstanding Hôtel Solvay by Victor Horta.[32] The push for depoliticization was a countermovement against the close contact between architecture and politics and its stupefying effect on the blind cycles of creative destruction in urban development, such as the so-called 'third world war' in Ghent or Brusselization in Brussels.[33] The early initiatives gave birth in the late 1990s to the founding of the VAi, functioning as watchdog for architecture culture, and also the Flemish Government Architect, a more institutional position advising the government when it comes to project definitions and the selection of architects.

Depoliticization is absolutely necessary and perhaps key to understanding the current recognition of Flemish architecture by the international architecture scene today. I am quite happy that the Caritas project is part of it. Still, the danger is that the depoliticization of architecture can lead to a totally post-political or even apolitical conception of architecture. The representation of work by Office KGDVS is, again, quite symptomatic. What to think about the exhibition title *Everything Architecture* that cuts the design loose from any social or cultural context, not even referring to assignments and clients, only numbering the work as Office 56, Office 57,
and so on.[34] The positioning of architecture as empty against an equally hollow backdrop comes close to the argument of Slavoj Žižek about the end of ideology: 'The big news of today's post-political age of the "end of ideology" is thus the radical depoliticization of the sphere of the economy: the way the economy functions (the need to cut welfare, etc.) is accepted as a simple insight into the objective state of things.'[35] The post-political mindset makes it possi-

ble to discuss circular villas in the Spanish Pyrenees designed by Office KGDVS without mentioning the context of the luxury holiday resort nor the design process circling so many starchitects.

The end of ideology in architecture is made possible by critics like Christophe Van Gerrewey, who lashed out in response to an essay by Lars Kwakkenbos on the new courthouses in Ghent and Antwerp. Kwakkenbos discussed how the required security measures and the difficult specifications had a strong impact on the design by, respectively, Stéphane Beel Architects and Richard Rogers. Van Gerrewey argued: 'The last two "issues" have nothing to do with architecture, but everything to do with "meeting", "managing" and regularly "sitting down together".'[36] What Van Gerrewey failed to notice was not only the philosophical difference between politics and the political, but also how these notions are always intertwined in everyday reality – at least, in the viewpoint of Chantal Mouffe, who wrote: '[...] by "the political" I mean the dimension of antagonism which I take to be constitutive of human societies, while by "politics" I mean the set of practices and institutions through which an order is created, organizing human coexistence in the conflictuality provided by the political.'[37] The very practical issues in the everyday negotiations of the design process – call it the daily politics of architecture – is always a way to organize in an orderly manner the antagonisms that linger in architecture. Conversely, the practicalities of politics might well function as a key to more fundamental political issues.

The attempts to reach straight to an absolute architecture does not depoliticize architecture, it merely distracts by discussing only scale, proportion, materiality and other formalities. Moreover, the desperate attempt to evacuate everyday politics from the architecture discourse misses out on as many entry points to discuss the political dimension of architecture – this is the logic of Chantal Mouffe. It happened to Christophe Van Gerrewey, him again, when he started to rant against the main players of Flemish architecture culture. The VAi was too busy with popular festivals, the Flemish Government Architect too busy with climate emergency, including poor me, the critic, too busy enlarging problems.[38] The only answer Van Gerrewey came up with was the cryptic dream '[...] to break the impasse, by making rational, passionate but informed choices, for or against buildings, for or against projects, for or against architects – and, above all, to make those choices open to discussion and a public topic'. In the suggestion of a radical architecture debate, the theorist failed to mention one concrete topic that eventually could function as an entry point for such a rational, passionate and informed choice – logically, all substance was lost after discharging every form of content as empty politics.

All art is subject to political manipulation, except art that speaks the language of the same manipulation, wrote Laibach in their Convenant.[39] The reverse logic is that architecture claiming to be free of politics might show itself as most entrenched in politics and unable to articulate the dubious attachments that function as a condition of possibility for architectural production. The best example is the close encounter of Office KGDVS with Jaspers Eyers Architects in many recent projects in Brussels, such the new headquarters for the VRT public broadcasting company and the redevelopment of the headquarters of the KBC Bank in Brussels.[40] Suddenly, the young gods of Flemish architecture, the proud heirs of the long struggle for architecture culture qua civil society in the past century, now appear as allies of the establishment that their great patrons rebelled against. The biggest challenge a critic faces is not so much the countercriticism advanced by opposing forces (which are actually just open invitations to work through); more difficult to overcome is the self-censorship that prevents architecture history and theory from assuming its agency within the larger debate on the city of tomorrow.

The quest for the depoliticization of architecture thus poses a paradox: saving architecture from dirty politics is only possible when we dare look into it – this is Parsifal's idea that 'the wound can only be healed by the very weapon that inflicts the wound'. Elsewhere, we listed the different ways in which architects are regaining a political dimension in the everyday design practice while respecting the overall framework of depoliticization in Flemish architecture culture, such as the strategies of the micropolitics of bending the brief, the para-architecture in the art world, the architecture of the project brief by Government Architects, the architecture civil society as a politics in its own right, the cultural operator, the architecture of the commons animated by the architect-mediator, the guerrilla tactics of activist architects and much more. 'How much politics can architecture take?' is the working title for another book awaiting conclusion and publication.[41] (The list was also the matrix for the chapter on activist architecture in the publication on Forms of Activism as Democracy in the City, written together with Lieven De Cauter, but here mainly dealing with international practices.[42]) Allow me to finish the retrospective on twenty years of critical interventions by BAVO by saying that the book the reader holds in his/her hand hopes to prove how criticism makes it possible equally to repoliticize architectural production while respecting the holy principle of depoliticization through a practice that starts from the strategy of overidentification and next visits every shadowy corner of the architecture discourse.

Notes
1. Guattari, *The Three Ecologies*, 25.
2. Laibach, '10 Items of the Convenant', item 3.
3. Žižek, *The Fragile Absolute*, 150.
4. Žižek, 'Why Do We All Love to Hate Haider?'.
5. Žižek, *The Parallax View*, 304.
6. Lieven De Cauter, 'Kunst en Activisme', *Rekto:Verso*, 15 Jun. 2015. Trans. by the author. The final version of the text is: Lieven De Cauter, 'The Space of Play: Towards a General Theory of Heterotopia (with Michiel Dehaene)' in *Entropic Empire On the City of Man in the Age of Disaster* (Rotterdam: nai010, 2012), 174-189.
7. Petrescu, 'Losing Control, Keeping Desire'.
8. Gideon Boie and Sofie De Caigny, eds., *Architectuurcultuur in Vlaanderen* (Antwerp: VAi, 2019).
9. Sofie De Caigny, 'Epilogue: On Architecture Culture and Building Culture', in *More Than a Competition*, ed. Maarten Liefooghe and Maarten Van Den Driessche (Antwerp/Brussels: VAi/Team Vlaams Bouwmeester, 2021). Gideon Boie, 'Flemish Architectural Culture for Beginners', *Archined*, 16 May 2022.
10. Roeland Dudal in a lecture on the practice of AWB in the elective master's course Architecture and Activism at the Faculty of Architecture KU Leuven, 15 Apr. 2016.
11. Gideon Boie, 'The Future Is (Not) Here', in *WTC Tower Teachings* (Brussels: KU Leuven Faculty of Architecture, 2019), 178-80. Gideon Boie, 'How much politics can architecture take?', unpublished manuscript developed in the master's course Criticism and Ethics at KU Leuven Faculty of Architecture. Boie, 'Seven Questions on Flemish Architecture'.
12. Peter Swinnen, *Zeven memo's voor een verlichte bouwcultuur. Ambitienota Vlaams Bouwmeester 2010-2015* (Brussels: Vlaamse Overheid, 2010). Peter Swinnen, 'De architect als beleidsfluisteraar', *A+ Architecture in Belgium* 261 (Oct. 2016), 48-50. Boie, 'Flemish Architectural Culture for Beginners'.
13. Paul Vermeulen, 'Dankrede bij de Vlaamse Cultuurprijs', *A+ Architecture in Belgium* 233 (Dec. 2011-Jan. 12), 52-53. Paul Vermeulen, Maarten Delbeke and Christophe Van Gerrewey, *Moderne Tijden: Teksten over architectuur: Vlees en beton 72* (Ghent: WZW Editions & Productions, 2007).
14. Guattari, *The Three Ecologies*, 23-24.
15. Lieven De Cauter and Michiel Dehaene, 'Meditations on Razor Wire: A Plea for Para-Architecture', in *Visionary Power: Producing the Contemporary City*, ed. Christine de Baan, Joachim Declerck and Véronique Patteeuw (Rotterdam: nai, 2007), 233-47.
16. Kersten Geers, Joris Kritis, Jelena Pancevac, Giovanni Piovene, Dries Rodet and Andrea Zanderigo, *Architecture Without Content* (London: Bedford Press, 2015). Moisés Puente, ed., *Kersten Geers, Without Content; 2G Essays* (Köln: Walter & Franz König, 2021).
17. Butler, 'Bodies in Alliance and the Politics of the Street'. Achille Mbembe, *Necropolitics* (Durham, NC: Duke University Press, 2019), 66-92. Originally published in 2003.
18. Žižek, *Looking Awry*, 3.
19. Petrescu, 'Losing Control, Keeping Desire'.

20. Boris Groys, 'On Curatorship'.
21. Petrescu, 'Losing Control, Keeping Desire'.
22. Loeckx, *Stadsvernieuwingsprojecten In Vlaanderen*.
23. Butler, 'Bodies in Alliance and Politics of the Streets', 75.
24. Rancière, *The Ignorant Schoolmaster*.
25. Petrescu, 'Losing Control, Keeping Desire', 45 and 54.
26. Gideon Boie and Lieven De Cauter, *Forms of Activism as Democracy in the City* (Brussels: BAVO/OXUMORON Books, 2021), 87. Gideon Boie, 'De ondraaglijke traagheid van het Brussels stedelijk beleid', *De Standaard*, 9 Jun. 2022, 26-27.
27. Žižek, *The Parallax View*, 304.
28. Lacan, 'Mirror Stage', 8.
29. Marshall McLuhan, *The Medium Is the Massage: An Inventory of Effects* (London: Penguin, 1967).
30. Sofie De Caigny, 'Epilogue: On Architecture Culture and Building Culture'.
31. Geert Bekaert, Mil De Kooning, Marc Dubois and Bart Verschaffel, *Architectuur als Buur: panorama van Gent en omstreken 1968-88* (Turnhout: Brepols, 1988).
32. Bekaert, 'Belgische architectuur als gemeenplaats'.
33. Bekaert, De Kooning, Dubois and Verschaffel, *Architectuur als Buur*. Isabelle Doucet, *The Practice Turn in Architecture*.
34. Office Kersten Geers David Van Severen, *Everything Architecture*, Bozar, Brussels, 4 Mar.-29 May 2016, exhibition. Office Kersten Geers David Van Severen, *Everything Architecture* (Cologne: Walther König, 2017).
35. Žižek, *The Ticklish Subject*, 353.
36. Van Gerrewey, 'Jaarboek Architectuur Vlaanderen 06-07, editie 2008'.
37. Mouffe, *On the Political*, 9.
38. Christophe Van Gerrewey, 'Wie over architectuur wil spreken, sta op en spreek over architectuur', *De Witte Raaf* 202, Nov.-Dec. 2019.
39. Laibach, '10 Items of the Convenant'.
40. Gideon Boie, 'Kwaliteit als katalysator van sloop', *De Architect : Vakblad voor de Architect, 48, no. 5* (2017): 164-65. Gideon Boie, 'Vernieuwing en gevestigde orde gaan niet samen', *De Standaard*, 28 Jun. 2021, 30-31.
41. Gideon Boie, 'How much politics can architecture take?'.
42. Gideon Boie and Lieven De Cauter, 'Architectural Activism', in *Forms of Activism as Democracy in the City* (Brussels: BAVO/OXUMORON Books, 2021), 123-74.

List of Abbreviations

AAA	Atelier d'Architecture Autogerée (Studio for self-managed architecture)
4Gs	Informal name used by FPS Justice in reference to the public-private partnership for four new prisons ('vier gevangenissen') within the Master Plan 2008-2016
ABN-AMRO	Algemene Bank Nederland – Amsterdamse en Rotterdamse Bank (General bank of the Netherlands – bank of Amsterdam and Rotterdam)
AG Vespa	Autonoom Gemeentebedrijf Vastgoed en Stadsprojecten Antwerpen (Autonomous city company for real estate and urban projects in Antwerp)
AMADA	Alle Macht Aan De Arbeiders (All power to the workers)
AWB	Architecture Workroom Brussels
CBK	Centrum Beeldende Kunst Rotterdam (Rotterdam centre of visual arts)
CDA	Christen-Democratisch Appèl (Christian democratic appeal)
CD&V	Christen-Democratisch en Vlaams (Flemish christian democratic party)
CIVA	Centre d'Information, de Documentation, et d'Exposition de la Ville, de l'Architecture, du Paysage et de l'Urbanisme de la Région de Bruxelles-Capitale (Centre for information, documentation and exhibitions on the city, architecture, landscape and urban planning in the Brussels-Capital Region)
CLiC	Circle for Lacanian Ideology Critique
DDW	Dutch Design Week
FPS Justice	Federal Public Service Justice
FPC	Forensisch Psychiatrisch Centrum (Forensic psychiatric centre)
FPÖ	Freiheitliche Partei Österreichs (Freedom party of Austria)
G30	Association of Architects asbl
HIC	High and Intensive Care model
IPCC	Intergouvernmental Panel on Climate Change
IWT	Agentschap voor Innovatie door Wetenschap en Technologie (Agency for innovation by science and technology)
LSR	Low Stimulus Room
NAi	Nederlands Architectuurinstituut (The Netherlands architecture institute)
NSK	Neue Slowenische Kunst
N-VA	Nieuw-Vlaamse Alliantie (New Flemish alliance)
MAS	Museum aan de Stroom (Museum by the stream)
MVRDV	Maas Van Rijs de Vries
OCPP	Opleidingscentrum Penitentiair Personeel (Prison staff training centre)
Office KGDVS	Office Kersten Geers David Van Severen
OMA	Office for Metropolitan Architecture

PAAZ	Psychiatrische Afdeling Algemeen Ziekenhuis (General hospital psychiatry department)
PvdA	Partij van de Arbeid (Labour party)
PVT	Psychiatrisch Verzorgingstehuis (Psychiatric care home)
PVV	Partij voor de Vrijheid (Party for freedom)
RAL	Revolutionaire Arbeidersliga (Revolutionary workers league)
SALK	Strategisch Actieplan voor Limburg in het Kwadraat (Strategic action plan for Limburg in the square)
S/AM	Stichting Architectuurmuseum (Architecture museum foundation)
SP.a	Socialistische Partij Anders (Socialist party differently)
UNESCO	United Nations Educational, Scientific and Cultural Organization
VAi	Vlaams Architectuurinstituut (Flanders architecture institute)
VOKA	Vlaamse Ondernemers Kamers Alliantie, Vlaams netwerk van ondernemingen (Flanders' chamber of commerce and industry)
VLAIO	Agentschap Innoveren & Ondernemen (Flanders innovation and entrepreneurship)
VRP	Vlaamse Vereniging voor Ruimte en Planning (Flemish association for space and planning)
VRT	Vlaamse Radio en Televisieomroeporganisatie (Flemish public broadcasting company)
VRT NWS	Nieuwsdienst van de VRT (News service of the VRT)
VVD	Volkspartij voor Vrijheid en Democratie (People's party for freedom and democracy)
VVGG	Vlaamse Vereniging Geestelijke Gezondheid (Flemish association for mental health)
WTC	World Trade Center
WTO	World Trade Organization
NMBS/SNCB	Nationale Maatschappij der Belgische Spoorwegen/ Société Nationale des Chemins de fer Belges (Belgian public railway company)

Bibliography

ADD, 'Maak van Colignonplein een terras', *BRUZZ*, 31 May 2020.
Jens Aerts, Gideon Boie and Annekatrien Verdickt, 'Naar de exit zonder auto', *De Standaard*, 12 May 2020, 33. Jens Aerts, Gideon Boie, Annekatrien Verdickt, 'Une nouvelle feuille de route pour une nouvelle mobilité', *Le Soir*, 12 May 2020. Jens Aerts, Gideon Boie, Annekatrien Verdickt, 'It is not desirable for our streets to be dominated by cars again', *The Bulletin*, 12 May 2020.

Giorgio Agamben, *What Is an Apparatus? And Other Essays* (Stanford: Stanford University Press, 2009).

Giorgio Agamben, *Where Are We Now?: The Epidemic as Politics* (Lanham, LD: Rowman & Littlefield, 2021).

Anarchitektur, 'On the Commons: A Public Interview with Massimo De Angelis and Stavros Stavrides', *E-Flux Journal* 17 (2010).

Alejandro Aravena, ed., *Reporting from the Front: 15th International Architecture Exhibition* (Venice: Marsilio Editori, 2016).

Inke Arns and Sylvia Sasse, 'Subversive Affirmation: On Mimesis as a Strategy of Resistance', in *East Art Map. Contemporary Art and Eastern Europe*, ed. IRWIN (London: Afterall /MIT Press, 2006), 444-55.

Nishat Awan, Tatjana Schneider and Jeremy Till, eds., *Spatial Agency: Other Ways of Doing Architecture* (London: Routledge, 2011).

Étienne Balibar, *Politics and the Other Scene* (London: Verso, 2002).
Verena Balz et al., eds., *Netwerken in Zuidelijk Holland: 1000 dagen Atelier Zuidvleugel* (The Hague: Provincie Zuid-Holland, 2008).

BAVO, 'When it Comes to Security, There Is No Normality: een klinische benadering van de hedendaagse beveiligings- en bewakingscultuur', *Archis* 3 (Mar. 2002), 36-42.

BAVO, *De onverdeelde stad en haar gewillige beulen* (The Hague: Stroom, 2003).

BAVO Research, 'Rediscover Your Wholeness! Vijf manieren om de spanning tussen economie en identiteit op te lossen', in *Geest en Grond, culturele planologie in de Duin- en Bollenstreek*, ed. Hans Venhuizen (Rotterdam: Bureau Venhuizen and Erfgoedhuis Zuid-Holland, 2003), 138-46.

BAVO and Dieter Roelstraete, eds., 'Spectres de l'Avant-Garde', *Andere Sinema AS* 176 (Sep.-Oct. 2006).

BAVO, 'From Political Games to Absolute Architecture ... and Back: The Architectural Avant-Garde Today', *Andere Sinema AS* 176 (Sep.-Oct. 2006), 42-61.

BAVO, 'Pleidooi voor een oncreatieve stad', essay part of the exhibition *Neo-Beginners* curated by Reinaart Vanhoe in TENT. CBK Rotterdam, Sep. 2006.

BAVO, ed., *Urban Politics Now: Re-Imagining Democracy in the Neoliberal City* (Rotterdam: nai, 2007).

BAVO, ed., *Cultural Activism Today: The Art of Over-Identification* (Rotterdam: Episode, 2007).

BAVO, 'The Murder of Creativity in Rotterdam: From Total Creative Environments to Gentripunctural Injections', in *MyCreativity Reader: A Critique of Creative Industries*, eds. Geert Lovink and Ned Rossiter (Amsterdam: Institute of Network Cultures, 2007), 153-64.

BAVO, 'Pleidooi voor een oncreatieve stad' (Plea for an uncreative city), an essay that was part of the exhibition *Neo-Beginners* curated by Reinaart Vanhoe in TENT. CBK Rotterdam, Sep., 2006. The paper was reworked as an article: BAVO, 'On Behalf of the Uncreative City', *Metropolis M* 28, no. 1 (Feb. 2007), 27-31.

BAVO, 'Neoliberalism with Dutch Characteristics: The Big Fix-Up of the Netherlands and the Practice of Embedded Cultural Activism', in *Citizens and Subjects: The Netherlands for Example*, ed. Rosi Braidotti et al. (Zürich: JRP-Ringier, 2007), 51-63.

BAVO, 'Kunst in de Grote Verbouwing: voorbij de collectieve conditie van interpassiviteit' (The Hague: Stroom, 2007).

BAVO, 'Take This Fucking Free House, You Creative Idiot!', *Architecture& Magazine* 1: Architecture & Property (Winter 2008), 15-16.

BAVO, 'The Dutch Neoliberal City and the Cultural Activist as the Last of the Idealists', in *Highrise: Common Ground, Art and the Amsterdam Zuidas Area*, ed. Jeroen Boomgaard (Amsterdam: Valiz, 2008), 217-52.

BAVO, 'Come With Us and Enjoy Geographical Schizophrenia', published in the *Euregional Paper* (Maastricht: Jan van Eyck Academie, 2008), pamphlet.

BAVO, 'Eigen Euregio Eerst' (Our own Euregion first), 2009, poster series.

BAVO, Dutch Design Lobby (2010), contribution to the exhibition *Tricksters Tricked: (Un)Covering Identity* at the Van Abbemuseum, Eindhoven, 16 Oct. 2010-06 Feb. 2011, curated by Freek Lomme and Hadas Zemer Ben-Ari.

BAVO, *Too Active to Act: Cultureel activisme na het einde van de geschiedenis* (Amsterdam: Valiz, 2010).

BAVO, 'The Necessity of Enthusiastic Leadership in the Formation and Activation of Creative Coalitions in the Netherlands', in *Power?... To Which People?!*, ed. Jonas Staal (Heijningen: Jap Sam, 2010), 25-34.

BAVO, 'Actieprogramma Kunstenaarsparticipatie', Bureau Kunstenaarsparticipatie, Rotterdam, exhibition piece, 2010.

BAVO, 'Maak liberaal kunstbeleid liberaal', *Metropolis M*, 8 Jun. 2011.

BAVO, 'Denkverbod op liberale kunst', *Joop.nl*, 18 Jun. 2011 and *Metropolis M*, 23 Jun. 2011.

Geert Bekaert in conversation with Johan Thielemans in the VRT documentary Eiland, Nov. 1985, on the occasion of the publication of Verzamelde opstellen.

Geert Bekaert, 'Belgische architectuur als gemeenplaats. De afwezigheid van een architectonische cultuur als uitdaging', *Archis* 9 (1987).

Geert Bekaert, Mil De Kooning, Marc Dubois, Bart Verschaffel, *Architectuur als Buur: panorama van Gent en omstreken 1968-88* (Turnhout: Brepols, 1988).

Geert Bekaert, 'Happy Anniversary: Office Kersten Geers David Van Severen at the 11th Venice Architecture Biennale', in *Rooted in the Real: Writings on Architecture by Geert Bekaert*, ed. Christophe Van Gerrewey (Ghent: WZW Editions & Productions, 2011), 230-40.

Geert Bekaert, 'Belgian Architecture as Commonplace: The Absence of Architectonic Culture as a Challenge', in *Rooted in the Real*, 90-96.

Walter Benjamin, 'On the Concept of History', originally written 1940, online English trans., https://www.sfu.ca/~andrewf/CONCEPT2.html.

Jan Bex, 'Denktank pleit voor kleinschalige aanpak gevangenis Leopoldsburg', *Het Belang van Limburg*, 22 Oct. 2014, 12.

Gideon Boie, 'Report by the Taskforce for Architecture and Administrative Modernisation: Here the Citizen is at Home', in *Flanders Architectural Yearbook 2006-2007: edition 2008*, eds. Katrien Vandermarliere et al. (Antwerp: VAi, 2008), 21-26.

Gideon Boie, 'Plea for Care Architecture', *Flanders Architectural Yearbook 2008-2009* (Antwerp: VAi, 2010), 249-66.

Gideon Boie, *Het Huis van de psychiatrie: verslag* (Antwerp: VAi, 2010).

Gideon Boie, 'Zorgarchitectuur is een opdracht', *Psyche* 23, no. 1 (Mar. 2011), 4-7.

Gideon Boie, 'A Lesson in Added Architectural Value', in *Flanders Architectural Yearbook 2008-2009* (Antwerp: VAi, 2010), 175-77. Later republished as: Gideon Boie, 'Wet89', in *Double or Nothing*, ed. 51N4E (London: AA Publications, 2011).

Gideon Boie, 'Waarom Bas Heijne een nieuwe baan moet zoeken', *Joop.nl*, 22 Sep. 2011.

Gideon Boie, 'A Lesson in Added Architectural Value', *Flanders Architectural Yearbook 2008-2009* (Antwerp: VAi, 2010), 175-77. The essay was later republished: Gideon Boie, 'Wet89' in *Double or Nothing*, ed. 51N4E (London: AA Publications, 2011).

Gideon Boie, 'Een slakkengang voor internering', *Psyche* 24, no. 3 (Sep. 2012), 20-21. Trans. and pub. as 'The Twists and Turns of Internment' on the occasion of the Conflict & Design Triennial at C-mine Genk, 15 Dec. 2013-9 Mar. 2014.

Gideon Boie, *Stad Limburg Projectnota Atelier Limburg Europa* (Hasselt: Architectuurwijzer, 2012).

Gideon Boie, 'Het werk moet nog beginnen', *Ruimte* 17 (Mar. 2013), 28-29.

Gideon Boie, 'Stad Limburg: baanbreker in de ruimtelijke ontwikkeling van Vlaanderen', *Ruimte* 19 (Sep. 2013), 64-67.

Gideon Boie, 'Architectural Asymmetries', in *Is There (Anti-)neoliberal Architecture?*, eds. Ana Jeinić and Anselm Wagner (Berlin: Jovis, 2013), 104-17.

Gideon Boie, 'Ikea komt naar... Stad Limburg', *Het Belang van Limburg*, 19 Oct. 2013, 16.

Gideon Boie, "'t Stad is ook aan de gevangenen', *Ruimte* 15 (Sep.-Nov. 2012), 58-62. Trans. and pub. by Prison Gear under the title 'The City also Belongs to the Prisoners' on the occasion of the Conflict & Design Triennial at C-mine Genk (15 Dec. 2013-9 Mar. 2014).

Gideon Boie, 'De gevangenis als oplossing voor internering', *Psyche* 26, no. 2 (Jun. 2014).

Gideon Boie, 'De Bouwmeester en de onheilsprofeten', *De Standaard*, 14 Aug. 2014.

Gideon Boie, ed., *Ruimteregie in Limburg: Atelier Limburg Europa* (Hasselt: Architectuurwijzer, 2014).

Gideon Boie, 'Het Penitentiair Verdriet van België', *De Standaard*, 27 Oct. 2015, 37.

Gideon Boie, complaint about the Haren prison village design addressed to the mayor of Brussels in the context of the public enquiry part of the urban building permit procedure, 8 May 2015.

Gideon Boie, 'Welke democratie zal Haren redden?', *BRUZZ*, 10 Jun. 2015.

Gideon Boie, 'The Only Good Architect Is a Dead Architect', *OASE* 96 (2016), 44-50.

Gideon Boie, 'Drie variaties op een monumentale buitenruimte', *Psyche* 28, no. 2 (Jun. 2016), 20-21.

Gideon Boie, 'Toiletemmers in werelderfgoed', *De Standaard*, 3 Jun. 2016, 38-39.

Gideon Boie, 'Pic Nic Architectuur', *A+ Architecture in Belgium* 264 (Feb. 2017), 22-24.

Gideon Boie, 'Kwaliteit als katalysator van sloop', *De Architect : Vakblad voor de Architect*, 48, no. 5 (2017), 164-65.

Gideon Boie, 'Moet de beurs een biertempel worden?', *BRUZZ* (3 Oct. 2017).

Gideon Boie, 'Wafels, bier en architectuur', *BRUZZ*, 1586 (4 Oct. 2017), 18-19.

Gideon Boie, 'Verslaafd aan architectuur', *A+ Architecture in Belgium*, 16 Oct. 2017.

Gideon Boie, *Gevangen in open landschap: Kempenlab Cahier 7* (Turnhout: AR-TUR, 2017).

Gideon Boie, 'Relational Architecture: Experiences from the Psychiatric Field', in *Urban Living Labs for Public Space: a New Generation of Planning? Proceedings of the Incubators Conference*, ed. Johan Verbeke (Brussels: KU Leuven, 2017), 49-57.

Gideon Boie, 'Francorchamps aan de Maalbeek', *BRUZZ*, 1600 (24 Jan. 2018), 22-23.

Gideon Boie, 'De onuitroeibare schaamteplek', *De Standaard*, 31 Jan. 2017, 29.

Gideon Boie, 'Design Your Symptom', in *Unless Ever People*, eds. Gideon Boie and architecten de vylder vinck taillieu (Antwerp: VAi, 2018), 186-223.

Gideon Boie, 'De geniale mislukking van de prikkelarme kamer', *Psyche* 30, no. 1 (Mar. 2018), 20-21.

Gideon Boie, 'Architectuur in de naam van de vader', *Architect: Vakblad voor de Architect*, 49, no. 1 (2018), 122-24.

Gideon Boie, 'Everybody Architect: The Authorship of the Square', in *Unless Ever People*, eds. Gideon Boie and architecten de vylder vinck taillieu (Antwerp: VAi, 2018), 228-45.

Gideon Boie, 'The Future Is (Not) Here', in *WTC Tower Teachings* (Brussels: KU Leuven Faculty of Architecture, 2019), 178-80.

Gideon Boie, 'Beste Brusselse politici: het hondsbrutale rijgedrag dat alledaags lijkt, is jullie gedeelde verantwoordelijkheid', *VRT NWS* (2 Apr. 2019).

Gideon Boie, 'Het gebrek aan politieke verbeelding houdt de Brusselse verkeersellende in stand', *VRT NWS* (20 May 2019).

Gideon Boie, 'Verkeersagressie los je niet op met een likje verf', *De Standaard* (21 Jun. 2019), 34-35.

Gideon Boie, 'Hardnekkige hardrijders mogen geen goedkoop alibi zijn voor de verkeersonveiligheid in Schaarbeek', *VRT NWS* (24 Jun. 2019).

Gideon Boie, 'La mente sociale – The Social Mind', *Domus* 1036 (Jun. 2019), 650-57.

Gideon Boie, 'Weg met de fietssuggestiestrook', *De Standaard* (27 Oct. 2019), 30.

Gideon Boie, 'Weg met de architectuurwedstrijden?', *De Standaard*, 31 Oct. 2019, 37.

Gideon Boie, 'Inspraak is geen technisch detail', *De Standaard*, 28 Dec. 2019, 41.

Gideon Boie, 'Werken aan de Brusselse verkeersveiligheid is een boulevard van gebroken beloftes', *VRT NWS* (16 Jan. 2020).

Gideon Boie, 'De nalatenschap van de architectuur', *Psyche* 32, no. 1 (Mar. 2020), 20-21.

Gideon Boie, 'De stad hertekenen, nu kan het', *De Standaard*, 15 Apr. 2020, 26-27.

Gideon Boie, 'De huis-keuken-en-tuin-besognes van een stad', *De Standaard*, 18 Jun. 2020, 26-27.

Gideon Boie, 'De onverschillige logica van het beddenhuis', *De Standaard*, 8 Jul. 2020, 28.

Gideon Boie, 'Here Comes the Architect-Entrepreneur', *A+ Architecture in Belgium* 287 (Dec. 2020-Jan. 2021), 84-87.

Gideon Boie, 'Een hinkelspel is geen parkeerplaats', *De Standaard*, 2 Dec. 2020, 36.

Gideon Boie, 'De fantasie van het Zoomonderwijs,' *De Standaard*, 19 Feb. 2021, 25.

Gideon Boie, 'Playboy-fantasie valt tegen', *De Standaard*, 18 Dec. 2020, 33. Also published in English: Gideon Boie, 'We're all playboys', *Domus* (29 Mar. 2021).

Gideon Boie, 'Een hinkelspel is geen parkeerplaats', *De Standaard*, 2 Dec. 2020, 36.

Gideon Boie, 'Vernieuwing en gevestigde orde gaan niet samen', *De Standaard*, 28 Jun. 2021, 30-31.

Gideon Boie, Vernieuwing en gevestigde orde gaan niet samen, *De Standaard*, 28 Jun. 2021, 30-31.

Gideon Boie, 'Flemish Architectural Culture for Beginners', in *The Persistence of Questioning: Critical Reflections on the Future, on Architecture and More – What Is The State of Architecture Culture?*, eds. Marina van den Bergen, Paul van den Bergh en Leonieke van Dipten (Rotterdam: Archined, 2022).

Gideon Boie, 'De ondraaglijke traagheid van het Brussels stedelijk beleid', *De Standaard*, 9 Jun. 2022, 26-27.

Gideon Boie, 'Ode aan het Caritas project', *Psyche* 34, no. 2 (Jun. 2022), 18-19.

Gideon Boie, 'Seven Question on Flemish Architecture', in *Seven Questions – ETH Studio Jan De Vylder: Universum Carrousel Journey*, eds. Jan De Vylder and Annamaria Prandi (Berlin: Ruby Press, 2022), 241-46.

Gideon Boie, *How much politics can architecture take?*, unpublished manuscript.

Gideon Boie and Sofie De Caigny, eds., *Architectuurcultuur in Vlaanderen* (Antwerp: VAi, 2019).

Gideon Boie and Lieven De Cauter, *Forms of Activism as Democracy in the City* (Brussels: BAVO/OXUMORON Books, 2021).

Gideon Boie and Roel De Ridder, 'Geef Blondeswinning terug aan de natuur', *Het Belang van Limburg*, 22-23 Mar. 2014, 14.

Gideon Boie and Matthias Pauwels, 'De creatieve stad – Stadsontwikkeling is politiek', *De Groene Amsterdammer* 7 (2007).

Gideon Boie and Fie Vandamme, 'Lijdt ook u aan ziekenhuispsychastenie?', *Psyche* 26, no. 4 (Dec. 2014), 20-21.

Gideon Boie and Fie Vandamme, 'Atelier Reigersvliet', in *Ruimteregie in Limburg: Atelier Limburg Europa*, ed. Gideon Boie (Hasselt: Architectuurwijzer, 2014), 59-80.

Gideon Boie and Fie Vandamme, 'Prison Gear', in *Conflict & Design: 7de Triënnale voor Vormgeving / 7th Design Triennial*, ed. Kurt Van Belleghem (Leuven: Lannoo, 2014), 152-53.

Gideon Boie and Fie Vandamme, 'Fit In, Stand Out! From Adjacencies to Agencies in Prison Architecture', in *Creative Adjacencies: New Challenges for Architecture, Design and Urbanism. Proceedings of the Conference 'Creative Adjacencies'*, eds. Yves Schoonjans et al. (Santiago de Chile and Brussels/Ghent, 2014), 455-63.

Gideon Boie and Fie Vandamme, 'Wat gebeurt er tussen paviljoen en schietveld?', *Psyche* 27, no. 2 (Jun. 2015), 20-21.

Gideon Boie and Fie Vandamme, 'Gevangenissen in België: de fabel van marktinnovatie', *De Architect* 25, no. 10 (Dec. 2015).

Gideon Boie and Fie Vandamme, 'De toekomst is aan het zorgerfgoed', *Psyche* 27, no. 1 (Mar. 2015), 20-21.

Gideon Boie and Fie Vandamme, 'Ruimte voor humane isolatie', *Psyche* 27, no. 4 (Dec. 2015), 20-21.

Gideon Boie and Fie Vandamme, *Ontwerp je eigen detentiehuis: Prison Gear* (Ghent: Faculteit Architectuur KU Leuven, 2016).

Gideon Boie and Fie Vandamme, *Vrouwen ontwerpen hun eigen detentie: Prison Gear* (Ghent: Faculteit Architectuur KU Leuven, 2016).

Gideon Boie and Fie Vandamme, 'Architectuur zonder dwang: drie ontwerpuitdagingen', *Psyche* 29, no. 3 (Sep. 2017), 20-21.

Gideon Boie and Annekatrien Verdickt, 'Een winterterras kan levens redden', *De Standaard*, 21 Oct. 2020, 35.

Kristiaan Borret, *Beleidsnota 2006-2011* (Antwerp: Stad Antwerpen, 2007).

Kristiaan Borret, 'Tijd om alternatieven voor Disneyficatie concreet te maken', *BRUZZ*, 25 Oct. 2017.

Nicolas Bourriaud, *Relational Aesthetics* (1998; Dijon: Les Presses du réel, 2002).

Jan Braet, 'Bouwen voor de broeders' (interview with Patrick Lefebure), *Knack*, 18 Feb. 2009, 38-41.

Judith Butler, 'Bodies in Alliance and Politics of the Streets', in *Notes on a Performative Theory of Assembly*, Judith Butler (Cambridge: Harvard University Press, 2015).

Judith Butler, Ernesto Laclau and Slavoj Žižek, *Contingency, Hegemony, Universality: Contemporary Dialogues on the Left* (London/New York: Verso, 2000).

Frans Buyens, 'Een mens genaamd Ernest Mandel (1972)', in Chris Den Hond, dir., *Ernest Mandel, een leven voor de revolutie* (Avanti Productions, 2005), video documentary.

Hans Claus et al., *Huizen naar een duurzame penitentiaire aanpak* (Brussels: ASP, 2013).

Hans Claus, 'De re-integratiegerichte gevangenisdirecteur. Een wedervaren', *FATIK* 147 (2015), 24-30.

Hans Claus and Ronny De Meyer, 'In een of ander huis. detentie op een keerpunt?', *A+Architecture in Belgium* 261 (Aug.-Sep. 2016), 81-85.

Crimson Architectural Historians, *Mart Stam's Trousers: Stories from behind the Scenes of Dutch Moral Modernism* (Rotterdam: 010, 1999)

Crimson Architectural Historians, *Too Blessed to Be Depressed: 1994-2001* (Rotterdam: 010, 2002).

Crimson and Felix Rottenberg, *WIMBY! Hoogvliet toekomst, verleden en heden van een New Town* (Rotterdam: nai, 2007).

Nadia Casabella, 'Nawoord', in *Netwerken in Zuidelijk Holland: 1000 dagen Atelier Zuidvleugel*, eds. Verena Balz et al. (The Hague: Provincie Zuid-Holland, 2008).

Liliana Casagrande, 'Ikea beter in Genk?', *Het Belang van Limburg*, 10 Oct. 2013, 8.

Wim Cassiers, ed., *Antwerpen, Werf van de Eeuw: Een nieuwe fase* (Antwerp: Stad Antwerpen, 2007).

Belgian Chamber of Representatives, notes of the first presentation of the Prison Act in the Committee on Justice, 24 Nov. 2004.

Beatriz Colomina, 'The Bed in the Age of Corona', *Vitra Magazine*, 19 Jun. 2020.

Wim Cuyvers, *Beograd – The Hague: About the Impossibility of Planning* (The Hague: Stroom, 2003).

Wim Cuyvers, 'The Belgian House: The Waiting Façade and the Field of Fire', *A+U* 392 (2003).

Wim Cuyvers, 'From the Dream of the Novel Turned to Stone to the Acknowledgment of Public Space', *OASE* 70 (Jun. 2006), 20-29.

Barbara Debusschere, 'Therapeut klaagt aan: Jeugdpsychiatrie bezorgt jongeren vaak méér trauma's', *De Morgen*, 30 Mar. 2015.

Sofie De Caigny, 'Het glazen plafond van de Vlaamse architectuur', *De Standaard*, 28 Nov. 2018.

Sofie De Caigny, 'Epilogue: On Architecture Culture and Building Culture', in *More Than a Competition*, eds. Maarten Liefooghe and Maarten Van Den Driessche (Antwerp/Brussels: VAi/Team Vlaams Bouwmeester, 2021).

Lieven De Cauter and Michiel Dehaene, 'Meditations on Razor Wire: A Plea for Para-Architecture' in *Visionary Power : Producing the Contemporary City*, ed by. Christine de Baan, Joachim Declerck, and Véronique Patteeuw (Rotterdam: NAI Publishers, 2007), 233-247.

Lieven De Cauter, 'Kunst en Activisme', *Rekto:Verso*, 15 Jun. 2015.

Lieven De Cauter, 'Utopia Rediscovered: A Redefinition of Utopianism in the Light of the Enclosures of the Commons', in *A Truly Golden Handbook: the Scholarly Quest for Utopia*, eds. Veerle Achten, Erik Schokkaert, and Geert Bouckaert (Leuven: Leuven University Press, 2016), 534-45.

Lieven De Cauter, 'Biertempel? Over our dead bodies!', *BRUZZ*, 11 Oct. 2017.

Lieven De Cauter, 'Waarom een verwaterde biertempel? Een antwoord aan Sven Gatz', *De Wereld Morgen*, 26 Oct. 2017.

Lieven De Cauter, 'The Space of Play: Towards a General Theory of Heterotopia (with Michiel Dehaene)' in *Entropic Empire On the City of Man in the Age of Disaster* (Rotterdam: nai010, 2012).

Lieven De Cauter, 'Coronalimbo', *De Wereld Morgen*, 27 Apr. 2020.

Lieven De Cauter, *Ending the Antropocene: Essays on Activism in the Age of Collapse* (Rotterdam: nai010, 2021).

Christophe De Rijcke, 'Immobel herontwikkelt hoofdzetel Proximus', *De Tijd*, 29 Oct. 2021.

Sara De Sloovere, 'Bescheiden steunactie 1030/0 en Gracq aan "stadstuintje" Schaarbeek', *BRUZZ*, 20 Jun. 2020.

Sara De Sloovere, 'Josaphatpark kreunt onder wildparkeerders: Schaarbeek ontkent gedoogbeleid', *BRUZZ*, 24 Apr. 2019.

Sara De Sloovere and Laurent Vermeersch, 'Beloftes zijn er, nu moeten ze worden waargemaakt', *BRUZZ*, 1637 (07 Nov. 2018), 12-15.

Lionel Devlieger, 'Law Court, Antwerp', *Flanders Architectural Yearbook 2006-2007: edition 2008*, eds. Katrien Vandermarliere et al. (Antwerp: VAi, 2008), 50-57.

Stefan Devoldere, ed., 'A+ 1907 After the Party', special issue of *A+ Belgisch tijdschrift voor architectuur*, on the occasion of the 2008 Venice Biennale.

Stefan Devoldere, 'Een stadsbouwmeester moet durven bluffen: interview met Kristiaan Borret', *A+ Belgisch tijdschrift voor architectuur* 209 (2008), 50-55.

Isabelle Doucet, *The Practice Turn in Architecture: Brussels after 1968* (New York: Routledge, 2015)

Marc Dubois, 'Het spook van de Gentse opera', *De Standaard* (3 Dec. 2018).

Maxie Eckert and Veerle Beel, 'De stoornissen van de Psychiatrie: de inspectieverslagen doorgelicht', *De Standaard*, 27 Jan. 2017.

Nan Ellin, ed., *Architecture of Fear* (New York: Princeton Architectural Press, 1997).

Eubelius attorneys, Registered letter sent to Gideon Boie and Dag Boutsen, dean of the KU Leuven Faculty of Architecture, 16 Dec. 2015.

EVG, 'Fietspad verdeelt de Wetstraat', *De Standaard*, 5 May 2020.

Sophie Fiennes, *The Pervert's Guide to Cinema: Presented by Slavoj Žižek*, documentary film, 2006.

Alain Findeli and Rabah Bousbaci, 'L'éclipse de l'object dans les théories du projet en design', *The Design Journal* 8, no. 1 (2005), 35-49.

Bruce Fink, 'The Master Signifier and the Four Discourses', in *Key Concepts of Lacanian Philosophy*, ed. Dany Nobus (New York: Other Press, 1998), 29-47.

Richard Florida, *The Rise of the Creative Class: And How it's Transforming Work, Leisure, Community and Everyday Life* (New York: Basic, 2004).

Michel Foucault, *History of Madness* (1961; London/New York: Routledge, 2006).

Michel Foucault, 'The Order of Discourse', in *Untying the Text: A Post-Structuralist Reader*, ed. Robert Young (Boston: Routledge & Kegan Paul, 1981), 48-78. Inaugural lecture at the Collège de France, given 2 Dec. 1970.

Michel Foucault, *Discipline and Punish: The Birth of the Prison* (1975; New York: Vintage, 1977).

Michel Foucault, 'Of Other Spaces', *Diacritics* 16, no. 1 (Spring 1986), 22-27.

Francis Fukuyama, *The End of History and the Last Man* (New York: Free Press, 1992).

Francis Fukuyama, *America at the Crossroads: Democracy, Power and the Neoconservative Legacy* (New Haven: Yale University Press, 2006).

Sven Gatz, 'We geven Beursgebouw terug aan de mensen', *BRUZZ*, 10 Oct. 2017.

GDC, 'Vijfjarige jongen zwaargewond na ongeval met vluchtmisdrijf', *BRUZZ*, 16 Jan. 2015.

Kersten Geers, Joris Kritis, Jelena Pancevac, Giovanni Piovene, Dries Rodet and Andrea Zanderigo, *Architecture Without Content* (London: Bedford Press, 2015).

Caroline Goossens, 'De Janssens Werken', in *35m³ BAVO*, eds. Katrien Vandermarliere and Moritz Küng (Antwerp: De Singel/VAi, 2008), exhibition brochure.

Goudvis, Season 1, Episode 2, VRT, 2009, television documentary.

GR, 'Wake voor in Schaarbeek verongelukte journaliste', *BRUZZ*, 09 Nov. 2017.

Ralph Gregoor, 'Limburg heeft 60.000 nieuwe woningen nodig', *De Standaard*, 22 Nov. 2012. Also published in Het Nieuwsblad, 22 Nov. 2022.

Félix Guattari, *The Three Ecologies* (London/New York: Continuum, 2008). Originally published as *Les trois écologies*, 1989.

Boris Groys, 'The Irwin Group: More Total than Totalitarianism', in *Primary Documents: A Sourcebook for Eastern and Central European Art Since the 1950s*, eds. Laura Hoptman and Tomaš Pospisyl (New York: Museum of Modern Art, 2002). Originally written in 1990.

Boris Groys, *Art Power* (Cambridge, MA: MIT Press, 2008).

Roger Hallam, *Common Sense for the 21st Century: Only Nonviolent Rebellion Can Now Stop Climate Breakdown And Social Collapse* (London: Chelsea Green, 2019).

Michael Hardt and Toni Negri, *Commonwealth* (Cambridge: Belknap Press, 2009).

David Harvey, *Rebel Cities: From the Right to the City to the Urban Revolution* (London: Verso, 2012).

Klaske Havik and Sebas Veldhuisen, 'Communisten, jongleurs en cliniclowns', *Archined*, 8 Apr. 2003.

Veronica Hekking, Sabrina Lindemann and Annechien Meier, *OpTrek in Transvaal: On the Role of Public Art in Urban Development. Interventions and Research* (Heijningen: Jap Sam, 2010).

Joris Hendrickx, 'Geestelijke gezondheidszorg zet voluit in op welzijn en comfort', *Media Planet*, Dec. 2016.

Kris Hendrickx, '27 van de 95 Brusselse flitspalen defect', *BRUZZ* (2 April 2019).

Kris Hendrickx, 'Ukkelse burgemeester: Test Ter Kamerenbos veel te radicaal', *BRUZZ*, 2 Sep. 2020.

Tine Hens et al., Architectuurnota 2009-2014 (Antwerp/Brussels: VAi/Team Flemish Government Architect, 2009).

Wouter Hertogs, 'Honderdtal mensen voeren actie voor veiliger verkeer na aanrijding kind (2)', *Het Laatste Nieuws*, 30 May 2020.

Stéphane Hessel, *Time For Outrage!* (2010; London: Quartet, 2011).

Susanne Hofmann, *Architecture Is Participation: Die Baupiloten – Methods and Projects* (Berlin: Jovis, 2014).

Hoge Gezondheidsraad, *Omgaan met conflict, conflictbeheersing en dwanginterventies in de geestelijke gezondheidszorg*, HGR 9193 (Jun. 2016).

Dirk Holemans, 'Radicale klimaatactivisten effenen het pad', *De Standaard*, 10 Nov. 2022.

Frank Hoornaert, 'Buurtbewoners komen na ongeval op straat in Schaarbeek', *BRUZZ*, 1 Jun. 2020.

Ineke Hulshof, *Poetic Freedom: Report on a Regeneration Project in the Neighbourhood of Spangen in Rotterdam* (Delft, 2008).

Ana Jeinić and Anselm Wagner, eds., *Is There (Anti-)neoliberal Architecture?* (Berlin: Jovis, 2013).

Charles Jencks, *Can Architecture Affect Your Health?* (Arnhem: ArtEZ Press, 2012).

Martin Luther King, *Where Do We Go From Here: Chaos or Community?* (Boston: Beacon, 1967).

Kollectief Zonder Dwang, 'Jeugdhulpverlening zonder dwang! Op zoek naar alternatieven voor eenzame opsluiting', press file, 4 May 2017.

Rem Koolhaas, *Delirious New York: A Retroactive Manifesto for Manhattan* (1978; New York: Monacelli, 1994).

Lars Kwakkenbos, 'Glass Under Siege: Two New Court Buildings in Flanders', *Flanders Architectural Yearbook 2006-2007: edition 2008*, eds. Katrien Vandermarliere et al. (Antwerp: VAi, 2008), 9-14.

Jacques Lacan, 'The Mirror Stage as Formative of the Function of the I', in *Écrits: A Selection* (1966; London: Routledge, 2005).

Jacques Lacan, *The Seminar of Jacques Lacan, Book XVII: The Other Side of Psychoanalysis* (1973; New York: Norton, 2008).

Transcript of the lecture by Jacques Lacan at Milan University on 12 May 1972 is published in: Jacques Lacan, 'Du Discours Psychanalytique', in *Lacan in Italia, 1953-1978, Lacan en Italie* (Milan: La Salmandra, 1978), 32-55.

Mierle Laderman Ukeles, *Manifesto! Maintenance – Proposal for an Exhibition*, 1969, artwork.

Laibach, '10 Items of the Convenant', *Nova Revija* 13/14 (1983). Originally created in 1982.

Bruno Latour, *Down to Earth: Politics in the New Climate Regime* (Cambridge: Polity Press, 2018). Originally published as *Où atterrir? Comment s'orienter en politique*, 2017.

Ihsane Chioua Lekhli and Floor Bruggeman, 'Wat is het antwoord van Bart De Wever (N-VA) aan de 35.000 klimaatspijbelaars? Niet geloven in doemverhalen', *VRT NWS*, 1 Jan. 2019.

Marlies Lenaerts, ed., *L'Autre Atelier / Het Andere Atelier* (Brussels: BRAL, 2021).

André Loeckx, ed., *Stadsvernieuwingsprojecten In Vlaanderen: ontwerpend onderzoek en capacity building* (Nijmegen: SUN, 2009).

André Loeckx, 'Labo Vespa,' in *Flanders Architectural Yearbook 2008-2009* (Antwerp: VAi, 2010), 217-48.

André Loeckx, 'Meesterzet in drie bewegingen: gesprek met Peter

Swinnen, Marcel Smets en b0b Van Reeth', *A+ Architecture in Belgium* 242 (Jun.-Jul. 2013), 90-94.

Marshall MacLuhan, *The Medium is the Massage: An Inventory of Effects* (London: Penguin Books, 1967).

Jeroen Maesschalck et al., 'De evolutie naar een nieuwe politieke cultuur in België: een beleidswetenschappelijke analyse', *Beleidswetenschap: kwartaalschrift voor beleidsonderzoek en beleidspraktijk* 16, no. 4 (2002),295-317.

Gerard Marlet and Clemens van Woerkens, 'Het economisch belang van de creatieve klasse', *Economisch Statistische Berichten* 89, no. 445 (11 Jun. 2004), 280-83.

Karl Marx and Friedrich Engels, *The Communist Manifesto: A Modern Edition* (1848; London: Verso, 2012).

Alexei Monroe, 'The Myth of the Slovene Stag: Neue Slowenische Kunst and the Reprocessing of Traditional Symbolism', in BAVO, *Cultural Activism Today*, 49-57.

Alexei Monroe, 'Full Spectrum Provocation: The Retrogarde Strategies of Neue Slowenische Kunst', *Andere Sinema* 176 (Sep.-Oct. 2006), 84-101.

Alexei Monroe, *Interrogation Machine: Laibach and NSK* (Cambridge MA: MIT, 2005).

Chantal Mouffe, *On the Political* (New York: Routledge, 2005).

MVRDV, *Metacity / Datatown* (Rotterdam: 010, 1999).

NN, 'Protest tegen megagevangenis Haren: Gespannen sfeer tijdens overlegcommissie', *BRUZZ*, 20 May, 2015.

NN, 'Tegenstanders megagevangenis bekladden huis Vervoort: Geen normale democratie', *BRUZZ*, 19 May 2015.

NN., 'Terugblik op de eerste Staten-Generaal van de Limburgse architectuur', report on the website of Architectuurwijzer, https://architectuurwijzer.be/staten-generaal-vd-limburgse-architectuur/ and https://www.facebook.com/pg/Architectuurwijzer/photos/?tab=album&album_id=10151488354544758.

Chris Nelis, 'Architecten vragen eigen Limburgse Bouwmeester', *Het Belang van Limburg*, 22 Nov. 2012, 46.

Maurice Nio, *You Have The Right To Remain Silent* (Amsterdam: 1001, 1998).

NLS, 'Geen uitgebreide terrassen op het Colignonplein', *BRUZZ*, 3 Jul. 2020.

Dany Nobus, 'What Are Words Worth? Lacan and the Circulation of Money in the Psychoanalytic Economy', *Modern Psychoanalysis* 38, no. 2 (2013), 157-88.

NOX, *Actiones in Distans* (Amsterdam: 1001, 1991).

NOX, *Biotech* (Amsterdam: 1001, 1992).

NOX, *Chloroform* (Amsterdam: 1001, 1993).

NOX, *Djihad* (Amsterdam: 1001, 1995).

Office Kersten Geers David Van Severen, *Everything Architecture* (Cologne: Walther König, 2017).

Merijn Oudenampsen, 'De pijnlijke scherpte van het cynisch idealisme', *Archined*, 25 Jan. 2011.

Merijn Oudenampsen, 'Too Active to Act: Review', *Open! Platform for Art, Culture & the Public Domain* 21 (2011), 164-65.

Jesse Pappers, 'Voor wie zijn de parken?', *De Standaard*, 30 Nov. 2020.

Matteo Pasquinelli, 'Immaterial Civil War: Prototypes of Conflict within Cognitive Capitalism' (Barcelona, Sep. 2006).

Matteo Pasquinelli, 'Beyond the Ruins of the Creative City: Berlin's Factory of Culture and the Sabotage of Rent', in *Skulpturenpark Berlin_Zentrum*, ed. KUNSTrePUBLIK (Berlin: Verlag der Buchhandlung Walther König, 2010).

Walter Pauli and Ewald Pironet, 'Voormalig Vlaams bouwmeester Peter Swinnen: Hoeveel visuele rommel kan een mens aan?', *Knack*, 13 Jun. 2018.

Doina Petrescu, 'Losing Control, Keeping Desire', in *Architecture and Participation*, eds. Peter Blundell Jones, Doina Petrescu and Jeremy Till (London: Spon Press, 2005), 43-65.

Kris Pieters, Dominik Renson and Wim Simons, 'Primeur binnen de GGZ: Rooming In', *Similes* 158 (Dec. 2016), 8-10.

Paul Poet, *Foreignors Out! Schlingensiefs Container*, film, Monitorpop, 2002.

Jef Poppelmonde, 'Een auto is oké, maar een tuintje dat mensen samenbrengt? Ho maar', *De Standaard*, 17 Jun. 2020.

Moisés Puente, ed., *Kersten Geers, Without Content; 2G Essays* (Köln: Walter & Franz König, 2021).

Jacques Rancière, *The Ignorant Schoolmaster: Five Lessons in Intellectual Emancipation* (1987; Stanford: Stanford University Press, 1991).

Jacques Rancière, *Disagreement: Politics and Philosophy* (Minneapolis: University of Minnesota Press, 2004).

Herman Reynders, *Rede van de Gouverneur 2013: De Stad Limburg Pleidooi voor meer stedelijkheid en samenwerking* (Hasselt: Provincie Limburg, 2013).

Herman Reynders, *De Stad Limburg II* (Hasselt: Provincie Limburg, 2014).

Serge Rooman, 'Voorwoord', in *Gevangen in open landschap: Kempenlab Cahier 7*, ed. Gideon Boie (Turnhout: AR-TUR, 2017), 7.

Herman Roose, 'Architectuur en zorg samen op zoek naar ruimte voor humane isolatie', Zorgwijzer 59 (May 2016), 23-25.

Herman Roose, 'Design Dialogue and Co-Authorship: A Social-Constructionist Approach', in *Unless Ever People*, eds. Gideon Boie and architecten de vylder vinck taillieu (Antwerp: VAi, 2018), 228-45.

Marc Santens and Jan De Zutter, *Het Vlaams Bouwmeesterschap 1999-2005: Een zoektocht naar kwaliteit in de publieke ruimte* (Antwerp: Houtekiet, 2008).

Yannick Schandené, 'Biertempel en activisten: mag het debat gematigder?', *BRUZZ*, 25 Oct. 2017.

Jack Segbars, *Rondom (All Around the Periphery)* (Eindhoven: Onomatopee, 2013).

Geert Sels, 'Eén of vijf Bouwmeesters?', *De Standaard*, 14 Aug. 2014.

Geert Sels, 'De jonge architecten zijn aan zet', *De Standaard*, 25 Oct. 2016.

Geert Sels, 'Eerste project van Rem Koolhaas in België', *De Standaard*, 22 Feb. 2020, 30-31.

SN, 'Straat door Josaphatpark wordt weer autoweg', *BRUZZ*, 21 Aug. 2019.

Edward W. Soja, 'Postmetropolitan Psychastenia: A Spatioanalysis', in BAVO, *Urban Politics Now*, 78-93.

Michael Sorkin, *Variations on a Theme Park: The New American City and the End of Public Space* (New York: Farrar, Straus and Giroux, 1992).

Michael Sorkin, 'Drawing the Line: Architects and Prisons', *The Nation*, 27 Aug. 2013.

Michael Speaks, 'Design Intelligence', in *Constructing a New Agenda*, ed. A. Krista Sykes (New York: Princeton Architectural Press, 2010), 204-15.

Jonas Staal, *The Geert Wilders Works* (2005-08), artwork.

Jonas Staal, *Post-Propaganda* (Amsterdam: Fonds BKVB, 2010).

Deyan Sudjic, *The Edifice Complex* (London: Penguin, 2006).

Malkit Soshan, *BLUE: Architecture of UN Peacekeeping Missions* (Barcelona: ACTAR, 2022).

Annemie Sour, *169 klushuizen: van experiment naar instrument* (Heijningen: Jap Sam, 2009).

Peter Swinnen, *Zeven memo's voor een verlichte bouwcultuur. Ambitienota Vlaams Bouwmeester 2010-2015* (Brussels: Vlaamse Overheid, 2010).

Peter Swinnen, 'De architect als beleidsfluisteraar', *A+ Architecture in Belgium* 261 (Oct. 2016), 48-50.

Erik Swyngedouw, 'A New Urbanity? The Ambiguous Politics of Large-scale Urban Development Projects in European Cities', in *Amsterdam Zuidas: European Space*, eds. Willem Salet and Stan Majoor (Rotterdam: 010, 2005).

TDN, 'Flitspalen op Lambermontlaan nog steeds defect', *BRUZZ* (8 Oct. 2019).

TDN, 'Burgercollectief vormt mensenketting voor veiligere Lambermontlaan', *BRUZZ* (5 Feb. 2019).

Johan Thielemans, *Eiland*, VRT, Nov. 1985, television documentary.

Henry David Thoreau, *On the Duty of Civil Disobedience* (1849; New York: Open Road, 2015).

Pieter Uyttenhove, 'De Janssens Werken (BAVO) en architectuur in Antwerpen – een paneldiscussie', *De Witte Raaf* 119 (May-Jun. 2009).

Lukas Vanacker, 'Immobel plant 400 woningen en koten in Proximus-torens', *De Tijd*, 14 Jul. 2022.

Maarten Van Acker, ''t Stad als vaccin, onze buurt als medicijn', *Gazet van Antwerpen*, 15 Apr. 2020.

Liesl Vanautgaerden, *T.OP Limburg – Ruimte voor groei. Nr. 1* (Brussels: Ruimte Vlaanderen, 2015), 7.

Liesl Vanautgaerden, 'Het Kolenspoor', *Ruimte* 31 (Sep.-Nov. 2016), 48-51.

Leo Van Broeck, comment on the post by Lieven De Cauter on *Facebook* (10 Oct. 2017), https://www.facebook.com/lieven.decauter/posts/pfbid02bGf54sBePTikBQj5KWm8xpmgkNFvPSXHPzNbQVhojZnYiQydY-1hLgaipNUbsTPsgl

Leo Van Broeck, 'Het gaat om kwaliteit, en kwaliteit alleen', *De Standaard*, 4 Dec. 2018.

Fie Vandamme, 'Recycle the Prisoners' (master's thesis, Brussels, KU Leuven Faculty of Architecture, 2013).

Fie Vandamme, 'Fit In, Stand Out: Een actieonderzoek naar architectuur als antwoord op mortificatie en recidivisme in de gevangenis' (Brussels: KU Leuven Faculty of Architecture, 2014).

Nikolaas Vande Keere and Regis Verplaetse, *De Psychiatrische Kliniek Ontmanteld* (Antwerp: UR Architects, 2009).

Sara Vandekerckhove, 'Psychiatrie moet sociaal zijn', *De Morgen*, 25 Feb. 2017.

Kevin Van den Panhuyzen, 'Flitspaal Lambermontlaan al tien jaar defect', *BRUZZ*, 13 Feb. 2019.

Kevin Van den Panhuyzen, 'Stadstuintje staat weer op parkeerplaats in Schaarbeek zonder toestemming gemeente', *BRUZZ*, 8 Jul. 2020.

Marina van der Bergen, 'De Dutch Design Lobby', *Archined*, 28 Oct. 2010.

Katrien Vandermarliere et al., eds., *Flanders Architectural Yearbook 1990-1993* (Brussels: Ministry of the Flemish Community, 1994).

Katrien Vandermarliere et al., eds., *Flanders Architectural Yearbook 2006-2007: edition 2008* (Antwerp: VAi, 2008).

Geert Van der Speeten, 'Gezocht: architecten voor 't Stad', *De Standaard*, 14 Apr. 2008.

Ries van der Wouden et al., *Ex Antetoets Startnotitie Randstad 2040* (The Hague: PBL Netherlands Environmental Assessment Agency, May 2008).

Elke Vanempten, *Manifesto for a productive landscape – Manifest voor een productief landschap* (Brussels: ILVO, Team Bouwmeester, Departement Landbouw & Visserij and Departement Omgeving, 2018).

Femke Van Garderen, Sara Vandekerckhove and Jonas Lampens, 'In een isolatiecel wordt niemand beter', *De Morgen*, 18 Feb. 2017.

Femke van Garderen and Sara Vandekerckhove, 'Te snel naar de isoleercel', *De Morgen*, 21 Feb. 2017.

Femke Van Garderen, 'In Diest mag je man mee in afzondering' (In Diest your husband can join you in the seclusion room), *De Morgen*, 24 Feb. 2017.

Steven Van Garsse, 'Ongeval op Lambermontlaan roept vragen op', *Brussel Deze Week* 1459 (28 Jan. 2015), 2.

Christophe Van Gerrewey, 'Architecture Is Itself: Een gesprek tussen Joachim Declerck, Kersten Geers & David Van Severen', in *35m³ Office Kersten Geers David Van Severen*, eds. Katrien Vandermarliere and Moritz Küng (Antwerp: De Singel/VAi, 2005), exhibition brochure.

Christophe Van Gerrewey, 'Jaarboek Architectuur Vlaanderen 06-07, editie 2008', *De Witte Raaf* 135 (Sep.-Oct. 2008), review.

Hans Teerds, Christophe Van Gerrewey and Véronique Patteeuw, eds., 'What Is Good Architecture?', *OASE* 90 (May 2013).

Christophe Van Gerrewey, 'Order, Disorder. Ten choices and contradictions in the work of OFFICE' in *OFFICE Kersten Geers David Van Severen: Volume 2*, eds. Kersten Geers, David Van Severen, Bas Princen, et al. (Cologne: Walther König, 2016), 7-14.

Christophe Van Gerrewey, 'Het saaiste ontwerp heeft gewonnen', *De Standaard*, 25 Oct. 2019.

Christophe Van Gerrewey, 'Wie over architectuur wil spreken, sta op en spreek over architectuur', *De Witte Raaf* 202, Nov.-December 2019.

Nicholas Vanhecke, 'Gebouw centrum geïnterneerden kampt met kinderziektes', *De Standaard*, 4 Dec. 2015.

Tom van Mierlo, Frits Bovenberg, Yolande Voskes and Niels Mulder, eds., Werkboek HIC: High en intensive care in de psychiatrie (Utrecht: De Tijdstroom, 2013).

Th. Van Ro, 'Official Report of the Public Enquiry Commission by the City of Brussels', Urbanism Department, Permit Section, meeting 20 May 2015.

Wouter Vanstiphout, 'Blame the Architect!', lecture organized by Stad en Architectuur (Leuven, STUK, 3 Mar. 2011). The title was used as general title for the autumn lecture series by Wouter Vanstiphout as Chair of Design as Politics at TU Delft in 2011.

Koen Van Synghel, comment on the post by Lieven De Cauter on *Facebook* (10 Oct. 2017), https://www.facebook.com/lieven.decauter/posts/pfbid02bGf54sBePTikBQj5KWm8xpmgkNFvPSXHPzNbQVhojZnYiQydY-1hLgaipNUbsTPsgl

Ward Verbakel and Joeri De Bruyn, *bMa: Man of Thoughts* (Mechelen: Public Space, 2014).

Heleen Verheyden, 'Een detentiehuis in my backyard' (A detention house in my backyard) (master's thesis, Brussels, KU Leuven Faculty of Architecture, 2017).

Paul Vermeulen, Maarten Delbeke, Christophe Van Gerrewey, *Moderne Tijden: teksten over architectuur: Vlees en beton 72* (Ghent: WZW Editions & Productions, 2007).

Paul Vermeulen, 'Dankrede bij de Vlaamse Cultuurprijs', *A+ Architecture in Belgium* 233 (Dec. 2011-Jan. 12), 52-53.

Immanuel Wallerstein, *Historical Capitalism with Capitalist Civilization* (1983; London: Verso, 1995).

Eyal Weizman, 'Matters of Calculation: The Evidence of the Anthropocene. Eyal Weizman in Conversation with Heather Davis and Etienne Turpin', in *Architecture in the Antropocene*, eds. Heather Davies and Etienne Turpin (London: Open Humanities Press, 2013), 66-82.

Kristof Windels, 'De Wever gooit stadsslogan in de kiesstrijd', *De Morgen*, 17 Sep. 2012.

The Yes Men, film starring Mike Bonanno and Andy Bichlbaum, MGM Distribution, 2003.

Slavoj Žižek, *The Plague of Fantasies* (London: Verso, 1997).

Slavoj Žižek, *Looking Awry: An Introduction to Jacques Lacan through Popular Culture* (Cambridge, MA: MIT Press, 1991).

Slavoj Žižek, *Pleidooi voor intolerantie* (Amsterdam: Uitgeverij Boom, 1998). Originally published as 'Multiculturalism, Or, the Cultural Logic of Multinational Capitalism', *New Left Review* 225 (Sep.-Oct. 1997), 28-51.

Slavoj Žižek, *The Sublime Object of Ideology* (London: Verso, 1989).

Slavoj Žižek, 'Why Are Laibach and NSK not Fascists?', M'ARS Moderna Galerija Ljubljana Magazine 3-4 (1993).

Slavoj Žižek, *Tarrying With the Negative: Kant, Hegel and the Cri-*

tique of Ideology (Durham: Duke University Press, 1993).

Slavoj Žižek, *Indivisible Remainder: On Schelling and Related Matters* (London: Verso, 1996).

Slavoj Žižek, *The Ticklish Subject: The Absent Centre of Political Ontology* (London: Verso, 1997), 171-245.

Slavoj Žižek, *The Fragile Absolute, Or, Why the Christian Legacy is Worth Fighting For?* (London: Verso, 2000).

Slavoj Žižek, 'Why Do We All Love to Hate Haider?', *New Left Review* 2, Mar. – Apr. 2000.

Slavoj Žižek, *The Fright of Real Tears: Krzystof Kieslowski between Theory and Post-Theory* (London: British Film Institute, 2001), 114-15.

Slavoj Žižek, *Enjoy Your Symptom! Jacques Lacan in Hollywood and Out* (London: Verso, 2001).

Slavoj Žižek, *On Belief* (London: Routledge, 2001).

Slavoj Žižek, *Repeating Lenin* (Zagreb: Bastard, 2001).

Slavoj Žižek, *For They Know Not What They Do: Enjoyment as a Political Factor* (1991; London: Verso, 2002).

Slavoj Žižek, *The Puppet and the Dwarf: The Perverse Core of Christianity* (Cambridge, MA: MIT Press, 2003).

Slavoj Žižek, *Organs without Bodies: Deleuze and Consequences* (London: Routledge, 2004).

Slavoj Žižek, *Iraq: The Borrowed Kettle* (London: Verso, 2004).

Slavoj Žižek, 'The Object a in Social Links', in: *Jacques Lacan and the Other Side of Psychoanalysis: Reflections on Seminar XVII*, eds. Justin Clemens and Russel Grigg (Durham: Duke University Press, 2006), 107-28.

Slavoj Žižek, *The Parallax View* (Cambridge MA: MIT Press, 2006).

Slavoj Žižek, *How to Read Lacan* (London: Granta, 2006), 79-90.

Slavoj Žižek, 'Some Politically Incorrect Reflections on Urban Violence in Paris and New Orleans and Related Matters', in BAVO, *Urban Politics Now* (2007), 12-29.

Slavoj Žižek, *Violence: Six Sideways Reflections* (London: Profile, 2009).

Slavoj Žižek, *The Year of Dreaming Dangerously* (London: Verso, 2012).

Slavoj Žižek, *A Left that Dares to Speak Its Name* (Cambridge: Polity, 2020).

ZUS and MAAT, Ontwerpend Onderzoek Territoriaal Ontwikkelingsplan Centraal-Limburg, commissioned by Ruimte Vlaanderen (Brussels: Vlaamse Overheid, Jun.-Dec. 2013).

Sander Zweerts de Jong, 'BAVO en het Bureau Kunstenaarsparticipatie', *CBK Magazine*, Mar.2010.

'De gestoorde procedure', Panorama, VRT, 21 Feb. 2013, television documentary.

'Weg van de waanzin', Koppen, VRT, 25 Nov. 2015, television documentary.

List of Images

- Cover: *Traces* by Ultima Vez, performance in the framework of Openstreets 22. © Ivan Put
- Introduction: /
- Chapter 1: Cinéma Jolia, *The dream labour with BAVO*, 2024 © Cinéma Jolia
- Chapter 2: Image accompanying the article by BAVO, 'Verslaafd aan creativiteit', *ZOUT Corporate Magazine KPMG* 06 (Aug. 2007), 62-67. © Nienke de Zwart
- Chapter 3: Hendrik-Jan Grievink, *VOC meets Louis Vuitton wall paper*, image made for HTV De IJsberg 68, 2008, guest-edited by BAVO. © Hendrik-Jan Grievink
- Chapter 4: Hendrik-Jan Grievink, page from 'Too Active to Act, beeldessay', 2010, graphic novel, published in BAVO, *Too Active to Act: Cultureel activisme na het einde van de geschiedenis* (Amsterdam: Valiz, 2010), 71-95. © Hendrik-Jan Grievink
- Chapter 5: Roberto Soto, image series reusing photography from the Provincial Archive for the publication of the workbook *Tien dingen die je gewoon moet doen*, Jun. 2007. © Roberto Soto
- Chapter 6: The 'De Janssens Werken' information box installed at De Singel, Antwerp, part of the exhibition series *35m³ Young Architecture* organized by De Singel and the VAi, 2008. © Jan Kempenaers
- Chapter 7: 'Bureau Kunstenaarsparticipatie' (Office for artist participation) organized an information booth in Rotterdam City Hall from 22 to 25 Feb. 2010, a parallel event part of the exhibition *The People United Will Never Be Defeated*, curated by Jonas Staal at TENT Rotterdam, 19 Feb.-28 Apr. 2010. © Lotte Stekelenburg
- Chapter 8: Presentation of the initial note *Building Up a Stronger Brand: Limburg Government Architect* (Hasselt: Architectuurwijzer, 2012) at the first Staten-Generaal (C-mine, 21 November 2012). The plenary evening debate was introduced by Herman Reynders, Governor of Limburg Province, and followed by a panel with distinguished guests. The host of the evening was Ianka Fleerackers. © Architectuurreportage
- Chapter 9: Photography series 'Prison in a protected landscape' by Karin Borghouts documenting the architecture of Merksplas and Hoogstraten prisons, exhibited in the chapel of Merksplas Colony, 4-28 May 2017. © Karin Borghouts
- Chapter 10: Kanunnik Petrus Jozef Triest Plein at KARUS, campus Melle, May 2018, design by architecten de vylder vinck taillieu © Filip Dujardin
- Chapter 11: The Low-Stimulus Room (LSR) in the Sint-Jan Acute admissions department of the Sint-Annendael Diest psychiatric hospital, image series part of the *Prikkels* (Stimuli) exhibition at Museum Dr. Guislain, Ghent, 20 Oct. 2018-26 May 2019. © Kurt Deruyter
- Chapter 12: Drawing of hopscotch, running track and labyrinth using the parking markings of Avenue Ambassador Van Vollenhoven in Schaarbeek, action by citizen movement 1030/0, 28 Nov. 2020. © Sien Verstraeten
- Conclusion: /

Acknowledgements

The theoretical exploration of the strategy of overidentification was initiated with Matthias Pauwels during our two-year stay at the Jan van Eyck Academie in Maastricht and further shaped through interaction with Koen Brams, Wim Cuyvers, Marc De Kesel, Aglaia Konrad and many other (advising) researchers. The academic friendship has its roots in our studies at the KU Leuven Faculty of Architecture and later at the Faculty of Philosophy of Radboud University Nijmegen and the Erasmus University Rotterdam. In these formative years, the teachings of Jacques De Visscher, Wim Cuyvers, Philippe Van Haute and Henk Oosterling left an undeniable mark.

The first critical interventions that made use of the strategy of overidentification and are described in Chapters 5 to 7 were a joint effort with Matthias Pauwels, co-founder of BAVO, and developed at the invitation of different actors. First, the 10 Must-Dos was a critical study commissioned by Atelier Zuidvleugel at the Provincie Zuid-Holland (thanks to Nadia Casabella), De Janssens Werken was an exhibition at the invitation of the Flanders Architecture Institute (VAi) and De Singel (curated by Katrien Vandermarliere and Moritz Küng) and the Bureau Kunstenaarsparticipatie was part of a group exhibition at TENT. Rotterdam (curated by Jonas Staal, commissioned by Mariëtte Dolle and Ove Lucas).

The work on the Provincial Government Architect in Limburg (Chapter 8) was initiated in conversation with Dimitri Minten and Tim Vekemans (RE-ST architects) and commissioned by Architectuurwijzer, a non-profit organization for architecture culture in Limburg active under the umbrella of the Hasselt arts centre Z33. Over the years, the project was guided through lively discussions with Roel De Ridder (UHasselt/KU Leuven) and other volunteers at the non-profit organization.

The work on prison architecture (Chapter 9) was initiated in the framework of research at KU Leuven Faculty of Architecture and was assisted at specific moments by Wim Vandendriessche, Rūta Valiūnaitė-Aleks, Paoletta Holst, Fie Vandamme and Heleen Verheyden (BAVO). The contribution to the triennial 'Conflict & Design' in C-mine (15 Dec. 2013-9 Mar. 2014) included studio work of KU Leuven master's students Maarten Moonens and Fie Vandamme. The exhibition was curated by Kurt Van Belleghem. The project at Merksplas Prison was a joint effort with Edith Wouters, artistic director of AR-TUR, and Serge Rooman, prison director and director of the Opleidingscentrum voor Penitentiair Personeel or OCPP (Prison staff training centre) of the Federal Public Service Justice (FPS Justice). The work was inspired through engagement with the non-profit association De Huizen (The houses) and interaction with prison director Hans Claus in particular.

The work at KARUS psychiatric centre (Chapter 10) originated in the context of research at KU Leuven Faculty of Architecture. The work was a joint venture with Fie Vandamme (BAVO) and would have been unthinkable without the support and trust of Herman Roose, general director of KARUS. The work was guided by work groups made up of psychiatrists, directors, staff *and* patients and owes a debt to a lot of people working and staying at the clinic. The collaboration with architecten de vylder vinck taillieu was crucial in the dissemination of the work. The installation *Unless Ever People: Caritas for Freespace* was a collaboration with architecten de vylder vinck taillieu and Filip Dujardin. It was shown in the central exhibition curated by Shelley McNamara and Yvonne Farrell at the 16th Venice Architecture Biennale in 2018. Steunpunt Geestelijke Gezondheid (Support centre mental healthcare, now called Psyche) was supportive throughout the years, especially editor-in-chief Rik Van Nuffel.

The research on the seclusion room in the Sint-Jan Acute admissions department of the Sint-Annendael Diest psychiatric hospital (Chapter 11) was a joint effort with Heleen Verheyden (BAVO) and was made possible through critical interaction with Dominik Renson, Wim Simons and Kris Pieters, respectively head nurse, head psychiatrist and psychologist. The work was guided by work groups made up of psychiatrists, directors, staff, experts-by-experience and patients. The study was continued in different clinics in collaboration with Vjera Sleutel (BAVO). The exploration of the topic took place as part of the Caritas project in collaboration with Fie Vandamme (BAVO). The research became part of the *Prikkels* (Stimuli) exhibition at Museum Dr. Guislain, Ghent, 20 Oct. 2018-26 May 2019. The exhibition came about with the help of Rosa Fens, Helen Van de Vloet (drawings), Kurt Deruyter (photography), Lieven Vanhove (film) and Dorine Demuynck (knitting).

The engagement with citizen movements 1030/0, Heroes for Zero and Filter Café Filtré in Brussels (Chapter 12) was inspired by the power of the commons, often people I didn't know, but with who I share the same desire for a safer, healthier, more social and more just organization of the public space in Brussels. Listing all the people I owe a debt to would be impossible, but some people stand out, in the case of Heroes for Zero: Pieter Fannes, Sophie Feyder, Kadri Soova and Wiet Vandaele. My engagements with Filter Café Filtré were inspired by Annekatrien Verdickt. The Van Vollenhoven action was inspired by Gerben Van den Abbeele, just as many other moments of activism in Brussels.

The doctoral research at KU Leuven Faculty of Architecture was supervised by Pascal De Decker, Hilde Heynen, Lieven De Cauter, Kristel Beyens and Yves Schoonjans. I am grateful for their trust at moments when the research went off down long and winding roads. Particular thanks go to Pascal De Decker for challenging me each time to focus on the methodology. You can see this book as a sort of overidentification. The result might come as a surprise, but Pascal has got what he wanted, not simply as an introductory chapter, but as a stand-alone volume that reflects on tactics for critical intervention.

A special mention goes to Lieven De Cauter, with who I had the pleasure of a joint teaching assignment at the KU Leuven Faculty of Architecture for many years. The research owes an immense debt to the weekly debates with countless students on such wide-ranging topics as politics, practice, aesthetics, activism, transgression, commons, deschooling and religion. Hilde Heynen therefore rightly described Lieven De Cauter as a *de facto* supervisor. The intellectual encounters, often triggered by disagreement, provided the inspiration and joy that have driven the research in all directions, including an awful lot of exciting parallel writings.

Credits

This publication is made possible with generous support of the Johan Verbeke Fund.

This book is a dissertation submitted in partial fulfilment of the requirements for the degree of Doctor of Architecture (PhD) at the Arenberg Doctoral School and KU Leuven Faculty of Architecture, campus Sint-Lucas Brussels, February 2024. Supervisors: Prof. dr. Pascal De Decker, Prof. dr. Hilde Heynen, Prof. dr. Lieven De Cauter. Members of the examination committee: Prof. dr. Kristel Beyens, Prof. dr. Fredie Floré (Chair), Dipl.-Ing. Nikolaus Hirsch, Dr. Annette Kuhk (Secretary), Prof. dr. Doina Petrescu, Prof. dr. Yves Schoonjans.

Cover illustration: *Traces* by Ultima Vez, performance in the framework of Openstreets 22. © Ivan Put
Copy editing: Patrick Lennon
Design: Joseph Plateau
Publisher: Eelco van Welie, nai010 publishers

© 2024 Gideon Boie and nai010 publishers, Rotterdam

All rights reserved. No part of this publication may be reproduced, stored in a retrieval system, or transmitted in any form or by any means, electronic, mechanical, photocopying, recording or otherwise, without the prior written permission of the publisher. nai010 publishers is an internationally orientated publisher specialized in developing, producing and distributing books in the fields of architecture, urbanism, art and design. www.nai010.com

Available in North, South and Central America through Artbook | D.A.P., 155 Sixth Avenue 2nd Floor, New York, NY 10013-1507, tel +1 212 627 1999, fax +1 212 627 9484, dap@dapinc.com
    Available in the United Kingdom and Ireland through Art Data, 12 Bell Industrial Estate, 50 Cunnington Street, London W4 5HB, tel +44 208 747 1061, fax +44 208 742 2319, orders@artdata.co.uk

Printed and bound in The Netherlands
ISBN 978-94-6208-899-3
NUR 648; BISAC ARC005080, ARC006000
Keywords:
Architecture criticism, commons, overidentification, political pilosophy, psychoanalysis, urban theory